Anthony Burgess

Anthony Burgess

THE ARTIST AS NOVELIST

Geoffrey Aggeler

THE UNIVERSITY OF ALABAMA PRESS

UNIVERSITY, ALABAMA

To Sondra

Library of Congress Cataloging in Publication Data

Aggeler, Geoffrey, 1939-
  Anthony Burgess: the artist as novelist.

  Includes bibliographical references and index.
  1. Burgess, Anthony, 1917-   —Criticism and
interpretation.
PR6052.U638Z53   823'.9'14   78-12200
ISBN 0-8173-7106-0

Contents

Acknowledgments

I am indebted to the following persons and organizations for granting permission to use material that has appeared elsewhere: to Professor Jack Garlington, for permitting me to base part of chapter 2 on material that appeared in *Western Humanities Review* 27 (Fall 1973) Copyright © University of Utah 1972; to Professor Robin Skelton, for permission to base parts of chapter 3 on articles that appeared in *Malahat Review* 10 (April 1969) and 44 (October 1977) Copyright © the *Malahat Review* 1969 and 1977, and to base chapter 6 on an article that appeared in *Malahat Review* 17 (January 1971) Copyright © the *Malahat Review* 1971; to the Swets Publishing Service, Amsterdam, for permission to base chapter 5 on an article originally published in *English Studies* 55 (February 1974) Copyright © Swets and Zeitlinger 1974; and to the Purdue Research Foundation for permission to base chapter 7 on an article that appeared in *Modern Fiction Studies* 18 (Winter 1972–'73) Copyright © 1973 Purdue Research Foundation. I would also like to thank Alfred A. Knopf Inc. for sending me the galley proofs of *MF* and an advance copy of *The Clockwork Testament.*

I am especially grateful for the invaluable assistance and support of Dr. Eric Graham, Royal Roads Military College, Victoria, B.C., which made possible my research during the summer of 1969 and an interview with Anthony Burgess in Stratford, Ontario. I would also like to thank the College of Humanities, University of Utah, for enabling me to visit Burgess in New York in September 1972. My largest debt, however, is to Mr. Burgess himself, whose generous encouragement of the book at every stage gave me the courage I needed to complete it. Additional support, in the form of unflagging patience and good humor, was provided by my wife Sondra.

Anthony Burgess

Title Abbreviations

AVOB, A Vision of Battlements
MT, Malayan Trilogy
DS, Devil of a State
WR, The Worm and the Ring
NLS, Nothing Like the Sun
IME, Inside Mr. Enderby
EO, Enderby Outside
CT, The Clockwork Testament
RA, The Right to an Answer
DIS, The Doctor Is Sick
HFB, Honey for the Bears
ESV, The Eve of St. Venus
TWS, The Wanting Seed
ACO, A Clockwork Orange
TI, Tremor of Intent
MF, MF
NS, Napoleon Symphony
OHC, One Hand Clapping
BRW, Beard's Roman Women

1

ENTER POSTERITY

And a very happy New Year to you, too, Mr. Burgess!

The wish, however, is wasted on both sides, for this, to your night visitors, is a very old year. We—whispering, fingering, rustling, creaking, about your roach-ridden West Side flat—are that posterity to which you hopefully address yourself. Congratulations, Mr. Burgess: you have already hit your ball smack over the pavilion clock, not to mention the left-field wall on this American side of the Atlantic. If you awaken now with one of the duodenal or pyloric twinges of your poet Enderby (which are to us as gruesome a literature-lesson spicer as Johnson's scrofula, Swift's scatophopia, or Keats's gallop of death-warrant blood), do not fancy it is ghosts you hear, sibilant and crepitant about the bed. To be a ghost one has first to die.

But you are still very much alive, Mr. Burgess, in spite of the eager North American scholars who would regard you as dead and ready for decent interment in an elegant sarcophagus of scholarly exegesis. I'm sorry, Priscilla, that I cannot recommend examples of "early," "middle," or "late" Burgess, for I cannot honestly say he appears to be anywhere near the end of his revels. You see, for about a dozen years, he has had a disease uncommon among writers of serious fiction: it is called *fecundity*.

I would call your attention, children, to the fact that there is in Mr. Burgess's appearance nothing to suggest a complacent sense of completed achievement. The photographs in recent articles that show a stocky little man are very misleading. If we could linger here until he rises in the morning, you would see he is about six feet tall and lean, without either the haunch or the paunch you might expect to see on a man who spends most of his time before that typewriter in the corner. No, Harold, Mr. Burgess does not write in the lavatory like Mr. Enderby, but maybe he should. Do you know what the word *impinge* means? Well, never mind, I'll tell you later.

You will notice, children, that his hands are rather large and powerful, more than strong enough to play a piano as well as an electric typewriter. Mr. Burgess, I might add, is very fond of typewriters, although, like a farmer, he dares not make a pet of one. But let us not talk of typewriters while we have the man himself slumbering before us. As you can see, his hair is half grey, but he still has it all and combs it forward Roman fashion across his high forehead.

Regrettably, his most arresting features are presently concealed beneath heavy lids. His eyes, when he opens them, are sharp grey and extremely penetrating, although reddened somewhat by an almost perpetual stream of cigar smoke. That should give you some idea of how he *looks,* children, but can you guess how he *sounds,* when he wakes in the morning, lights his first cigar, and brews his first five-bag cup of tea? What's that, Priscilla? Like anyone else from England, you say? Like those announcers on NET who sound sort of vaguely superior? Yes and no, Priscilla. He does indeed sound very British, but one tends to be less aware of the Britishness, if you will, than the deep resonance of his voice. The sound of his voice rather enhances an overall effect of tremendous virile energy awaiting release. In fact, as one listens to him, one soon becomes less astonished that so many books have flowed out of him in such a short time.

You could not, of course, derive any sense of Mr. Burgess's dynamism from watching him at this moment. But if we could stay through the morning, you would surely see him at work, if not at that typewriter, then lecturing on some campus in Texas or Missouri, or conferring with theatre associates in Minneapolis or New York, or being interviewed by some professor with a tape recorder. About this word *impinge,* incidentally—what's that, Melanie? Yes, I realize tomorrow is your holiday. Of course, Mr. Burgess never takes a holiday; whether he is in Malta, Rome, Sussex, or New York City, he works seven days a week. No, Harold, he doesn't drink like Mr. Hemingway or Mr. Fitzgerald. Sometimes he does leave that machine humming to itself while he brews himself a strong cup of tea, but his rest breaks are few. Strong tea and cigar smoke are about all he will consume during a working day. Actually, he enjoys cooking and relishes fine wines, but any indulgence that might slow him down he leaves for after working hours.

Why does he do it? You mean, why this sense of urgency? Well, I suppose it's partly a vestige of his "terminal year." He was, you know, told that 1960 would probably be his last year on earth, and he spent that year producing as many books as he could before a supposed brain tumor did its work. But I tend to see in his commitment something more than a sense of life's brevity. What appears to be a more compelling motivation is simply creative desire itself—a determination to bring forth all the books within him. Regretting what he considers a late beginning as a writer, he means to leave you not only new fiction but as much drama, poetry, translation, and criticism as his remaining years will allow.[1]

Although for some years, he has spent less time in England than in Italy, the United States, or Malta, he is, "in spite of everything," still British. He was born in Manchester on February 25, 1917, the son of Joseph and Elizabeth Burgess Wilson. His full name, which he seldom uses, is John Anthony Burgess Wilson. Anthony is his confirmation name; Burgess is his mother's maiden name. His nom de plume omits the other two names, which he shed when he was bringing out the three novels that comprise the *Malayan Trilogy.*

At the time, he was an education officer with the British Colonial Service in Malaya, and it was regarded as indiscreet for one in his position to publish realistic fictional portrayals of actual events and personalities under one's own name. Besides, as he says, there were "already enough Wilsons writing." Some years later, having observed the Laborite government of Prime Minister Harold Wilson, he became even less attached to his surname and considered abandoning it legally.

His family is an old Lancashire family whose Roman Catholic heritage reaches well back through the centuries. The people of Lancashire, in fact, led the Pilgrimage of Grace in Henry VIII's time. When the Reformation came, it failed to penetrate the northwestern part of the country; nevertheless, many Lancashire Catholics suffered severely for their faith during the dark, penal days of the Reformation, and one of Burgess's ancestors, also named John Wilson, was martyred during the reign of Elizabeth I. Moreover, the family, being Catholic, lost what land it possessed. Its later history parallels that of other steadfastly Roman Lancashire families. During the Civil War, it "hid its quota of undistinguished Royalist leaders in Lancashire cloughs, and supported the Pretenders after 1688." Burgess's Catholicism is not, then, the Catholicism of Evelyn Waugh or Graham Greene, both freshly ignited converts, but part of an ancient regional and family heritage. Like many Lancashire Catholics, however, he has some Irish blood. There was a tendency for Lancashire Catholic men to marry Irish brides because there were not enough native Catholic women to go around. One of his grandmothers, whose maiden name was Finnegan ("a kind of Joycean tieup there, I suppose"), was a native of Tipperary.

The family again acquired land during the eighteenth century and again lost it. Most of his more recent forebears were tradespeople: his grandfather kept a tavern, and his father, like Mr. Enderby's, was a wholesale tobacconist. His mother, Elizabeth Burgess, was a golden-haired singer and dancer who, as a performer on the British musical comedy stage, was styled tautologically "the Beautiful Belle Burgess." She and Burgess's sister—then three years old—both died in the influenza epidemic of 1918/19, and he was left alone with a father who sought to provide him with a new Catholic mother by marrying into a totally Irish family. Burgess thus acquired two stepsisters and an Irish stepmother, a woman of very meagre cultural attainments. His relationship with his stepfamily was never very warm, and years later, his portrayal of Mr. Enderby's gross, illiterate stepmother, who appeared strongly to resemble his own, chilled it completely.

His father's second marriage effectively absorbed both of them into a huge Irish community of tradespeople, publicans, and laborers, none of whom maintained much in the way of cultural or artistic interests (although in 1967 one member of the new family became the archbishop of Birmingham). Burgess's early youth was "mostly a matter of rebelling against a strongly philistine and superstitious tradition," and it was a lonely rebellion, for the most part. His father, a cinema pianist, had introduced Burgess to music but was not really interested in passing on the art to his son, and he was simply unable to teach him anything about other arts or literature. On his own, the boy learned how to play the piano and how to read and write music. Also, having learned to read words before his fourth birthday, he was able to explore serious literature at a fairly early age. His first artistic successes, however, were neither musical nor literary. When he was not composing or writing, he was sketching, and he was only about eleven years old when he had a drawing published in the *Manchester Guardian* for which he received the then handsome sum of five guineas. A short time later, he had another drawing published in the *Daily Express,* which also brought him five guineas. Not surprisingly, he was fired with an ambition to become a professional cartoonist, but this did not really replace his most persistent youthful ambition: to become a composer. Manchester was blessed with what many believed to be the finest orchestra in Europe, the Hallé Orchestra, and Mr. Wilson looked after his son's cultural growth to the extent of introducing him to the Hallé concerts presented in the Free Trade Hall. The boy attended them regularly, and most of his daydreams concerned great orchestral and choral creations. He even sought to realize them in the actual composition of numerous "very jejune" works.

A passion for classical music is the only thing young Burgess shared with the teenage gang-leader protagonist of *A Clockwork Orange.* Burgess had friends but, like most potential artists, was more of an introvert than an extrovert and spent most of his spare time either in solitary creative activity or taking advantage of Manchester's cultural opportunities. However, the city in no way resembled the setting of *A Clockwork Orange,* as some critics have suggested. There were no rat packs or teddy boys or hoodlum police. Rather, it was "a fine industrial city. Rather dirty. With a kind of raffish nobility about it." It was full of German Jews, who built its culture, not the least of their contributions being the Hallé Orchestra. There was a great deal of theatrical activity, and young Burgess was aware of it even when he attended mass at the Church of the Holy Name. Since most of the theatrical lodgings were just around the corner and most of the theatrical people were Catholic, he came to associate mass with being surrounded by theatrical people. He frequently found it a heartening musical experience as well. Considering Manchester's culture, it is not surprising that congregations at the Holy Name should be entertained and edified by music of quality. The church had a fine choir and orchestra, and during the early days, the Carl Rosa opera company sang there regularly. One of the organists was Leslie Stuart, who later achieved fame as the creator of *Floradora.* Stuart, like Burgess, saw the theatrical aspects of the church, and when he was working out the choreography for the famous double quartet ("Tell me, pretty maiden") in *Floradora,* he had in mind the motions of the priests at High Mass before the altar in the Holy Name. (Herein of course lies another tangential Joycean tieup in that *Ulysses* contains snatches of song from *Floradora* as well as references to Father Bernard Vaughan, one of the great preachers associated with the Holy Name in earlier days.) There was, as Burgess says, "a good rich sort of Catholic tradition in that part of Manchester—very powerful."

The first school he attended was the Bishop Bilsborough Memorial School, named for one of the English martyrs. There he was brought up by nuns "who were pretty sadistic." Being advanced in reading skills, he was not taught much but was often assigned to tutor slower youngsters. In those days, one attended elementary school until the age of fourteen, unless one was clever enough to win a scholarship to a secondary school. At the age of eleven, Burgess won two scholarships and was sent to a Catholic public school, the Xaverian College. It was and is a good school, pleasantly situated in an isolated green enclave within the otherwise highly industrialized city of Manchester. Young Burgess enjoyed it. The masters were Xaverian Brothers, and, paradoxically, it was from them that Burgess learned to question Catholicism. This came about partly because some of the brothers were losing their faith even though they were supposedly giving the boys sustaining religious instruction. Some had joined the order solely to acquire a free education, and once they had it, they left. Burgess remembers in particular an Irish history master who encouraged discussion of problems of belief. It was largely from him that Burgess learned how to lose his own faith. The school syllabuses also had something to do with it. While young Burgess was studying European history, he became interested in Luther and the Reformation. He began reading philosophy and studying metaphysics on his own, and about the age of sixteen, he decided he was through with Catholicism. But it was a renunciation that gave him little joy; although intellectually he was convinced he could be a freethinker, emotionally he was very much aware of Hell and damnation. He still is to some extent.

When he was seventeen, Burgess left school, having taken the Higher School Certificate. In one year, the headmaster had put him and his class-mates through a two-year program that was roughly the equivalent of the intermediate stage in the British university course. But after receiving his certificate, Burgess was encouraged by the headmaster to repeat the year to secure a state scholarship to a university. He had just finished a course of study focusing mainly on English literature, history, and Latin, but he decided to switch to music, much to the astonishment of the school authorities who were totally unaware of either his musical inclinations or capabilities. He won a distinction in music but no scholarship, which was not surprising since there were only three state scholarships and only one corporation scholarship offered in the whole city of Manchester. Although courses at the nearby University of Manchester were subsidized, one still had to pay some tuition, and Burgess's family simply could not afford to pay it. So for about two years, he drifted in "a kind of Limbo world of private study," during which he helped his father in the wholesale tobacco business, studied languages, did odd jobs, earned a little money, tried to write music, and felt totally lost. Finally he persuaded his family to add enough to the little he had saved to send him to the University of Manchester.

He wanted to study music at Manchester, but he lacked the science background required by the music department, which laid a heavy emphasis on physics, meaning acoustics. So he took English language and literature. The university was quite small then, and the English department was housed "in a literal house" that had formerly been used by the Tiller Girls, a well-known theatrical troupe. The head of the department was Professor H. B. Charlton, author of *Shakespearean Comedy* and other scholarly works and a man whom Burgess did not greatly admire. Burgess's personal tutor, whom he did admire, was Dr. L. C. Knights, author of *Drama and Society in the Age of Jonson,* coeditor of *Scrutiny,* and one of the leading members of the F. R. Leavis school of criticism. Through Knights, Burgess met Leavis and came under his influence, as well as that of I. A. Richards. He was very much struck by their method, which enabled one to assess a novel critically by closely scrutinizing a single page instead of reading all of it. Leavis was regarded as a charlatan by Professor Charlton, but in Burgess's view, "Charlton was the real charlatan."

Burgess managed to get through the required courses without much effort, but he tended to neglect subjects other than English. When it came time for the *viva voce* examination at the end of his degree course, he didn't know whether he was being "groomed for a first class degree or a bottom second" (nearly thirty years later, he found it was indeed a first). The energy he failed to spend on course work he poured into editing the university magazine, *The Serpent,* and into the dramatic society: "Manchester was a great city for drama. The Rusholme Repertory Theatre had produced actors like Robert Donat and Wendy Hiller, and amateur drama societies had plenty of professional stimulation." Unlike many of his contemporaries who were intensely involved in some form of political activity, Burgess had no interest whatever in politics. The university's Socialist society had no more appeal for him than its Fascist society, and he maintained, as he has maintained since the age of about fourteen, a stance neither radical nor conservative nor anything but "just vaguely cynical." (This is of course the point of view that manifests itself in his fictional conflicts between "Pelagians" and "Augustinians.")

Long before his university days, he had begun reading James Joyce. At age fifteen, he had been frightened out of his wits by the mission sermon in *A Portrait of the Artist,* and the following year, he had begun reading *Ulysses.* During Burgess's university days, Joyce was not well known in academic circles. Although Knights had read Joyce, other academicians, such as Charlton, seemed hardly even to have heard of him. Occasionally Burgess found his knowledge of Joyce to be an advantage in his literature courses, especially when he was able to adduce parallels between Joyce and other writers that would not have occurred to examiners.

While he was at Manchester, he met a Welsh girl, Llewela Isherwood Jones, a distant cousin of Christopher Isherwood. She was four years younger than Burgess and an economics honors student at the university. They were married in 1942, and the marriage was to last until her death in 1968, after many years of severe illness.

For Britain and most of her allies, World War II began in September 1939. To complete his work for a degree, Burgess had to appear before a tribunal and obtain an exemption from being called for service with his age group. The exemption was grudgingly granted, and in June 1940 he received a degree in English language and literature. There followed a long period of waiting to be called, during which time he had various odd jobs. One of them involved tutoring the son of a wealthy garage proprietor, and thanks to the generosity of the boy, who pressed his own lavish pocket money on him, Burgess's last two months as a civilian were taken up with "riotous living."

Burgess joined the army in October 1940, having managed through the influence of a girl friend in the Department of National Services to get himself called ahead of schedule. Against his wishes, he was put into the Royal Army Medical Corps and sent to Scotland. For Burgess and his comrades, basic training was especially dismal. Britain, like most of the enemies of the Axis, was ill-prepared for war, and there was a desperate shortage of equipment and facilities. Even in late 1940, with the bombs falling on London, Burgess and his training mates were dressed in civilian clothes, which they were unable to change for prolonged periods, and the camp was lacking in essential facilities, such as lavatories.

In 1941, having completed his training, Burgess was posted to a field ambulance unit in Northumberland. From there he was sent to the head-quarters of the 54th Division as a pianist and arranger with a small entertainment group. The group, all of whose members except Burgess had been professional entertainers, gave concerts at camps and lonely batteries, relieving the boredom of soldiers who were sick of the "phoney war." Burgess found his job satisfying and enjoyable, but he was soon transferred to the Army Educational Corps, a branch whose roles were not as "cushy" as the name suggests, since it was in fact a cover for intelligence work. Before the formation of the Intelligence Corps in 1942, most cipher work was done by this Educational Corps. Burgess was sent to Gibraltar in 1943, and there he remained until 1946. The story of Richard Ennis in *A Vision of Battlements* is fairly close to his own story. Like Ennis, Burgess lectured to the troops and taught them useful skills such as map reading and foreign languages. Unlike Ennis, however, he was involved with Army Intelligence in cipher work. It was a frustrating, dreary time for him. He composed a good deal of music, including a symphony and a concerto, but very little literature.

His first year on the Rock was made especially miserable by the news that his wife was hospitalized in London with severe injuries. During the blackout, she had been assaulted on the street as she was walking home from work.

Her attackers were American GI's, deserters bent on robbery, who had seized her handbag and beat her up when she screamed. She was carrying a child at the time and aborted; thereafter she was ill, and this led, Burgess believes, to her eventual death. His initial reaction was understandably one of consuming rage against all American soldiers and a yearning to return to England for vengeance. This feeling soon subsided as he forced himself to reflect that the attackers could as easily have been Free French, Poles, or anyone else, but his horror of the action itself, senseless male violence on a defenseless woman, remained undiminished. Clearly, it was the inspiration for the most shocking scene in *A Clockwork Orange,* the brutal assault on the writer and his wife, as well as the woman-beating incidents in *The Right to an Answer.* In the latter novel, the protagonist's mistress is assaulted by American teenagers, dependents of air force personnel stationed in Japan.

Finally in 1946 Burgess was able to return to his wife after being discharged from the army at the rank of warrant officer class one. His wife had repeatedly urged him to apply for a commission, but his military ambition had been satisfied by arrival at the summit of the noncommissioned ranks. One could not, after all, rise any higher without a commission, and he simply "didn't fancy the idea of being a subaltern."

During his first few years back in civilian life Burgess's career oscillated between music and teaching. For a time, he was a pianist with a little-known jazz combo in London, and he also played the piano and did arrangements for Eddie Calvert, "the Man with the Golden Trumpet." Then he became a civilian instructor at an army college of education, where young men and women were trained as teachers, and, upon graduation as sergeant/ instructors, were sent to teach the troops. During the years 1947–48, there were a great many troops to be taught. Churchill had given his famous "Iron Curtain" speech and Britain still saw herself as an embattled nation. A huge army awaited demobilization, and yet people were still being called for service. After this, he was hired as a lecturer in an emergency training college, one of the schools set up in what were previously American army camps to provide thirteen-month crash courses for potential teachers. There he taught drama and phonetics for two years. He also wrote music, directed a number of plays (including *Hamlet*), and was generally happy. But then the whole educational scheme broke down, and Burgess had to seek another position. He found one as a senior master in a grammar school located in Banbury, Oxfordshire, where he remained for four years.

The situation of grammar-school teachers in England was, as he says, "ghastly beyond belief in those days." Negotiations were going on for a new salary scale, but nothing came of them, and Burgess's salary was so wretched that he found it "increasingly impossible to live." Both he and his wife did spare-time teaching, but they were merely breaking even financially while getting nothing out of life. His dismal situation was in most respects the same as that of Christopher Howarth in *The Worm and the Ring.* Discouraged and desperate, he, like Howarth, kept applying for jobs to better himself. Then one night in a drunken stupor, he "quite unconsciously" scrawled out an application for a teaching post in Malaya, and a short time later, he was astonished to receive a summons to the Colonial Office to be interviewed for a position in the Far East. He was subsequently offered a post on the staff of a public school for Malays in Kuala Kangsar, Malaya, which he accepted with little hesitation.

Burgess's literary career really began in Malaya. In 1949 he had written a fictional account of his Gibraltar experiences, but this did not appear as *A Vision of Battlements* until 1965, and his Banbury experiences were not molded into *The Worm and the Ring* until 1961. He began writing fiction during his Malayan years, "as a sort of gentlemanly hobby, because I knew there wasn't any money in it." *Time for a Tiger,* his first published novel, appeared in 1956. Thanks in part to the encouragement of reviewers and his publisher, it was followed in 1958 by *The Enemy in the Blanket. Beds in the East,* which appeared the following year, completed the *Malayan Trilogy.* The trilogy, by far his finest early achievement in the novel, was his attempt to record the fantastic cultural and linguistic mélange that he saw, as well as the interracial strife and chaos he foresaw with the passing of the British raj. Unlike other British writers who have tried to reveal life in Malaya, he researched his subject beyond the confines of the English-speaking community. He acquired a perfect knowledge of Malay and actually got to know members of the various ethnic groups. His impatience with other writers who have not bothered to do this spade work before they hold forth on Malaya is considerable. Of Alan Sillitoe, he has said:

> He wrote a book called *Key to the Door,* which was about his national service in Malaya and it totally misrepresented the case. I know because I was there myself. He said what the Malays want is what the Chinese want, a Communist revolution. You see, this is what they all want but the British are preventing it from happening. This is totally untrue. The Chinese and Malays didn't want a Communist revolution because they had too much to lose. They were all capitalists, all businessmen. The Malays are not interested in politics. In any case, they're Moslems and Communism would presumably fight against Islam. What all the Malaysan people wanted was just to go on as they were with the British there in the background administering the war, building roads and doing the dirty work. But Sillitoe—so ideological in that way—totally misrepresented the entire picture. You see again I get mad at the man who was so full of humility, *so* interested in the people. He never learned the bloody language even; he never *talked* with the Malays. He never knew what was going on in the Malay's mind.[2]

Burgess adapted well to the country and even considered becoming a Malaysian citizen. As he remembers this stage of enchantment, it was a brief one, during which he was "probably drunk"; nevertheless, he recalls:

Malaya appeared to be a reasonable community at the time, an interesting, multiracial community, and a warm country, with a certain measure of intellectual freedom and a tremendous stimulation from the fact that all these things—Hinduism, Islam, Christianity and free thought—were working together. There were two very good universities in Singapore. Colleges were being built in Kuala Lumpur. I was engaged in education, and it was a stimulating time, very stimulating indeed. I felt that if the new world was going to be made, it might well be made in Malaysia. But now I see that the prophecy of my own book [the *Malayan Trilogy*] has been fulfilled; the Chinese and Malays are killing each other again, and I have no more hopes there.[3]

Although he eventually abandoned hopes for a better world in Malaya, he believes the impact of his experiences there affected his life permanently. Learning an Oriental language for the first time broadened his awareness enormously and made him see that "all our bloody stupid notions of the universality of linguistic categories, which I think John Stuart Mill first put forward—you know, 'the eight parts of speech are a universal reality'—all this was nonsense." He studied Chinese as well as Malay, but unlike Ezra Pound and Ernest Fenollosa, he was not enthusiastic about the possibilities of the Chinese ideogram as a medium for poetry. He could not share their confident hope that it would provide a way of returning to a "classical" kind of verse and of getting at "the thing itself":

I've never been excited about the Chinese ideogram. I think it's been over-glamorized. That's what [Marshall] McLuhan is doing at the moment, over-glamorizing the ideogram. Frankly, I think the Chinese way of writing is a stupidly outmoded, insufficient technique. It would serve as a medium only for a totally non-auditory verse, a verse or pure ideas which couldn't be read aloud. I mean the only virtue of Chinese script is that it unites many dialects. I've seen Chinese of different provinces talking to each other and not making themselves understood. They either turned to English or wrote down everything they had to say in Chinese ideograms. Everyone can understand a Chinese newspaper, but if a man from the North and a man from the South start reading to one another, they're hitting two different languages. The unifying power of the ideogram is of great interest, of great value, but from the point of view of a writer who has always been troped to the auditory, Chinese has no appeal. The sounds of Chinese are different because there you use musical intonations to determine meaning, and this has always been tremendously interesting to me, but I was drawn more to the Islamic culture and the languages of Islam.[4]

Indeed, the appeal of Islam was such that Burgess considered becoming a Muslim. He was struck by the reasonableness of the religion: "You believe in one God. You say your prayers five times a day. You have a tremendous amount of freedom, sexual freedom; you can have four wives. The wife herself has a commensurate freedom. She can achieve divorce in the same way a man can." However, for Burgess, as for Rupert Hardman in *The Enemy in the Blanket,* Islam soon "ceased to seem reasonable" and he returned to what he calls a "renegade Catholic" religious stance.

Certainly the most important effect of this mind-opening exposure to new religions, languages, and philosophies was that he was being stimulated to write, to express in one artistic form or another the incredible composite world he was seeing. Although he might have become a major novelist without going to Malaya and writing the trilogy, the importance of this experience in his development as a novelist was in many ways analogous to the importance of *Endymion* in Keats's development as a poet. His success in capturing so much of Malaya's cultural variety in an extended piece of fiction seems to have been a tremendous impetus for him toward writing other fiction dealing with other worlds he either knew or imagined. Unlike Keats, he also had the encouragement of perceptive critics.

Like Victor Crabbe, the linking protagonist in the trilogy, Burgess enjoyed his teaching in spite of his tendency to clash with administrative superiors. After a quarrel with one headmaster, he was posted to Malaya's East Coast as a senior lecturer in a training college. Then in 1957 Malaya gained her independence and the future of British expatriates grew doubtful. Shortly thereafter the Malayan government generously provided each erstwhile colonial with a sum of money and courteously threw him out of the country. But Burgess soon found another teaching post in Brunei, Borneo. The favorable reception of his Malayan books notwithstanding, he did not view himself primarily as a novelist, but as a professional teacher who simply wrote novels "as a kind of hobby."

In Borneo, as in Malaya, he refused to join the rest of the British colonials in their lofty isolation from the native community. His perfect Malay and genuine interest in the people and their problems enabled him to mix freely with them, and, at the expense of antagonizing his fellow colonial officers, he won their trust and respect. This led to an invitation to lead the people's Freedom party, which he refused. Even so, rumors about his loyalty began to circulate within the British community, and he was stuck with the appellation "bolshy." The antagonism of his fellows and superiors was further augmented by an incident during a garden party in honor of Prince Philip, who was in Brunei on an official visit. As the prince wandered dutifully from group to group, he inquired casually about local conditions: "Everything all right?" All the dazzled colonials replied appropriately that indeed everything was as it should be—all, that is, except Burgess's fiery Welsh wife, who, according to other rumors, was supposed to be Aneurin Bevan's sister. She replied very bluntly and rather insultingly that "things bloody well weren't all right," and moreover that the British were largely to blame. After this, Burgess's days in Brunei would probably have been few even without the physical breakdown that finally sent him back to England.

Not long after the garden party, Burgess was giving his students a lecture on phonetics, when he, like Edwin Spindrift in *The Doctor Is Sick,* suddenly collapsed on the floor of the classroom. He now suspects it was "a willed collapse out of sheer boredom and frustration." Whatever the cause, with incredible dispatch, he was loaded aboard a jet airliner for England, where doctors at the National Hospital for Nervous Diseases diagnosed his ailment as a brain tumor. The neatness with which he was thereby eliminated as a source of official embarrassment in Borneo leads him to guess that his hasty removal had as much to do with his general intransigence and the garden-party incident as with his collapse on the classroom floor.

The political situation in Borneo was now among the least of his worries. The existence of the brain tumor had been determined primarily on the basis of a spinal tap, which revealed an excess of protein in the spinal fluid. Other excruciating tests followed. Initially the doctors considered removing the tumor, and Burgess was apprehensive, lest "they hit my talent instead of my tumor," but then they decided that removal was impossible. Burgess was told that he would probably be dead within the year, but that if he managed to live through the year, he could infer that the prognosis had been excessively pessimistic and that he would live. His situation was extremely dismal in that he had no pension, was unable to get a job, and saw no way of providing for his prospective widow. Fortunately they had been able to bring a bit of money with them from the Far East. His wife, Llewela, having graduated in economics from the University of Manchester, was knowledgeable in money matters, and she shrewdly invested on the stock exchange the sum of £1,000 they had taken out of Malaya. The stock exchange was a free organization in those days; one could buy and sell on margins, and, in a few years, she had doubled, then quadrupled, the original sum. The initial sum enabled them to live through the year, from 1959 into 1960, that Burgess had been told would be his last. But instead of moping about in self-pitying depression, he began writing novels, chiefly to secure posthumous royalties. Surprisingly, he felt more exhilarated than depressed, and his "last year on earth" was one of the most productive he has ever known. The five novels he produced—*Inside Mr. Enderby, The Wanting Seed, The Doctor Is Sick, The Worm and the Ring,* and *One Hand Clapping*—include some of his best work, and they were not the only things he wrote. Thus he launched himself as a professional novelist under much less than favorable and indeed quite accidental circumstances. But, as he says, "most writers who actually do become novelists do so by accident. If a man deliberately sets out to become a novelist, he usually winds up as a critic, which is, I think, something less."[5]

His productivity astonished the critics and, paradoxically, alarmed his publisher. The fecundity of writers such as Dickens, Trollope, and Henry James had long been forgotten in England, where it was generally thought that writers of quality followed the example of E. M. Forster and produced a canon of perhaps four or five books over a period of eighty to ninety years. Fecundity, Burgess found, was looked upon as a kind of literary disease. His publisher suggested he conceal the malady by taking another pseudonym, and so it happened that *Inside Mr. Enderby,* one of his comic masterpieces, and *One Hand Clapping* were published under the name Joseph Kell. But the two books had few reviews and sold poorly, mainly because no one had ever heard of Joseph Kell. Since then both novels have been reissued profitably under the name Anthony Burgess. A comical result of the Kell business was that Burgess was asked to review one of his own novels. The editor who sent him the book did not know he was Joseph Kell. Appreciating what he took to be the editor's sense of humor, Burgess wrote the review—and was never again allowed to write for that journal.

As the novels came out, his health improved steadily, and he began to take on various nonfiction-writing chores as well. For a time, he was both music critic for *Queen*—a British glossy read in the United States—and drama critic for the *Spectator.* One of the trials of this dual role was being dogged by spies assigned "to see whether I really saw an opera and a play on the same night." He also wrote a number of television scripts, including one on Martinú, one on Shelley and Byron in Switzerland, and one on Joyce. Other projects included a play written at the request of the Phoenix Theatre, London, another one for the BBC, and still another for Independent TV, as well as a new translation of Berlioz's *Enfance du Christ.* In addition, he was becoming more and more in demand as a book reviewer, and his average yearly output in reviews alone was estimated by one reporter at 150,000 words.[6]

But Burgess was and is primarily a writer of fiction, and most of his boundless energy during the early sixties went into the writing of novels. He also wrote some short fiction and, although he finds the short story a constricting form, contributed a sizable number of stories to the *Hudson Review, Argosy, Rutgers Review,* and other periodicals. In regard to his verse contributions, anyone who has read much of his fiction does not need to be told he is a poet. His prose, like that of Joyce, is charged with a music that cannot be appreciated fully unless read aloud. But not all his lyric effusions are woven in with his prose. While he was writing fiction, drama, criticism, and music, he was also contributing verse to a number of periodicals, including the *Transatlantic Review, Arts and Letters,* and the *New York Times;* the last named commissioned him to write a poem on the landing of Apollo II.

He did not, however, remain rooted to his writer's chair. Always restless, he traveled a great deal, and so far as his fiction is concerned, one of his most productive trips was a visit to Leningrad in 1961. His purpose in going "was to experience life in Leningrad without benefit of Intourist—i.e., as one of the crowd." Before the trip, he spent about six weeks reviving his Russian, acquired during the war, and this enabled him to gain a great deal from the experience. One of his first discoveries in Russia was that it was possible to enter the country without a passport. One simply left the ship long after everyone else and the immigration officials went off duty. If one were really willing to live dangerously, one also could reap a tidy profit selling smuggled Western goods. One could even smuggle a man out of the country by securing a deluxe cabin with a bathroom in which he could be hidden. On top of all this, one could even get to know the secret police on a friendly basis. Late one evening, these stock villains of Western spy thrillers were kind enough to take Burgess home, drunk, in one of their cars. This and other experiences finally led him to conclude that "the Russian soul is all right; it's the state that's wrong."[7]

One of the fruits of this hair-raising "research" was *Honey for the Bears,* a hilarious entertainment in which an unconsciously homosexual ("gomosexual") antique dealer goes to Russia to sell smuggled drilon dresses and in the process loses his wife to a lesbian. Another product was *A Clockwork Orange,* a seriously philosophical picaresque tale narrated by a demonic young hoodlum who could be Russian or English or both. Burgess and his wife encountered some of his prototypes late one evening outside a Leningrad restaurant. As they were finishing their meal, they were startled to hear loud hammering at the door. Having been filled with the usual Western propaganda, they immediately had the terrifying thought that the hammerers were after them, the capitalist enemy. Like Paul Hussey, he was reminded of a Biblical phrase: "Bring us the strangers, that we may know them." In fact, these hardfisted young toughs, called "stilyagi," were after different prey. When the Burgesses wanted to leave the restaurant, the stilyagi courteously stepped aside, allowed them to pass, then resumed their hammering. Burgess was struck by the Nabokovian quality of the incident, the way in which their conduct reflected the "chess mind": "Even lawless violence must follow rules and ritual." He was also struck by their resemblance to the English teddy boys of the fifties, whom indeed they were copying, and he went home with an even sturdier conviction that "Russians are human." (When he described this incident during a lecture, he accidentally said "Humans are Russian," but he would not correct the slip, considering it "ben trovato.")[8]

As the years passed and his "terminal year" receded, he became less worried about his own health but more about that of his wife. She had never fully recovered from the injuries she received in 1943 and the years in the Far East had been hard on her. She began to deteriorate both physically and mentally, attempted suicide in 1960, and finally died in 1968 of portal cirrhosis, brought on partly by alcoholism but mainly by years of vitamin starvation in Malaya and Borneo. Somehow the news of her death reached a film producer with whom Burgess had been working on a script, and the man immediately invited him to Hollywood. His intentions were the kindest and Burgess was deeply touched. However, when he went to Hollywood in January and March of 1969, he found the reality of her death even harder to accept than it had been when he was home. Imagining that home was what it had been, he found himself buying gifts for her. Although he had been unable to do much to ease the pain of her last years, he was still burdened with a strong residue of guilt about her death.[9]

Some months after his first wife's death, he married a lovely, dark-haired

Italian contessa, Liliana Macellari, whom he had known for several years. Liliana is a philologist and translator, whose works include Italian translations of Thomas Pynchon's *V* and Lawrence Durrell's *Alexandria Quartet*. Burgess finds the latter project "hard to forgive," not because of the quality of her translation, but because he considers the original hardly worth translating, especially into this language, which he knows and reveres. At present he and Liliana are looking forward to working together on a project of appalling complexity—translating *Finnegans Wake* into Italian. Liliana has taught at various colleges and universities in Europe and the United States and, at the time of her marriage to Burgess, was a member of the linguistics department at Cambridge involved in the development of a scientific approach to Italian. Burgess had met her while she was working for an Italian publisher who commissioned her to write annual reports on current happenings in English literature. With their son Andrea, the Burgesses moved to Malta, where they lived, between lecture tours and a teaching stint at North Carolina, for nearly two years.

Burgess had a number of reasons for leaving England, not the least being the need to have a year or two unburdened by heavy taxes. He had had to pay the staggering sum of £7000 in death duties on his first wife's estate, largely because of the amazing production of his "terminal year," whereby he had sought to provide for her. He had also just received a windfall with a couple of film scripts, which he anticipated losing almost wholly in surtax. Incredibly, at that time, the British tax structure made no allowance whatever for fluctuating incomes, and there was no provision for spreading earnings in any just or equitable manner. Whatever a writer received in a given year would be taxed in one devastating bite as an ordinary year's income, even though it might be the financial fruit of several years labor. This helps to explain why so few long novels have come out of England in recent years. Moreover, the *working* writer especially was, and is, liable to be discriminated against, in that tax-free prizes, such as Arts Council awards, have a way of falling to the unproductive. By the end of 1968, Burgess's productivity had gotten him into such a financial tangle that he had to pour most of his energies into journalism just to pay his taxes. Although he enjoyed journalism—writing essays and critical reviews for an immediate audience—and although he was managing to pay his bills, he saw the situation as an unhealthy one for a serious novelist. In Malta, where the tax situation was easier, he hoped to return to novel writing as a primary job.

The Burgesses would have preferred moving to Italy in 1969, but there were some obstacles preventing that, including the fact that sterling could not be exported. Malta, being within the sterling area and only fifty minutes by air from Italy, seemed to be an ideal second choice. However, the Burgesses soon found it had little to recommend it besides its Mediterranean climate. The repressive rule exercised by a church-dominated government made life exceedingly dreary if not intolerable. Burgess could never even be certain he would receive books or periodicals mailed to him. The same puritannical sensibility that would not allow his wife to wear a sleeveless dress on the street might cause a mail clerk to seize a book or a magazine with a vaguely erotic cover.

Because of these nuisances, the Burgesses welcomed invitations to travel and lecture abroad: During the fall of 1969, he was a visiting professor of English at the University of North Carolina. Most of the winter and the following spring were spent on a tour through Australasia for the British Council. During the academic year 1970–71, he taught in the Princeton Creative Arts Program. The academic year 1972–73 he spent as a visiting distinguished professor of English at the City College of New York.

If Burgess's attempt to find a fertile writing retreat in Malta was a failure, it was one only by his own incredible standards of productivity. During his brief, unhappy residence on the island, he managed to produce two books: a biography of Shakespeare and his novel *MF,* which is set in the United States and a tyrannically ruled Carribean island called "Castita." The striking resemblance this supposedly chaste little island bears to Malta would appear to be more than coincidental.

In 1971 the Burgesses purchased a flat in Rome (the flat that appears in *Beard's Roman Women*) and acquired a house in the nearby lakeside town of Bracciano. (The house appears in the conclusion of *MF.*) Between tours and visits abroad, they lived alternately in the two residences until 1976. Although they found the atmosphere in Rome a good deal more civilized and bearable than that of Malta, after five years, they felt compelled to move again. Italy, Burgess believed, was on the verge of civil war. There was a state of general chaos, prices were rising intolerably, and shortages were becoming more than irksome. In addition, there was the omnipresent danger of his son Andrea being kidnapped. With the rash of kidnappings in Italy in recent years, Burgess felt especially threatened because of the Italian tendency to believe all foreigners, especially foreign writers, are rich and capable of paying high ransoms.[10]

To escape these nuisances and threats, Burgess moved his family to Monaco and purchased a flat in Monte Carlo on the rue Grimaldi within sight of the royal palace. Soon they will be moving again, into a house on the Var in the little town of Callian. Monaco has advantages in terms of its location between France and Italy. In spite of all its troubles, the Burgesses visit Italy from time to time and still maintain the house in Bracciano.[11]

Burgess's frequent visits to the United States in recent years have involved him as much in American show business as in American academia, and, for the most part, he has enjoyed it thoroughly. In 1970 he was asked to do a new translation of Edmond Rostand's *Cyrano de Bergerac,* to be played at the Guthrie Theatre in Minneapolis with Christopher Plummer in the title role. The invitation seems to have come about partly because a number of actors and stage directors connected with the Guthrie had read Burgess's Shakespearean autobiography *Nothing Like the Sun,* a novel that has appealed to actors and stage people generally. Burgess's sympathetic understanding of Shakespeare and his feeling for the period in which Shakespeare wrote suggested he might be able to do a translation/adaptation of *Cyrano* that would be closer in spirit to the early seventeenth century, when the events supposedly took place, than to the late nineteenth century, when the play was written. He completed the translation, but then Plummer was not available to play Cyrano. Production went ahead nevertheless with another actor playing the lead, and it turned out to be an amazing success. It was especially well received by the young, which is not really surprising since, as Burgess observes, "Cyrano is a great rebel, a man who in some sense chooses failure, chooses a sacrificial role, despite his tremendous potency, his tremendous skill as a fighter, his masterfulness."[12]

Although it did not take the Guthrie out of the red, the play was an indisputable financial triumph, bringing in more money at the box office than anything played there before. This raised hopes that it might be turned into a successful musical. Burgess was again called upon to perform the challenging tasks of adapting the play and writing lyrics for it. He spent more than a year reducing the enormous text to something more manageable and building, in collaboration with the composer, lyrics out of the situations within the play.

The musical *Cyrano* was staged in 1973 with Plummer in the title role, and Burgess was immensely excited by the achievement, believing he had been involved with an art form in which his particular set of talents could be fully employed. He calls himself "a sort of failed musician and a sort of failed poet," a combination that "often makes a good lyric writer. Lyrics are not poems, they're merely exercises in verbal engineering. They're supposed to be witty, apt and relevant to particular instants in the play. I enjoy doing this work."[13]

In addition to his *Cyrano,* Burgess has completed the book, lyrics, and score for a musical entitled *Blooms of Dublin,* based on Joyce's *Ulysses,* and a new musical called *Trotsky's in New York,* "which may or may not come to something off-Broadway."[14] He feels a kind of fulfillment in this form of creation, and to those who suggest it is not "the highest form of art," he offers no apologies:

> It does represent a very exacting kind of craft. I think it would do a lot of high-flying poets and novelists good to get into the theatre, where their words, their constructions have to come up against the hard facts of box-office reality. One can't start saying, "well, these words are too good for the audience." If they're too good for the audience, the audience doesn't come in. One has to try and effect a compromise between one's own literary aspirations and what the public can take. And when all's said and done, this is what Shakespeare did. Shakespeare was a popular, highly successful dramatist in his own day, and his skill seems to have lain in being able to appeal, on a primary level, to all sections of the Elizabethan community, whereas on other levels, deeper elements were

at work, which could or could not take on significance according to the member of the audience that took them in. The men from the Inns of Court and the universities appreciated the plays on levels which the groundlings did not. I'm not saying that one can do this in musicals. The musical is a much more popular form than the Shakespearean tragedy, or even comedy, but when all is said and done, we are not, when we're writing, solely trying to communicate with an ideal audience. We're trying to communicate with an actual audience. And to get on the stage, to hope that an audience will come in night after night and make the whole project worthwhile, should not be despised by the high priests of literature. Although I seem to be stepping down by engaging in this kind of work, I don't think I really am. I think that one has to try and please a public and at the same time try and please oneself, and the real skill lies in doing both.[15]

Whether or not the high priests of literature agree with Burgess, they can hardly accuse him of being uninvolved with serious drama. Another project for the Guthrie Theatre was a translation/adaptation of Sophocles' *Oedipus Tyrannus*. Burgess's feelings about this achievement are somewhat ambivalent. That is, he is both elated by and vaguely ashamed of what he considers its "unscholarly" character. He completed it in Rome, working from the original Greek text and consulting only an Italian/Greek lexicon. Thus he minimized English intrusions, and the resulting translation into English has for him a magical, dreamlike quality. This is partly because of his own state of mind during its composition, which, incredibly, took him only about a week. He recalls being in a curious "trancelike" state in which he was able to compose with amazing speed and fluency. The meanings of some of the speeches are no longer entirely clear to him, but he remembers they had very definite meanings at the time; hence he is unwilling to make any emendations that might destroy some of the "peculiar magic" that seems to surround the whole rhythm of the play.

Like the novel *MF*, Burgess's *Oedipus* reflects the influence of the anthropologist Claude Lévi-Strauss, who was the first to clarify the connections between riddling and incest within not only the Oedipus myth but various non-Greek myths as well. Thanks to Lévi-Strauss's application of his doctrine of shared archetypes (structuralism), we understand the meaning of incest better than the Greeks themselves did. We know it means something in terms of the structure of a society. The act of incest is naturally associated with various phenomena, such as eclipses and earthquakes, with what Lévi-Strauss calls *chaviré*, the turmoil of a people. Some of these elements appear in Burgess's *Oedipus*. Beyond this, the influence of Lévi-Strauss appears in the way Burgess has related the nature of the riddle of the Sphinx. The arithmology of the riddle is four-two-three: what animal goes on four legs in the morning, two legs at noon, and three in the evening? The answer of course is "man," but Burgess finds the arithmology itself significant. The four-two-three is cyclical and capable of going on forever. It also suggests musical intervals and rhythms. Oedipus, when he discovers he doesn't know his parentage, relates himself to the rhythms of the turning year. Thus the riddle can be seen to apply to him. In one sense, he is himself a riddle, although this does not come out in the original Sophoclean version.

A related element is the play's attempted reconciliation of the two Thebeses—the Greek and the Egyptian—whereby the audience is led to think of a race that is "neither Egyptian nor Greek nor anything but just remotely Indo-European." Burgess enhances this effect by choruses that are not in Greek or in any known language but in his own reconstruction of Indo-European. To accomplish this, he combined the Indo-European roots, as they have been discerned through linguistic scholarship, with imagined declension endings. In the choric speeches, one hears first the roots and then the endings mumbling away into nothingness. The effect is a peculiar sense of remoteness, a sense of "getting back to our roots." He has not, in short, attempted to produce an *Oedipus* that is either classical or traditional but one that "fuses various of our cultures, certainly various of our types of thinking about culture." The result, he believes, should be "at least rather moving." Reviews of the Minneapolis production suggest he has achieved his end: according to *Time* reviewer Melvin Maddocks, audiences have been "shaken . . . to the bottom of their atavistic souls" by "an *Oedipus* that bleeds and thus lives."

Although Burgess's appetite for musical comedy and other dramatic creation has increased with his achievements on the stage, his appetite for any sort of involvement in cinematic creation has diminished. The main reason for this is his own history of wasteful disappointments in Hollywood, a history he considers more typical than atypical of the present day. Although it may have been possible during the 1930s for novelists such as William Faulkner and Aldous Huxley to achieve something working with filmmakers in Hollywood, such fruitful liaisons are no longer common. More often, they prove to be abortive, as in the case of the projected film that first brought Burgess to Hollywood in 1968.

Warner Brothers had invited Burgess to write the script for a major film on the life of Shakespeare. This he soon completed, producing a five-hour script that he intended to reduce for a three-hour, "hard-ticket" film. The script was approved and all necessary arrangements had been made. Joseph L. Manckewicz was to direct. There was going to be a magnificent cast, with Maggie Smith as Anne Hathaway, her husband, Robert Stephens, as Shakespeare, and a host of big names in the theatrical world playing lesser parts. But then, as so often happens in the film world, the company changed hands, and under the new owners all existing projects either were shelved, passed over to other people, or put into the archives. Among the projects shelved was the Shakespeare film, although there is a possibility it may still be done sometime in the future. For Burgess the only fruitful result of this abortive association was being asked to cobble dialogue in some period screenplays and to do English voice-over for the dubbing of Italian films into English. He thus managed to achieve something from his scriptwriting labors.

Burgess's major connection with the film industry came with Stanley

Kubrick's adaptation of *A Clockwork Orange,* completed in 1971. There is a widely held belief that every novelist's dearest wish is to have one of his books turned into a major film, which if successful will make the novelist and everyone else involved in the film instant millionaires. But the history of *A Clockwork Orange* from novel to major film was, financially and otherwise, a disappointing affair that Burgess now views as "symptomatic of the way things go between the author and the film world." The novel was first published in 1962, and an English pop group, the Rolling Stones, then proposed that they make a film of it and act the roles of Alex and his droogs. Since pop-singing quadrupeds such as the "Stones" are in some ways natural developments from street-fighting groups of the same size, this would not have been entirely inappropriate. The group was even willing to put up a little money for the project. But Burgess wanted to see his novel made into a film of some value. The fact that the "Stones" would probably have made it a commercial success—just as the films of the Beatles and Elvis Presley were invariably commercial successes—did not matter to him. He thought a film version of value might best be done by an underground company working on a low budget, and thus he was prepared to take very little for the film rights and finally sold them for about $500.[16]

Because of the problems of censorship, however, it appeared the film might never be made. Only in the last few years have permissive conditions made it possible for filmmakers to undertake honest adaptations of books depicting sexual as well as other forms of violence, and *A Clockwork Orange* was wisely reserved for this time. The film rights were owned by a New York attorney who lived in London. When Stanley Kubrick wanted to film the novel, Warner Brothers paid the attorney approximately half a million dollars for the rights. Thus an investment of $500 paid off rather handsomely for the lawyer, but the man who had created the book reaped next to nothing.

There were bigger disappointments yet to come. Burgess earned a little money writing a script for the film, but then Kubrick decided he wanted to write his own screenplay. Burgess's script had been purchased with the film rights in a package deal and it eventually became part of the material used by Kubrick in composing his own script. Indeed, much of Burgess's script is present within the finished film, although without acknowledgment.

Thus the whole experience was disappointing to Burgess, and not merely from a financial standpoint. Far more depressing was the sense of being demoted to the level of "a mere provider of raw material for a great filmmaker," the sense of being a lowly hod carrier, as it were, for creative genius. Throughout the year of the film's release, it became more and more evident to Burgess that he was regarded as the secondary or even tertiary creator of *A Clockwork Orange,* and that Kubrick was regarded as the primary creator, the real source of the ideas, characters, and language. One of the more irritating manifestations of this popular misapprehension was a grotesque proposal from *Playboy* magazine that Burgess should go to England while Kubrick was there, follow him around like a dog, and produce the definitive article on Kubrick and "his" work. Not surprisingly, Burgess's reply to *Playboy* was that they might as well ask Kubrick to do the same thing for him.

Burgess's sense of demotion was more than personal. He felt the tendency to regard Kubrick as primary creator was symptomatic of a popular inclination to give the art of the novel less than its due. A common view at present is that the visual arts, especially films, are somehow more real and therefore more important than the lower-toned arts such as prose fiction. A writer's descriptions, no matter how precise or evocative, are viewed as only potentially real and as being in need of the filmmaker's life-giving touch. Burgess is distressed by this because he has no doubts whatever that written fiction is a far richer and potentially more rewarding art than filmmaking:

> When all is said and done, the thing one writes is the thing one means. Literature is a superior art to the film. The film is too explicit. It can't indulge in ambiguities. It can't indulge in overtones, whereas literature still does provide one with these vast areas in which the imagination can move. One can see a character as one wishes. One can interpret a scene as one wishes. There is room for symbolism and linguistic play. Whereas the film is a rigid form that will permit little of this. And it's becoming increasingly visual, increasingly the medium for the cameraman. The interplay of light and shade and shape is everything.

The films of the 1930s, he recalls, bad though some of them were—banal, stagey, oversimple, prudish—tended at least to move with genuine literary logic from beginning to end. Now this is no longer the case. Filmmakers no longer feel the need for logic in plotting, and one result is that they are apt to regard books as "just the rawest kind of material" for their shaping hands. Burgess is no longer inclined to supply this "rawest kind of material" to filmmakers. He wants his books to "maintain their own integrity and not be diminished by people who see a cinematic interpretation of them." After his experience with *A Clockwork Orange* he wanted nothing more to do with films if he could possibly avoid it: "The lure of the money is not even there. In the newspapers one encounters rumors of millions of dollars changing hands, but it just isn't true."[17] Since then, however, his attitude has changed a little, to the extent that he is again willing to permit some of his novels to be made into quality films.

Burgess, as an artist, is still committed primarily to prose fiction—fiction to be appreciated for its own sake. Indeed, he is seething with ideas for new novels, wanting only the time to write them. His most recent major novel, just completed, is an attempt to fuse his two major interests, the novel and music. Although there have been many fanciful attempts in the past to musicalize literature—Eliot's *Four Quartets* and Aldous Huxley's *Point Counterpoint,* for instance—Burgess's fusion of the two was intended to go well beyond anything previously accomplished in this line. His novel *Napoleon Symphony* presents the life of Napoleon Bonaparte, from his marriage to Josephine until his death, in the "shape" of Beethoven's *Eroica* Symphony. What this means is that he has deliberately matched the proportions of each of four "movements" within the novel to each of the four movements within the symphony. He began the project by playing the symphony on the phonograph and timing the movements. He then worked out a kind of proportionate correspondence of pages to seconds of playing time. He even worked with the score of the *Eroica* in front of him, making sections within his prose movements match sections within the *Eroica* so, for instance, a passage of so many pages corresponds to a passage of so many bars. Beyond this, he sought to incorporate the actual dynamics of the symphony, the same moods and tempo. The project probably would not have astonished Beethoven, for, as Burgess observed while he was in the process of writing *Napoleon Symphony:*

> Beethoven himself was a more literary composer than many people imagine. He was a great reader of Plutarch's *Lives,* which of course always deal with two parallel lives. And he seems to have done something like this in the *Eroica,* though we have no external evidence to prove it. It has seemed to many musicologists that the first two movements of the *Eroica* deal with a sort of Napoleonic man. We see him in action, then we hear his funeral oration, and after that we get away from the modern leader and back to the mythical. The scherzo and the finale of the *Eroica* both seem to deal with Prometheus. In the last movement Beethoven puts all his cards on the table because it is a series of variations on a theme taken from his own ballet music about Prometheus and his creatures. So this leaves me with the task of writing a set of variations on a Promethean theme. Napoleon in my novel turns into a sort of Prometheus in the last two movements. The problem is a vast one and not purely a gratuitous question of seeing if it can be done. It's a question of using musical form to cover a vast amount of material, the whole course of Napoleon's life from the marriage to Josephine to his eventual death. Music enables me to get away from strict chronology and deal mainly in mood and theme, so that the novel need not end with his death on St. Helena. In fact it will end with a resurgence of the old triumphant mood, with Napoleon crowned for having, despite all obstacles, at least partly fulfilled his dream of a united Europe. But the technical problems involved are immense. In order to achieve something like compression, I've had to use verse as well as prose. I've had to use diagrammatic constructions, immensely compressed dialogue and subchapters which are only half a page long, so that a great deal of agility will be required of the reader.[18]

None of this should suggest that reading *Napoleon Symphony* will be more work than pleasure. Napoleon emerges as a human being in a way he never before has been allowed to emerge from lengthy historical tomes or even other works of historical fiction. Like Coriolanus, he is simultaneously tragic and ridiculous, a grand comic creation demanding sympathy as well as laughter. We see him from within engaged in spectacular rationalization and romantic self-delusion, and from without through the eyes of the lesser creatures who follow his fortunes—cynical political observers in Paris, wretched foot soldiers in Egypt and elsewhere, and his faithless empress. The disastrous effects of his Promethean efforts are in no way softened, but there is sympathy for the dreams inspiring the efforts.

Napoleon Symphony was followed by *The Clockwork Testament,* which outraged so many New Yorkers, and two novellas, *Beard's Roman Women* and *ABBA ABBA.* The latter two works represent, as he said recently, "a sort of farewell-to-Rome phase." In *Roman Women,* he draws upon his experiences as a scriptwriter and, as he does in *The Clockwork Testament,* puts cinematic art in its proper place, well below literature, in the hierarchy of artistic achievement. Within the hierarchy of Burgess's own artistic achievement, these shorter recent works are relatively minor. *The Clockwork Testament* occupies a place in his canon that might be likened to the place of *The Loved One* in Evelyn Waugh's. *Beard's Roman Women* might similarly be likened to *Scott King's Modern Europe* or *Love Among the Ruins.* They are funny, provocative little books that reward rereading. We are grateful and reassured to see them, and they whet our appetites for Burgess's next major novel, *Christ the Tiger.* *ABBA ABBA* is primarily a collection of sonnets by the blasphemous dialect poet Giuseppe Giocchino Belli (1791–1863), which Burgess himself translated, maintaining the Petrarchan form ABBA ABBA CDC CDC. The collection, seventy-two of Belli's nearly three thousand poems, is introduced by a brief novella about John Keats dying in Rome and his possible meeting there with Belli in 1820 or 1821. Another poetic exercise recently published is a long original poem in free verse entitled *Moses.* As Burgess explains, the poem was actually the "source" of the script for the television epic *Moses the Lawgiver,* starring Burt Lancaster, which in turn became a film for the cinema: "I was trying to get a rhythm and a dialogue style, and verse-writing helped."[19]

The *Moses* epic was part of what Burgess calls his "TV tetralogy," which also includes specials on Shakespeare, Michelangelo, and the widely acclaimed *Jesus of Nazareth.* As a result of the highly favorable reception of these productions, he has been asked to write scripts for several others, including a six-hour TV epic on "Vinegar Joe" Stillwell, who hated the British; a Persian film on Cyrus the Great; and the next disaster epic by Zanuck and Brown of Universal, "ultimate, really, since it's about the end of the world."[20]

His disgust with filmmakers has diminished a little, and he is no longer quite so resistant to having his novels turned into films. He was in fact elated when Carlo Ponti proposed making a film of *The Wanting Seed,* with Sophia Loren in the role of Beatrice-Joanna.[21] But his attitude regarding the inferiority of film to literature as an art form remains essentially unchanged, as we may gather from *Beard's Roman Women,* in which he sets up a rivalry and confrontation between a novelist and a scriptwriter. The novelist Pathan sneers at the scriptwriter Beard as one "who writes for the great crappy demotic media." Pathan's narrowly contemptuous view of the scriptwriter's art is not Burgess's, but when the cinema and the scriptwriter's art have been given their due, Beard is forced to recognize his own inferior status as an artist. Burgess has thus represented two very different modes of creative commitment in which he himself has been engaged and has revealed the somewhat antithetical nature of the relationship between them. It is the business of a novelist to exploit language fully. A novelist who becomes a scriptwriter must in effect restrain his art. Pathan scornfully describes what the novelist must do: "Crisp nervous dialogue. Don't use many words, but repeat the ones you do use. Lesson number one, as administered to Scott Fitzgerald and William Faulkner" (*BRW,* 61).[22]

Burgess's next major novel, *Christ the Tiger,* has been completed and is scheduled to appear in French and Italian translations but, strangely, not in English—at least not yet.[23] It was originally planned as a retelling of the life story of Jesus Christ through the mouth of a follower, a kind of drug-taking hippy of the period who uses a language of his own, a specially made dialect based on Semitic roots. The language itself is an ambiguous vehicle designed to convey "a very ambiguous image of Christ." Moreover, the point of view of the narrator allows readers to view Him in various unconventional ways, even as a diabolical being not unlike Charles Manson.

Another novel with a religious subject is already well underway. Tentatively entitled *The Affairs of Men,* it focuses on a character who resembles the late Pope John XXIII. Burgess felt neither reverence nor admiration for this pope. He has referred to him as a "Pelagian heretic" and an "emissary of the Devil" who caused the Church enormous damage by raising unrealistic hopes that there would be radical doctrinal changes to accommodate the pressures of twentieth-century life. The Pope John figure in his novel will be a kind of antichrist, and thus Burgess suspects the book is "likely to be vastly unpopular." While working on this, he is also writing a novel, to be entitled *The Pianoplayers,* in the naïve, unlettered style of a young girl. Burgess has not lost the ability, shown most vividly in *A Clockwork Orange,* to convey the voices of the young, and he can still communicate with even the very young, as his children's book *A Long Trip to Teatime* shows.

Burgess has enough projects in fiction and scriptwriting to keep him more than fully occupied as a writer even if he did nothing else. But he is involved with a good many other writing projects as well. His biography of Shakespeare appeared in 1971 and, more recently, a 30,000-word article for the *Encyclopaedia Britannica* on "The Novel," as well as a linguistic study of Joyce called *Joysprick.* Other scholarly works planned or commissioned include a biography of Hemingway, a book on Orwell's *1984,* and a treatise on creative writing. He intends to revise and update *The Novel Now* to include more American novelists and others he thinks he may have slighted unjustly in the first edition.

Certainly the most awesome scholarly task that awaits him is the translation of *Finnegans Wake* into Italian, an endeavor he and his wife will undertake jointly. As a scholar/translator in her own right, her qualifications so perfectly complement his own that he feels they must have been "both predestined to work together on it." They will begin by translating Burgess's abridgment, *A Shorter Finnegans Wake.* If that works, they will attempt the complete original. The undertaking has the blessing and encouragement of a major Italian publisher, but when he asks how much money they will want for it, the Burgesses are simply unable to answer because obviously no amount of money could possibly recompense the time and energy it will take. As Burgess says,

> . . . the problems are unspeakable, the problems of telling a Dublin dream in Italian. But then again if one looks at the text, one finds that there is already a great deal of Italian in it—Triestini Italian—and a kind of fusion of Trieste and Dublin. One finds that there are various motifs in Italian life which Joyce found in Dublin life. For instance, in Dublin he found the publishers Browne and Nolan, whom he introduces in *Finnegans Wake.* Their names are useful, for "Browne" can be Italianized to "Bruno" and the philosopher Bruno came from Nola. In fact, Joyce refers to him in an earlier work as "the Nolan." One sees as well a relationship between the Tiber and the Liffy. And one sees also that various new puns can be developed by bringing Italian and English together in ways that Joyce did not. The tentative title of the whole work is *Forbicetta,* but in our spelling it will be *pHorbiCEtta,* with the H, C, and E in capitals to indicate the hero, Humphrey Chimpden Earwicker. The word "forbicetta" means "ear-wig." In the middle of it is "orbi" meaning "to the world"—HCE in his Pope manifestation. Even this single word encourages one to believe that something can be done in this way with Italian which will work as well as Joyce's own English, or "Pun-Eurish," as I call it, seems to work. But it's a tremendous undertaking. God knows when it will be finished. Nevertheless it has to be done—by somebody—and we're the two people who must do it. We both feel that Joyce has been a tremendous revivifier—of more than English. His early works—*The Portrait of the Artist as a Young Man* and *Ulysses*—had a strong influence on contemporary Italian novelists. But Italian writers have not yet been willing to go the whole hog and enter the region of dreams, and we hope that an Italian translation of *Finnegans Wake* will help to stimulate Italian fiction into new directions. This would give me immense pride, to have some say in the literature or language of an alien country.[24]

It appears that Burgess's revels are nowhere near an end, although he is now sixty and in the senior ranks of British novelists. But few people realize that exhaustion of the creative vein is by no means the only major obstacle that can discourage an established writer. Even when a writer's pen is surging with life, life itself is extremely difficult, especially for a British writer. In addition to the discouraging nuisance of inequitable taxation, there are always printers' strikes to delay a book's appearance and the venom of underpaid reviewers when it does appear. For instance, some critics could not understand what Burgess was doing in *The Wanting Seed* and *A Clockwork Orange* because they simply had not bothered to read them through to the end. *Nothing Like the Sun,* a truly brilliant achievement by any fair critical standard, was dismissed by one reviewer as a mere "potboiler" designed to capitalize on the Shakespeare quadricentennial. But the favorable critical response to Burgess's books far outweights the unfavorable. *Devil of a State* was a Book Society choice, and the British literary establishment thought enough of his work in general to make him a fellow of the Royal Society of Literature. Nevertheless, the "sneers of the impotent" in hastily scribbled reviews have a way of damaging a book's sales; also, there is always the possibility that one's novel may bring a lawsuit. Any reader who happens to detect a vague resemblance to himself in some character in a novel may get a ready hearing in the British courts. Burgess has been especially unlucky in this regard. The entire first edition of one of his best early novels, *The Worm and the Ring,* was withdrawn and pulped up because of a purely coincidental resemblance of events and characters, and his publisher was obliged to pay £100 in damages in an out-of-court settlement.

In truth, writing novels and scholarly nonfiction for a living is a hazardous, sometimes painful occupation, and for the most serious writers it is far from lucrative. If money, not genuine literary creation, is the objective, a writer can grind out pornographic artifacts. But this has never tempted Burgess. A more tantalizing and far more respectable temptation would be to take a position as a writer-in-residence, a "kept" creator, at a wealthy American university. William Faulkner, e e cummings, John Barth, and many others have not been above yielding to this one. Burgess, however, is proud of his identity as a professional writer and so far has managed to resist this temptation, too, even though the University of Buffalo and other schools, not to mention his own severe financial pressures, have made it very attractive for him. He accepts visiting professorships mainly because he enjoys teaching:

> It's a mode of direct communication which is comforting and stimulating after sitting in a state of solitude before a typewriter communicating with the ghosts of readers or readers unborn or nonexistent readers or some abstract notion of a reader.[25]

He has taught widely in the British Commonwealth and Europe as well as in the United States, and he is fairly impressed by the quality of American students "from a human point of view":

> They're good and sincere, aspirant and very different from their parents. They do question everything. But it worries me that they lack basic equipment. They haven't read very widely. I don't mind their cutting themselves off from the 1930s or '40s, but I do object to their cutting themselves off from the Graeco-Roman and Hebraic civilizations which made our own. It means that if one is

giving a lecture on Shakespeare or Marlowe, one cannot take it for granted that they know who Niobe was, or Ulysses, or Ajax. And this is undoubtedly going to get worse in America; may indeed lead to the entire cutting off of America from the whole current of culture which gave it birth. A man like Benjamin Franklin, a great American, may become an unintelligible figure to modern Americans. This is very frightening.[26]

He objects as well to the utilitarian view of literature held by many American students, their insistence that it is to be valued primarily in terms of the "messages" it conveys and their concomitant tendency to regard a purely aesthetic aim as "irrelevant," "sinful," or "reactionary."

Although he enjoys university teaching, he does not see himself as any sort of intellectual ("If I am one, I'm fighting against it all the time"). He does not want to become too much a part of the rarified, cerebral campus atmosphere in which the enwombed academic thrives. His attitude stems largely from his view of the nature of literature and indeed reality itself. To some extent, he agrees with the Shakespeare/Burgess composite hero in *Nothing Like the Sun* that literature is "an epiphenomenon of the action of the flesh":

I don't think it's an intellectual thing. It's not made out of concepts; it's made out of percepts. People often think you're being trivial or superficial if you think it's important to describe a bottle of sauce or beer as neatly, as cleverly, as evocatively as you can. It's really more important to do that than to express an idea or concept. I believe the world of physical things is the only world that really exists, and the world of concepts is a world of trickery, for the most part. Concepts only come to life when they're expressed in things you can see, taste, feel, touch, and the like. One of the reasons I have a sneaking regard for the Catholic Church is that it turns everything into tangible percepts. There's no mystical communion with God as there is in Hinduism or Buddhism. Instead you get God in the form of a meal, which is right, which is good. When you die, they shove oil on your body. Oil is something your body has always given out, exuded. You're getting it back again. It's a Mediterranean idea, using this staple of life, this nourishing thing, oil. And I like the ring in marriage. One gets a shock in countries like Italy to find the old Fascism alive and people who talk about mystical concepts, about what Mussolini *really* meant, about *l'umanita, lo spirito umano,* and all that sort of thing. These are horrible metaphysical concepts which mean bugger all. You find this summarized best at the end of *Finnegans Wake,* where they're waiting for the coming, where you get this Berkeley-Bulkily-Buckley character who talks an idealistic mumble. Then you get St. Patrick with the shamrock. There it is, the God-given, the *Dieudonné,* the physical object. It's a thing in itself, just as the Cross is a thing in itself, but it's also a symbol of something bigger. These bloody far eastern religions with their lack of physicality, their incorporeal substances, they're sickening.[27]

With regard to religion, Burgess still maintains a "renegade Catholic" stance that is oddly conservative in some respects. He despises liberal Catholicism, which seems to have become another religion in the process of gaining acceptance in the modern world. The ecumenical movement repels him, as do the liturgical changes and the use of the vernacular. He is disgusted by these innovations, as he says, "very much from the Catholic angle":

> But when I say that I am a Catholic now, I mean solely that I have a Catholic background, that my emotions, my responses are Catholic, and that my intellectual convictions, such as they are, are very meager compared with the fundamental emotional convictions. Certainly, when I write, I tend to write from a Catholic point of view—either from the point of view of a believing Catholic, or a renegade Catholic, which is I think James Joyce's position. Reading *Ulysses,* you are aware of this conflict within a man who knows the Church thoroughly and yet has totally rejected it with a blasphemous kind of vigor.[28]

To an extent, he subscribes to the Manichean heresy, although he agrees with the Church that it should be condemned as heresy. He shares the Manichean belief that there is a perpetual conflict between two forces that dominates the affairs of the universe, and whether the forces can be accurately labelled "good" and "evil" is by no means certain. They might as reasonably be designated by terms such as "right" and "left," or "x" and "y," or even "hot" and "cold." All that is certain is that the opposed forces exist, are in conflict, and that earthly turmoils, such as the present conflicts between East and West, are relatively trivial affairs that merely "figure" the great cosmic clash. Like his character Hillier in *Tremor of Intent,* he believes that the man who is aware of this conflict and yet deliberately and cynically refuses to involve himself in it is a contemptible self-server. Although even America and Russia are beginning to realize that the Cold War has just been a game, and although the possibility of nuclear war between them is perhaps steadily diminishing, Burgess believes their rivalry reveals "an unconscious recognition that this is the nature of life—the two opposed forces, as exemplified in these big political blocs, the West and the East and their opposed ideologies. In this respect, I call myself a Manichee. I believe, if you like, that God and the Devil are possibilities, but it is not forseeable, it is not inevitable that God should win over the Devil."[29]

Although Burgess's world view is in many ways a pessimistic one, it has not prevented him from enjoying fully what the world has offered him. The spectacle of humanity in all its infinite variety of race and language is a constant source of wonder and pleasure to him, and the love he has known in human relationships is a great solace. Then there are the pleasures, although sometimes excruciating, of artistic creation, which for him include music as well as literature. He still composes music and has had the pleasure of hearing his own Concerto for Strings, some sonatas and quartets, and the incidental music for some plays and motion pictures performed. Most recently, his Symphony in C was performed at the University of Iowa. There is also for him the great sensual pleasure of listening with a trained ear to the works of others. The bitter disappointments, frustrations, and pain he has known cannot diminish the consolations of love and art, and indeed his view of life itself is wholly affirmative, even while his pessimistic view of the world allows the possibility that the "wrong god" may gain the upper hand in the great cosmic struggle. Like Christopher Howarth in *The Worm and the Ring,* he believes life must be blessed and praised in spite of every misery it may bring. The reader who shares to any extent this capacity to accept life on its own tragicomic terms will find his fiction an enriching experience.

2

IN QUEST OF A DARKER CULTURE

Many of Burgess's novels have a recurrent motif related to his dualistic concept of ultimate reality: his work thus portrays cultures that embody, either literally or metaphorically, some forms of "darkness" and cultures that lack this darkness. The protagonists of these novels tend to be derived from the latter and drawn to the former. For example, in *A Vision of Battlements*, Richard Ennis is caught between the cultural values represented by his fair Protestant English wife and the love he finds with a Spanish Catholic girl in Gibraltar. Other aspects of a darker culture, including the Rock's Moorish heritage, which he seeks to capture in music and his own residual Catholicism, draw him to this Mediterranean darkness and increase his sense of alienation from the culture he has left. In *The Long Day Wanes*, the darkness of Malaya draws Victor Crabbe into itself and reveals the mystery of a dark girl he had loved and killed. An obsessive desire to be reunited with this girl causes him to give himself wholly to the country. In *Devil of a State*, on the other hand, darkness is a negative thing for Lydgate, a means of escape from responsibility and guilt. In fleeing his past, he seeks shelter in various dark corners of Asia and Africa before he is finally caught in a dark little state called "Dunia." Unlike the protagonists in those novels, Christopher Howarth in *The Worm and the Ring* is not actually shown within a darker civilization. But his residual Catholicism deprives him of any sense of community in fair Protestant England, and he finally decides to leave it for a darker Catholic Mediterranean community. One can find the same theme treated in different ways in *The Right to an Answer, Tremor of Intent, Nothing Like the Sun,* and *One Hand Clapping,* but this chapter focuses only on those novels in which this motif appears dominant.

A Vision of Battlements

Burgess's first novel, *A Vision of Battlements,* did not appear until 1965, well after his Malayan books and others had begun to establish his reputation.

It had been written during the Easter vacation of 1949, partly as an experiment in extended creation (could he compose such a prose piece without getting bored?), and partly as an attempt to exorcise the "dead weight of Gibraltar." As a soldier stationed on the Rock, he had found three years to be "a long long time," and "a work of fiction seemed the best way of breaking it up, pulverizing it, sweeping it away."[1] However, the protagonist's story is close to his own story, and the attempt to exorcise the pain and loneliness he was experiencing merely served to call it back.

There is much more to *A Vision of Battlements* than the mere dreariness of soldiering on the Rock. Much of it is riotously entertaining, and Burgess's gift for comic description is evident throughout. The book also contains partial treatments of philosophical and religous themes that become central preoccupations in his later work. Also, in some respects, it anticipates later developments in the novel generally. Its form, for instance, is that of a mock epic quest structured around the misfortunes of an antihero of the type introduced by Kingsley Amis and others during the fifties. Although it is by no means one of Burgess's finest achievements in the novel, it is a very respectable apprentice piece; moreover, it deserves recognition as one of the more successful attempts to capture satirically an aspect of a war that inspired surprisingly little in the way of significant fiction.

As Burgess tells us in the introduction, the epic he most closely paralleled and parodied was Vergil's *Aeneid.* But he was perhaps influenced less by Vergil than by Joyce; in fact, he was consciously paying a small tribute to Joyce, who had, by use of the *Odyssey,* simultaneously reduced Odysseus to the stature of a little man named Bloom and exalted Bloom to Odysseus.[2] The outlines of a Joycean comic-epic quest can also be perceived in several of Burgess's later books, including *The Long Day Wanes, The Doctor Is Sick,* and *The Wanting Seed.* In each of these novels, his sense of the comic possibilities of such a framework becomes more evident. However, he takes an increasing amount of liberty with this framework, fleshing it out with dystopian satire, antiromance, and other comically enriching elements.

The fact that Burgess chose to parody the *Aeneid* tells us a great deal about how we should read this novel. Vergil's masterpiece is a sublime tribute to Rome and the austere ruler who had managed to reunite a country devastated by civil war and was striving with much less success to halt the corrosive progress of society's decadence. Like Horace's Roman Odes, the *Aeneid* glorifies the old-fashioned patriotic ideals and moral values upon which supposedly the past and future greatness of Rome depended. Aeneas's piety and unswerving stoic commitment to moral purpose cause the gods to smile upon him and the empire he will found. Some readers have thought Vergil effectively dehumanized Aeneas by sanctifying him to suit the taste of Augustus. Certainly, in comparison with fun-loving Odysseus or even Achilles or Roland, he seems like a cold fish, but this is largely because, unlike them, Aeneas is invariably able to subordinate all selfish inclinations to a higher end: the founding of a new Troy. Like Shakespeare's Henry V, he is not without strong passions, but his blood and judgment are so commingled that his sense of duty is never seriously threatened, even when he is with Dido. He also is amply reassured that his devotion to duty is well worth what it costs. Vergil obviously intended his readers to be filled with a sense of Roman greatness, past and present. Although he was surely aware of the discrepancies between Augustan moral and religious ideas, and the realities of Augustan society, this awareness did not inhibit his presentation of the ideals in his epic. The fact that Aeneas's direct descendant was on the imperial throne was in itself proof that the God-sanctioned greatness of Rome was still a reality.

When a writer such as Burgess, living in another empire, chooses to burlesque such an epic by reducing Aeneas to a bumbling sergeant and his Mediterranean wanderings to the Rock, we can see that his diminishing irony extends beyond characters and events to the tradition-hallowed, imperial self-images and ideals that inspire the creation of national epics. The passing of the empire is not itself one of Burgess's main focuses in this novel, as it is in the *Malayan Trilogy* and *Devil of a State,* but it is an important part of the backdrop against which we watch the antiheroic exploits of Sergeant Richard Ennis. For this empire, which had so drained itself in the fight against fascism that its ability and will to preserve itself against other foes had gone, Ennis is an appropriate Aeneas. In short, it is not merely the antiheroism of an individual we are seeing, but the antiheroism of Britain herself at the end of the war. Vergil could overlook debauchery at court and other blemishes and still celebrate Roman greatness, but few writers who had experienced World War II could overlook its dehumanizing effects and still sing in traditional heroic terms of arms and men.

The novel opens with Ennis's landing on the Rock. Like Aeneas, he is memory haunted by the wife he left behind, a dead father, and a burning city. His assignment to the Rock with the Army Vocational and Cultural Corps is enviable in terms of safety, but he is destined to face service as trying in its way as the action he has seen at Dunkirk and Crete. His CO is a tyrant and his messmates are men with whom he has little in common. The principal cause of Ennis's misfortunes, however, is no one other than Ennis himself. He is an artist, a musician whose art has a habit of "getting in the way" and preventing him from fitting smoothly into his assigned role as a purveyor of culture and officially sanctioned inspiration. When, for example, he is supposed to be inspiring a gang of hardhanded dockers with a discourse on "the future of the British Empire," his artistic soul and vaguely liberal leanings cause him to accept the role of bardic mouthpiece for the downtrodden and inarticulate. He is trapped by his own rhetoric into abandoning the lecture hall and leading the men into a drinking shop. In thus allowing his art to orchestrate his thoughts to the exclusion of what the world calls "duty," Ennis anticipates one of Burgess's later creations, the poet Enderby.

Like Mr. Enderby, Ennis need only let himself go and a vaguely left-wing indictment of the Establishment will flow out, complete with a hazy vision of a golden age to come. Unlike Enderby, however, Ennis is oppressed by a heavy sense of guilt over his failure to become an accepted part of any Establishment, and his guilt makes him rather feeble as a rebel and an artist. He really would like to be a good soldier. Even more, he longs to be worthy of his wife, Laurel, a social-climbing patrician whose letters to him are either "Dear Johns" announcing divorce or guilt-heaping missives prodding him on to higher things in "my world." Another great Establishment also beckons with a guilt-heaping hand—the Catholic Church, which he has abandoned but cannot escape. Somehow, even though "he desperately wanted conformity, stability," his art will not permit him to mold himself to a form admissible in any of these venerable realms.

Ennis's life on the Rock is not all pain and loneliness. Venus provides him with temporary consolation—a dark-skinned Spanish Dido named Concepción who offers all that a man could ask. If Ennis were truly capable of rebelling and submerging his sense of social and religious restraint, he would not follow the dutiful example of Aeneas and abandon her after loving her. But the same yearning for conformity and stability combined with a Catholic horror of divorce and fear of ostracism cause him to leave her to lingering misery and death. Having done this, he is tormented by longing and an awareness of the absurdity and shallowness of the conventional values that cow and control him:

> Ennis was seeing, projected on to the bare staves of his manuscript paper, Concepción in a cold England, shivering over the fireless grate, jaundiced-looking against the snow, Concepción in the fish queue, the "bloody foreigner" in the English village, the "touch of the tar brush" from the tweeded gentry. He foresaw the ex-prisoner-of-war Luftwaffe pilot, flaxen, thick-spoken, playing darts with the boys ("That were a bloody good one, Wilhelm"), Concepción and himself in the cold smokeroom ("That foreigner that there Mr. Ennis did marry"). Finally he saw Laurel meeting Concepción, Laurel slim and patrician, sunny hair glowing under the floppy hat, over the flowered frock, at some garden party: "But she's terribly sweet; that accent is *most* attractive; such an unusual, such a perfectly fascinating biscuit-coloured complexion; I'm sure we shall be *great* friends." (*AVOB,* 71)

Another temporary consolation is provided by the very art that gets in his way. As he broods over the loss of Concepción, a *Passacaglia* stirs within him and, while the Rock celebrates final victory over Japan, Ennis brings it forth. He is temporarily borne aloft by a heady sense of personal victory over the "philistine sods" who have oppressed him. An orchestra is gathered and he has the services of a magnificent flamenco singer as well as an epicene ballet dancer who happens to be his bunkmate. His sense of triumph increases as the evening of the concert performance approaches. But the philistines are destined to triumph. Ennis's CO, a tyrant with that capacity for vengeful sadism characteristic of the envious impotent, orders Ennis to teach classes in elementary shorthand on the evening of the concert. Since Ennis happens to be the conductor, the concert is doomed. For the first and only time in the book, he engages in authentic rebellion; with "his Church and Army training battling against Prometheus and Satan," he responds with a *non serviam* that places him under close arrest.

Curiously, Ennis makes no attempt to reschedule the concert later, and the reasons for this are revealed in a sort of postmortem analysis by Ennis and a sneering fellow sergeant who happens to be a psychologist. They agree that Ennis's residual Catholicism has quenched his will and made defeat acceptable. The tyrannical CO is a kind of God figure, a "gangster god," and his authority has for Ennis something like an eschatological sanction. He evokes Ennis's sense of Hell. At this point, the psychologist deliberately switches off his interest in the case, and he justifies his own submission to tyranny in terms of scientific interest. This gives Ennis his turn to sneer:

> "You scientists," said Ennis. "You'll never raise a hand to strike down a Caligula or a Hitler. Your excuse is always the scientific interest of the abnormal. 'We need morbid types to justify the existence of morbid psychology.' You make me sick sometimes." He said this without rancour. (*AVOB*, 92)

This conversation reveals Burgess's early preoccupation with the themes he would develop in several later novels. The Church's tyranny even over individuals in whom faith is a residual presence is treated in *The Worm and the Ring* and *Enderby*. Other questions raised in the conversation are probed extensively in one of the most brilliant of his later novels, *Tremor of Intent*.

To some extent, Ennis prefigures the secret agent protagonist of *Tremor of Intent* who returns to Rome with a faith renewed by the experience of evil. This can be seen not only in Ennis's contempt for the moral idiocy of the so-called scientific attitude but also in the Manichaeism he arrives at through his experiences with his CO. He adjusts himself to "a world of perpetual war. It did not matter what the flags or badges were; he looked only for the essential opposition—Wet and Dry, Left Hand and Right Hand, Yin and Yang, X and Y. Here was the inevitable impasse, the eternal stalemate" (*AVOB*, 55). The sneering psychologist prefigures the scientist in *Tremor of Intent* whose efforts to escape divine judgment through Promethean achievement fail to provide him with any really important answers. The psychologist's antagonism toward Roman Catholicism also foreshadows the main conflict in *A Clockwork Orange* between the social planners who seek to impose goodness on individuals through behaviorist technology and their opponents who hold to the ancient Catholic belief that such an imposition is evil. Interestingly enough, Ennis's companion asserts flatly that he is not a behaviorist, not a watcher of watering dogs' mouths; he is "interested in the mind." Ennis finally concludes that the psychologist's revulsion toward Catholicism grows out of a strong attraction. When a psychologist becomes truly "interested in the mind," he's apt to stumble onto something called "faith."

Burgess includes a number of these stimulating dialogues in his "Enniad," including one on Pelagianism discussed below (in chapter five) in connection with his dystopian books. Some of the dialogues may appear to be digressive; his material is not as smoothly integrated in this novel as in later ones, but since we are reading a kind of epic, long digressions are in order. Moreover, even a comic epic hero must be aware of being involved in events of more than imperial significance. Ennis's sense of earthly conflict as a mirror of cosmic opposition is very much in the tradition.

The trials of Ennis are by no means finished with the abandonment of the *Passacaglia*. Like long-suffering Aeneas, he has much to endure even as he nears the end of his quest. Aeneas's final trials at the site of the new Troy are mixed with the pleasures of anticipation. The fair Lavinia awaits him, a mate more fit in the eyes of the gods than Dido to be the consort of an empire builder. Ennis, too, meets a Lavinia who seems to represent all that the gods of stability and conformity demand, a lovely, golden-haired English girl who possesses "that cool aseptic English charm which . . . was like a clear note from which all the harmonics had been eliminated" (*AVOB*, 109). Her striking resemblance to his patrician wife is part of her attraction, but she is no snob and she even shares his artistic interests. Unfortunately, since she does represent for Ennis that cool aseptic world and its conventions, which he can neither accept nor ignore, he feels compelled to seduce her in conventional, insincere terms. But since she is in fact a girl who prefers a frank, animalistic approach to a dishonest detour through aesthetic discussion, he is doomed to yet another failure. She doesn't deny him the pleasures of her body, but his own body, feeling the intimidation of his spirit, will not respond. Then, without malicious intent, she also plants seeds of doubt in his mind about his potency as a musician. At first he tries to resist this dawning sense of impotence in love and art. When he finally does accept it, after a thoroughly cheerless visit with a Sybil, he has the somewhat dismal consolation of feeling ready for a regeneration in which potency doesn't matter: "That's all I'm fit for, I suppose. Whom art rejected, whom love rejected, God rejected not" (*AVOB*, 171). Again, a main theme in *Tremor of Intent* is foreshadowed, but in that novel, the theme of potency and religious regeneration is handled differently.

This exegesis of plot and themes in *A Vision of Battlements* is distressingly inadequate as a description of the novel. Indeed, the book is a philosophical, sometimes melancholy, satire, but it is also very funny. Take, for instance, this picture of Ennis's troopship approaching Gibraltar out of the stormy Atlantic:

> The storm died down, and there was already in the clearer air the smell of a warmer climate. The rolling English drunkard had come to the Mediterranean by way of the Viking whale roads. The ship woke to life again, the decks were busy with arms drill, P.T., a succulent drawled lecture on venereal disease. Wrens, dapper in flapping bellbottoms, provocative with Sloane Square vowels and wagging haunches, minced up and down. . . . Only a few bodies still lay prone and supine, rejecting the hard-boiled breakfast eggs and the lyrical call of life. As to some faunfife or Triton-horn, the colleagues of Sergeant Ennis rose from their beds, back to perpetual games of solo, and their harsh vowels cut the mellow cultured flutings of the Intelligence Corps contingent. Though the vowels of Sergeant Agate, ballet-dancer, one-time Petrouchka praised by Stravinsky and patted by Diaghilev, were far from harsh. (*AVOB*, 15–16)

This same epicene sergeant becomes Ennis's most reliable comrade, his Achates. Burgess, unlike some writers who cannot seem to treat homosexuality without exhibiting a pathological fear of infection (at least in the minds of their readers), makes Agate an endearing character and uses him to achieve some hilarious effects. The combat sequence, for instance, in which Ennis vanquishes Sergeant-Major Turner, his Turnus, is made even more ludicrous by Agate's utterly unexpected and devastating assault on the manhood of Turner's supervirile simian cohorts.

A Vision of Battlements is indeed a very respectable apprentice piece. Comparison of the book with acknowledged classics about the war, such as Mailer's *The Naked and the Dead* and Evelyn Waugh's *Sword of Honour* trilogy, is hardly fair, although in terms of characterization and use of language, it is about even with Mailer's book and not too far beneath Waugh's. What places it beneath both is a certain confusion of purpose. Mailer's novel is integrated about the one great theme of futility—the inevitable emergence of a new fascism out of the victory over the fascism of the Axis. Waugh's treatment of the wartime progress of Guy Crouchback is similarly integrated about his vision of the passing of an old order and all its values. Burgess's novel is a kind of potpourri of subjects—the plight of the artist oppressed by a philistine Establishment, the attractions of Manichaeism, the inescapable hold of Catholicism, the Pelagian heresy in the twentieth century—that he treats fully and brilliantly in his later novels but that are not intimately related here except in the mind of Ennis and his chance conversations with others. Although, to an extent, this can be justified in terms of the comic epic form, inclusion of too much intrusive, loosely related material has a vitiating effect on a book that seeks to present an author's vision of what World War II meant to one nonheroic participant and, by implication, what it meant to the weary victors generally. This is not to say that the subjects are not in any way relevant to each other or to his main focus. They can in fact be related closely, as Burgess himself shows in *Tremor of Intent, Enderby,* and other later novels. It seems, however, that Burgess had not fully thought through the connections when he was writing *A Vision of Battlements*. Still, he introduces his material in an intriguing fashion, and while he is entertaining us with respectable comedy, he whets our appetites for later, fuller treatments of the same material.

The Long Day Wanes

Burgess's first three published novels—*Time for a Tiger, The Enemy in the Blanket,* and *Beds in the East*—deal with life in Malaya as he saw it in the midfifties and late fifties. The British were still engaged in a long, bloody, ultimately successful campaign against communist guerrillas, but the long day of British colonial domination was clearly waning. The trilogy, subsequently published in one volume entitled *The Long Day Wanes,* encompasses not only the actual passing of the British raj a year before it occurred but some of the less happy events that were to follow the birth of Malaysian independence.

Burgess had found the country a fascinating, indeed fantastic, cultural and linguistic mélange, and he was eager to record what he saw. As a musician, his first impulse was to orchestrate it, and he actually composed a symphony in which the different ethnic groups revealed themselves in snatches and strains. But the symphony was not well received, and he sought another medium. The resultant oeuvre may itself be likened to a symphony or perhaps a giant canvas upon which Burgess has painted portraits representing most of the generic types he had known. We are introduced to Malays, Chinese, Tamils, Sikhs, and Eurasians, as well as to a largely maladapted collection of British colonials. Our vocabulary is increased by the addition of numerous words and expressions in Malay, Urdu, Arabic, Tamil, and Chinese. A glossary is included in the back of the book, but, as he does in *A Clockwork Orange,* Burgess weaves the strange vocabulary into the context so the meaning is readily apparent.

The trilogy is unified by Malaya itself and by the presence of Victor Crabbe, a young British schoolmaster who has come to the Far East in search of a new life. Like Richard Ennis and other Burgess protagonists, Crabbe is guilt ridden, oppressed by the memory of a wife he accidentally drowned in an English river, and, like so many of the protagonists, he feels the inexplicable pull of a darker civilization:

> But it was also right that he himself should draw great breaths of refreshment from the East, even out of the winds of garlic and dried fish and turmeric. And it was right that, lying with Rahimah, he should feel like calling on the sun to drench his pallor in this natural gold, so that he might be accepted by the East. And, if not right, it was at least excusable if he felt more loyalty to these pupils than to the etiolated, ginger-haired slug in the Headmaster's office. His indiscretion was based on something better than mere irresponsibility. (*MT, 49*)[3]

Since Crabbe's presence links the trilogy, we become very involved with him at times. But because the focus of the book is much broader than any individual, Crabbe is seen primarily as a witness. Our attention is focused mainly on the people he meets and their experiences, which reveal the heart of Malaya itself.

The first novel of the trilogy, *Time for a Tiger,* concerns the hilarious trials and adventures of one of Crabbe's most remarkable acquaintances, a gigantic colonial police lieutenant named Nabby Adams. One should always note the significance of names in Burgess's novels. In this case, it happens that "Nabby Adams" is very close to *Nabi Adam,* which is Arabic for the prophet Adam, and Nabby is indeed a true son of Adam. Within the thematic framework of the novel, he seems to represent the condition of man. He also helps introduce Crabbe to the East and reconciles him to "going forward," despite his name. Nabby has already achieved what Crabbe longs for: acceptance by, indeed absorption into, the East. But Nabby's East is India, not Malaya, and he longs to return there. Having mastered Urdu and Hindustani, he is in the process of losing his English through disuse. A far more serious liability, however, is a dependence on drink that the term *alcoholic* cannot adequately describe, for drink is not a crutch for Nabby, or an anaesthetic: it is his raison d'etre. He will drink virtually anything, but his favorite nectar is a local beer named "Tiger" (hence the novel's title). Unlike Crabbe, he is not troubled by concupiscible urgings, but his passion for Tiger is comparable to what other men feel for women: "His real wife, his houri, his paramour was everywhere waiting, genie-like in a bottle. The hymeneal gouging off of the bottle-top, the kiss of the brown bitter yeasty flow, the euphoria far beyond the release of detumescence" (*MT,* 62).

Assuaging "six feet eight inches of thirst" is a formidable task requiring the full commitment of Nabby's wits during every waking moment. He must outwit disapproving superiors, unpaid *kedai* keepers, and anyone else who might be a source of drinking money. His perilous quests for Tiger drive readers to uncontrollable laughter along with a bit of lip-licking sympathy stirred by Burgess's evocative descriptions of his thirst and the orgasmatic ecstasy of gratifying it. Indeed, although Nabby is a cheat, a liar, and a sponge, he is irresistible, and a reader must inevitably find himself accepting the big man's simple hedonistic standards. After all, what could be more frustrating than being rewarded by a *kedai* keeper with only *one small* bottle of Tiger after you have paid five dollars of your bill of a few hundred? What could be more heavenly than being virtually drowned in Tiger and brandy by wealthy Chinese businessmen eager to show their appreciation for the dedicated service of the police?

Accompanying Nabby on his thirsty wanderings is his assistant, a little Punjabi corporal named Alladad Kahn. The two converse in Urdu and have little to do with the British community until they meet Crabbe and his attractive blonde wife, Fenella. Although Nabby is attracted by Crabbe's well-stocked sideboard and his wallet, Alladad Kahn is mainly interested in Fenella. He is one of several dark-skinned characters in the trilogy who feel the erotic and cultural pull of a lighter civilization, and through him we gain some insights into the Islamic culture that so fascinated Burgess. To an extent, Alladad Kahn feels the same weak twinges of guilt about disregarding the ways of this culture that Crabbe feels about "letting down the side" as a British colonial:

> He was not a very orthodox Muslim. He had ideas which shocked his wife. He had once said that the thought of eating a pork sausage did not horrify him. He liked beer, though he could not afford much of it. He could afford even less of it now that Adams Sahib insisted on taking him around. He had seen kissing in English and American films and had once suggested to his wife that they try this erotic novelty. She had been horrified, accusing him of perversion and the blackest sensual depravity. She had even threatened to report him to her brother. (*MT,* 42)

The feeble restraints of Muslim mores are dashed away completely when Alladad Kahn gains acceptance by Fenella Crabbe. After awhile, he stops trying to win her heart and settles for her kind, pitying, motherly attention. If the troubadours had been translated into Urdu or Malay, he would be able to recognize some similarities of sentiment and situation. To him, she is a divine creature whose pity is a healing balm, a regenerating spiritual force, but to Crabbe, she is merely a wife, to be taken for granted and excluded from the romantic context in which he thinks about his mistress.

Oddly enough, it is Alladad Kahn and the giant alcoholic wreckage of a man he follows who make life in Malaya worth enduring for Fenella. She is devoted to Crabbe and willing to sweat with him in a tropical purgatory apart from the rest of the British community, but she senses that Crabbe's love for the girl he drowned will never let him love anyone else. He simply does not need her, and, until she mets Nabby Adams and Alladad Kahn, she is almost ready to accept his suggestion that she return to England. But she happens to be a poetess with a sense of the archetypal, and Nabby stirs her imagination:

> He fascinated her, he seemed a walking myth: Prometheus with the eagles of debt and drink pecking at his liver; Adam himself bewildered and Eveless outside the Garden; a Minotaur howling piteously in a labyrinth of money worries. She treasured each cliché of his, each serious anecdote of his early life, she even thought of compiling his sayings in a book of aphorisms. (*MT,* 110)

As Burgess introduces Malaya through the experiences of these characters, he reveals some of the reasons why the British raj must pass. The Crabbes and, to an extent, Nabby Adams gain the affection and respect of segments of the native population, but they do so at the expense of alienating the rest of the British community. Crabbe sees this clearly:

> The side had been let down. He had broken the unwritten laws of the white man. He had rejected the world of the Club, the weekend golf, the dinner

> invitations, the tennis parties. He did not drive a car. He walked round the
> town, sweating, waving his hand to his Asian friends. He had had an affair with a
> Malay divorcee. And of course Fenella was no better. She had rejected the
> white woman's world—*mah jong* and bridge and coffee parties—for different
> reasons. (*MT*, 77)

Most of the British colonials are content to remain with each other in lofty
isolation from the native community. In some cases, this is due to a pathological revulsion toward dark skins and a concomitant reluctance to assume any
white man's burden other than that of simple exploitation. We see this in the
drunken ravings of a planter who views the entire non-European community
as "niggers" whom he would like to "lash," "beat," "nail to the door," and
"pepper with hot lead." A less violent, although equally unloved, type of
colonial is represented by the headmaster at Crabbe's school, a yawning slug
of a man who complacently views the same vast community, as well as some of
the European masters under him, as "wogs." Except for puritanically punish-
ing a bit of fancied fornication, he exhibits no real interest in his young
charges. His only concern is maintaining the approval of his superiors in
Kuala Lumpur, and when his ignorance and incompetence lead to a humiliating pupil revolt, he immediately blames Crabbe.

Nevertheless, although Malayans may not have much reason to love the
British, they do have some reasons to be grateful. Beyond the relatively safe
confines of the cities, the jungle is infested with communist guerrillas who
emerge to ambush travellers in autos and terrorize plantations. They "appear
capriciously, at unpredictable intervals, to decapitate tappers or disembowel
them—a ceremony followed by harangues about the Brotherhood of Man
and the Federation of the World" (*MT*, 35). Thanks to the British, this threat
is destined to diminish and finally end. Malayans also have reason to thank the
British for maintaining some degree of interracial harmony. The Chinese,
Indians, and Malays despise each other, but the British presence gives them a
kind of unity in resentment. Unfortunately, the departure of the British will
immediately liberate all the old antagonisms. Crabbe's school is a microcosm
of Malaya and a vision of its future. In it "the problem of rule seemed
insuperable. A sort of Malayan unity only appeared when the discipline was
tyrannous; when a laxer humanity prevailed the Chinese warred with the
Malays and both warred with the Indians and the Indians warred among
themselves" (*MT*, 33). On the adult level, the attitude of Crabbe's Malay
tutor is typical. When Crabbe asks him about the roles of native Chinese,
Indians, and Eurasians in a free Malaya, he replies without hesitation: "Dey
do not count. . . . Dey are not de friends of de Malays. Malaya is a country for
de Malays!" (*MT*, 76–77). Crabbe's attempts to reason him out of this racial
chauvinism only bring forth a torrent of slogans and catchwords: "*Merdeka!
Merdeka!* Freedom, independence, self-determination for de Malays!" (*MT*,
77). Such outbursts should give Crabbe some insights into the future, but he is

a liberal and therefore an optimist, a believer in human reasonableness. In *Beds in the East,* however, he will finally begin to lose hope that racial strife will yield to reason.

Through the experiences of Crabbe, we are made aware of the "political themes" of *Time for a Tiger*—the cultural tensions and currents of feeling affecting Malaya as a whole during this critical period of its history. Presenting these tensions and currents as they reveal the beating heart of the country was obviously one of Burgess's main concerns in this novel, as it was in the two sequels. But just as the political themes in Shakespeare's *Henry IV* plays are overshadowed by the figure of Falstaff, so the political themes of *Time for a Tiger* are overshadowed by the giant "vice" figure of Nabby Adams. Burgess does not, however, have to make his novel bear the same sort of didactic burden as the *Henry IV* plays; hence, although the riotous disposition of Falstaff must be punished by rejection, there is nothing to prevent Burgess from letting Nabby triumph gloriously over all obstacles to alcoholic delight. As the novel concludes, the future is uncertain for the Crabbes and for Malaya, but Nabby is a Prometheus freed from his rock by the Herculean hand of wealth.

Burgess's career as a novelist really begins with this first novel of his *Malayan Trilogy.* In it the promise of *A Vision of Battlements* is richly fulfilled. Not only does he manage to picture convincingly some rather fantastic characters, he also enables us to view life in their terms. Nabby Adams, for instance, compels a reordering of standards: having shared his thirst and frustrations, we rejoice with him when fortune permits him to drink the rest of his life away in Bombay. If there were little in the novel besides Nabby, it would still be a comic masterpiece. But there is much more: we have seen part of the rich canvas of Malaya, its warm bright colors and its shadows, and we are eager to move on.

The problems of adjustment to a darker civilization are dealt with lightly in *Time for a Tiger.* Crabbe chooses to "let down the side" and Nabby Adams drowns himself in Tiger. In *The Enemy in the Blanket,* Burgess deals with more complex cases. The novel opens with Crabbe on his way to a new post as head of Haji Ali College in the state of Dehaga. The stale news of his affair with a Malay divorcee has finally found its way to Fenella, and this together with the crapula engendered by Chinese New Year hospitality makes the flight to Dehaga a dismal one. Their marriage will in fact dissolve, although not because of this particular affair. Fenella will find the love she deserves with a man of another race, and Crabbe will be left with his memories, his guilt, and a sense of loyalty that makes the guilt bearable. Before this happens, however, they meet some characters with interesting adjustment problems of their own.

There is no one to meet the Crabbes at the airport in Dehaga, but they are assisted by a man of their own race, a "very white man" named Rupert

Hardman. Hardman is a young lawyer, an alumnus of Crabbe's own university, and at the time of Crabbe's arrival, he is about to become, somewhat reluctantly, absorbed into the Islamic culture. The case of Hardman shows how Islam might lose its enchantment for an Englishman, as it once did for Burgess, even if he has much to gain by embracing it. Hardman, like Nabby Adams, is under desperate financial pressure. Having abandoned the unsavory Singapore law firm that brought him to Malaya, he is trying with little success to make an honest fortune practicing on his own. He would return to England if he could, but as he sinks further into debt, the prospect of escape from Malaya grows more remote. He could escape the debt, but not the East, with 'Che Normah, a fiery, voluptuous, and wealthy Malay widow who has him marked for her third and last husband. His status as a professional man and his albinoid complexion, indisputable proof of his racial identity, are among her principal attractions for her. In return for these social assets, she offers her wealth and the pleasures of a marvelously formed and insatiable body. Unfortunately for Hardman, who derives no pride whatever from being an albino, she is also a strong-willed and very orthodox Muslim. His white, "very white," skin and his profession are about the only vestiges of his former self she will permit him to retain. His Catholic religion, most of his harmless pleasures and habits, and even some of his friendships must be discarded. He deludes himself into believing the marriage is only a temporary, expedient arrangement; when he has established his practice and paid her back for taking care of his debts, he will avail himself of the simple Muslim means of obtaining divorce. But it becomes clear that 'Che Normah is indeed "no Cho Cho San."

One of the friendships that Hardman must discard—his closest Malayan friendship—is with a French Catholic priest, Father Georges Laforgue. Father Laforgue is alarmed by Hardman's plunge into Islam, but it is difficult for him to counsel Hardman effectively because he, too, has been so completely absorbed into the East that his own Catholicism is somewhat "equivocal." As a missionary in China, he had been seduced intellectually by Chinese philosophy and emotionally by the Chinese way of life. Aside from his contacts with the Chinese community, life in Malaya is meaningless for him. He is "so sick for China" that nothing else seems to matter if he cannot devise a means of returning. Eventually he does find a most unlikely means, as a deportee with a shipload of communist guerrillas.

Burgess does not focus exclusively on colonials in this novel. He is as much or more concerned with presenting the native community, but there is one more colonial who takes up considerable attention and who provides a great deal of hilarity: Talbot, a fat, moon-faced creature who exhibits the same sort of devotion to food that Nabby Adams had to drink. As with Nabby, most of Talbot's sexual drives seem to have been either rechanneled or replaced by the demands of other viscera. He is perpetually gorging himself, but far more nauseating than this is his lyric poetry, in which he celebrates the pleasures of the table. A sample:

> . . . Cracks open the leaden corncake sky with
>   crass, angelic
> Wails as round as cornfruit, sharp as crowfoot, clawfoot,
> Rash, brash, loutish gouts of lime or vinegar strokes
> Till the crinkled fish start from their lace of bone. . . . (MT, 201)[4]

Talbot's wife, Ann, clings desperately to her sanity, chiefly by means of affairs with other men, and it is inevitable that she and Crabbe will have an affair. Ann is a small, dark-haired girl, physically like Crabbe's dead wife. One of the means whereby Crabbe placates his former wife's "unquiet ghost" is making love to vague images of her such as Ann. This is what drew him to the Malay divorcee, and indeed he hopes to find his dead wife reincarnated again and again as he becomes absorbed into Malaya.

Crabbe is the only colonial on the staff of Haji Ali College. The teaching staff under him is made up of Malays, Indians, Chinese, Tamils, and Eurasians. Supervising their work is the sort of chore that would age any conscientious man rapidly, and Crabbe *is* conscientious. Listening to the classroom learning process is especially trying, as it is, for instance, when he looks in on a history lesson and hears the following account of colonial brutality from the Tamil instructor:

> . . . And the British hate the Indians so much they built a prison called the Black Hole of Calcutta and they put thousands of Indians in this very small dark room where there was no air and the Indians died. . . . (MT, 225)

He moves on to an English lesson and hears an exhortation from a Malay:

> . . . For fuck's sake if you are going to speak this bloody language, take your finger out. And work I give you you do not bloody well do. I stand here in great pain because I am a sick man, and I see you little bastards doing no bloody work at all grinning at me like fucking apes as if it did not matter. (MT, 225)

The teacher happens to be a veteran of the British navy, and in reply to Crabbe's tactful remonstrance, he asserts, reasonably enough, that he is teaching "English as it is spoken, not from dusty books."

Crabbe also has to contend with the vigorous hostility of some subordinates. Jaganathan, a not-very-bright Tamil senior master who had been bribed with the promise of the headship before Crabbe's appointment, ceaselessly intrigues against him. He finds an unwitting ally in Hardman, who indiscreetly mentions Crabbe's undergraduate leftist activities at their university. This leads to the resurrection of Crabbe's Marxist juvenilia in old issues of the student magazine and their circulation in typed copies among members of the staff and community. With the communist guerrillas still at their bloody work in the jungles, such relics of his youth could be as troublesome for Crabbe as pink mud from a witch-hunting senator. Jaganathan's smears are not even the worst threat. Thanks to the thievery of his Chinese cook, Crabbe has actually been feeding the guerrillas. Oddly enough, though, these dangerously embarrassing associations are part of an incredible chain of accidents that eventually ingratiates him with the natives. His undergraduate utopianism proves attractive to some who are supposed to be scandalized and a large group of communist guerrillas surrenders to Crabbe, considering him their benefactor. It is one of the few times in the trilogy that he is actually able to do something for Malaya. For the most part, he has no real control over events and, all his benevolent efforts not-withstanding, he can only watch the coming of independence with helpless concern, unable to make any meaningful contribution.

Aside from 'Che Normah, perhaps the most interesting native character is the Abang, a feudal lord of Dehaga whose rule, along with that of the British, is about to pass. This does not distress him greatly, for he has managed to salt away enough wealth to enjoy a glamorous exile on the Riviera or anywhere he chooses. The Abang is an enlightened man who has a clearer understanding than most Malays of what the British mean to Malaya:

> Haughty, white, fat, ugly, by no means *sympathique,* cold, perhaps avari-
> cious—you could call them all these things, but Malaya would be empty without
> them. The common enemy was also the common law-giver; coldness could
> mean justice. It was too late to be friendly, too late to try to learn. But one could
> at least dislike with sympathy and smile through one's valedictory jeers. (*MT,*
> 248)

He is especially sympathetic toward Crabbe, for he intends both to cuckold him and to appropriate his automobile, which happens to be of a type not represented in his royal fleet. He views Fenella as a kind of transitional conquest between the long series of blond women he has enjoyed in his own country and those he intends to have in exile; therefore he "would treat her kindly, he would revere her as a symbol, his seduction of her would be civilized, delayed" (*MT,* 248). In fact, when she gives up her loveless, meaningless existence with Crabbe, the Abang takes her along into exile. Ironically, Fenella, through her relationship with the Abang, will probably come closer to knowing the heart of Malaya than Crabbe.

Burgess also entertains us riotously in this novel with a group of shiftless Sikhs. In Malaya, as in India, the Sikhs, if they are not already night watchmen or farmers, are drawn to careers in the police or the military. But Mohinder Singh aspires to a higher calling, that of shopkeeper. He believes that, by diligent effort, he can succeed as well as those commercial masters, the Chinese. Unfortunately, his effort is delayed by two fellow Sikhs, an incredi-bly lethargic night watchman named Teja Singh and a police constable named Kartar Singh upon whom Burgess lavishes some magnificent lyrical comic description:

> Kartar Singh was so fat as to generate in the beholder a re-orientation of
> aesthetic standards. His was a fatness too great to be gross, a triumphant fatness

somehow admirable, an affirmative paen, not a dirge of wasted muscle and overindulged guts. This fatness *was* Kartar Singh: it was the flesh singing, in bulging cantilenas and plump pedal-notes, a congenital and contented stupidity, a stupidity itself as positive as the sun. (*MT,* 232)

The two easily persuade Mohinder Singh that he needs time off, and as they swill *samsu* in a *kedai,* Mohinder Singh puts off commercial glory to the future.

The Sikhs provide some disquieting glimpses of the future. They have a lordly disdain for other races and it is returned. Malays in particular look with contempt on them and dream of the day of independence when they can exterminate them along with white men, Tamils, and, above all, their pork-eating Chinese creditors. The sense of foreboding engendered by these glimpses of interracial loathing prepares us for the scenes of actual strife in *Beds in the East.* Against this, Crabbe hopes to be a voice of sanity and reason, a spokesman for sound Western "values." Hardman, who has his own illusions about himself in the new Malaya, tries to disabuse Crabbe with brutal sneers:

> You'll never teach them how to think. And you know damn well they've got their own values, and they're not going to change those for any high-minded, pink-kneed colonial officer. They're ready to take over now. It's probably going to be a hell of a mess, but that's not the point. Whether the fruit's going to be good or rotten, the time is ripe. (*MT,* 255)

But the good fortune that makes Crabbe temporarily a hero of the people allows him to continue in his liberal optimism. As the novel concludes, he is preparing to take a new assignment, an important administrative post in which he hopes to accomplish something before he is replaced by a Malayan. His wife leaves him with his memories, just as Talbot's wife leaves him with his food and poetry, and Hardman makes an unlucky escape from 'Che Normah—unlucky in that the plane that Hardman pilots to freedom apparently crashes.

Again, Burgess has given us a brilliant living picture of a setting and characters unlike anything that most Western readers would ever encounter. After this novel and *Time for a Tiger,* one feels close to an understanding of this fantastic composite culture and the people from outside who are drawn to it. But there is a great deal more to come in the equally splendid concluding novel of the trilogy.

Beds in the East begins with a description of a Malay family arising for one of the last days of British rule and concludes with a description of a lovely Tamil girl wiping away a tear for Victor Crabbe as she is pulled onto a ballroom floor. Nearly all of the novel is concerned with native Malayans, members of groups Burgess introduced briefly in the first two books. For them it is the "dawn of freedom," a shedding of light to illuminate all the problems of freedom. As anticipated, the only change in interracial relationships is an intensifying of mutual hostilities. In the opening scene, Syed Omar, a Malay police clerk, looks back with little remorse on the previous evening when he had completely upset a farewell dinner for a Tamil chief clerk by denouncing him and all of his race. That same day, he seeks out the Tamil and follows his verbal assault with a physical one. His grudge against the clerk is personal, but it is felt all the more deeply because of his unshakable conviction that Tamils "are a lot of bastards" (*MT,* 336).[5]

The Tamils have the same regard for the Malays, and Burgess then focuses on his victim and other members of "the élite of the Jaffna Tamils": young government officers and professional men, all single because of their inability to find "women of good caste and of the right colour, worthy of professional men." The most interesting member, a state veterinary officer named Vythilingam, is willing to risk disgrace, but the woman he has in mind, a lower caste Christian Tamil girl named Rosemary Michael, is not interested in him. She is a girl whose dark beauty is so perfect it is "absurd," the absence of any flaw itself "a kind of deformity." It is not merely her caste but also her reputation for looseness with British colonials that makes her, in Tamil eyes, unworthy of Vythilingam. She is a "colonial widow," loved and left by a formidable list "ranging from the District Officer to the manager of the local Cold Storage." Determined to marry a European, she offers sensuous treasure to all white takers, but not to Vythilingam or any other dark-skinned Asian. (On one occasion, after a brief rationalization involving geography and exotica, she does yield to a fat, asthmatic Turk.) This determination causes Vythilingam to loathe them all, especially the British. As a member of a proud caste, he is even more sensitive than most Asians to the slights and insults of colonial masters, and his intense hatred for them derives from a long history of indignities. It is in no way diminished by the fact that his widowed mother has married an Englishman. Like a kind of black-skinned Hamlet, he is filled with revulsion and hatred for her, which he intends to express in part by marrying Rosemary. It will be a deadly cut to their family honor, for the aristocratic Tamil code of honor is not unlike that of Renaissance Italy or Spain:

> And yet in his choice of a wife there was something masochistic. Rosemary's reputation was known; he would, by obscure logic, become retrospectively a cuckold. Her caste, as her name, the name of a Christian, proclaimed, was of the lowest, and that hurt, and yet that would hurt his mother more, and yet perhaps it would not, because what had she done but marry a Christian? (*MT,* 339)

Vythilingam is actually a bundle of contradictions. He is a communist, and this together with his hatred for the British should send him into the jungle to join the guerrillas. But, with the racial chauvinism characteristic of the country, he is held back by his dislike for the Chinese; moreover, he has an aversion to violence that "reeked of Hinduism." Indeed, his whole attitude toward Rosemary "reeks" of religion and morality, the "bourgeois device of oppression." At a critical moment, however, his hatred for the colonial oppressor triumphs over his gentler inclinations, and the colonial who suffers is, ironically, Victor Crabbe. Just as it is seldom the professional agitator but nearly always the relatively innocent and well intentioned who suffer the wrath of outraged authority, so it is not usually the sneering, cursing exploiter but more often the rare colonial devoted to serving the natives who feels their wrath. (Burgess's Malaya seems to be not unlike the Congo in this respect.) Near the end of the novel, Vythilingam, a kind of emblem of Malaya itself, stands by a river in studied unconcern while Crabbe and all of his dreams are literally devoured.

Before his miserable death, Crabbe engages in a number of benevolent activities that are little appreciated, including a daring attempt to promote interracial harmony by bringing together members of the principal ethnic groups. With little success, he has urged the Malay who is taking over his post and others to think in terms of Malayan unity and community. Their lack of enthusiasm does not discourage him and he actually arranges a multiracial cocktail party. He plans it carefully, down to the porkless, beefless hors d'oeuvres. The absurdly beautiful Rosemary acts as hostess, having convinced herself that the whole thing has really been arranged for a showing of her new engagement ring. The élite of the Jaffna Tamils are invited, along with a few Malays, Chinese, and Eurasians. Indeed, all would probably go well enough if it were not for the arrival of an uninvited guest, Syed Omar, freshly fired from his job, full of liquor, and aching for revenge on the Tamils. Because of his fondness for the dramatic, Syed Omar's occasions and places of attack on his black-skinned enemies are invariably those that provide both spectacle and direct involvement for the maximum number of innocent bystanders. One moment Crabbe is discoursing eloquently to his guests on the necessity of breaking down racial barriers and a few moments later there is pandemonium. One of Omar's fellow Malays attempts to calm him, but he is goaded on by drunken, half-conscious gibes from Vythilingam, who also provides an oddly appropriate musical background with "the song the Japanese had sung in celebration of the fall of Singapore." So much for one more benevolent colonial effort.

A potentially far more effective scheme for promoting racial amity presents itself in Robert Loo, an eighteen-year-old Chinese boy who happens to be a bona fide musical genius. Robert is capable of giving Malaya what Burgess himself had sought to give it, a musical monument. As in *Nothing Like the Sun* and *Enderby*, the goddess has descended, and this boy, "a rather dreary boy, not very intelligent, emotionally less mature than he should be" is "strapped to a talent which had, quite arbitrarily, chosen him, driving him to teach himself to read music at fourteen, pore over Stainer, Prout, Higgs,

Forsythe at sixteen, at eighteen produce two works which, Crabbe thought, were probably works of genius" (*MT*, 352). He is, Crabbe feels, capable of becoming Malaya's answer to Sibelius and de Falla. Although he lacks any of their patriotic feeling, he has created pieces that reproduce on wind and strings the rhythms of the many languages and cultures among which he has grown up. The most ambitious of these is a symphony that Crabbe hopes to have performed in Europe, if he can pull the right strings and persuade the right people, including Robert Loo himself. But everyone, including the boy, is indifferent to the idea of promoting national harmony through art. When Crabbe insists that "music can be a big thing to a country finding itself. Music presents a sort of image of unity," the boy is simply unable to understand him. Crabbe doesn't have much more luck with the Malay administrator he tries to interest in the symphony, especially after he reveals the composer is Chinese. ("Do you think he'd object to having a Malay what-you-call? You know, something like Abdullah bin Abdullah? It would make quite a bit of difference up in Kuala Hantu" ([*MT*, 373]). But he is not to be discouraged.

Crabbe's motives for promoting this not too likeable boy and his work are thoroughly misunderstood by the native community. Even his friends simply assume his motives are pederastic. The Malays in particular, sons of Islam for whom "celibacy is not merely unknown" but "unintelligible," are unable to imagine anything else. Actually, Crabbe is in the process of deliberately abandoning his sexuality completely along with whatever else remains of his youth, but the natives are correct that there is more to his interest than a love of music and a desire for Malayan unity. Again, this is really a tribute to his dead wife. That she is identified in Crabbe's mind with Malaya itself is clearly suggested by some old love letters Rosemary Michael discovers among his handkerchiefs. The dead girl's signature is indecipherable but appears to be "Mal, May, Maya, something like that" (*MT*, 436). She had been a gifted musician, and by fostering this hope of a great national symphony for Malaya, he is paying her the finest tribute of which he is capable. This benevolent scheme, like all of his others, is destined to fail, but Crabbe, thanks to his violent death, is mercifully spared complete knowledge of the failure.

In *A Vision of Battlements* Burgess deals with the situation of the artist vis-à-vis an unsympathetic, impinging world, a subject he deals with in various novels and most extensively in the *Enderby* books. In all of them, he is as much concerned with what unmakes as with what makes an artist, and the story of Robert Loo is yet another treatment of the melancholy theme of creative genius's fragility. As with the poet Enderby, Robert Loo's undoing as an artist begins when the great world begins to "impinge." His father decides to stimulate the drinking trade in his little shop by installing a jukebox, and this ear-splitting presence makes it impossible for Robert to continue composing while he minds the till. Since his father is also too thrifty to let lights burn after working hours, Robert must forsake his goddess, must leave her with her violin, "bow at the ready, smiling patiently but clearly puzzled at the delay" (*MT*, 379). Except for a brief interval while he is at odds with his father, the thought of leaving home for the sake of his art is simply unthinkable and, from the conservative Chinese point of view, "blasphemous." Still, he might be able to achieve a reunion with the lady, in spite of the jukebox, were it not for another woman, namely, Rosemary Michael. He first encounters her in his father's shop, in company with Crabbe, and as he gazes at merely one splendid limb of this delectable, empty-headed creature, it is the beginning of the end for his art:

> Robert Loo saw himself looking, for the first time, at a woman's hand. It was a well-shaped hand—the beauty of any one isolated part of Rosemary's body was a divine wonder: it was only the totality, the lack of the animating soul that failed to impress: the kinship of the sublime and the absurd. Robert Loo's eyes were led, as in an artfully composed picture, up from the long delightful fingers to the cunning of the wrist, up to the smooth round brown arm to the bare shoulder. This was the real world impinging. (*MT*, 391)

A few hours later, having secretly "maimed" the jukebox for the sake of a day's blessed silence, he "hears" a concerto and sees how he will sketch its first movement, but then suddenly, with the same mind's eye, he sees Rosemary and hears "no music": "Seeing the long elegant brown arm again, he groaned, remembering Crabbe's curious word 'impinge' " (*MT*, 392).

Burgess's marvelous gift for interrelating without apparent contrivance a widely varied collection of fascinating characterizations and themes is apparent throughout the trilogy but especially in this novel. The romance of Robert Loo and Rosemary, which ultimately destroys the boy's art, would seem to be a most unlikely possibility since he is a rather "dreary boy," and she despises the touch of Asians. But circumstances bring them together in the house of Crabbe, while he is absent, and for a torrid half hour, Crabbe's dream of interracial harmony is realized, in a small way at least, on his own bed. There can of course be nothing for Robert Loo beyond this marvelous interlude. Even this has been made possible only because of a number of accidents, including Rosemary's acquaintance with an incredibly Anglophile Chinese gentleman whose Oxonian voice and manner permit "the entrance of Asia." Other factors, especially her recent abandonment by a white man, turn her toward her native East, with the result that "time and grief had handed the key to a dull and harmless Chinese boy" (*MT*, 438). When the door swings wide, however, it is not for the key bearer but for the long-suffering Vythilingam. Unfortunately for that black Hamlet, he is to be sundered from his Ophelia by parental machinations, forced to flee upcountry to avoid a marriage arranged by his mother. By the time he returns, Rosemary is again hopefully offering herself as a delectable colonial pastime.

Through Rosemary, Robert Loo tastes the fruit of what he calls "love," but it is more likely codish adolescent romanticism. However, he feels compelled to express this strange new feeling—strange, indeed, by its strength alone—

in his music. But the sort of composing he has been doing—remarkably competent, honest work, which is both his own voice and Malaya's—is inadequate for expressing what he feels, or thinks he feels, for Rosemary. Not only does the insipid stuff blasting out of the jukebox no longer shock him, he believes it is closer to what he should be composing for his lady than his early work:

> And, yes, he would, he would! He would revert from this stage of hard-won mastery of counterpoint, of orchestration, of thematic development, to breathed clichés of wind and voice for her, for her. All the ore that waiting lay for the later working he would melt before its time to make her ornaments for a day. (*MT,* 443)

Even Rosemary's humiliating rejection of him fails to counteract this corrosive new attitude. Like any other self-conscious adolescent discarding toys and other embarrassing childhood relics, he destroys his early work. When opportunity finally knocks, thanks to Crabbe, and two Americans eagerly summon him in hopes of finding someone who can musically recreate the sounds of Malaya with authenticity, someone upon whom a scholarship can be bestowed, he permits them to view only work that is "second-rate cinematic romantic stuff, complete with big Rachmaninoff tunes on the violins and chords banging out on the solo piano" (*MT,* 505). The Americans, having not "come out these thousands of miles to see a distorted image of ourselves in a mirror," are quite uninterested in the musical potential of Robert Loo. So much for yet another benevolent scheme on behalf of Malaya.

Crabbe's most miserable disappointment awaits him upcountry at a remote estate in the communist-infested jungle where he is sent to investigate the murder of a native headmaster. The manager of the estate is an affable but insufferably complacent patrician who represents all of the colonial attitudes and values Crabbe despises. The unbearable revelation he receives from this man concerning his first marriage is the cruelest irony of all in a book that is full of cruel ironies. Just as his belief that he is truly needed by Malaya is shown to be illusory, so his perfect relationship with the girl who is figured in his mind by Malaya is shown to be an illusion. It is unlikely that Crabbe would ever have recovered from this shock even if he had lived. As it happens, he dies accidentally a few minutes after he learns the miserable truth, either drowned or devoured by a crocodile. But the explanation of suicide, accepted by the estate's superstitious coolies, would be plausible to anyone who knew fully what he had experienced.

A reader is liable to be jolted by Crabbe's wretched exit, but he cannot deny that Burgess has prepared him for it in various ways throughout the trilogy. All along, although Crabbe is no fool, he has had a tendency to cling to illusions, especially with regard to his potential as a human benefactor and problem solver. The communism of his undergraduate days was discarded long before his arrival in Malaya, but the utopianism that made him a communist remained a part of him, and, like most optimistic utopian thinkers, he tended to let his sensibility mold the reality of which his dreams were to be made. He resisted the thought that he might be digested by Malaya without leaving any trace of his benevolent efforts, a thought first prompted near the end of *Time for a Tiger* when a Ceylonese teacher named Mr. Raj, who appears again in *The Right to an Answer,* prophesies that Crabbe will lose both "function and identity" and "be swallowed up" by the country. Mr. Raj's words come back to him during his fatal journey upcountry, but he shrugs them off, thinking how "there was plenty for him to do still, all over the dwindling Colonial Empire" (*MT,* 452). However, Crabbe means very little to the natives or anyone else. His death is "little mourned," although "resented by a few" who had hoped to take advantage of him in some way. Until then, all his generous actions are misinterpreted, as, for instance, when he bails Syed Omar's son out of jail and it is assumed he has a perverted interest in the boy or perhaps in Syed Omar himself. For all his years of service, his knowledge of Malay, his sympathy, and his interest, he is less *sympathique* than the ignorant beer salesman with whom he travels upcountry. Like Vythilingam, he is a kind of emblem of his country, which, as the Abang of Dahaga realized, had given Malaya a great deal even as it had sought to gain. But all that can be hoped for in return is a bit of sympathy mixed in with the jeering farewells.

As the Abang had predicted, there is an emptiness left by the British departure, but it is partially filled without delay by a culture that is in many ways an affront to revered colonial tradition. From the United States come teams of specialists in everything from music to speech therapy, and the process that one Spanish writer has called "the Coca-Colization of the world" begins in Malaya. It is of course ironic that the British should have paved the way for Coca-Cola. Schools such as the one where Crabbe was first assigned had, at the same time they were making "the alumni despise their own rich cultures," sought to provide at least "a show of resistance" to the inevitable global spread of American culture. The Americans, like the British, have little understanding of the natives, but their bumbling efforts to win friends at least amuse the people without antagonizing them greatly, and occasionally the skills of specialists are applied with impressive, gratitude-gaining effect. One of the most grateful natives is a member of the Tamil élite whose voice, a humiliating eunuch's squeal, becomes a manly boom thanks to a bit of speech therapy. A few feats of this kind, some opportunities on the payroll of the United States Information Service, and wide circulation of the story of the Boston Tea Party accomplish a great deal.

The terrorist threat in the jungle continues and the newly independent Government of the Federation of Malaya acts promptly to "carry, posthumously as it must be supposed, the White Man's Burden." However, there is hope that other threats to stability will be diminished. Some Malay and

Chinese youths seem unwilling to keep alive the hatreds of their fathers, and, incredibly, at least one gang is formed consisting of not only these two groups but a Tamil and some off-duty British soldiers as well. Uniformly clad in the Edwardian costume of the teddy boys, the gang turns out to be "a sodality that was to prove more fruitful in promoting inter-racial harmony than any of Crabbe's vague dreams" (*MT,* 502). But Crabbe himself is utterly forgotten, except for a brief, not-too-tearful lament by Rosemary: "Poor Victor . . . poor, poor Victor." Thus Burgess in characteristically tragicomic terms ends his first major achievement in fiction, the *Malayan Trilogy.*

The trilogy is less sophisticated in some ways than his later work. The characters are not very complex psychologically, and all of them, including Crabbe, function primarily as representatives of generic types. But this is how Burgess wanted them to function. They are figures on the giant canvas of Malaya in all its cultural richness and variety. Burgess's focus throughout is on the cultures rather than the uniqueness of the individuals who represent them. Even characters like Nabby Adams and Talbot, who have been likened, rightly, to Dickensian eccentrics, are also colonial types. The result is a grand comic pageant, a kind of symphony, with all the earmarks of a classic of the colonial novel. One might object, as indeed one reviewer did, that the book is excessively negative and pessimistic. The glimpses of Malaya's future offer very little cheer. Even more depressing is the way Crabbe, the character with whom the reader is made to sympathize most fully, is led by the most redeeming elements in his own nature, his capacity to love and his willingness to entertain hope for his fellow human beings of a darker culture, toward nothing but humiliating disillusionment and painful death. Crabbe's punishment for dreaming seems to be so excessive that one's sense of fitness may well be outraged. But then again, considering how offensive life itself is liable to be to one's sense of fitness, the punishment becomes easier to accept.

The critical response the trilogy received encouraged Burgess to write, as he says, for "a cultivated readership," whatever that is. At least he has managed to reach a readership representing a very broad range of cultivation. Burgess speaks to a much wider audience than, for example, the campus. Recently, I sent a copy of the trilogy to a friend who is currently serving aboard a merchant tanker hauling oil between Singapore and Manila. I should have sent a hardback, for after the book had been passed from my friend to the skipper, to his officers, and finally down to the deckhands, it was simply worn out. Happily, some aspects of the book that I had completely over-looked were illuminated for me as a result of conversations between my friend and the first mate. I was also fortunate in meeting recently a Canadian Air Force noncom with little formal education but plenty of exotic travel under his belt, who had read and admired the trilogy. A wide-ranging appreciation from those who can articulate less but have lived more, especially those who have seen what the writer has seen, is an important test of a writer The penalty for failing to earn it is the sort of humiliation suffered by the novelist in Hemingway's *To Have and Have Not* when he bellies up to a bar and asks a hard-living veteran what he thinks of his books. Burgess will probably never be stung by the sort of four-letter rebuke this man receives, unless it is from someone who has lost the ability to appreciate the rich, tragicomic drama of life itself.

Devil of a State

Devil of a State was a Book Society choice when it first appeared in 1961; like so many of Burgess's novels, it had a mixed critical response. *A New Statesman* reviewer observed that its comic devices would have been more effective "if Mr. Burgess hadn't been Scooped long ago."[7] He and others had noted that the book seems to echo Evelyn Waugh's early satires, *Scoop* and *Black Mischief*. Indeed, the African setting and the sardonic detachment with which Burgess presents the chaos of life in a newly emergent state are liable to give a reader of the Waugh satires a sense of déjà vu. Certainly Burgess has acknowledged a general indebtedness to Waugh, as well as to Joyce, Sterne, and Nabokov. But the book is essentially Burgess's own vision of life in such a state, and he quite likely saw the the same sorts of things in the Far East that Waugh saw in Africa. "Dunia," the imaginary caliphate in *Devil of a State*, is, Burgess tells us, "a kind of fantasticated Zanzibar,"[8] but one senses the real setting may be Borneo, just as one senses the Caribbean island of "Castita" in *MF* may actually be Malta.

Devil of a State, like his earlier novels dealing with states of transition in British colonial territories, presents a richly comic gallery of natives, Europeans, and various ethnic mixtures. Again, much of our attention is focused on the trials of a guilt-ridden Englishman haunted by the memory of his first wife, whom he believes is dead. But Lydgate, the fifty-year-old protagonist, has very little in common with Victor Crabbe besides guilt, bad luck, and a fondness for darker, warmer civilizations. He is essentially an adventurer who has tried everything from importing in Nairobi to gold-prospecting in Malaya. Also, unlike Crabbe, he has few altruistic impulses. Thoroughly selfish, he tends to use other people as means rather than ends and to dodge responsibilities. He had married his first wife, an older woman, for her money only to find life with her utterly impossible. Unable to endure her religious fanaticism, he had deserted her and much of his wandering from place to place has been continual flight to avoid her. When he believes she is dead, he remarries only to be divorced and remarried again.

As the novel opens, Lydgate is still bound by this third marriage, but it appears to be as hopeless as the first two. Lydia, his third wife, is a voluptuous Australian girl whose only fault seems to be her desire to be treated as a person by Lydgate. They have been separated but she has come to Dunia in hopes of a reconciliation. Their reunion is promising enough, but soon

Lydgate is asking himself, "Why did women want to be people?" Earlier he had reflected on the difficulty of maintaining an attitude that has come to be associated with male chauvinism:

> But was there really anything except women? He saw his tragedy quite clearly, or thought he did. He expected too much from women, and too little. Heaven, which they could give, was surely a passive thing, static, marble, light, air. But the heaven was enclosed in an irrelevant apparatus with a hellish high-powered will of its own. The trouble with women was that they wanted to be human beings. (*DS*, 151)[9]

His only genuinely happy relationship with a woman has been with a black mistress by whom he has had two children, but here, too, his essential selfishness manifests itself. As a passport officer, he is in a position to betray her by keeping her and their children out of Dunia, and when it suits him to do so, he does not hesitate.

For all his problems with women, Lydgate adjusts to Dunia more easily than most of the Europeans in the novel. Among the more sympathetically drawn and pathetic characters is the Honorable Mr. Tomlin, United Nations adviser, a competent, conscientious veteran of the British colonial service. Mr. Tomlin has the impossible job of advising the caliph on problems of government and use of resources and the equally impossible job of promoting harmony and goodwill among the various native factions in the state as well as between the natives and visitors from various places outside the state. He must strive to promote understanding among people who despise each other nearly as much as they despise him. He must worry about revolutionaries from neighboring territories. He must see that head-hunting cannibal tribesmen upriver have the opportunity to attend school and learn about civilization. When a terrified district adviser seeks to abandon his post upriver, Mr. Tomlin must drive him back to it, and when the man's head becomes a trophy and his body a feast, Mr. Tomlin must blame himself. It is a thankless, man-killing job that causes him to speculate fruitlessly from time to time on the nature of "reality."

One can see in the presentation of British administrators in this novel a bit more sympathy than was shown in the *Malayan Trilogy*. Burgess, himself a former colonial education officer, may have become a bit fed up with the abuse heaped on the British by those who had gained from them as much or more than they had lost. During a disastrous luncheon at the UN adviser's mansion, the doomed subordinate adviser snarls his exasperation at the assembled guests, including a visiting Czech painter who exhibits an intolerable, suspiciously Teutonic frankness; a lecherous Italian marble worker; and an extremely troublesome black revolutionary:

> "We try to do our bloody best. . . .We won the war, didn't we? Try to give 'em peace and show 'em how to behave? Isn't that right? No good German but a dead un," he said. "Hitler was a bloody painter. A bad un like you," he said to

Smetana. ("Czech," chessed Smetana.) "Race of bloody organ-grinders," he said to Nando Tasca. "Black bastards," he said to Patu. "You'll have your own bloody way, but what do we get out of it? Sitting there smug on your arses, having a crack at the poor bloody British. Income tax fifteen bob in the pound. Fags five bob for twenty. Purchase tax on every bloody thing. Can't afford whiskey. So that all you smug bastards can sit comfortable on your arses and have a smack at the British." (*DS*, 91)

Although one cannot imagine that these are anything like Burgess's own sentiments, one can see how a colonial servant could be driven to utter such words and, given the insolence and bad manners of the guests, there is something gratifying in his outburst. The UN adviser can rebuke his subordinate, but he cannot console him for the bad time he has had and will have upriver except to say, "that's what you were sent here for. The British are supposed to have a bad time. That is their destiny" (*DS,* 91–92). Later, after the tribe upriver has lost it head, Mr. Tomlin, too, will indulge in a gratifying outburst against the caliph himself.

This novel is more comic than bitter, and some of the most hilarious effects are provided by the Italian, Nando Tasca, and his son Paolo, who have been brought to Dunia to complete the marblework on a new mosque. The relationship is as utterly without either filial or paternal devotion as one could imagine. The son feels wronged by the father, the father by the son, and each looks forward to a day of retribution. For Paolo, it will be the day when he has the courage to rise up against his father and assert his superior strength and virility. For the father, it will be the day when Paolo takes a job arranged for him on a coconut estate where he is almost certain to be killed by terrorists. In the meantime, the father weakens the son by starving him until he has barely enough strength and energy to work the marble-cutting machine. Paolo submits to this tyranny, sometimes stealing a little food and things to hock for food and occasionally embarrassing his father by publicly discussing the old man's weaknesses for whoring and beer. But he does little to merit Nando Tasca's recurrent accusation that he is "a very very very bad a boy"—until he falls under the influence of revolutionaries who see in him a potentially moving symbol of the plight of the downtrodden working classes.

At a meeting designed to inflame dark-skinned workers with hatred for all white masters, Paolo is prompted to present his grievances against his "fader," a term that to black revolutionaries immediately signifies "the oppression of paternal white rule." The crowd has already been fired up by a skilled demagogue from a neighboring state and dazzled by his indescribable vision of "Liberty, Progress, the *Zeitgeist.*" It takes little besides this, a stirring up of old racial antagonisms and Paolo's unfinished indictment of paternal tyranny, to set off a riot. But this is by no means Paolo's most spectacular feat on behalf of the dark-skinned proletariat. Later, while fleeing from his father with the old man's best suit on his back, he ascends the spiral stairs of the new minaret and locks himself inside the muezzin's golden cage, which happens to be equipped with a microphone. From there he broadcasts his woes throughout Dunia, and again the revolutionaries are able to use him as a symbol and are quick to inflate the family quarrel into one of profound political significance:

> Even in Ceylon he was known: Mr. Bastians referred to him in a speech, and the newspapers had brief references to a young Italian fanatic, self-appointed leader of ragged malcontents, emulating Simon Stylites to shame the white men into granting immediate autonomy to Dunia. (*DS*, 219)

Burgess's experiences with revolutionaries in Borneo, including an invitation to lead their Freedom party, may have had something to do with Paolo's hilarious elevation to glory. Such conjectures about the relevance of his experiences in Borneo are based on the predominance of Asian types in the novel and the fact that most of Burgess's fiction is based on his own experience. One is tempted to toy with possible etymological connections between "Brunei" and "Dunia." Perhaps Burgess is dropping a hint that he has transferred a "brown" culture from the East Indies to Africa. Actually, *Dunia* is the Arabic word for "the world" in its Far Eastern form, but one might still view it as a kind of Joycean etymology making Brunei and Dunia at least dream cognate.[10] Carrying this further, in connection with the dark-versus-light motif that appears so frequently in Burgess's fiction, it is significant that Lydgate has come to Dunia in his long flight from responsibility.

In *The Worm and the Ring,* the "brown" embodied in a woman named Hilda (short for Brunhilde) is symbolic of "neutral pleasures" the hero must forsake before he can progress spiritually. In *Tremor of Intent,* self-serving "neutrality" is shown to be the only truly contemptible human condition. Also in that novel, as in Dante's *Inferno,* "neutrals" are shown to be undeserving of any dignity, even that of damnation among their betters, the committed servants of one of the great cosmic forces. The story of Lydgate in Dunia seems to be yet another treatment of the theme of neutrality versus commitment. Dunia is full of self-servers, from the caliph who carries on in a genteel civilized manner the plundering tradition of his pirate ancestors, down to the lowly half-caste assistants of the United Nations adviser who fatten themselves on bribes and information sales. It is an appropriate hiding place for Lydgate, a self-server who longs to escape all responsibility for treating people, especially women, as human beings.

Unlike other self-serving neutrals in Burgess's fiction, Lydgate is not very self-satisfied. Neither his own conscience nor his contacts with other people will allow him to be, and, not paradoxically, this sense of guilt makes his condition more damnable even than that of the womanizing, treacherous, self-indulgent Nando Tasca. The two are compared in Lydgate's troubled mind as he tosses in bed and yearns for "a sempiternal quietus." As in parts of *Nothing Like the Sun,* the voice of conscience here is Godly and unmistakable:

> Thou hast a sense of guilt, meseemeth, which thy neighbor lacketh. Thy neighbour is saved. He hath thrown his guilt on to the shoulders of One Who

will bear the guilt of all mankind, and that gladly. And, indeed, thou feelest that thy failure in thy past ambitions, the enemies about thee, are not the random bestowings of a malign and potent destiny. Was there not something in thy past, some sin, which, like Cain, thou wanderest through distant lands to forget? We shall not know till thou speakest, and speak thou wilt not.

Thy Italian neighbours, having spent some of the night in loud and rapid altercation in their own musical tongue, are now most still in sleep. The father snoreth and the son at times calleth out from the prison of his slumber some Italian name or other, belike a woman's. But thou snorest not and no woman's name escapes thy open lips. *(DS,* 68–69)

We can see here another contrast between what Burgess terms "Augustinian" and "Pelagian" attitudes. Lydgate, in many ways a typical Englishman, leans toward a Pelagian belief in self-sufficiency, which leads him into despair whenever his conscience is aroused. Not surprisingly, the Godly voice of conscience seems to be vindicating the Augustinian thesis regarding human potentiality and the avenue to salvation. It is a thesis more acceptable to a man of Nando Tasca's hot-blooded Latin temperament. In another, related respect, Burgess's Shakespearian autobiography *(Nothing Like the Sun)* throws light on the condition of Lydgate's troubled soul. Shakespeare's "great crime" is love, which is "both an image of eternal order and at the same time the rebel and destructive spirochaete." He is destroyed by it, but without it, his achievement would have been much less. Lydgate cannot love, hence his inability to find any sort of meaning in his existence or relationships and his consequent yearning for escape even from the responsibility of living. The same troubling voice reminds him that life has offered him much in the way of color and excitement. True, he is less secure materially than men who have led more pedestrian lives, but he is most ungrateful to call upon the Author of Life to release him from it.

A disagreeable experience sets off this nagging conscience. Under the pretext of inviting him to an evening of bridge, some of the Christian members of the non-European community attempt to coerce him into openly confessing his sins. Through Lydgate's confidential file, helpfully provided by a God-fearing, frequently bribed, half-caste clerk, the group has gained some sense of the nature of Lydgate's sinfulness, but they want the whole story. The brand of Christianity they subscribe to has a distinctly Western, even Calvinistic, flavor. When Lydgate admits he has never made any money, the Chinese who leads the group is gratified: "That," said Carruthers Chung, "is the sulest sign of sin." When Lydgate refuses to play their penitential parlor game, the group permits him to leave unsaved yet troubled by an aroused conscience. They will, by a startling process of deduction, eventually determine precisely the nature of the sin that weighs upon him like Cain's mark. But this does not occur until near the end of the novel, when Lydgate is about to find himself beyond redemption in a living hell.

Lydgate's progress, like that of backward-looking Victor Crabbe, is toward a terrible reckoning with his past, and it is set, like Crabbe's, against the chaotic progress of a former British colony toward independence. Although in *The Long Day Wanes,* we become involved with Crabbe and the Malaya he loves, in *Devil of a State,* Burgess does not permit us to become involved with Lydgate and Dunia. He compels us to remain sardonically detached from the horribly comic spectacle of irresponsibility and its fruits both on the individual and the state level. According to one *Saturday Reviewer,* "the book is heavily facetious and too pointlessly sardonic. It never decides whether to be farce or parable," but this reviewer obviously has little feeling for satire. *Devil of a State* is indeed both farce and parable. Like the satire of Swift, it is pointed in an overwhelming variety of directions. For certain types of subjects, including life in a fantastic colonial setting, such satire is eminently suitable. The reader is detached and moved primarily to mocking laughter, and the only way in which a writer can fail in this vein is by inconsistency, by failing to sustain his irony throughout. But Burgess does not fail in this way; he is consistently, brilliantly ironic in his presentation of the farce of life in Dunia and the horribly funny practical jokes that life plays on men like Lydgate. Irresponsibility and emergent-state confusion are also presented in Waugh's *Black Mischief* with appalling horrible hilarity, and Nicholas Monsarrat deals with much the same material and themes, although in a dreadfully earnest fashion, in *The Tribe that Lost Its Head.* Presumably, Burgess knew both of these books and judged quite rightly that heavily sardonic satire that is both farce and melodrama can be far more interesting and effective than melodrama. Although *Devil of a State* may not quite equal Waugh's achievement in *Black Mischief,* it is far beyond Monsarrat's wearisome novel. Burgess's description of Waugh's *The Loved One* as "a satire . . . told heartlessly but brilliantly"[11] would fit *Devil of a State* very well, and a less sentimental reader might find it more satisfying than *The Long Day Wanes.*

The Worm and the Ring

The year 1951 was the year of the Festival of Britain, a time for Englishmen to celebrate. It was also a time of grinding austerity that made celebrating difficult for some. Ironically, the educators, upon whom the preservation of British culture largely depended, were among those who suffered the most. Burgess was then teaching at Banbury Grammar School in Oxfordshire, and he recalls the time wryly: "Tradesmen were spending fortunes in pubs, standing everyone rounds of whisky and gin, while teachers and musicians had to drink draught cider at twopence halfpenny the glass."[12] The bitterness of *The Worm and the Ring,* one of the five novels produced during what was supposed to be his "terminal year," derives mainly from his memory of this wretched situation, but the scope of its social criticism is much broader than the treatment of teachers. Indeed, the undervaluing of teachers is shown to be symptomatic of a national drift toward philistinism. England has "spewed up the old values" and there remains little to celebrate.[13]

Like *A Vision of Battlements,* his novel *The Worm and the Ring* is a kind of mock epic. More exactly, it is a mock opera, a burlesque of Wagner's *Der Ring des Nibelungen.* Wagner's allegorical struggle for power between Nibelung dwarfs, giants, and gods is translated into a struggle for the control of a grammar school in a little English borough. Wotan, ruler of the gods, becomes Mr. Woolton, headmaster of the school and an old-fashioned liberal humanist. Fafner, the giant who seizes all and turns himself into a dragon, is "Dr." Gardner (Gard=drag=dragon), a cynical academic Babbitt who has managed to ingratiate himself with members of the business community. With these back-slapping connections, the prestige of a doctorate (earned with stolen treasure, a plagiarized dissertation), personal wealth, and a Machiavellian ruthlessness, he is bound to triumph. Woolton has no allies among the smug burghers of the town, who despise not only his weakness and inefficiency as an administrator but all the humanistic values he represents. They want Gardner and, as the novel reveals, they deserve him.

The first character we encounter is a repulsive schoolboy named Albert Rich, one of the little "scatophagous hawks" who make up the student body. Like the Nibelung dwarf Alberich, whose renunciation of love opens *Das Rheingold,* he has had no success with girls, but he continues to hope. When the schoolbell rings, he pants across the schoolgrounds in pursuit of his female classmates with vague intentions of gratifying his boy's lust. When one of these pubescent Rhine maidens accidentally drops her diary, he seizes it, reads an entry, and realizes he has a chunk of gold that may be molded into an instrument of great power. It contains the girl's fantasy of being seduced by Woolton in his study. Rich is a pug-faced, acne-blotched pygmy, but like his counterpart in *Das Rheingold,* he dreams large: "Power. With that book he would have her where he wanted her, when he wanted her. And as for him. . . . He had lain awake last night dreaming of blackmail. But how much better to be the only one in the school who could, with a wrist-flick, send packing the man at the top. If he wanted to" (*WR,* 50).

The diary very nearly falls into the hands of one of Woolton's few allies, the protagonist, Christopher Howarth. A kind of ineffectual Siegfried, Howarth is a thirty-nine-year-old assistant master who teaches German and leads a generally ungratifying existence. In addition to feeling the conflict between Woolton and Gardner (whose dissertation is actually one of his own essays), Howarth is under a number of personal pressures. His relationship with his wife, Veronica, is extremely tense, partly because of their lack of money but mainly because of her total submission to the rules of the Catholic Church. Howarth is a lapsed Catholic and she views him as a threat to the spiritual welfare of their son, Peter. Because of the difficulties she experienced giving birth to Peter, she has an overpowering fear of pregnancy, but she is the sort of Catholic for whom birth control is a gross violation of the Law of Nature.

Her fear of pregnancy and revulsion at the apparently damned state of her husband cause her to be frigid. Howarth must look elsewhere for love and he does not have to look far. Hilda Connor (Brunhilde), another teacher, is frolicsome and curious to see if his residual Catholic guilt can extinguish her appeal. His only genuinely happy relationship is with his son, who is a pupil at the same grammar school. Thanks to his mother's influence and that of the Church, young Peter is well on his way towards acquiring a full burden of orthodox fear and guilt, but this does not prevent him from loving and admiring his father.

Howarth misses the opportunity to save Woolton by seizing the diary, but some hope is kindled briefly when it falls into the hands of an aging science teacher, Mr. Lodge, who is above school politics and would never dream of using it against Woolton. Unfortunately, he is also above the distracting concrete reality of school life generally, and although like the fire god Loge he knows how to gain the treasure by cunning, he soon forgets about it. Instead of returning the diary to the girl as he had intended, he absent-mindedly leaves it on the floor of the staff room where it is picked up by Gardner. Again Howarth has the opportunity to seize the diary, but having just accepted a gift of £10 from the treasure-laden dragon, he hesitates to act until it is too late.

Gardner's dreams of power, like those of Rich, are fed by the toothsome fantasies in the diary, and he proceeds to employ some insidious tactics in his campaign for mastery. Woolton begins to receive anonymous letters charging him with moral turpitude, as well as inefficiency, and demanding his resignation. Rumors of his lechery begin to circulate widely, rumors that Woolton feeds unwittingly by one small indiscretion: he is unlucky enough to be "caught" in the well-intentioned act of lending his shoulder to a personable young female teacher who is sobbing inconsolably over her sense of failure in the jungle warfare of the classroom. The girl, Miss Fry, is thus unwittingly made, like Freia in *Das Rheingold,* an offering to the giants. Meanwhile, the young girl who could reveal the fictitious nature of the diary is intimidated by the dragon into standing by its contents as fact. By the time Howarth finally acts, entering the dragon's lair to seize the diary, its contents have been bruited so widely that the document itself is no longer necessary, and Gardner is clever enough to turn its loss to his advantage by suggesting to everyone that Howarth is Woolton's instrument.

As one might gather simply from the fact that Gardner, a dragon who is wormlike in every respect (Anglo Saxon *wyrm* = serpent, dragon), is destined to emerge triumphant, unscathed by the hero, the ruler of the gods, or anyone else, this is a very pessimistic, bitter version of the *Ring.*[14] Its bitterness extends beyond the arena of school politics. The wretchedness of Howarth's genteel poverty, the stupid tyranny of mindless Catholic orthodoxy, and the philistinism of the little English borough are all presented with angry force. But Burgess's anger does not cause him to present any of his criticisms simplistically. If the society is drifting toward philistinism and the rule of the worm, the drift is not entirely due to the strength or cunning of philistine "giants."

The liberal humanism of Woolton, his unshakable faith in human goodness, gives him excuses to shirk responsibility. In the face of the insidious, slanderous intrigues of Gardner, which contradict his whole liberal view of human nature, he retreats into his books and makes no attempt to defend either himself or his humanistic intellectual values on the battlefield of public opinion. The philistine community might not be so readily taken in by Gardner if they could associate Woolton with something besides his alienation from an age of material values and the fact that he prizes "inefficiency as the last of the human virtues" (*WR*, 25). But he is not without courage. His defiant ringing speeches to the school governors express his philosophy nobly and illuminate their stupidity with brilliant sarcasm. However, again he is not really doing anything that will help preserve what he values within the grammar school. Indictments from a man as notorious for other-worldliness and inefficiency as Woolton have no sting. Woolton acknowledges his failure and sarcastically admits he is less fit to rule than someone like Gardner: "Only the man incapable of completeness in himself can be accepted as a leader of others; only he can sink to the unexpected lowness of the governor's chair" (*WR*, 191). But Woolton never realizes how completely he has paved the way for Gardner and a new philistine order by discrediting his own ideals.

Burgess's treatment of Woolton's reptilean antagonist is similarly balanced. Gardner is repulsive, more like a worm or an insect ("a quick smart darting beetle") than a man, but unlike Woolton, he is capable of ruling the Valhalla of education, and he is unhampered by any illusions about human nature. An epilogue provides us with a depressing glimpse of the school's future under his rule. By appealing to the "genteel cupidity" of the starving teachers, he persuades them to accept a new, unified state school system that will both increase his own power and dilute the quality of the education. No rival will emerge from this staff to challenge him and he will tolerate little interference from the community: "Most people," he reflects to himself, "were uneducable, like those stupid little yappers and sniffers of the borough: they would soon have to be brought to heal. When he ruled the Valhalla of education he would rule the borough as well. Top-dog. God-pot" (*WR*, 271). A dismal prolepsis, indeed. But the feeble liberalism of Woolton has failed to provide any alternative that would satisfy the community's craving for stability.

This balanced critical treatment of the extreme of rule based on liberal idealism versus the extreme of cynical autocracy agrees with what we find in Burgess's other novels. As he does in his dystopian books, Burgess again exposes the inadequacies and dangers of both views as governing philosophies. At the same time, he suggests that Western society is becoming increasingly incapable of accepting a sane, realistic mixture of the two philosophies that would insure the preservation of individual human dignity. That he intends this power struggle in the grammar school to have these much broader political implications is indicated in the thoughtful responses of two of the teachers to Gardner's announcement that under the new state plan designed to ensure "the realization of a genuinely democratic educa- tion," all pupil segregation will be eliminated. In reply, one teacher remarks "how the pushing of a thing to its logical limit seems to turn into its opposite . . . real democracy is anarchy, and anarchy is Hobbes's state of nature, and then we have to have a large police force to keep the chaos in check, all the apparatus of totalitarianism" (*WR,* 270). Ennis of Gibraltar, protagonist of *A Vision of Battlements* and a music teacher, picks this up and cautions against some of the dangers of egalitarian enthusiasm:

> "We should leave well alone," said Ennis. "Approximate democracy is the only safe kind. I shudder to think what will happen to this country when the common man is really taken seriously."
> "That sounds like fascism," said Keyte sternly.
> "On the contrary," said Ennis, "You get fascism, collectivism, whatever you like to call it, only when this concept of the value of the common man is pushed so far that the common man starts crying out for a leader, and, as the state has been so busy manufacturing common men, only a common man can lead, and he makes an uncommon mess of it. The uncommon man, of course, is never allowed to emerge. Who have been the real defenders of liberty? The few. The odd boy or girl whom we've encouraged and been able to watch emerge out of the mediocrity. Now we're going to get big factories, churning out common men by the thousands. The brilliant uncommon exception will be overlooked in the crush." (*WR,* 270)

This rather Platonic meditation illuminates the symptomatic importance of what has happened in the grammar school. Just as the school has made an abrupt but easy transition from the lax rule of Woolton to the autocratic reign of Gardner, so England herself, having "spewed up the old values," seems ready to embrace a tyranny of mediocrity in the guise of democracy.

Burgess's eschewal of simple answers can also be seen in his treatment of Howarth's rending religious conflicts. Howarth's marriage is nearly wrecked by his wife's fanatical Catholicism, but its salvation does not lie in a total rejection of Catholicism. For one thing, Howarth himself cannot reject it totally. As it has with so many Catholics, Catholicism has molded his con- sciousness so he views life in eschatological terms. His casual conversation in the staff room has a way of turning into discourses on sin and heresy. He is uplifted by the sight of a church spire, believing he is "near to a solid comfortable bed, the Middle Ages." But then he is brought to earth by the depressing awareness that the world of "the winecup . . . for jolly roisterers in a tavern as well as the sacramental chalice. Eschatological and scatological world" is "gone for ever" *WR,* 11). He no longer has any faith, but his

Catholic responses give him a sense of alienation in his own country that has nothing to do with its growing philistinism. He thinks he can live without faith, but he yearns to be part of a community that is no longer possible in England: "But if only there were some community in which one could be accepted, somewhere one could feel really at home" (*WR,* 12). Eventually, his quest for Catholic community leads him to a darker, Mediterranean civilization in which he can feel at home even without faith. He is persuaded to go to Italy by an American Catholic who has felt the same sense of alienation in the United States, although for somewhat different reasons:

> "You want to be in the middle of life to be a Catholic. You need dirt and disease and smells. You need just what America can't give. You don't want chlorophyll and wrapped food and underarm depilatories. You want a particular kind of sun and the old phallic dances and a bit of wailing to a guitar. America's too darn clean. It's aseptic. I'd gotten to the stage of believing that when you got to the top of a girl's legs you'd find just nothing there."(*WR,* 175)

Howarth's decision to accept the American's offer of a position with his winery in Italy comes with the realization that he, too, can never be "in the middle of life" where he is. Even his sins lack a satisfying darkness. Hilda Connor represents "neutral pleasures" and "gay suburban freedom, cold copulation with the English voices of summer evening cyclists ringing and circling outside." Her name is intended to be a contraction of "Brunhilde" and, like Wotan's favorite Valkyrie, she lends support to the god ruler's enemies. Her affair with Howarth is something more for the scandal hungry to blame on Woolton's administration. The god ruler is not the one to punish her, but she is destined nonetheless to be imprisoned on a rock, stationed on Gibraltar with her army-officer husband. The "Brun" in Brunhilde refers to her place within the motifs of light and darkness that run through the book. She is for Howarth a kind of "brown" between the bleak light of graceless enforced chastity and the darkness of illicit love known fully. Appropriately, their Easter holiday romance takes place in Paris, between the fair Protestant culture of England and the dark Catholic culture beyond the Alps.

Howarth would in fact prefer his own dark-haired wife, even as he prefers the Catholicism that has made her frigid, but the flesh-despising attitude of both is an insuperable barrier. Hilda is an avenue of release, a much needed means of purely earthly purgation. Veronica, sensing Howarth's relief, assumes he has received Easter absolution in a confessional in Paris. She is not, however, totally naïve, and her awareness of a danger to her marriage along with the news that pregnancy will no longer be a threat causes her to reassess her whole position as a Catholic. She suddenly realizes "that the Church was a man's Church, that it was unfair to women. Virginity and maternity were the only two desirable states for a woman, so the Church seemed to say; the Church saw woman as an instrument, not a soul in her own right" (*WR,* 183).

When she reorders her priorities in terms of a fuller, unrepressed life, it is possible for Howarth to reject the cold, neutral gratification of Hilda.

A careless reading of *The Worm and the Ring* might suggest that its religious themes are either indictments of the Catholic Church or pleas for liberalization. In fact, the book contains neither. What keeps Howarth away from the Church in England, in addition to his loss of faith, is the conviction that it is no longer the Church of his Catholic ancestors. The clergymen he knows exhibit an appalling ignorance of theology and the ancient heresies that still survive under various labels to threaten orthodoxy. Perhaps if he could find the Church in something approximating its medieval form in Italy, he would rejoin it. Even if he did not, he would certainly be comforted by its presence. He has nothing but contempt for liberal Catholicism, which seems to have become something other than Catholicism in the process of gaining acceptance in the modern world. Similarly, Burgess declared in a recently published interview that:

> I go mad at the various changes of the church very much from the Catholic angle. I hate this ecumenical business and I hate the use of liturgical changes and the use of the vernacular. I loathe it but who am I to loathe it? I've no real stake in the church at all now.[15]

Still, *The Wanting Seed* can be read, Burgess admits, as a vindication of Pope Paul's most unpopular encyclical.[16] Burgess has also written a Dantesque/Augustinian spy thriller, *Tremor of Intent,* in which the protagonist returns to Rome by way of Manichaeism. Although Burgess may have no stake in Catholicism, he cannot bear to see it watered down or modified in the name of progress. His contempt for this "progress" shows itself again in a later novel, *Enderby Outside,* where we find a Catholic priest ministering as a spiritual advisor, a kind of Maharishi, to a group of loutish pop singers. Thus it would be strange if Burgess were beating a drum for updated, liberalized Catholicism in *The Worm and the Ring.* Instead, what he is presenting through his characterization of the Howarths are the stresses and anxieties that burden Catholics generally, as well as the sense of alienation they must feel even in a twentieth-century Protestant, although lax and tolerant, culture.

The Worm and the Ring is one of Burgess's better novels, not merely because it is such a memorable record of conditions that should have generated national shame in the year of the Festival; it also reveals Burgess's extraordinary capacity to make absorbing dramatic entertainment out of the most unlikely material. The hidden comedy and pathos of life in the dreary little grammar school are revealed with sensitivity, sympathy, and irresistible wit. In addition to the main characters—Howarth, Woolton, Gardner—there are some splendidly drawn minor portraits. One of them is Mr. Lodge, whose humdrum existence as an uninspired purveyor of elementary scientific truths would seem to be most unpromising material for hilarity or pathos; yet

Burgess manages to evoke both. In the jungle warfare of the classroom, some of the teachers are nearly destroyed by the dwarfs, but Lodge's utter detachment holds them with a magical power:

> "Silence." They became silent, frightened of his abstraction and indifference, which they did not understand. Noise, rage, pleading: these were different, part of the heroic world of Grendel and Beowulf, Hector and Achilles, who were each themselves, after all a sort of schoolchild, Grendel not unlike Gilpin [a marvelously ugly child]. (*WR*, 48)

With the same grave, lofty detachment, Lodge comforts a sobbing child: " 'Don't cry,' he patted the boy's shoulder. Like patting a bicycle. Children were so unreal" (*WR*, 50). The pathos of Lodge's existence becomes apparent with his growing realization of its utter meaninglessness. A belated interest in literature arouses this distressing awareness, but at the same time provides him with a new mode of comfortable detachment. As Gardner outlines the new order of things to his uneasy staff, Lodge sits "indifferent to all that had been said, reading with wonder and child-like joy a school edition of *Gulliver's Travels*" (*WR*, 271). Like Wagner's fire god, he remains a detached observer. It is rather doubtful he will ever be able to see the ways in which the school exemplifies the objects of Swiftian satire. A kind of houyhnhnm himself, he will neither realize nor care that the unrealistically "rational" houyhnhnm rule of Woolton has prepared the school for a demagogic yahoo dictatorship and a yahoo-geared "genuinely democratic education."

Some of the minor female characters are equally well drawn, especially the three women who are as much of a trial to Woolton as Gardner. One of them, his wife, Frederica, is, like Wotan's wife, Fricka, a jealous guardian of marriage vows. She is in the midst of her climacteric, convinced that Woolton is unfaithful, and constantly burdening him with her fears that "the whole town was littered with the thrown-away victims of his satyriasis" (*WR*, 26). In this delusion, she is encouraged by a genuinely horrible spinster named Alice who seeks in this mischievous fashion to promote her own amorous designs on Woolton. His other female burden is his mother, whose stage in life is not the sort of thing most writers could describe comically, but Burgess's comic touch is irresistible:

> She had arrived at that blessed destination—the railway terminus where she must now wait indefinitely for the private car. The man would come to collect her soon, but nobody knew quite when. All she had to do was to flip through magazines (hardly worth while starting a book now), look around, pity those still anxious about train-times, and eat. Woolton envied her her old woman's greed, her old woman's scant need for sleep. She was also dispassionate, unsympathetic, crackling with energy. (*WR*, 29)

Somehow it becomes genuinely comic when Woolton's dying mother and his ailing wife both arrive in the same hospital at the same time.

Finally there are the children. The novel is filled with sharply evocative descriptions of these adolescent dwarfs, and we hear them clearly in the snatches of speech that are part of the discordant symphony of the school. In addition to Alberich, we can see Wagner's Nibelung dwarf Mime in the figure of a boy named Mimms. Mimms is not as important in the novel as Mime is in the *Siegfried,* but he is, like Mime, a victim of the hero, or more exactly the hero's irresponsibility, when he is injured by a car while Howarth is engaged elsewhere with Hilda Connor.

Young Peter Howarth—Siegfried junior—is not really a part of this dwarf world. Like his father, he feels alienated by his religion and is, in fact, bullied by the dwarfs because of it. It is through Peter, not the Brunhilde figure of Hilda, that Burgess introduces his variant of the motif of expiation that concludes *Götterdämmerung.* Hearing of his father's adultery, Peter becomes even more confused and guilt ridden than before. The spectacle of his father's sins is awesome, but he cannot bring himself to love him any the less because of it. Nor can he bring himself to love God and the Church more than his father. While he is in this state of miserable confusion, he very nearly suffers a kind of martyrdom for both his faith and his father. Galled by anti-Catholic taunts from Rich and his dwarfish comrades, he recklessly climbs a drainpipe in pursuit of a softball. The temporary victory of reaching the ball thrills him with the feeling "he had witnessed for the faith of his fathers." Moments later, he falls and is impaled on a spiked railing. As he begins to fall, he is comforted fleetingly by thoughts of expiation: "He offered up what was coming now for his father, that part of his father in himself." (*WR,* 230). Thinking he is dying on the spikes, he reflects: "A good act of contrition didn't matter now; he was safe" (*WR,* 230).

Peter's nearly fatal expiation occurs while his father is supposed to be on yard duty but is in fact closeted with Hilda Connor. The accident marks the end of Howarth's affair with her—the end, as it were, of an era of lust. While the boy is recovering and Howarth is beginning to recover from grief and remorse, the Howarth marriage begins to recover as well. Veronica is freed of the worry of pregnancy, a good deal less worried about the letter of Church law, and ready to begin a new life in Italy. For all three Howarths, there has been atonement for the parents' sins of spiteful selfishness, lust, and failure to love.

For Woolton, too, there is a dawning of a new era of love. His wife emerges from her climacteric completely purged of her distemper, repentant, and eager to begin a new life with him. This new life is made possible by an unexpected and sizeable inheritance from his mother, who finally arrives "at that blessed destination." Woolton is free to surrender the headmaster's ring and Tarnhelm to the giants. With his new wealth, he will be able to build his own private school, one that will offer his ideal of a liberal, humanistic curriculum with Greek and Latin as a basis. His stress is at an end, even as Wotan's stress ends with the destruction of Valhalla. The school has been a sordid empire under his weak rule, and although the reign of Gardner may not be one of love, the dragon is, we are told, "loved and feared by the children" and the forces of lust and ambition will not be tempted to overthrow him.

The Worm and the Ring draws to its conclusion with something like a Wagnerian affirmation of hope in the power of love. The epilogue, though, ends it on a bitter, depressing note, as Gardner outlines plans for the new Valhalla of education. But this is preceded by a reflection on the consolations of human existence in a dragon-dominated world that tempers the bitterness considerably—a reflection that may express something of Burgess's own credo:

> But, as the beer warmed, as the minute-hand stole imperceptibly towards the last drinking second, Howarth lost none of his optimism, his trust in his own future based upon the past. There would be wine and love and the self-renewing cycle. And, above all, God and the various swordsharp manifestations of God. For, despite death and toothache and the young men tossing on their frustrated beds, the silly man with the gun and the short-necked men brooding over maps, the sour morning mouth and the agony of the martyrs, the crumble of towers and town walls, life had to be blessed and praised. Blessed and praised from the ring of marriage and the ring of the horizon, the ring of the universe, down to the worm crawling through the greening earth. But, crawling home in the dark, he foreknew tomorrow's crapula and an empty pocket, the agony of change, of saying good-bye to so much. Still he said, heartburn in his throat like a dirty word, "Amen," meaning it. (*WR,* 265–66)

Even when the wrong God—"Top-dog" or "God-pot"—has the upper hand, even when one has been told that death is imminent, life still has much to offer the man who can love. Burgess's mock opera is bitter in a way *Der Ring des Nibelungen* is not, but it is, proportionately, as full of an affirmation that cannot be overshadowed by the rising of a new and tawdry Valhalla.

3

DESCENT OF THE GODDESS

As a musician, Burgess is troped to the auditory. His prose, like that of Joyce, is filled with music, and its full sensual reward cannot be gained until it is read aloud. Much of it is what some Greek scholars in their panegyrics on Plato call "poetical prose." But not all his poetry is woven into his prose. Over the years, he has contributed lyric verse to a number of periodicals on both sides of the Atlantic, and some of the pieces he considers most worthy of preservation are included in the *Enderby* novels. In these novels and his magnificent Shakespearean "autobiography," *Nothing Like the Sun,* he treats the formidable question of what makes a poet. He had touched upon this question lightly in *A Vision of Battlements* and other early works, but in the *Enderby* novels, it is his central focus.

Unfortunately, the reception of *Nothing Like the Sun* and the *Enderby* novels, like some of his other books, suffered initially from the strictures of obtuse critics. *Nothing Like the Sun* was undervalued by some because they failed to see what Burgess was doing with the two main personae, Shakespeare and Burgess himself, although the asides and stylistic hints are certainly clear enough for any sensitive reader to follow. The *Enderby* novels distressed others because, for one thing, the novelist had not explicitly told his readers which of Mr. Enderby's poems were supposed to be "good" poems and which were "bad." Such is the state of some contemporary criticism.

Nothing Like the Sun

The setting is a classroom somewhere in Malaya or Borneo. The narrator, Burgess informs us in a kind of prologue, is "Mr. Burgess," who has just been given the sack by his headmaster, and it is time to bid his students farewell. His farewell speech, a last lecture, will be primarily for the benefit of those "who complained that Shakespeare had nothing to give to the East." It will be a very long discourse, but fortunately he will be well fortified with a potent Chinese rice spirit called *samsu,* a parting gift from his students. The *samsu* and his considerable knowledge of Shakespeare will enable him to transport himself and his class back into sixteenth-century England. In a sense, however, he will also bring Shakespeare forward into the twentieth century through identification with himself. As his lecture progresses, accompanied by much *samsu* swigging, the identification becomes stronger and stronger until finally, in the epilogue, we are able to hear the voice of a Shakespeare/ Burgess composite hero.

The lecture begins with a vision of an adolescent Master Shakespeare at home in Stratford. He is "growing into a proper young man, ripely pout- mouthed and with a good leg, quiet of speech but flowery withal, a fair seller of fine gloves."[1] Understandably, he is also extremely restive, yearning for fulfillment and the release of creative energy surging within him. Occasion- ally, since he is "already a word-boy," his yearning and energy bear fruit in pieces of verse, but he doesn't view poetry itself as fullfillment. Rather, it is merely one of many activities—creative, procreative, or both—inspired by his "goddess," a lady who dwells in his dreams. She is his muse, his ideal of beauty, his forbidden fruit, and eventually a disease that will burn and rot the life out of him. "Naked, gold, glowing, burnished, burning," she waits for him wherever his dreaming mind wanders. Sometimes she waits over the seas in the fabulous lands just being discovered, at other times, within his idealized image of "proud high London." Most often, though, she is quite literally embodied in dark-complexioned country maidens whose maidenhood yields readily to the demands of "a most importunate Adam" thrusting and crowing "out of the fork of this gentleman."

The goddess will eventually descend in all of her terrible glory when Shakespeare's body has been prepared by disease. In these early boyhood scenes, however, her arrival is foreshadowed. On one occasion, as he strug- gles to complete the final couplet of a sonnet amidst the confusion of the household, his henpecked father, in a rare rage, seizes the paper. WS (Shake- speare) fights to keep it and suddenly, in the midst of the struggle, his goddess seems to descend, "rushing down the chimney in a wind, making the fire flare gold." As he wrestles with his father for possession of the thirteen completed lines, the last line comes to him and the sonnet is complete:

Fair is as fair itself allows,
And hiding in the dark is not less fair.
The married blackness of my mistress' brows
Is thus fair's home for fair abideth there.
My love being black, her beauty may not shine
And light so foiled to heat alone may turn.
Heat is my heart, my hearth, all earth is mine;
Heaven do I scorn when in such hell I burn.
All other beauty's light I lightly rate.
My love is as my love is, for the dark.
In night enthroned, I ask no better state,
Than thus to range, nor seek a guiding spark

And, childish, I am put to school of night
For to seek light beyond the reach of light. (*NLS,* 25–28)

Isolating the first letter of each line reveals the acrostic FATIMAH-HAMITAF. It will be many years before WS meets the dark lady who bears this name. His boyish sonnet is addressed to a dark-haired country girl named Ann Whateley. It appears that Burgess is suggesting a typically Elizabethan identification of "will" with "fate." Significantly, a witness to the row in the Shakespeare household is a syphilitic passerby. ("He had no nose, love's disease").

Shakespeare's insatiable appetite for dark ladies mirroring the image of his goddess would seem to exclude the likes of the pale, auburn-haired Ann Hathaway, but the determination of a "love-mad older woman" is something he is ill-equipped to resist, especially after a heavy drinking bout and a severe beating. Like the Adonis of his first poem to Southampton, he is "set upon" and overcome. Anne is not, however, entirely to blame. After the initial rape, he had sought her out again, and as Burgess, lapsing into Elizabethan parlance, observes,

He was in a manner tricked, coney-caught, a court-dor to a cozening cotquean. So are all men, first gulls, later horned gulls, and so will ever be all men, amen. It was easier to believe so, yet the real truth is that all men choose what they will have. (*NLS,* 37)

After "another little drop" of *samsu,* Burgess tells of "WS the married man." Anne's nymphomania leaves him neither time nor energy to write much in the evenings, but it is clear that his yet unrealized art will ultimately benefit. She teaches him all he can stand to know about woman at her most bestial and bitchy. Her appetite is insatiable, but the feast is stale for her without some admixture of degradation or violence. She must assume various regal guises, walk on WS as on a carpet, and then be brutally raped. One night, the spectacle of an old woman being torn to shreds by a witch-hunting mob drives her into a bizarre frenzy of desire, and WS, having reached a point beyond which even his satyriasis will not carry him, shrinks from her in horror and nausea. Anyone who has seen a production of *King Lear* in which Regan seems to achieve orgasm during the blinding of Gloucester will see part of the poet's debt to Anne. She is also, as Joyce suggests in *Ulysses,* a model for Gertrude in *Hamlet* and various other ladies whom the gods inherit "but to the girdle."

A position as a Latin tutor enables WS to escape for a time from Anne and the glove-making trade, and it is this experience that gives birth to Shakespearean comedy in *The Comedy of Errors.* Like many of his contemporaries, WS looks to Plautus and Terence for models, but in his case, "imitation" is necessary because he leaves his pupils' editions of Plautus in a Bristol whorehouse featuring fascinating negroid courtesans, "dark ladies" who haunt his dreams thereafter.

A careless bit of pederasty ends his teaching career, but the play enables him to join a touring company of players with something in hand. Soon we find him with Henslowe's company, the most illustrious members of which are ranting Ned Alleyn and jigging Will Kemp. The indifference of Kemp to the constraints of a playwright's actual utterances is annoying to WS, as is Henslowe's apparent assumption that Talbot, in *1 Henry VI,* is more Alleyn's creation than his own. His departure from this company is inevitable. However, during his stay with Henslowe, a number of events occur that are destined to influence his art. One is a bloody uprising of apprentices that gives him material for his treatment of the proletariat in the Roman plays, as well as the Jack Cade scenes in *2 Henry VI.* But perhaps the most momentous is his meeting with Harry Wriothesley, third earl of Southampton. This extravagantly attractive young man, "Mr. W. H.," will exert an influence far beyond the poems addressed or dedicated to him. He is overbearing, treacherous, frequently sadistic, and degenerate, but he is also the sole surviving heir of a great and wealthy house, and WS is eager to regain somehow his family's lost honors. He persuades Wriothesley to accept the dedication to a projected poem about Venus and Adonis that, when finished, is actually semiautobiographical:

> In a double figure it presented both a country poet set upon by a love-mad older woman and a pampered godling of an English earl nagged to leave his sports and marry. (*NLS,* 101)

The young man is delighted with it, and in time he comes to mean more to Shakespeare than a means of advancement. The love the poet professes in the sonnets is sincere and ardent. He becomes both a father and a lover, seeing in the young man another image of his goddess.

Like the poet himself, Harry is sexually ambiguous, and when he seems to favor other effeminate young lords, WS is wracked by "jealousy that, in the quietness of his own chamber, he must unload into verse to be torn up after." When Harry also seems to favor a rival poet named Chapman, WS experiences professional jealousy as well. Anyone who has read much of Chapman's work will appreciate the probable accuracy of Burgess's portrait of him. It is not hard to imagine him patronizingly telling WS that *Venus and Adonis* "was well enough. There was a sufficiency of lusty country matter in it. Each of us has his own way. One way is not another. We must do as we can, remembering the parable of the talents" (*NLS,* 120). The jealousy aroused by Chapman is, however, a good deal less unsettling than the secret envy stirred by two other fellow playwrights, Christopher Marlowe and Robert Greene. After Marlowe's assassination, Wriothesley tauntingly consoles WS with the thought that he is now "without peer."

Even more unsettling is the passing of Greene, "decayed master of arts, master of decayed kidneys." WS had admired Greene a good deal more than he cared admit because, although Greene's life was wretched and his plays were failures, he was unquestionably a poet: "His work was clogged with poetry: poetry held up action, drove all differentiation from the characters: all mouths became lyric bird-beaks" (*NLS,* 90). When this man, repentant and bitter in the face of death, bequeathes to other learned but failed playwrights a warning against upstart players, especially one "Upstart crow, beautified with our feathers," WS is stung. Suddenly, mere popular success as a playwright is not enough for him. He must also show himself a poet. Before this, he had been content to rate himself beneath Greene and even further beneath Marlowe, and he had largely accepted the idea that poetic talent had little to do with successful playwrighting. Even now, it is through *Venus and Adonis* and *The Rape of Lucrece,* rather than his plays, that WS seeks to establish himself as a poet.

As he rises to prominence as both playwright and poet, WS is guided and drawn on by occasional glimpses of his goddess. He is determined not to betray her as Greene, fearing hellfire, had apparently betrayed his. For the most part, she exists, as before, in his dreams or in rare objects such as W.H. in which he beholds true beauty. No longer an unsophisticated country boy, he doesn't see her embodied in every dark-haired wench. But when he catches a glimpse of Fatimah, more commonly known as Lucy Negro, a brown-gold girl from the East Indies, the old yearning to know his goddess fully in the flesh overwhelms him again. His conquest of this dark lady is a long and arduous process, and when it is finally accomplished, he knows that the bones of other explorers must be littered about somewhere. But she becomes a fever raging within him, and reason, his physician, is by no means able to enforce any saving prescription.

In defining WS's relationship with this devouring-goddess image, Burgess is guided by the sonnets, where, as Stephen Dedalus observes, "there is Will in overplus." It is an "expense of spirit in a waste of shame." There is no meeting of the minds whatever. The action of the flesh is all, but WS is totally unable, and indeed unwilling, to rise about it. His body withers as he loses himself in an enchanting world of "browngold rivercolour riverripple skin with its smell of sun." He cannot live unless he is "dying" with her. Meanwhile, another fleshfast soul, Richard II, "jogs on towards his foul death" in a play written "in despair of the power of words."

His deliverance from this enchantment is terribly painful and disillusioning. His two "angels" (as he describes them in Sonnet 144) meet each other and, knowing the lady's courtly ambitions and Wriothesley's voluptuous nature, he must ere long "guess one angel in another's hell." With this betrayal and loss, he sinks into Baudelairean ennui, a state of spiritual sloth in which he is unable to write anything but a few lines about the agonies of his poor soul, the center of his sinful earth. In addition, he is oppressed and inhibited by a heightened awareness of the wretchedness of the world around him with its "wrack, filth, sin, chaos." The country is in terror of a new Armada, mysterious portents, and the thought of what the queen's impending climacteric may bring. In London, apprentices are rioting again and being brutally put down by the Knight Marshal's Men. Out of this chaos, he would coax "images of order and beauty," plays like those he has written before, but he cannot.

At this point, the narrating persona is altered slightly. An Elizabethan audience might associate the tone of the new voice and the language with a fire-breathing Calvinist preacher such as William Perkins. But neither Perkins nor any other hellfire Elizabethan preacher would lubricate his tongue for a Godly discourse with a swig of *samsu*. No God-fearing Puritan would know the drama and popular literature well enough to be able to chide WS for writing badly and filching lines. The voice can only be that of Shakespeare's nagging conscience, its Godly tone not surprising if we are mindful of the Elizabethan view of conscience as "a little God setting in the middle of mens hearts." It is also the voice of a *samsu*-swigging schoolmaster, but the identification of Burgess with Shakespeare has become so strong by this time that we are not surprised to hear him discoursing from within the poet's conscience, troubling his dreams:

> I have news for thee, snorer. There is one, a God-fearing true Christian named F. Lawson Gent., who has been vouchsafed, by God's holy grace, a vision of these poets screaming in hell, the which he has set down in a treatise called *A Watchword against Wickedness and the Lewd Trumperies of Poetified Sneerers,* wherein he recounteth the horror of their deathless punishment in hellfire (as seen by him in his vision), a burning stinking brewis of venomed maggots and toothed worms that do gnaw to the very pia mater. Thou dost well to stir and sweat in thine unwholesome sleep.
>
> God is almighty and all-just. Yet, in his all-mercifulness, he will oft chastise and castigate and chasten the sinner in this life as a warning of what is to come if he leave not off. This poor play thou writest of King John—it is no more than a quincunx of botched nonsense, creaking stuff. Account that to thy sin. Are not the personages therein stillborn, ditch-delivered by a drab of a whining muse, even the Bastard a roaring emptiness of meaningless rant? Are not thy best lines, such as they are, filched from pamphleteers that write on the present troubles? (*NLS,* 163)

He wakes to "a great shaking," the news that his son Hamnet is dying. As he hastens to Stratford over roads filled with soldiers triumphantly drunken after the Cadiz raid, he thinks of the living poem his dying son might have been. He would have been the ideal young courtier—gentle, witty, melancholy, with a stoic contempt for the world and its self-seeking viciousness and a distrust of women that would prevent his every marrying. WS recognizes in this image his own desire for sterility and a kind of self-annihilation. He is not thinking about plays now, but this image and his anguish over the loss of a son he had never really known will be the genesis of one of his greatest tragedies.

Although he can do nothing for his son, WS raises his father's spirits considerably with his decision to buy New Place, "the hub and core and flag and very emblem of Stratford gentility." With the acquisition of New Place and the granting of a coat of arms, both fruits of the ungentlemanly labor of play writing, the Shakespeare family's gentility is restored. WS does not stay long after the funeral of his son. His long neglected wife has taken to reading tracts and her natural shrewishness has been much augmented by freshly ignited puritanical righteousness. The thought of taking her back to London with him makes him shudder: "What would the gentlemen of the Inns say? Ah, hast seen his Juliet? His Adriana thou wouldst say, his Katherina" (*NLS*, 171).

Upon returning to London, he is reconciled with Wriothesley, whose affair with Lucy Negro has been terminated by a pregnancy for which WS is probably responsible. The beautiful young man is ailing physically with venereal disease, and WS perceives in him an ailing spirit as well: "the free boy's spirit had changed to the crafty, seeking, politic soul, tending to meanness and spite, that Essex was teaching men at court to endue" (*NLS*, 183). W.H. had never been free of corruption, but this new spiritual as well as physical deterioration has a profound effect upon the poet. Along with the many other symptoms of decay in the kingdom, it stirs within him a new sense of the dark reality of human life. He is not yet able to articulate this reality, but he senses "what might be done if the words and craft could descend in a sort of pentecostal dispensation of grace" (*NLS*, 183). The vessel of this grace will be his goddess, but he will not receive it until he has suffered much more, been more bitterly disillusioned, and has felt dark reality devouring his very flesh.

In the meantime, he can only produce polished, vaguely bitter comedies, such as *All's Well*, which delight his audiences but leave him far from satisfied. It is the real drama at Court as much as anything that makes him aware of their inadequacy: "A sort of masque of evil was being played out at court, but the mere fact of great seals and jostling for place, gold chains of office, the farce of worshipping as a sort of Titania a queen pock-marked, unwashed, posturing like a nymph before mirrors, reduced the quick scurrying nastiness to unhandily played mirthless comedy" (*NLS*, 183). Eventually, when the goddess has descended, he will have the "grace" to render accurately this sort of nauseous reality in such black mirthless comedies as *Troilus and Cressida* and *Measure for Measure*.

In preparation for this divine infusion, WS has much to undergo. His sense of the world's all-permeating rottenness has not yet been adequately developed, but he may find some consolation in the knowledge that his rivals in the theater are failing even more dismally in their efforts to render human reality. The Burbages would have him "out-Chapman Chapman" in the writing of humor plays, but he will have no part of "singing one air over and over and then turning to another," the dishonest presentation of human souls as thoroughly predictable entities (*NLS,* 185). Later he will come to envy the man who does actually "out-Chapman Chapman," the burly bricklayer who is "able to take the world skin-deep—humours and manners—to know that the world takes itself skin-deep," although not according to Jonsonian laws and systems. By then WS will have suffered "the fateful lesion" and been vouch-safed the truth about the world.

It happens that Jonson is indirectly responsible for accelerating WS's painful progress toward knowledge. *The Isle of Dogs,* his first effort in satirical drama, directed against "City and Court and Council and everyone" (*NLS,* 187), causes all London theaters to be shut down, and WS takes the opportunity to pay Stratford a surprise visit. He is eager to ride back bearing his new gentility and eager to see his family installed in New Place. Burgess the lecturer then prepares his class for painful discovery. Some details of the ride are given, including an "image" that keeps us simultaneously in both the sixteenth and twentieth centuries. Beneath the Clopton Bridge, there is "the spurgeoning of the back-eddy" (*NLS,* 190). It is not really surprising to find a man who has transported himself back into the 1590s in the very person of Shakespeare should yet maintain his awareness of twentieth-century Shake-spearean criticism, and what could be a more appropriate fate for Miss Caroline Spurgeon, author of a book entitled *Shakespearean Imagery,* than being transformed into an image? The poet is a bit nervous but filled with a gratifying sense of his new worth and the homage that is his due as a landed gentleman. Disconnected thoughts of lascivious Tarquin, *The Metamorphosis of Ajax,* and Dick Burbage flit through his head. WS is vaguely uneasy when he finds New Place apparently deserted, and he is totally unprepared for the vision that greets him in the bedroom. What awaits this newly landed gentle-man is "the cuckold's unspeakable satisfaction, the satisfaction of confirma-tion," the sight of his aging but still love-mad wife preparing to receive the whining cripple who had been his model for Richard III (*NLS,* 191). From now on, as Stephen Dedalus remarks, "the theme of the false or the usurping or the adulterous brother or all three in one" will always be with WS in nearly everything he writes.

He rides back to London, a kind of cuckolded ghost, like King Hamlet. His "cornuted manumission" dazes him and causes sexual impotence, but there is still surging life within his pen. The Lancastrian plays are growing into a Henriad, and Wriothesley, struck by the apparent topical relevance of *1 Henry IV* and *Richard II,* comes to solicit his aid on behalf of Essex. The resultant bitter exchange between WS and the young man exemplifies a recurrent motif in Burgess's fiction, the clash between "Pelagian" optimism and "Augustinian" pessimism. Essex and Southampton are believers in social progress through revolution. They would drag the aged queen from her throne and, with the help of their enthusiastic young followers, "cleanse" the

state. WS tries desperately to cure Wriothesely's self-inflicted blindness to
the real nature of Essex's revolutionary plans. He perceives such blindness is
due largely to the haze of fancy, abstraction, and noble sentence about the
commonweal's good with which men such as Essex always cloak the concrete
evils of their actions. When Wriothesley speaks to him in terms of "duty," he
replies in a speech that reveals how his sense of ubiquitous evil has increased
since his humiliating homecoming:

> I am old enough to know that the only self-evident duty is to that image of order
> we all carry in our brains. That the keeping of chaos under with stern occasional
> kicks or permanent tough floorboards is man's duty, and that all the rest is
> solemn hypocrite's words to justify self-interest. To emboss a stamp of order on
> time's flux is an impossibility I must try to make possible through my art, such as
> it is. For the rest, I fear the waking of dragons. (*NLS,* 199)

This is the voice of Hobbesian/Augustinian pessimism, fully accepting original sin and all its consequences, fully aware that unregenerate humanity must
be coerced into virtue and social responsibility, and consequently fully aware
of the futility and pointlessness of attempts to overthrow tyrannical political
structures.

His refusal to support the Essex faction with his pen terminates his relationship with Wriothesley. The spectacle of universal insanity of which the
young man's headlong rush to self-ruin is but a part deepens his awareness of
the world, but he is still not yet ready to receive the goddess in all her terrible
splendor. He has yet to "draw down on himself the right pain, achieve the
right releasing agony. The goddess, he was convinced, abode in the air, an
atomy, ready to rush into a wound, were the wound deep enough." Although
the goddess herself may abide in an airy realm, the wound she inflicts must be
more than spiritual, must afflict his flesh as well as his soul, and although she
herself is a vessel of creative "grace," she must use another, nonairy "vessel"
to prepare WS for her divine dispensation.

Fatimah, discarded and repentant, returns to Shakespeare. Although he
welcomes her and takes her under his protection, the ever-present memory
of his discovery in New Place prevents immediate renewal of their former
relationship. However, after some months have passed, on the same day that
another "brave erection," the Globe, is complete, his manhood is restored.
Once again, he is borne off on a golden vessel to the fabulous realms of the
East, and this time his voyaging is even more marvelous because it is utterly
"without disgust or guilt or the gnaw of responsibility." In addition to
midwifing the rebirth of his manhood, Fatimah provides some consolation
for the loss of Hamnet. The golden son she has borne him will be raised as a
gentleman and eventually sent to her homeland. The poet is exhilarated by
the thought that "his blood would, after all, flow to the East." But the lady has
been sent by the goddess to wound even more than she restores. She bears

within her "hell" the fatal spirochete, a gift of Mr. W.H., which will complete Shakespeare's preparation for the "pentecostal" descent of the goddess.

With the poet's discovery that he is syphilitic, Mr. Burgess is near the end of both his lecture and the *samsu*. In the "Epilogue," the voice of the poet merges completely with that of the writer/lecturer, and, although the latter is not himself syphilitic, he describes how the disease molded "his" subsequent art even as it ravaged his body. Burgess has observed that students of serious literature may owe as much to the spirochete as they do to the tubercle bacillus. Tuberculosis and syphilis would seem to be the most "creative" diseases, and it is significant that Keats, who had "an especially good hand," had both. The list of syphilitic poets is long, including widely differing talents such as Baudelaire and Edward Lear, and to this list Burgess would add the greatest name of all. His reasons are based chiefly upon close study of the poet's later works and the actual experience of seeing genius flower in individuals suffering the last stages of the disease. In *Time for a Tiger,* a character recalls a wartime experience that was actually one of Burgess's own:

> In the early days of the war he had been in an Emergency Hospital, a temporary establishment which had taken over a wing of a huge County Mental Hospital. Most of the patients suffered from General Paralysis of the Insane, but the spirocaete [sic], before breaking down the brain completely, seemed to enjoy engendering perverse and useless talents in otherwise moronic minds. Thus, one dribbling patient was able to state the precise day of the week for any given date in history; no rationative process was involved: the coin went in and the answer came out. Another was able to add up correctly the most complicated lists of figures in less time than a comptometer. Yet another found a rare musical talent blossoming shortly before death; he made a swanlike end. (*Time For a Tiger* [1964 ed.], p. 48)

In *Nothing Like the Sun,* WS finds syphilis an avenue to truth about the world and the omnipotent evil dominating human affairs. Though he still believes men choose what they will have, he now sees that they must choose in the dark, drawn on irresistibly by diseased flesh. This is unfair, of course, but God Himself—"a sort of roaring clown full of bone-cracking japes," as crude a comic as Will Kemp—has so arranged it. Eventually this miserable discovery is followed by another: since man's will is formed with an inclination toward something God could not have made, there must be an opposite to God. This discovery comes about as a result of his own Godlike attempts to place man in Eden and the frustrating realization that "he would not stay there: he must needs leap out to his plotting and blood-letting and sniggering nastiness." The poet, second only to God in creation, agonizes toward clearer and clearer knowledge of the appalling omnipotence of the opposite that he "as God, could not have made." As he watches the ghastly progress of the disease in his own body and sees its symptoms in others, it becomes for him a true mirror of the organism that Spenser and others had idealized as a cleansing fountain, although it was in fact the most noxious putrescence in the kingdom:

> I reeled with my discovery of what I should have long known—that the fistulas and impostumes, bent bones, swellings, corrupt sores, fetor were of no different order from the venality and treachery and injustice and cold laughing murder of the Court. (*NLS*, 228)

The most wretched discovery of all follows this: the realization that the rottenness of the Court is utterly beyond the control of its members. What had infected the Court and hence, in the Elizabethan moral view, the entire kingdom was an evil gushing from "an infinite well of putridity from which body and mind alike were driven, by some force unseen and uncontrollable, to drink" (*NLS*, 228).

At last he is ready to receive the goddess, and she comes to him in the night bearing a grace that will enable him to articulate his vision. For the first time, he sees that language is "no vehicle of soothing prettiness to warm cold castles that waited for spring, no ornament for ladies or great lords, chiming, beguiling, but a potency of sharp knives and brutal hammers" (*NLS*, 230–231). He understands the nature of the goddess herself "—no angel of evil but an uncovenanted power" drawn into a kind of alliance with evil to be its articulatrix.

We do not see the poet at work on the great tragedies, but we have seen their true genesis. In the opinion of WS's physician son-in-law, standing by his deathbed as the spirochete completes its work, Shakespearean drama deteriorated as the poet's obsession with evil grew. The poet himself, fully reincarnated in the person of Mr. Burgess, answers him with his own "summary." His "great crime" had been love, but how can one be blamed for giving oneself wholly to what is "both an image of eternal order and at the same time the rebel and destructive spirochaete"? He has nothing but contempt for the incorporeal pretensions of his most gifted contemporary:

> Let us have no nonsensical talk about merging and melting souls, though, binary suns, two spheres in a single orbit. There is the flesh and the flesh makes all. Literature is an epiphenomenon of the action of the flesh. (*NLS*, 234)

The metaphysics of Donne and indeed the whole world of concepts are trickery. They only come to life when they're expressed in tangible things. The poet's own flesh had drawn him to love, and evil had been waiting with love ready to claim his flesh for its own. When evil and the goddess had come to dwell within him, he had been granted a vision and scourged by a compulsion to articulate it.

Is there nothing but evil in the last plays? What about the preoccupation with grace and forgiveness in *The Winter's Tale* and *The Tempest*? WS/Burgess would not deny it. The last comedies express an infinite compassion and hope that has grown with his knowledge of evil. Understanding man's utter helplessness has engendered hope of forgiveness, and the poet/lecturer's "one last last last last word" is an agonized supplication, "My Lord."

Nothing Like the Sun is Burgess's finest achievement so far in the novel. His rendering of Elizabethan idiom is faultless; yet the book is lucid enough to be enjoyed fully by the average reader. The only difficulty it may present is in the shifting personae and the novelist's identification with the poet. If the reader, like some of the critics, ignores the opening announcement that the book is "Mr. Burgess's farewell lecture to his *special* students," he may not be fully aware of what is happening, and it is mainly for the assistance of these readers that the book is summarized here in some detail.

Another source of distress to some readers will be the portrait of WS and its utter humanity. Again, like some of the critics, they may have entertained an image of Shakespeare as some sort of ethereal being who, through a mysterious process, was granted unparalleled understanding of the human condition without being a part thereof. Or they may have thought of him as a good, solid burgher cranking out money-making dramas about the power of evil he had never felt merely because that was as they liked it and what they willed. These readers would benefit by close study of the sonnets, *Troilus and Cressida, Hamlet, Timon of Athens,* and *King Lear.* They should give special attention to mad Lear's speeches, which sane Edgar labels "reason in madness." Burgess understands WS as few academic scholars do, and I am convinced of the comparative worth of his contribution to our understanding of Shakespeare. One cannot document the poet's syphilis with reference to parish records any more than one can "document" Joyce's provocative theories about him in *Ulysses.* But there is a ring of truth in the "unscholarly" disquisitions of both Dedalus and Burgess's drunken persona. The portrait of the man himself may not be entirely accurate. He may not have had syphilis (cancer perhaps?). But the man we are given in these novels is the kind of man who could have created the Shakespeare canon. He loves, suffers, and beholds the face of evil as surely as Shakespeare must actually have done.

This is not to suggest that Burgess simply used his imagination in lieu of doing his homework. His knowledge of the period and its well-documented events is considerable, and by his deft use of allusion and descriptive detail, he has given us an extremely convincing picture of the vigor, violence, filth, and color of Elizabethan town and country life. We see how amply WS could have been provided with material within the limited world he knew. As a youth, he is made aware of the religious and political controversies rending the country. Later he witnesses plagues, riots, and various shameless displays of heartless cruelty, including the ghastly execution of Dr. Lopez. He knows brothels, taverns, and the houses of the great. He also knows many of his notable contemporaries, and Burgess has included some remarkably convincing portraits of them. Especially memorable are dour Florio, quoting Montaigne and stoically disdaining "sweetness," and wretched Robert Greene, as he appears in WS's mind's eye:

> late rising, cursing in crapula, from a bed soiled with his body's incontinence. Cutting Ball, the thief and killer that loved him, would be ready to fill a cup sour with last night's dregs from the Rhenish bottle, if the Rhenish had not all gone; if it had, then the pen must race at once, over a growling belly, through the first pages of some new coney-catching pamphlet, these to be hurried to the printer as an earnest of the whole, Ball the messenger to translate at once the meagre advance into wine. (*NLS,* 89–90)

His characterizations of these writers, like his portrait of WS, are based as much upon what they wrote as what has been recorded about them. Although they may not be entirely accurate, they show us the kinds of men who could have written the works assigned to them.

Even if one is totally unacquainted with Elizabethan England and its literature, one can still derive enjoyment from the sheer verbal mastery exhibited in every page. We have Burgess's prose at its most poetical, and as one reads, one is frequently delayed by the impuse to commit passages to memory. Take, for example, the following entry in WS's diary under February 14:

> This is St. Valentine's Day, twittering feast of the low-bending blessing bird-bishop. Tawny bird with white bird on couch close-lying. Ah God, what fluttering tweeting tricks she has already taught me, lore and crissum and alula aflame. We fly, I swear we have flown, I swear we have taken wing and soared through a ceiling that has become all jellied air and floated then among puce and auriferous nebulae. It is the glorification of the flesh, the word made flesh. She calls down strange gods with strange names: Heitsi-eibib and Gunputty and Vitzilpitzli and the four archangels surrounding the god of the Musulmans. In a fever I take to my play-making and theatre business. (*NLS,* 152)

Indeed, the whole novel is a glorification of the flesh and its most glorious literary fruition. The reader who can get through it without sharing some of the poet/novelist's boundless capacity for sensual and intellectual response must be well removed from any "action of the flesh."

Inside Mr. Enderby

From Shakespeare's Globe to the water-closet study of Mr. Enderby is a long leap indeed; the protagonists have virtually nothing in common besides the practice of poetry. The fact that they have both been created by Burgess and both in a sense represent aspects of his own poetic genius indicates the breadth of his vision of the poetic process. Shakespeare's achievement had been largely the result of satyriasis, the supreme illustration of the dictum, "literature is an epiphenomenon of the action of the flesh." The Shakespeare canon grew, as it were, out of the groin of the master.

The Enderby canon grows, as it were, out of a very different visceral base. The poet/protagonist, Mr. F.X. Enderby, is a shy, harmless, flatulent little man, middle-aged yet somehow adolescent by reason of the secluded life he has led. Freed by a modest inheritance from the need to work for a living, he lives alone and devotes all his energy to writing poetry that is read with admiration by the few rare individuals who still maintain an interest in poetry in the latter half of the twentieth century. Like WS, Enderby has a goddess, but he does not meet her in the flesh until near the conclusion of *Enderby Outside*. She speaks to him frequently, however, prompting him irresistibly with a compulsion to arrange on paper words with or without meaning to him. This compulsion is liable to strike him anywhere at any moment, but he cannot actually yield to it and write until he has situated himself in the proper creative surroundings: he must rush to the nearest lavatory, lower his trousers, and poise himself on the toilet seat. He prefers his own study, with its handy bathtub repository of notes and rough drafts, but in a pinch, any other lavatory will do.

His contacts with the world outside his flat are minimal. Each day he emerges long enough to attend to simple necessities and to have a friendly whiskey or two with a few acquaintances who know or care little about poetry. With fellow poets or literati generally, he has no contact whatever. Neither does he make any serious attempt to keep up with current fashions in verse. He reads very little and in his own verse tends to favor traditional forms, especially the sonnet. His productivity-in-isolation flatly contradicts the popular assumption that the quantity and quality of a poet's work depend upon the range of his worldly experience. As Enderby puts it, "There are quite enough images in half a pound of New Zealand cheddar. Or in the washing-up water. Or . . . in a new toilet-roll" (*IME,* 61).[2] If one possesses a lyric gift, one need not wander about the world in search of matter for poetic treatment. His goddess, "playful kitten or tiger fully-clawed, finger-sucking idiot child or haughty goddess in Regency ball-gown," will visit him wherever he is and inspire creation with whatever matter is handy or remembered.

Enderby's monastic existence should offend no one. It is not what Western society generally regards as a "useful" existence, but neither is it harmful to anyone. He is completely self-sufficient, asking nothing from his fellow men except a little recognition as a poet. Ironically, such recognition leads to his undoing. He is selected by a famous firm of chain booksellers to be the recipient of its annual poetry prize, a gold medal and fifty guineas. Receiving the prize necessitates his leaving his womblike surroundings for a day while he attends the ceremony in London; unfortunately he does not heed certain inner warnings that would keep him away.

For some reason, unknown even to Enderby, he creates a scandal at the ceremony by suddenly spurning the award. Having failed to prepare an acceptance speech, he simply allows a speech to flow out of him with the same spontaneity as his lyric verse, and the words somehow manage to arrange themselves into an extremely rude refusal woven in with apparently irrelevant pleas for social justice. Within moments, he has managed to antagonize much of the London literary establishment, and for another moment or two, his remorse is quite intense. But antagonizing the literati is really not the sort of thing to depress Enderby for long. Unheroic as he appears, he is yet heroic enough to stand (or rather sit) alone and practice his art with or without their blessing. After a few more unpleasant adventures in London, his only wish is to return to his lavatory and the lonely craft of verse.

Although his London experiences do not in themselves have much impact on his art, the ceremony has brought him into contact with two people who are destined to exert a fatal influence on it. One of them is Rawcliffe, a ruined poet inordinately proud of the fame accruing from one short piece "in all the anthologies." Jealous of Enderby's continued productivity, he taunts him with reminders that the lyric gift is even more frail and mortal than the singer who possesses it. But a more serious threat to Enderby's art is an attractive young widow, Vesta Bainbridge, who immediately develops a strong maternalistic interest in him. Enderby's sex life has been almost purely masturbatory. His drives are heterosexual, but all women have been ruined for him by his hideous stepmother. Her gross manner and body had been nauseously overpowering, and she had bequeathed him, along with his financial independence, a Prufrockian horror of even the slightest bit of feminine grossness. Just as J. Alfred shrinks from the sight of an arm "downed with light brown hair," Enderby can be rendered impotent by feminine flatulence, belching, ear picking, or any little indelicacy reminiscent of his stepmother. In addition, he has had years of adolescent dreaming and conjuring on hollow seats, "possessed in imagination houri after houri of a beauty, passivity, voluptuousness no real woman could ever touch," as well as the furtive enjoyment of "too many pictures." (*IME,* 164). This puerile, illusory sex life is all his muse will allow him. His poetry, unlike that of WS and other lyric greats, can only suffer as a result of genuine sexual experience. Had Vesta Bainbridge remained out of his life, his gift might well have survived into his old age, the lyric flow from the lavatory, along with dyspepsia and the flatulence generated by a bachelor poet's unbalanced but adequate diet.

When, by mistake, Enderby sends this woman an extremely erotic poem, coldly written on behalf of someone else "as a pure poetic exercise," he unwittingly launches a whirlwind courtship that soon transforms him into a kind of child-husband, helpless in her motherly care. As he grows to know this woman in various ways other than a Biblical "knowing," he is horrified to find in her some noxious reminders of his stepmother. The loathsome association is made especially strong by her efforts to prod him back into the fold of the Catholic Church, which in his mind "is all tied up with that bitch, superstitious and nasty and unclean" (*IME,* 169). Although the spirit of his stepmother has always hovered about him like a foul fury, he cannot bear to live with her in the flesh. For the sake of his sanity and his art, he must escape. Unfortunately, this realization comes too late to save his art.

His stepmother/wife has brought him to Rome for their honeymoon in hopes that the atmosphere will strengthen her efforts to coerce him back into the arms of Holy Mother Church. But since Vesta's Holy Mother Church is in Enderby's haunted mind the unholy Stepmother Church, her efforts are doomed. Equally futile are her efforts to force him into sexual maturity. While she lies naked in his arms, desirable and willing, he tries to respond, but his flesh is unwilling: "all was quiet there, as though he were calmly reading Jane Austen" (*IME,* 164). However, although she fails to reform him, her efforts are not without effect. She has managed to exert pressures and create doubts that will inhibit him severely as a poet even after he has abandoned her and returned to England.

Another inhibiting presence in Rome is Rawcliffe, who mockingly assures Enderby that the departure of his lyric gift is long overdue. He is in Rome to make a low-budget horror film that, unknown to Enderby, is based upon the plot of Enderby's most ambitious effort in verse, an unpublished allegorical narrative describing the role of original sin in Western culture. After Rawcliffe's departure, the wretched experience of seeing his poem thus transformed on the screen effectively kills Enderby's interest in it. All these Roman experiences and his relationship with Vesta are just too much for his muse to bear. When he finally escapes to England, she has already, as Rawcliffe says, "booked her one-way flight to Parnassus or wherever Muses live."

The full realization that she has departed comes with the tepid critical reception of his first volume of poems since his flight from Rome. For Enderby this is a catastrophe not to be borne. The loss of the lyric gift means the loss of all purpose or meaning in life itself. Any other vocation or activity is unthinkable, and there is nothing left for him but suicide, which he attempts via a large bottle of aspirin. It is an earnest attempt, but he is saved by a sudden ghastly vision of his stepmother welcoming him into Hell, "farting prrrrrrp like ten thousand earthquakes, belching arrrp and og like a million volcanoes, while the whole universe roared with approving laughter. She swung tits like sagging moons at him, drew from black teeth an endless snake of bacon-rind, pelted him with balls of ear-wax and snuffled green snot in his direction" (*IME,* 205–6). Not approaching death itself but the vision of eternity with this horror causes him to cry out for help.

His suicide attempt leads him into the benevolent hands of psychiatrists who "save" him by giving him an entirely different self. Every aspect of his former self, including even his name, must be discarded. Instead of Enderby the antisocial lavatory poet, he must become Hogg the "useful citizen." Poetry must be nothing more to him than a dim memory welling up from his adolescent past. In a kind of testimonial, Enderby describes his "salvation":

> "Enderby," said Hogg, "was the name of a prolonged adolescence. The characteristics of adolescence were well-developed and seemed likely to go on for ever. There was masturbation, liking to be shut up in the lavatory, rebelliousness towards religion and society."
> "Excellent," said Dr. Wapenshaw.
> "The Poetry was a flower of that adolescence," said Hogg. "It still remains good poetry, some of it, but it was a product of an adolescent character. I shall look back with some pride on Enderby's achievement. Life, however, has to be lived." (*IME,* 215)

When he is not undergoing treatment or some kind of therapy, he entertains himself with boy's books about Colonel Bill and his faithful Spike or else television westerns in which he sees the conquest of new territory and the destruction of the "evil antisocial" as "an allegory of his own reorientation." In this state, he is capable of listening without any interest whatever to a radio discourse on modern poetry that includes an assessment of his own contribution ("a good minor poet in the tradition"). At last he is ready to become a "useful citizen." The name he bears is his mother's maiden name, and it fits the new man he has put on, a plump domesticated creature with all the poetry gone out of him.

The fact that the psychiatrists are having their way as *Inside Mr. Enderby* concludes suggests this is one of Burgess's more melancholy comedies. His attitude toward behavioral engineers who seek to replace antisocial "selves" with dutifully conforming "not-selves" may be inferred from *A Clockwork Orange,* in which a fiendish protagonist triumphs gloriously over will-sapping behaviorist reformers and regains his humanity. The behaviorists are destined to be vanquished again in the sequel to *Inside Mr. Enderby* as Hogg regains his lyric gift and returns to the practice of poetry. Abandonment of his art is an essential part of his rehabilitation, and his publication of a poem drives Dr. Wapenshaw into a rage bordering on lunacy.

The insanity of psychiatrists, however, is not the principal focus of either of the *Enderby* novels. Burgess is primarily concerned with the condition of poetry and the poet in the latter half of the twentieth century. He intended *Inside Mr. Enderby* to be "a kind of trumpet blast on behalf of the besieged poet of today—the man who tries to be independent, tries to write his poetry not on the campus, but in the smallest room in the house,"[3] where he can have some privacy. Again and again, he emphasizes that the poet must be independent. Enderby's lavatory may well be, as his psychiatrists tell him, a kind of womb substitute, but it is nonetheless an atmosphere within which he can work without being caught up in the insanity and the meaningless activity of the great world outside. One cannot always say as much for the campuses within which many of today's poets lead a kind of fetal existence. Enderby is free to find imagery lurking within the concrete realities of toilet rolls and wash water, but campus poets may lose themselves in the quest of conceptual reality or various ephemeral elements and issues. Moreover, they may feel considerable pressure to adhere to current fashions in verse and to abandon unfashionable traditional forms. Enderby, however, freely chooses forms to suit whatever lyric effusions happen to be welling out of him, and since he, unlike some of his fellow singers of the present day, is saturated in the works of the masters, he is liable to choose traditional forms generally thought to be outmoded.

The campus promotes or at least tolerates the writing of verse, but the great world that impinges on Enderby's privacy and drives him eventually to suicide is much larger and less sympathetic. This world is made by and consists of people like Dr. Wapenshaw, Vesta, and Enderby's illiterate step-mother. None of these three types of people has any real regard for poetry, and they simply can't tolerate someone like Enderby for whom poetry is something more than a harmless weekend hobby. The big-brotherly Dr. Wapenshaws, who have such a large voice in human affairs nowadays, feel compelled to remold humanity in various likenesses of textbook "normalcy." Enderby's "adolescence" threatens no one, but since he happens to be forty-five years old, he must grow out of it even if this means his becoming a bartender instead of a poet. A mere "hobby" is a small price to pay for a beneficial adjustment that will make him a "useful citizen." The Wapenshaws of this world pay some lip service to the value of poetry, as do the Vestas, but in their hearts both types are essentially philistine. Just as the Wapenshaws are preoccupied with normality, the shedding of complexes, and proper toilet habits, the Vestas care only about what is fashionable or socially acceptable. Vesta may, as Enderby suspects, "want to go down to posterity as the woman who reorganized Enderby's life, faith and works." Certainly, as *Enderby Outside* reveals, she is without any real taste or culture of her own. Like so many of her supposedly cultured contemporaries, she is ready to replace poetry with pop singing. Perhaps the least harmful of the three types is the bestial proletariat, such as Enderby's stepmother. At least this type of crea-ture has no cultural pretensions and generally makes no attempt to interfere with the practice of poetry by trying to turn the poet into a more sociable animal.

As a "trumpet blast," *Inside Mr. Enderby* may not shake the walls of conventional thinking surrounding the practice of poetry, but it is, as one critic has said, "a little masterpiece." The uncontrollable laughter it arouses somehow increases our sympathy for Enderby and artists like him. He presents a ludicrous figure as he scribbles away under the watchful gaze of the mice inhabiting his bathtub or wards off an intruder with his faithful toilet seat. But the great world, which is in many ways more ludicrous than he is, cannot see the humor. It can only bend a stern, stepmotherly gaze on him and coerce him into a more "serious" way of life. Before this is accomplished, he is an extremely lovable character, even though there is very little love in his life, and his forced conversion to useful citizenship is quite as painful as the conversion of Alex in *A Clockwork Orange.* Although we cannot help laughing at Enderby, we also cannot help but share Burgess's intense anger at the enemies who surround him. In a sense, he is doing for the besieged artist what Somerset Maugham did in *The Moon and Sixpence,* but Burgess's trumpet blast is the more powerful because it shows just how vulnerable the artist really is. Maugham's hero, Strickland, is a towering, indestructible figure who sneers triumphantly at bourgeois society and is not brought low by anything until he feels the touch of disease. But how many artists have the endurance of a Paul Gauguin, the model for Strickland? How many have the courage to resist all the pressures of the philistines, the pseudocultivated, and the conformity-minded do-gooders? For that matter, even Gauguin had to escape to his island and withdraw into an Eden of his own making. The example of Enderby is more typical. His muse is the mother he willed to replace his stepmother, but she is also his mistress, and when he yields to irresistible pressures to become reconciled with the world through another stepmother, he betrays her. She will not forgive him until he detaches himself fully from her worldly rivals.

Enderby Outside

Enderby Outside, like *Inside Mr. Enderby,* can stand alone as a little comic masterpiece, but ideally the two novels should be taken together in the form in which they appeared in the United States, as a single novel entitled *Enderby.* Burgess himself rates "the whole *Enderby* book in its American form, which is the form I always wanted," as his highest achievement so far in the novel: "It's the book in which I say most, mean most to myself about the situation of the artist."[4] Initially he had to publish *Inside Mr. Enderby* under the pseudonym Joseph Kell "to hide evidence of over-production. Critics and publishers alike look sourly on the prolific writer, forgetting how large was the output of men like H. G. Wells, Henry James, Hugh Walpole and—to go farther back—Anthony Trollope, Sir Walter Scott, and Charles Dickens."[5] The sequel appeared five years later under Burgess's own name, for he had clearly established himself as one of the most gifted novelists writing in English and, in the opinion of some (including myself), deserved to be ranked with the best of the writers mentioned above.

The sequel carries his investigation of the condition of modern poetry well beyond the situation of besieged creators such as Enderby. Enderby himself is again the center of attention, but his sphere of acquaintances is much larger in this novel, including various types of present-day claimants to the title of "poet." The question of whether Enderby himself or any of these claimants have what it takes to write poetry of major significance is raised and answered unequivocally.

As the novel opens, Hogg is engaged in useful activity as a barman in a London hotel. Occasionally poems still "twitch" feebly within him, but he doesn't give much serious thought to a reconciliation with his muse. For one thing, he has little hope that she will return, and for another he is absolutely obedient to the injunctions of Dr. Wapenshaw, who has strictly forbidden all "adolescent" activities engaged in by his former self. He does, however, allow himself a last, as it were, "posthumous" fling that he hopes to conceal from his savior. A sonnet he had begun before his "cure" somehow twitches itself into proper final form, and he cannot resist the impulse to let a poetry magazine publish it under "that former, forbidden name." When this unforgivable *incivisme* is revealed to Dr. Wapenshaw, Hogg is summoned to the doctor's office to give an accounting. In the ensuing judgment scene, he finds he has been as important to Dr. Wapenshaw's stability as Wapenshaw has been to his.

The psychiatrist has proudly included Hogg's "cure" in a triumphant volume of *Rehabilitations* he is about to publish, and the poem would make a most embarrassing footnote since it reveals the existence of a vestige of that former, forbidden, antisocial self. The scene itself is one of the most brutally funny in the book, but Burgess's aim is deadly serious. Wapenshaw, one of Western society's revered guardians of mental health, has resolved all human problems to his own satisfaction in terms of general formulae. For him the thought that they may not be universally applicable is unthinkable. He has sought to "rehabilitate" people like Enderby by transferring them from one social category into another without having any real awareness of them as individual human beings. His total ignorance of Enderby/Hogg's case is revealed by the confused "history" he is about to publish, which includes a supposed sexual fixation the poet had on his stepmother! The scene reveals, moreover, that Wapenshaw doesn't really care about what is actually in Enderby's psyche (or probably anyone else's) so long as Enderby responds to therapy and helps prove Wapenshaw's hypotheses about human behavior. When Enderby/Hogg, having failed to conform to the restrictions of his assigned therapeutic formula, meekly suggests inserting an erratum slip in the *Rehabilitations,* Wapenshaw stages a spectacular temper tantrum and throws him bodily out of the office. The unregenerate poet then mildly rebukes him and his benevolent kind with a suggestion that Burgess has made elsewhere: "You take too much on yourselves, if you don't mind me saying so" (*EO,* 22).[6]

Enderby/Hogg's disillusioning interview with Wapenshaw does not cause an immediate relinquishment of the "self" Wapenshaw has given him. He is still, to all outward appearances at least, Hogg the useful barman, and in this capacity, he meets a group of young men whose pretensions to major significance both as poets and musicians are taken seriously by many influential and supposedly cultured people. The Crewsy Fixers, as these young louts style themselves, are pop singers whose rock 'n' roll contributions to British culture have won them worldwide acclaim. Their leader, Yod Crewsy, who has won the Heinemann Award for a book of poems, is to be made a fellow of the Royal Society of Literature. A luncheon ceremony is to take place in the hotel where Enderby is a barman, and many notables, including the prime minister, will be in attendance. The rather strong resemblance these overly magnified yobs bear to the Beatles is probably not entirely coincidental.

As a serious musician who composed concerti and put together jazz arrangements before he started writing novels, Burgess has been baffled by the critical adulation accorded the Beatles and other such groups. His contempt for their pretensions as musicians showed in his earliest novels, and it did not diminish in the ensuing years as more and more critics climbed on the rock bandwagon. In *The Doctor Is Sick,* he gives this delightfully malicious description of a pop singer:

> A sloppy young man was greeted with ecstasy. He sang of teenage love, how that and that alone was the real thing, and how life ended at twenty. He treated the microphone as a very thin teenage girl and, after bestowing various caresses upon it, he threw it to the floor and lay upon the long rod of the stand, kiss-singing into the mouthpiece while his body made perceptible rutting movements. The girls' screams became orgiastic, orgasmatic. An austere age, thought Edwin, an age of economy. The opulence of *Tristan* had once been required to produce a like effect in an older generation, though a tactile effect only. (*DIS,* 164)

Similarly, Alex, the demonic protagonist of *A Clockwork Orange,* whose taste in music is hard to fault, speaks distastefully of "pathetic pop-discs" moaned by "horrible yarbleless like eunuchs whose names I forget."

Enderby/Hogg's first exposure to such singing occurs while he is mixing drinks on the day of the award luncheon: "Out of stereophonic speakers there excreted (Hogg could think of no other word) pseudo-music composed and performed by the guests of honour. . . . Hogg considered that he had never in his whole life heard anything so, at the same time, obscene, noisy and insipid" (*EO,* 34–35). In Dr. Wapenshaw's waiting room, he had read a critical panegyric on such music in which it was argued that "the miracle of this uncomplicated monody with its minimal chordal accompaniment is not diminished by our hindsight knowledge that it had been there waiting, throughout recorded history, yet unnoticed by the creaking practitioners of the complex." Youthful performers, "being unburdened by traditional technical knowledge," were able to triumph where all the old masters had failed. Their triumph is but another glowing proof that "the answer to all problems, aesthetic as much as social, religious, and economic, resides, in a word, in Youth" (*EO,* 14–15). This little bit of *merde universalle,* as another Wapenshaw patient aptly characterizes it, does not excite Enderby/Hogg unduly.

Burgess's main concern with pop singers in *Enderby Outside* is their claim to significance as poets, which even *Time* and *Life* magazines began to take seriously during the late sixties, but which Burgess obviously considered even more fantastic than their musical pretensions. Barman Hogg, standing by his post during Yod Crewsy's reception into the Royal Society of Literature, has the rending experience of hearing his own verse being clumsily read by pop singer Crewsy. The mystery of how this could happen and indeed the whole mystery of the young man's recognition as a poet are readily solved. Hogg has just had the miserable experience of seeing Vesta again, radiant in the glow of Crewsy's greatness. Having failed at managing a poet, she has found a new way to go down to posterity by managing the Crewsy Fixers and other pop groups. Thrifty Scotswoman that she is, she has not wasted the relics of her life with Enderby, namely some unpublished poems in a manuscript he had left behind. These have been published under Crewsy's name, hence the Heinemann Award and his fellowship in the Royal Society of Literature. Crewsy's ghastly recital of Enderby's verse is followed by a crude piece of noisy rock, which is suddenly interrupted by a shot fired by another artist whose work, like Enderby's, had gone unacknowledged into Crewsy's making. But Enderby finds himself holding the smoking gun. The frame is too neat to shake off, for indeed he had had "desire and motive and opportunity." He must flee for his life.

Somehow Enderby manages to escape on a tourist flight to North Africa via Spain, and it is at this unlikely time that his muse chooses to forgive him and return. Like the golden goddess in *Nothing Like the Sun,* she chooses another lady to be the vessel of her grace. Enderby (no longer Hogg) finds himself on tour with a dowdy little woman named Miranda Boland. The name is significant, although Professor Kermode is somewhat wide of the mark when he associates her with Shakespeare's Miranda and "brave new worlds." The Arabic/poetic for "moon" is *merenda* (مرندا) and the Malay for "moon" is *bulan* (بولان).[7] Miss Boland actually becomes for Enderby a kind of revivifying moon goddess, her identification with the moon greatly strengthened by the fact that she is a selenographer whose conversation tends to be full of the moon. The identification is significant in terms of the novel's thematic development.

Later in the book, Enderby's old enemy Rawcliffe refers to "the bloody man in Mallorca" and his observations on the moon goddess, meaning Robert Graves and his study of the poetic impulse, *The White Goddess.* According to Graves, the most familiar icon of Aegean religion is "a Moon-woman, a Star-son and a wise spotted serpent under a fruit tree—Artemis, Hercules, and Erechtheus." A poet would tend to identify himself with the Star-son; his hated rival was the serpent, with whom he identified himself only when he was writing as a satirist. The sole theme of a poet's songs was the woman in her divine character, as the Triple Muse. Graves notes that "in Greece, when the Moon-woman first became subordinated to the Thunder-god as his wife, she delegated the charge of poetry to her so-called daughter, her former self as the Triple Muse, and no poem was considered auspicious that did not begin with an appeal to the Muse for inspiration." Eventually, of course, the Triple Muse became a ninefold Muse, and in the course of this transformation these nine daughters lost many of the powers of the Triple Muse. They did, however, remain the sole source of poetic inspiration, even though Apollo was the God of Poetry and their leader, and they retained their erotic tendencies.[8] The reader's enjoyment of Enderby's affair with Miss Boland, as well as his comprehension of what Enderby's muse tries to accomplish at the end of the novel, may be greatly increased by his awareness of these mythological associations.

Like Vesta before her, Miss Boland is drawn to this strange little man, and in the appropriately charged atmosphere of Seville, Don Juan's town, she works to revive him sexually. Unwittingly, she actually helps revive his poetic potency, and suddenly, at *the* most inopportune moment, he leaps from the bed, over which "the Don himself seemed to hover," and rushes into the bathroom to catch his "ejaculation of words" on toilet paper. His companion, thus abandoned in midorgasm, wails dismally, unable to appreciate the miracle she has wrought, while Enderby, naked except for swathes of toilet paper, triumphantly molds a sonnet.

After this pathetic but hilarious episode, the dowdy little moon goddess ceases to be helpful and, in fact, becomes a definite threat to the extent that Enderby must leave the tour in Marrakesh. His ultimate goal is Tangier, where he hopes to stain his hitherto bloodless hands with the blood of another parasitic corrupter of art, the poet-turned-plagiarizing-screenwriter Rawcliffe. On the plane, Enderby had seen an advertisement for a Tangier restaurant concluding with the slogan "IN ALL THE ANTHOLOGIES!" Since he will probably be imprisoned anyway for shooting Yod Crewsy, he might as well have something to show for it.

Travelling from Marrakesh to Tangier, he meets various members of the underworld, including a fellow Britisher whose principal business is trading narcotics for PX goods at American army bases. Burgess has always had a true linguist's interest in underworld dialects, and the language this fellow speaks is an amazing concoction of underworld forms: multilingual in origin but less immediately comprehensible than the "nadsat" language invented for *A Clockwork Orange;* yet still understandable, especially to a poet whose ear is attuned to imagery and onomatopoeia. The following, for instance, is clear to Enderby as a proposition whereby he will exchange his precious British passport for a lorry ride to Tangier via the army bases:

> "See that. Right right. Gobblers watching at the airport and on the shemmy. Clever bastard that cab-nog, then. Ahmed, must have been. Well," he said, fanning Enderby with Enderby's passport, "give me this and you can come up the lemon pip by the long road. Fix you up in Tangey up the hill. No questions, get it? The gobblers leave it strictly on the old antonio. Wash me ends, though. Right up to you, brad. Never clapped mincers on you, get it?" (*EO,* 119)

Even this shady character has some pretensions as a connoisseur of poetry, and he regales Enderby with verse in his dialect that isn't nearly as nonsensical as the verse Enderby will encounter in Tangier.

Rawcliffe is not in Tangier when Enderby arrives, and he is forced to hide out in an upper room of a brothel with three homosexuals whose erotic explorations are uproariously funny to the reader but intolerably nauseous to Enderby. In sheer desperation, the poet crawls out of hiding and wanders into a nearby café where he confronts still another type of singer, the poet spawned by the so-called psychedelic revolution. A group of *soi-disant* literati lounging about the café, mostly expatriate Americans, are trying to induce creativity with drugs. One of them favors Enderby with a short piece of verse addressed to "mod" and "rocker" on behalf of "peyote chiefs," "Zen roshis" and other "psychedelic guides." Untactfully, Enderby says the poem, if it is a poem, sounds "rather old-fashioned" since "mod" and "rocker" have become archaic terms, and, moreover, such verse exemplifies the "danger, you see, of trying to make poetry out of the ephemeral" (*EO*, 140). The indignant literati then challenge Enderby to offer some of his own verse. He replies stoutly with a few stanzas from a Horatian ode he has been writing. The only response is a brief, flatulent statement from the posterior of one of the listeners and contemptuous smirks from the others. Enderby is distressed by this response, and, although he has no respect for their verse, he is led into searching questions concerning the status of his art in the 1960s. He wonders if perhaps these acid-inspired makers are not closer to the truth than he is: "Was it right that art should mirror chaos?" (*EO*, 158). He wonders whether McLuhan's widely accepted pronouncements on media and the universe have not made the whole business of putting words together in some sort of ordered, meaningful relationship a pointless exercise. "That Canadian pundit," however, does not trouble him greatly. Poetry based upon a McLuhanesque vision of the relevance of all things in the universe to each other (e.g., "Helmeted in grass, the perspex spider spits with toed antenna, a noise like fish, the cognac keyboard.") would be "too elegant . . . too much like Mallarmé or somebody. Old-fashioned too, really. Surrealist" (*EO*, 159).

But Enderby's questions are not really answered satisfactorily before the return and miserable death of Rawcliffe. If one takes a providential view of the personal histories of poets, perhaps it could be said that the gods scourge Rawcliffe horribly for being a plagiarizing parasite and a diluter of art. The word "cancer" is never used, but the disease ravaging Rawcliffe could be no other. As it does in *Nothing Like the Sun*, disease here readies the way for a descent, "pentecostal" or otherwise, of a goddess. But Rawcliffe's goddess comes too late; she is a busy lady, what with all the pretenders to the title of "poet" scribbling about the world today and invoking her through various hallucinogenic or other media. By the time she arrives at Rawcliffe's little seaside café in the form of a beautiful young girl, the disease has completed its work. There is no one to greet her but Enderby, who, ironically, has become heir to all of Rawcliffe's possessions, including even his name. That she mistakes Enderby for Rawcliffe is clearly suggested by her almost sadistic recitations of Rawcliffe's juvenilia, the paternity of which Enderby frantically denies.

This mistake on the muse's part and the novel's appendix, which suggests a merger of the Rawcliffe canon with the Enderby canon, reminds us of something we might otherwise forget. For all their differences as individuals, Enderby and Rawcliffe are essentially the same kind of tradition-oriented minor poet. Both are saturated in the works of the masters, and both eschew radical departures from traditional forms. This in itself would not necessarily make them minor poets, but in their cases it is symptomatic of an overall impotence. The view that literature is an epiphenomenon of the action of the flesh is implicit throughout the *Enderby* novels, as in *Nothing Like the Sun,* and this *would* limit the achievement of both poets. For Enderby, the action of the flesh is limited to flatulence and masturbatory gratification enhanced by pornography. Rawcliffe was a homosexual and, Walt Whitman's achievement notwithstanding, therefore unacceptable to the muse, who, "unlike Ariel," is "no airy slave of indeterminate sex but a woman, very much a woman." Rawcliffe, like Enderby, was also capable of finding satisfaction in the vicarious thrills of pornography. In fact, part of Enderby's inheritance, along with "all the anthologies," is a rather embarrassing "hard-core" library.

Since the two poets are limited in similar ways and consequently both unable and afraid to achieve genuine satisfaction, either sexually or poetically, it is not surprising that the revivifying therapy Rawcliffe's muse prescribes for him is also suitable for Enderby. Acceptance of the therapy and full recovery would be rewarded with lasting enjoyment of the lady herself. Indeed, for any poet who has both the requisite courage and the finesse, she is always there for the taking. She will not, however, tolerate either fear or illusory gratification, for both are avenues to impotence. She tells Enderby/Rawcliffe:

> "You lack courage. You've been softened by somebody or something. You're frightened of the young and the experimental and the way-out and the black dog. When Shelley said what he said about poets being the unacknowledged legislators of the world, he wasn't really using fancy language. It's only by the exact use of words that people can begin to understand themselves. Poetry isn't a silly little hobby to be practised in the smallest room of the house." (*EO,* 214)

However, even after this devastating indictment, she tries to rescue him for poetry. Like the caricature of Marston in Ben Jonson's *Poetaster,* Enderby is forced to purge himself of useless verbiage, to "get all these old things" out of his system, and then to "push on." Purgation and poetry have always been closely associated in Enderby's mind, and he is able to begin the prescribed evacuation. But "pushing on" is another matter entirely. It requires, among other things, a discarding of fear and some form of commitment to life. The lady offers herself as a delectable golden avenue to commitment, but Enderby, visualizing himself "puffing in his slack whiteness," is paralyzed with fear. This last failure effectively defines his limitations:

> "Minor poet," she said. "We know now where we stand, don't we? Never mind. Be thankful for what you've got. Don't ask too much, that's all." (*EO,* 226)

The question of whether Enderby and others like him have what it takes to write truly great poetry has been answered. It would appear that Burgess expects as little in the way of great verse from fearful little men like Enderby and Rawcliffe who have "opted to live without love" as he expects from the chaos-obsessed, the acid-inspired, or the rock singers. The hope for poetry, if indeed there is any hope, would seem to lie in a synthesis of the qualities and artistic points of view of these pretenders. Enderby himself possesses the most vital prerequisites: technical skill and saturation in the works of the masters. But he lacks courage and fears "the young and the experimental and the way-out" and the type of evil represented by "the black dog" in his dreams. In contrast, the rock singers and the acid heads have youth and a kind of reckless courage but lack skill and knowledge. As they are now, Burgess implies, little can be expected from any of these would-be makers. In the concluding chapter, a strange persona leading a tour of schoolchildren through Tangier sneers: "They are small artists, all. Here there is a *rue* Beethoven, also an *avenida* Leonardo da Vinci, a *plaza* de Sade. But no artist here will have a square or thoroughfare named for him. They are nothing" (*EO,* 233). This persona and her obnoxious little charges appeared earlier, in the opening pages of *Inside Mr. Enderby,* and it takes no great imaginative exertion to see that this "schoolmarm" with "snotty kids trailing round the monuments" is posterity itself, the minor poet's last forlorn hope. There seems, however, to be little hope that posterity will make minor poet Enderby into a major poet.

What began, then, as a trumpet blast on behalf of artists besieged by the great world has become an overall assessment of the condition of modern poetry—a pessimistic assessment, to be sure. But just as there is at least implied optimism within Swift's generally pessimistic assessment of humanity, *Gulliver's Travels,* so there is some basis for hope in *Enderby Outside.* Though neither Enderby nor any of the other would-be poets have what it takes to make love to the muse, at least she is available—downing champagne in cafés, swimming naked in the surf, throwing four-letter words at cab drivers, walking the dirty streets. Poetry is there for the making in all these places and things. If and when a poet arrives, the goddess will have her orgasm and poetry will be made.

Enderby Immolatus: *The Clockwork Testament*

Burgess's first two *Enderby* novels comprise his most complete positive statement concerning the role of the artist. The duties of that role are to maintain one's responsibilities to one's art, which means essentially committing oneself to the fullest extent of one's talent and energy and resisting social and other pressures from the great world that would "impinge" and interfere with this commitment. In *MF* Burgess defines the role in another way, by opposition. The "incestuous" works of "Sib Legeru" represent everything that art is not, and the attitudes of the admiring narrator/protagonist in search of "Sib Legeru" reveal the irresponsibility of the antiartist who cultivates chaos.

Burgess's choice of a black American protagonist and an American setting for the first part of *MF* was dictated largely by his perception of an incestuous pattern in American racial consciousness that mirrors incestuous yearnings in art or "antiart." In the third *Enderby* novel, *The Clockwork Testament or Enderby's End,* he again uses an American setting and places within it his besieged true artist, the poet Enderby. In this novel, it is not the artist that is besieged so much as art itself. In *Inside Mr. Enderby,* the great world had done its worst by fetching Enderby out of the womblike creative security of his water closet and forcing him to become a "useful citizen." In *Enderby Outisde,* he had, with the unwitting aid of the revivifying moon goddess Miss Boland, regained his lyric gift, temporarily lost and assiduously cultivated out of the new "useful" identity imposed by his psychiatrist Dr. Wapenshaw. That novel concludes with another identity problem for Enderby when the mysterious young woman, apparently either the muse or her representative, confuses him with Rawcliffe. This, however, does not inhibit Enderby's creativity. Some of her injunctions, though meant for Rawcliffe, are profitably received by Enderby. Among other things, she tells him to get back to work:

> "Get all these old things out of your system first. Then push on. . . . "It's time," she said, "you started work on a long poem." (*EO,* 214)

In *The Clockwork Testament,* we follow Enderby through his last day of life, during which he is shown still "pushing on," struggling with the composition of a long poem about Pelagius and Augustine while he endures an appointment as a visiting professor of English at the "University of Manhattan." It is a common practice for English departments in the United States to offer such appointments to working writers in hopes they may, while visiting, initiate students into the mysteries of "creative writing." What is uncommon about Enderby's appointment, however, is that although his poems are not unknown, the real reason he has been "considered worthy" by the university is his small association with "a great demotic medium," the film.

Having contributed an idea and a filmscript based on Gerard Manley Hopkins' poem *The Wreck of the Deutschland,* Enderby has achieved fame beyond anything his poems would ever bring. But the film, as released, hardly resembles his script, much less the poem. His script had preserved much of Hopkins' language and indeed had been intended by him "as the tribute of one poet to another." Naïvely he had assumed that "people would see the film and then go and read the poem. They would see the poem as superior art to the film."[9] However, most viewers are aware of only the "overexplicit scenes of the nuns being violated by teen-age storm troopers," "a great pink sexual encounter" of Father Hopkins with the nun Gertrude, and Gertrude's "end, in a posture of crucifixion on the Kentish Knock . . . as near nude as that of her Master" (*CT,* 16). Thus, through the interpolations of rewrite men, the mandatory titillation of successful filmmaking is achieved and, for a few viewers at least, something else besides—inspiration. Stirred by the film, a few teenagers in England and America seek to emulate the young storm troopers, and there are two widely publicized instances of "nunslaughter" allegedly motivated by the film. Although Enderby was not responsible for any of the film's sensationalism, he is willing to defend the entire cinematic achievement in that it is art, however "demotic" and inferior to the original hieroglyphics of Hopkins.

When Enderby's opportunity comes to assume the role of art's champion, it is on a field of honor whereon the odds are hopelessly against him: as a guest on a televised "talk show." The presiding genius of the show, one "Sperr Lansing," whose name is apparently derived from Hopkins' last sonnet ("The fine delight that fathers thought; the strong/ Spur, live and lancing like the blowpipe flame, . . .") is a master of vulgarity and what, here, might best be termed "antiwit." Also on the show is an actress, Ermine Elderly, whose films have titles derived from Hopkins. Since she seems to represent a typically American fear of aging, it is appropriate that she should star in something entitled *The Leaden Echo Mortal Beauty Rockfire.* The "Leaden Echo" song of Hopkins' poem *The Leaden Echo and the Golden Echo* could have been addressed to her, along with the little poem *To his Watch:* "Mortal my mate, bearing my rock-a-heart. . . ."

Having been a guest on several talk shows, Burgess knows the quality of entertainment they provide varies considerably, ranging from the urbane and interesting exchanges of the Dick Cavett show and the earnest wit honing of William F. Buckley's *Firing Line* to the unsurpassed inanity and vulgarity of the more popular shows. During one of his appearances on the Cavett show, Burgess remarked that Cavett's was one of the very few talk shows in which host and guests seemed to care about language, and he contrasted it with a show featuring "a sort of thin man with a fat jackal" engaged in conversation consisting largely of "yeah." In *The Clockwork Testament,* Enderby assumes he is being contacted by this latter show but is told he will instead be on a show that "is, well, *different*" (*CT,* 27). The difference between the two is merely a veneer of interest in serious issues maintained by the inclusion of nonshow-business guests with the usual show people. The essential vulgarity is actually the same, and any attempt to discuss a serious issue intelligently is doomed to failure.

Because of the film's alleged influence on the young, Enderby is expected to defend art against the charge of inciting violence. Actually, he is being set up as a foil for a more famous academic commentator on the problem of violence, "Professor Man Balaglas." Even without the echoes and direct quotes from *Beyond Freedom and Dignity,* one could recognize Professor Balaglas as a caricature of B.F. Skinner. The name "Balaglas" is actually that of a place Hopkins visited on the Isle of Man in 1873,[10] but it also serves to emphasize with heavy irony the Skinnerian conception of man as a crystalline sphere whose mystery and mechanism may be plucked out by the scientific gazer who has sufficient data and control of the environment. The name also has a subtle Dostoevskian echo. Skinner, who actually quotes Dostoevsky's "Underground Man" in *Beyond Freedom and Dignity* as expressing the kind of "sufficiently fanatical opposition to controlling practices to generate a neurotic if not psychotic response,"[11] is a would-be creator of the "Palace of Crystal," used by Dostoevsky in *Notes from Underground* as a symbol of the Western belief in science and technological progress.[12] Erection of the palace heralds the imminent creation of an "extra-ordinarily rational," mathematically ordered, although perhaps "frightfully dull," utopia to be founded upon the utilitarian assumption that man will act as his "reason and advantage" dictate. One is struck by the prophetic quality of the *Notes.* The Underground Man sounds as if he is railing against Skinner over a century before the publication of *Beyond Freedom and Dignity.* But there is nothing uncanny about this. For Skinner shares with the scientistic utopians and optimistic utilitarians of the nineteenth century a set of simplistic assumptions concerning the nature of man, as well as a pragmatic ethical system. Professor Balaglas's given name, "Man," is a heavy reminder of Skinner's apparent inability to think of *man* as anything but an abstract concept. Largely on the basis of his achievements with lower animals, he would have us accept on faith his definition of *man* as a "machine" to be redesigned in terms of the alleged survival needs of a culture.[13]

Burgess's attack on Skinnerian doctrine began some years ago with *A Clockwork Orange.* Although that novel was aimed more directly at well-meaning British politicians who advocated conditioning would-be teddy boys to revere the state, it may, as I indicate in another chapter, be read as an answer to Skinner's *Walden Two.* By remarkable coincidence, Stanley Kubrick's faithful film version of the novel appeared in the same year that Skinner's polemical restatement of his ideas, *Beyond Freedom and Dignity,* was published. In Burgess's splendid little satire, *A Fable for Social Scientists,* some students lounging on a campus of the future consider what the Skinnerian dispensation would mean for art and conclude that since there would be no pain, there could be no art, or, at most, "calligraphic art."[14]

In *The Clockwork Testament,* Burgess permits Skinner to speak for himself, as Professor Balaglas quotes at length from *Beyond Freedom and Dignity:*

> "What is being abolished is autonomous man—the inner man, the homunculus, the possessing demon, the man defended by the literatures of freedom and dignity."
>
> "That's it, you bastard," Enderby said, "you've summed it all up."
>
> "His abolition has been long overdue. He has been constructed from our ignorance, and as our understanding increases, the very stuff of which he is composed vanishes. Science does not dehumanise man, it de-homunculises him, and it must do so if it is to prevent the abolition of the human species. Hamlet, in the play I have already mentioned, by your fellow-playwright, Mr. Summers, said of man, 'How like a god.' Pavlov said, 'How like a dog.' But that was a step forward. Man is much more than a dog, but like a dog he is within range of scientific analysis."[15]

Skinner's defenders can hardly term this an unfair representation, and his critics may be tempted to echo an old saying of critics of former President Richard Nixon: to quote him is to slander him.

Balaglas/Skinner is representative of one kind of academic enemy of art, the scientistic social scientist with a sense of messianic mission who believes he must persuade humanity to accept a bit of secular grace and put on a new *man* that will enable it to fit into a utopian scheme. The Skinnerian scheme, as Burgess suggests in *A Fable for Social Scientists,* is the academy itself, Walden Two being simply "one of the better state universities. Shorn of lectures, essays, and examinations."[16] More insidious academic antiartists are found in departments whose very existence is a by-product of art, whose main business supposedly is leading students to an appreciation of great art and the ability to distinguish it from minor art and antiart. Professor Keteki in *MF* is this type, arousing student enthusiasm for incestuous pseudoart while carrying out his own research on "Volitional Solecisms in Melville."[17] The English department that invites Enderby "to come and pass on some of his Creative Writing skill to Creative Writing students" appears to be not without its Ketekis. The fact that Enderby has been hired primarily because of his association with the film suggests that the department, not unlike many English departments in the United States, has been influenced by the popular view that the film has become a more important form of art than poetry or prose fiction. Although few literary scholars would agree wholly with this view, the willingness of many to regard film study as their proper concern suggests acceptance, at least partial acceptance, of this view. These departments do not feel compelled to acquaint students with outmoded literary forms or indeed the literature of past ages more distant in time than the 1950s. Having thus encouraged student indifference to the past and the literary models of the past, these departments should not be astonished to encounter the consequences, especially in the works of their "creative writing" students. The English department at the University of Manhattan hopes that Enderby will shoulder some of its own neglected responsibilities:

> His penchant for old-fashioned and traditional forms might act as a useful corrective to the cult of free form, which, though still rightly flourishing, had led to some excesses. One postgraduate student had received a prize for a poem that turned out to be a passage from a vice-presidential speech copied out in reverse and then seasoned with mandatory obscenities. (*CT,* 17)

Since the students Enderby encounters in his creative-writing class are products of a culture and an academic system that does more to encourage than discourage such achievements, it is hardly surprising that Enderby, the potential "corrective," is received with hostility. Prompted perhaps by the muse who had visited him in Tangier, he tries to persuade his pupils to focus on the valid and proper concerns of the poetical enquiry:

> "The urgencies are not political or racial or social. They're, so to speak, semantic. Only the poetical enquiry can discover what language really is. And all you're doing is letting yourselves be ensnared into the irrelevancies of the slogan on the one hand and sanctified sensation on the other." (*CT,* 78)

He has just been analyzing the "rather sloppy and fungoid" erotic excretion of one student and "a sort of litany of anatomic vilification" by another, a black youth who fulfills in this way his "whitey"-castrating fantasies. To persuade these young poets that "poetry is made out of words," not simply emotions, is a hopeless task. When, in response to a kindly sounding student request, he offers a passage from what he considers a *"good* pome," the black student responds with a new torrent of abuse: "You bastard. You misleading reactionary *evil* bastard." Enderby has revealed his "evil" by uttering poetry that conveys nothing more than a graceful tribute to the beauty of the moon. The black student's reaction appears to be caused partly by Enderby's refusal to accept abuse with the docility that the student has probably come to expect from liberal white academics, but also because he has a utilitarian view of literature. Enderby's feelings are not necessarily those of his creator, although Burgess, like Enderby, has been irritated by the students' utilitarian attitudes toward literature. According to Burgess,

> They [the American students he has taught] find it hard to understand that one can write from a purely aesthetic aim; one merely wants to create a beautiful shape. They regard this as irrelevant, sinful and reactionary. I object very strongly to their utilitarian approach to literature. They feel that literature should do something to the world, to the state. And of course it can't, except indirectly.[18]

Burgess has also been disturbed that American students have "cut themselves off completely from the past, from the whole of the past."[19]

Enderby discovers this same lack of curiosity about the past and actually takes advantage of it when he is supposed to be teaching a class in minor Elizabethan drama. Having forgotten which dramatist he had intended to discuss, he simply allows his poetic imagination to invent one: "Gervase Whitelady . . . 1559–1591." Having invented Whitelady, he invents a Whitelady canon that includes a comedy, a history, and a tragedy. When the students call for a "specimen," he is ready with a soliloquy from still another invented play that, while ostensibly the testimony of a disillusioned scholar in Elizabethan London, actually sounds like an Elizabethan view of New York City:

> Aye, 'tis a knavish world wherein the whore
> And bawd and pickpurse, he of the quartertrey,
> The coneycatcher, prigger, jack o' trumps
> Do profit mightily while the studious lamp
> Affords but little glimmer to the starved
> And studious partisan of learning's lore. (*CT*, 62)

Although most of the students are taken in, Enderby derives little satisfaction from the feat, for it has brought him a dismal epiphany, a showing forth of certain truths concerning the meaning of his own life as an artist. A few hours before, he had suffered a slight heart attack, accepted the fact of approaching death, but consoled himself with the thought that his work, like that of Horace or that of even "the lousiest sonneteer that the Muse had ever farted onto," was *perennius aere,* a "death-cheater." Now he is not so sure, not sure that this is sufficient consolation. The creation of Whitelady and his canon, which he has dismissed as "nothing," has made him depressingly aware of the possible fate of his own posthumous reputation and that of his canon. Like Whitelady, Enderby is a minor figure whose immortality will depend to a large extent upon the interest of scholars who consider him important enough to bring his work to the attention of students. Like Whitelady, he will come in time to be a product of the imagination: "Oh God yes, I remember Enderby, what a man. Eater, drinker, wencher, and such exotic adventures" (*CT*, 53).

Dropping all pretence, Enderby tries to explain to his students, for whom he feels a sudden uprush of compassion, the real difference between imaginatively created people and those who have actually lived. It is not a matter of "identity," as it worries American youth, for this may be conferred upon both by the creative imagination. Enderby has conferred it upon Whitelady and posterity will confer it upon Enderby as his character gets "blurred and mingled with those of other dead men, wittier, handsomer, themselves more vital now that they were dead" (*CT*, 53). What cannot be conferred by either the artist or posterity is life itself, which is to say "sensation, which includes thought, and the sensation of having sensations" (*CT,* 64). For the loss of this, life as experience, the poet needs more consolation than *"perennius aere,"* for he, like any artist, has been more "alive," in this truest sense, than other men. He has sensed and thought the world, sought to capture it in his words, and created what he could from his experience. The price of his greater sensitivity to the value of life is a commensurately greater sensitivity to the pain of loss when he must think of leaving it. The Elizabethans understood this—how a heightened awareness of death increases sensitivity to the richness of sensual experience—and Enderby, a dying poet, enjoins his students of Elizabethan drama to value life, the life that cannot be invented.

In his creative-writing class, Enderby enjoins the students to value language, to "stock" their minds with "language, the great conserver, and poetry, the great isolate shaper," against the time when they will all be jailed by "the big bastards of computerized organizations" (*CT,* 78). If we recall what the muse's representative said about poetry at the end of *Enderby Outside,* these injunctions may be viewed as complementary, for it is only through language that these students may hope to gain the self-knowledge and awareness that will enable them to experience life fully. If or when the time comes for all to be jailed, it will be language alone that will preserve them against the dehumanizing, life-quenching effects of confinement. Hence it is painfully ironic that he is judged by them to be "antilife," caught up in "all this artsy-shmartsy crap" for which the time has not yet come. In vain he would persuade them that if the time for "high and neutral art" is not now, "it's not ever" (*CT,* 79).

The art Enderby defends, indeed that which he practices as a poet, is "high and neutral" only in that it is not committed to, that is, in the service of, ephemeral causes, slogans, or sensations—which is not to say it is above or indifferent to the human condition. In fact, Enderby's poem in progress on Pelagius and Augustine necessarily involves him in the most vexing questions concerning the human condition. In other novels, notably *The Wanting Seed* and *A Clockwork Orange,* Burgess presents the Pelagian/Augustinian debate as an endless controversy, manifesting itself in action, concerning the nature of man, whether he is by nature disposed to good or evil.[20] But for Enderby in *The Clockwork Testament,* the central issue is not the natural inclination of man but whether he is free. Pelagius had argued that man is free. Although God has given him the ability to choose, volition itself and the choice of action are wholly within man's control:

> Therefore man's praise lies in his willing and doing a good work; or rather this praise belongs both to man and to God who has granted the possibility of willing and working, and who by the help of his grace ever assists this very possibility.[21]

Augustine, too, explicitly asserted that man is free, but his doctrine of grace and predestination, springing from his personal experience of conversion and from his sense of his own helplessness and dependence on God, in effect denies that man is free to choose and persevere in the good without divine assistance:

> Freedom of choice then avails us for the performance of good works if it receive divine assistance; and this comes about by praying and acting with humility. But, if a man is deprived of divine assistance, then, be he never so excellent in knowledge of the Law, he will in no wise be firm and solid in righteousness, but blown up with the deadly swelling of irreverent pride. The Lord's prayer itself teaches this. For it were vain for us to pray to God and say "Lead us not into temptation" if this had been put in our power, so that we could fulfil our petition with no aid from him. . . .[22]

As Luther perceived, a will that has no power without grace is not free:

> Now then, I ask you: if God's grace is wanting, if it is taken away from that small power, what can it do? It is ineffective, you say, and can do nothing good. So it will not do what God or His grace wills. Why? Because we have now taken God's grace away from it, and what the grace of God does not do is not good. Hence it follows that "free-will" without God's grace is not free at all, but is the permanent prisoner and bondslave of evil, since it cannot turn itself to good. This being so, I give you full permission to enlarge the power of "free-will" as much as you like; make it angelic, make it divine, if you can!—but when once you add this doleful postscript, that it is ineffective apart from God's grace, straightway you rob it of all its power. What is *ineffective* power but (in plain language) *no* power?[23]

The Augustinian position on human freedom is of course very much in harmony with Augustinian doctrine concerning the effects of original sin, as reviewed in chapter 5. As a result of original sin, man is in a "penal" condition wherein he is unable to overcome the urgings of the flesh. Having freely abandoned the state of freedom and innocence he enjoyed before the fall, he lacks both freedom and goodness.[24]

Enderby, a firm believer in original sin, is greatly irritated that people are unable to perceive that it, not the filmed work of art he helped create, is the real generator of the violence being done against nuns. But Enderby is also, as he demonstrates in his debate with Professor Balaglas, a firm believer in human freedom. The problem he faces in his poem is reconciling the two beliefs. Again, this same problem manifests itself in Burgess's fiction. Burgess "accepts the myth of Eden and the Fall of Man,"[25] and in his characterization of Alex in *A Clockwork Orange,* he has presented the joy of evil at its most destructive in a terrifyingly convincing manner. Yet this same character is finally shown, at least in the original British version of the novel, choosing to reform himself and abandon evil. Burgess is no Pelagian liberal optimist, but the implication of the last chapter in *A Clockwork Orange,* not included in American editions, is that the individual is capable of learning through suffering and error and choosing goodness. Suffering, fallen human beings, not behavioral technology or the revolutionary schemes of idealists, bring goodness into the world.

Like Graham Greene, Burgess is much concerned with the need to sepa-rate the categories "good" and "evil" from "right" and "wrong," and one of the innumerable interruptions that prevent Enderby from completing his long poem is an interview by one of his "creative writing" students that generates a discourse on the real meaning of these terms. From Enderby's point of view, understanding the meaning of evil presents no problem since everyone must be aware of original sin, at least in terms of its ubiquitous manifestations. Defining "good" is a more difficult problem because of the popular tendency to confuse ethical with nonethical good, especially the nonethical good that is aesthetically pleasing. The distinction is especially difficult to clarify for American students, whose utilitarianism causes them to apply a "moral" yardstick of nonmoral "good" achieved to artistic endeavor that is essentially "neutral, outside ethics, purely aesthetic" (*CT,* 39). "Right and wrong," according to Enderby, may be best defined as simply what "the government" does or doesn't like at the moment. All this is addressed to a coed student who is not incapable of understanding it but is simply uncon-cerned with anything but her grade in Enderby's course. Enderby is offered a "lay for an A"; appalled by "the sheer horrible innocence of it," he breaks down and weeps.

Like his appearance on the talk show and his class meetings at the univer-sity, Enderby's interview by the A–hungry coed demonstrates his total inabil-ity to communicate with America verbally. Communication of a kind he finally does achieve during a subway journey when he defends an unsavory-looking matron against "gerontal violation" by three teenagers. One of the numerous items he has inherited from Rawcliffe is a swordstick or cane that conceals a rapier, and, with a few well-placed thrusts, Enderby manages to rout the young toughs. This fight scene is rather emblematic, mirroring in some ways the rest of the novel: Enderby, weakened by one heart attack and destined shortly to have another, "wearing a suit evocative of an age of decency when gentlemen thrashed niggers but paid their bills," thrusting and lunging, opposes a length of good steel to the worst that high-spirited American youth and their violent culture can provide. Like the gaseous blast he vents from a square mouth at some ill-mannered black coeds earlier in the day, his rapier thrusts express his disdainful, anachronistic defiance of a culture that cannot respond to the more civilized modes of communication.

The sensation of wielding a rapier "Elizabethanly" evokes for Enderby images of another age in which violence and cruelty were, if not more prevalent, more openly relished: "LOPEZ 95 MARLOWE 93 BONNY SWEET ROBIN 1601," and he even has a fleeting vision of his Elizabethan mirror-image Whitelady looking on in amazement from an advertisement. He becomes, imaginatively, an Elizabethan, and not for the first time. Near the beginning of *Enderby Outside,* a quarrel with a Spanish barman had caused him imaginatively to don a ruff and grow a spade beard while he chided the Spaniard with reminders of the Armada's destruction. It appears that he shares with Howard Shirley in *One Hand Clapping* a Kierkegaardian sense of the paltriness of life in this era,[26] especially when compared with the life of the Elizabethans. His involving himself in the defense of the weak is itself as anachronistic as the weapon he wields and the suit he wears.

The framing structure of *The Clockwork Testament,* like that of *A Vision of Battlements, The Wanting Seed, The Doctor Is Sick,* and several other novels, is Joycean mock Homeric. Enderby's last day has begun in the apartment of an antinymph, "a rabid ideological man-hater" who works out her fantasies in novels, "androphobic mistresspieces" in which men are castrated and mocked for their impotence. The woman, a kind of composite parody of Calypso and Circe, has a specially designed bed, circular in shape because "the traditional quadrangular bed was male tyranny," and Enderby commits the gratifying outrage of leaving a large semen stain on it. As he rises to resume work on his poem, his odyssey continues imaginatively with Pelagius from Britain to Rome. The coed who interrupts him to offer up her young body for an A is a Nausicaä whose "horrible" innocence he will not violate. His class on minor Elizabethan drama may be viewed as a kind of Cyclops' cave from which he escapes by an exercise of cunning, blinding the students with the discourse on Whitelady. The "creative writers" are boulder-heaving Laestrygones who would destroy him as an unwelcome intruder. Tiresias, blind seer, and Aeolus, wind god, are brought together in the encounter with Balaglas and Sperr Lansing. The subway, entered by way of the "Times Square subway hellmouth," is an underworld he must visit to find his way home, and, like Odysseus, he is granted there a dismal epiphany concerning the plight of man. The hoodlums he drives out of the subway at swordpoint become symbolic: "The door closed and their faces were execrating holes out there on the platform. The human condition. No art without aggression" (*CT,* 120). Finally his quest, like those of Odysseus and Leopold Bloom, terminates with a return home and a meeting with a woman who has been faithful to him in her rather curious fashion.[27]

With the entrance of a strange lady from Poughkeepsie, who feels as miserably bound to Enderby as Molly Bloom does to her husband, Burgess completes his mock-epic structure. Not that this mysterious figure, whom Enderby cannot even recognize, corresponds closely, if at all, to Molly Bloom. In fact, Enderby's actual marriage mate, Vesta Bainbridge, has long since remarried, and a reunion would not be likely. But Enderby's real mate was not Vesta but the muse, "playful kitten or tiger fully-clawed, finger-sucking idiot child or haughty goddess in Regency ball-gown" (*IME,* 84), a moody, unpredictable lady who will not tolerate a rival and who abandons

him when he marries Vesta in *Inside Mr. Enderby.* Her return to Enderby in
Enderby Outside is presented as her triumph over both the state that would
rehabilitate the poet (making him a "useful citizen") and the woman who,
representing womankind, has sought to force a standard of sexual maturity
and normality upon him. Her seductive appearance in the flesh near the end
of the novel, if indeed she is the muse, would seem to emphasize that service
to her, although it may inhibit normal sexual relations, is not a rejection of life
as sensual experience.

Comparison of this lady's visit with Enderby in Tangier with the visit
Enderby receives in New York from the lady from Poughkeepsie is revealing, and it is probably a comparison that Burgess intended his readers to
make. The contrast, indeed the complete opposition of the two ladies in
terms of what they seem to represent and their attitudes toward Enderby,
suggests that the lady from Poughkeepsie is a kind of antimuse. Unlike the
muse in Tangier, she does not confuse Enderby with anyone else. She arrives
with Enderby's poems in hand, having committed some of them to memory.
Also in hand is a small automatic pistol with which she forces Enderby to do
her will. That she loathes Enderby and his work is apparent, but the precise
reasons for her loathing are never made clear. Having been introduced to
Enderby's poems by her estranged husband, an equally mysterious figure, she
insists that she is held in bondage by them and must be freed to do her "own
things." Like an avenger in an Elizabethan revenge play, she will not be
satisfied with merely inflicting bodily death. She would kill the spirit as well,
in a sense, by putting Enderby through a process of total degradation, forcing
him to strip himself naked and micturate on his own poems, whereupon,
presumably, she will murder him. Her apparently "mad" conviction is that
her freedom can be achieved only in this way.

Enderby suddenly realizes "that *mad* was a very difficult term to define"
(*CT,* 132). This realization comes hard upon another, that the lady is not
merely Enderby's enemy but the enemy of art itself. The sins she would
punish Enderby for are the sins of all artists—their overriding concern with
fulfilling responsibilities to their art and to themselves and a concomitant lack
of "responsibility" as the great world conceives it. Her contempt and loathing
extend even to the subject matter of art: " 'There you go,' she gun-pointed.
'Interesting. So tied up in yourself and your so-called work you're just *interested. Interested* in how it happened, and all that crap about youth and beauty
and the other irrelevancies' " (*CT,* 133).

She is, then, an antimuse bent on nothing less than the utter negation of
Enderby and his achievement. Her contempt for his commitment to his work
puts her in direct opposition to the girl in *Enderby Outside* who has contempt
for anything less than real commitment to poetry. The two ladies are also
meaningfully contrasted in terms of Enderby's sexual responses in ways that
illuminate their symbolic opposition as muse and antimuse. The girl in
Tangier we may recall, offers her naked beauty to Enderby, and it is at this

moment that Enderby seems to see her as the muse incarnate: " 'Come on, take me, darling. I'm yours, all yours. When I give I give. You know that.' He did know it" (*EO*, 225). Intimidated by thoughts of his repeatedly proven impotence and assuming she, too, must be aware of it, he will not accept her invitation, and, for her at least, his fearful refusal defines his significance as a poet: " 'Minor poet,' she said. 'We know now where we stand, don't we? Never mind. Be thankful for what you've got. Don't ask too much, that's all' " (*EO*, 226). Enderby's response to the gun-toting lady from Poughkeepsie is very different from this, so different that it might well be termed out-of-character. Despite the threat of the gun and the lady's sneering reminder that he is "sexless," he assaults her and enjoys the first sexual triumph of this kind in his life.

The novel's concluding scenes defy, perhaps intentionally, anything like a tidy scholarly exegesis. However, Burgess has expressed contempt for fiction that offers an easy job to the exegete. Of the novels of John Barth, he has said: "I think that *The Sot-Weed Factor* is a very important novel. Don't think *Giles Goat Boy* is. It's fake; its allegory is too easy. The whole symbolism shells out much too easily."[28] Whatever else can be said of *The Clockwork Testament*, it certainly cannot be said that its symbolism shells out too easily (nor, for that matter, does the symbolism of the preceding *Enderby* novel). This chapter offers one interpretation of Enderby's adventure with the girl in Tangier, an interpretation not supported by Burgess's own remarks concerning Enderby's sex life. To an interviewer's suggestion that "the muse is working counter to the woman" in *Enderby,* Burgess replied: "There's a lot in that, though it's dangerous to work up a symbolism too strictly. But the idea is that the muse isn't quite Graves's White Goddess; it is a *female* force, highly capricious. And may well be the inhibitor of normal sexual relations, which explains the irregularity of Enderby's sexual life."[29]

In the same interview, Burgess discussed a film in the works based on *Enderby:* "In the film we're making, he achieves fruition. That's the idea, that he actually copulates. In the book he doesn't, he becomes a major poet. . . . The idea is all right. It's a good filming idea but goes against the true concept of the novel."[30] This may mean that we need not accept the assessment of Enderby's achievement by the girl, for she is not herself the muse, but simply another woman working counter to the muse. This *may be* the case, but we should not rule out the strong possibility that she is the muse incarnate. As Burgess remarked during another interview, "she knows too much."[31] He has put into her mouth statements concerning the role of the poet that are rearticulated by Enderby and illustrated by his example. Although she may think she is addressing Rawcliffe when she tells Enderby he is a minor poet, Enderby accepts the judgment, imagines an anthology of the future, "*Minor Poets of the Twentieth Century* (OUP, 8₄s), with a couple or three of his well separated, because of the alphabetical order, from that one of Rawcliffe" (*EO*, 227), and consoles himself with the hope that posterity might make him something more than minor. If the girl is the muse, and Enderby seems to think she is, we should perhaps view his refusal of her offering as symbolical, mirroring his refusal to attempt the kinds of achievement that might make him a major poet. At one point, she says to Enderby, "You lack courage. You've been softened by somebody or something. You're frightened of the young and the experimental and the way-out and the black dog" (*EO*, 214). She reminds him of what Shelley said concerning the role of poets as "unacknowledged legislators."

Heeding Burgess's own warning, we should not attempt to "work up a symbolism too strictly." Still, the sharply patterned opposition of the humiliation in Tangier with the triumph in New York City must provoke some conjectures regarding their possible symbolic import. What is most readily noticeable about the lady from Poughkeepsie, in addition to her attitude of loathing toward Enderby and his poems, is the way in which she is strongly associated with death. Again, this places her in direct opposition to the girl in Tangier who embodies, quite literally, all the joys of sensual experience. The gun toter from Poughkeepsie may indeed be viewed as symbolic of death itself. Significantly, she is described by the schoolmistress Posterity, during the guided tour that concludes *The Clockwork Testament,* as "skeletal." In Enderby's eyes, however, she is extremely attractive, capable of arousing a strong phallic response by her every action, including that of whizzing bullets past him.

We might recall, in connection with this strange love scene, that Enderby has been occasionally, like Thomas Lovell Beddoes, a misplaced Elizabethan. The love/death nexus is strong in the Elizabethan consciousness to the extent that "love" and "death" can mean the same thing. When Donne tells his mistress, "Wee dye and rise the same,"[32] he is fully exploiting ambiguity. Enderby's successful rape would seem to represent an encounter with death itself, from which he emerges *"triumphans, exultans,"* though destined soon to suffer a third heart attack and soon after that to meet his end. The combination of qualities and attitudes identifying the lady as antimuse with her implied identity as death seems to suggest she personifies all the forces Enderby has managed to either overcome or outrage by a life of commitment to his art. Her attempted degradation of him is a futile effort to defile what he has produced, as futile as the attempts of "a filthy unspeakable world," whose curiosity has been aroused by the infamous film, to defile or diminish the achievement of Hopkins by analyzing his sexuality. Enderby's sudden potency, the first he has ever experienced with a woman, is shown to be due to the thrilling proximity of death, but it must also be viewed symbolically, as a token of "impending victory" over not only death but the art-despising, art-defiling forces of the great world that have threatened Enderby throughout his career.

Enderby's victory is undiminished by the fact that he will never finish the long poem about Pelagius and Augustine. Unable to concoct symbols to represent the raw doctrine that is his subject, he has abandoned the project. But his yearning to see the subject dealt with artistically remains strong, so strong that it generates a consoling dream. While the lady from Poughkeepsie snores on the circular bed, enjoying the sound sleep of the well swived, Enderby switches on the television and proceeds to browse through his works, which have been brought by the lady for defilement. A passage from one poem, addressed apparently to someone with an Epicurean disregard for either teleology or eschatology, appears unfamiliar to Enderby:

> You went that way as you always said you would,
> Contending over the cheerful cups that good
> Was in the here-and-now, in, in fact, the cheerful
> Cups and not in some remotish sphere full
> Of twangling saints, the-pie-in-the-sky-when-you-die
> Of Engels as much as angels, whereupon I. . . . (*CT,* 146)

Whether this is addressed to Enderby himself is hard to say. ("Cheerful cups" could hardly refer to the stepmother's tea that has fueled Enderby throughout his lonely career.) What the passage presents clearly, though, is a point of view regarding what is "good" that is neither Augustinian nor Pelagian. The archetypal revolutionary vision of heaven on earth, stemming ultimately from Pelagian faith in human goodness, is rejected along with the Augustinian eschatological vision of the City of God that cannot be realized as the City of Man. It is doubtful the passage was ever written by Enderby. It would appear instead to be part of a dreamt poem that prepares him for the artistic treatment of Pelagius and Augustine that he is about to see on television. Its significance would seem to be simply that it does present an alternative view of the "good," a view especially congenial to the artist. We might recall how Enderby's problem of reconciling an Augustinian view of original sin with a Pelagian belief in human freedom seems to mirror Burgess's own difficulty with the same problem.

I will argue in chapter 5 that Burgess's own point of view is neither Pelagian nor Augustinian.[33] The implication of his dystopian books especially is that both Pelagians and Augustinians are hopelessly myopic in their analyses of the human condition. The true artist will find it difficult to commit himself wholly to either philosophical stance, partly because they both impose constricting views of "man," but also because they lead to constricting views of the "good" as being merely the ethically good. The artist is necessarily preoccupied with the nonethical good, which is to say, with the beauty he may capture in his "neutral" art. His perception of beauty, the transient "here-and-now" beauty that may be apprehended by his senses, must remain unclouded, undistorted by the promptings of his moral sense. This is not to say the artist must be immoral or amoral. (Enderby himself happens to be extremely, indeed fatally, scrupulous, as is shown in the matter of paying his subway fare.) It is a matter of priorities. For the artist, the highest good must be the nonethical, aesthetic good. Significantly, Enderby had told the A-hungry coed that "if God's good, if God exists that is, God's probably good in that way," which is to say, "neutral, outside ethics, purely aesthetic" (*CT*, 39). This is also reflected in his angry retort to the lady from Poughkeepsie's expression of contempt for youth and beauty: "I won't have that. Beauty and youth are the only things worth having" (*CT*, 133).

Enderby is understandably relieved to see that someone else has taken on the problem of dealing with Augustine and Pelagius artistically and there is "no need after all for him to worry about finding an appropriate poetic form." The television play he watches, or presumably dreams, effectively presents the problem of reconciling Pelagius's optimistic beliefs concerning man's ability to exercise "sweet reason" with the palpable evidence to the contrary that Pelagius himself must have encountered. Its concluding scene reveals the Goths sacking Rome, watched from a hill by Pelagius and by Augustine, who is trying literally to shake Pelagius out of his optimism and naïveté. The problem remains unresolved and unresolvable.

The last voice we hear in *The Clockwork Testament* is that of the first persona we encountered in *Inside Mr. Enderby,* the schoolmistress Posterity leading her snotty little charges, who are now on a tour of New York, "a vicious but beautiful city, totally representative of the human condition." Her implied assessment of Enderby's achievement seems to resolve doubts raised in the preceding *Enderby* novel about whether he is finally to be judged a "great" or a "minor" poet. Unlike the "small artists" of Tangier she had sneered at in *Enderby Outside,* which seemed to include Enderby, Enderby is one of the "great."

The Clockwork Testament is by no means one of Burgess's major achievements in the novel, and one suspects it was never intended to be. His treatments of the same themes in other novels are richer, more complex, and comparison with these other longer novels can only make this one appear rather slight. Readers interested in Burgess's view of the creative imagination, revealed somewhat in the Whitelady episode, should read—and "listen to"—*Napoleon Symphony,* a magnificent celebration of the creative will that appeared in the same year as *The Clockwork Testament.* Those who are ready for a fuller, subtler satiric treatment of American culture should read *MF.* Of course, the role of the artist receives its fullest definition in the two novels that appeared in the United States as one *Enderby* novel. This is not to say that *The Clockwork Testament* is not worth reading. It is a superb little satire, animated throughout by a fine rage and an unwearying wit. It occupies a place in the Burgess canon very much analogous to that of *The Loved One* in Evelyn Waugh's canon—slight when compared with the major novels but a brilliant minor work. Like *The Loved One,* it grew out of a disillusioning American experience, the climactic outrage of which involved the American film world. Waugh of course refused to let Hollywood have its way with *Brideshead*

Revisited and thus prevented its becoming a film, but the association was not unprofitable, for it gave him the material he needed for *The Loved One*. Burgess's impulse to write *The Clockwork Testament* came presumably from the experience of being "demoted" as an artist by the filming of *A Clockwork Orange*. It is his answer to those who would so demote him and the art of fiction itself. Like the rapier thrusts of Enderby on the subway, the thrusts of its multipronged satire are shrewdly placed.

4

LOVE AND DECAY IN
THE WEST

The Right to an Answer

In a group of novels written between 1960 and 1964 Burgess presented assessments, from various points of view, of the quality of life in midtwentieth-century England. One of them, *The Worm and the Ring,* discussed in chapter 2, seems to be primarily concerned with the ways in which an Englishman can be drawn away from his native country into a darker, foreign culture. The others include *The Right to an Answer, The Doctor Is Sick, One Hand Clapping, Honey for the Bears,* and *The Eve of St. Venus.* Not all of these novels are set in England, but the one that is not, *Honey for the Bears,* is in fact largely concerned with English attitudes and values and the question of love.

Of this group, *The Right to an Answer* is by far the most impressive as a novel. Burgess's astonishing skill as a stylist and his feeling for character are brilliantly exhibited, and his mixture of tragedy and comedy, harsh irony and pathos, is faultlessly blended. He admits that this novel was "much influenced in its language by Nabokov," but one is not likely to get any sense of imitation. Rather, one is delighted by the urbane, precise flow of the language—in itself Nabokovian, I suppose, but unweighted by Nabokovian pedantry. Aside from *Nothing Like the Sun* and *A Clockwork Orange,* this novel is perhaps the most memorable first-person narrative Burgess has written.

The narrator/protagonist, Mr. J. W. Denham, does not at first glance appear especially memorable. He is just a plump, balding, middle-aged businessman who takes what he can out of life in terms of pleasure and novel experience. The story he tells us is mainly concerned with his experiences in England during a series of visits. He is an Englishman, but his long career as a businessman in the Far East has made him feel like a stranger. This feeling of strangeness troubles him vaguely:

> It began to worry me to feel that I could never possibly settle in England now,
> not after Tokyo nude-shows and sliced green chillies, brown children sluicing at

the road-pump, the air-conditioned hum in bedrooms big as ballrooms, negligible income-tax, curry tiffins, being the big man in the big car, the bars of all the airports of Africa and the East. Was I right to feel guilty? Who was I to talk about the irresponsibility of modern England? I watched the grey villages limp by, the wind tearing at torn posters of long-done events. What I needed, of course, was a drink. (*RA*, 35–36)[1]

But what troubles him more is the spectacle of "irresponsibility" and instability in "hideous, TV-haunted England." What he has seen of life in East and West has given him a somewhat Hobbesian view of human affairs. He values stability more than freedom and is convinced that "you definitely can't have both." Although his story is not intended to be a sermon, with regard to the question of stability, it is definitely not without a didactic burden. Like the teachers in *The Worm and the Ring* who fear the dangers of excessive democracy in education, Denham views the abandonment of older, undemocratic value scales as a threat to the stability upon which the integrity of Western society depends:

You suffer from the mess, the great democratic mess in which there's no hierarchy, no scale of values, everything's as good—and therefore as bad—as everything else. I once read a scientific article which said that perfect order can only exist in matter when the temperature's low. Take your food out of the deep-freeze and it soon goes bad. It's escaped the grip of the cold which gave it a pattern; now it becomes dynamic enough, seething like a political meeting, but you have to throw it away. It's a mess. But the horror is that you can get used to rancid food, used to a mess. It catches up on you, however. Mithridates must have been the only poison-eater to die old. Those who blaspheme against stability don't last very long. (*RA*, 9)

Although the scenes of action in *The Right to an Answer* range from England to Japan and back again, with stops in places such as Singapore, Colombo, and Aden, much of the action originates in a single drinking spot within the "rather large smug Midland city" where Denham goes to visit his retired father. This spot is a popular little establishment known as the Black Swan or "Mucky Duck" . . . "what was known locally as a 'Flayer's ace' (a house run by Flower's of Stratford-on-Avon, presumably)" (*RA*, 11). It has in fact a very real Shakespearean connection that is also its most important customer-drawing asset, the landlord himself, an extremely likeable man named Ted Arden. Arden's connection with the family of Shakespeare's mother is proclaimed by both his appearance and an irresistible charm that effectively transforms what is actually a dreary little pub into a place where one feels privileged to spend one's money. He exhibits no interest in drama and is in fact nearly illiterate, but to Denham, a keen observer who is both very literate and a regular patron of the Black Swan, the atavism is unmistakable. Just as Shakespeare had a gift for bringing out the generosity of the earl of Southampton and others, so Ted Arden is able to make people feel deeply gratified to be able to do anything for him. Denham, for one, is honored to have his wallet drained as he buys rounds after hours for the host, his wife, and his helpers and receives nothing on the house in return. It happens, however, that Denham can afford to be generous, and his association with Arden and the Black Swan turns out to be as amply rewarding as it is disturbing in terms of what he learns about the drama of English life.

Denham usually visits the Black Swan in company with his father after they have been partially lobotomized by an evening in front of the telly. There they encounter other patrons, including some who have spent the evening in the same way and some who have spent it in an even more sordid fashion. The so-called suburban switch, considered by some Americans to be a peculiarly American institution, is shown to be a British pastime as well. On one of his first visits to the Black Swan, Denham sees an unwholesome "tennis" four-some, which includes a fun-loving, partner-switching electrician and his wife, a fine, heavy-thighed Nordic blonde named Alice Winter, or Winterbottom (a name discarded because her husband dislikes being called "coldarse"), and a single man who is attached for the evening to the electrician's wife. Alice Winter's husband, a rather helpless young fellow who doesn't "like tennis," is relegated to the role of mere observer. But he is destined to play a major comi-tragic role in the drama witnessed by Denham.

As often happens, at the end of this particular evening Denham has the "very high honour" to be invited by Ted Arden to stay on after hours for a "little arf" with him and the refined, rather intimidating woman who is his "missis." Not only does the high honor include buying rounds for host, wife, and helpers, but the privilege of being able to sweep up cigarette butts and polish glasses as well. There are three helpers named, incredibly, Cedric, Cecil, and Selwyn, of whom the last is apt to make the most distinct impression upon the reader. At first glance, he appears to be merely an idiot, but further attention reveals in him some "peculiar gifts." He turns out to be a kind of mystic, a Tiresiaslike blind seer. The blindness is actually an illusion caused by the way in which his glasses tend to catch the light, but his ability to see what others cannot is no illusion. One wonders if Burgess intended to suggest an Eliotian/Poundian reference with this character. One is apt to think of Pound's autobiographical poem *Hugh Selwyn Mauberly,* especially if one happens to have seen the Wyndham Lewis sketch of Pound in which Pound's spectacles are like Selwyn's "idiot's spectacles filled with light." *Mauberly* is an indictment of modern materialism, as is another long poem Pound influenced, Eliot's *The Waste Land,* in which we find the blind seer Tiresias. The major themes of these poems—the sterility and philistinism of modern culture, the loss of values and meaning accompanying a lack of belief in anything—are certainly treated in *The Right to an Answer,* and one thing the novel seems to be demonstrating is that such indictments are even more valid in the age of television than earlier. However, this is all fanciful conjecture based on little more than Selwyn's name, his glasses, and his startling visionary gifts. The characterization also seems to tie in with the Shakespearean element represented by Ted Arden. "Selwyn" happens to be a Welsh name and Selwyn himself gives us some curious echoes of the Welsh chieftain Glendower in *1 Henry IV*. Like Glendower trying to impress Hotspur, he calls attention to the drama of his nativity: "Ah wus born between the nart and the day." Also like Glendower, he is "profited in strange concealments" and has a sense of being "not in the roll of common men." Staring up at the moon, he announces: "Ah can see pipple oop thur. An ah sin pipple wot lives at back of it. Grinny-blue air they as. In drims ah sin 'em" (*RA,* 31). The truth of this cannot be tested in the Black Swan or Mucky Duck, but some of his later visions are amazingly accurate.

When the pub has been tidied up and Denham is in the process of getting everyone (including himself) roaring drunk, Winter (or Winterbottom) is discovered sitting alone in the water closet enduring the misery of being locked out as well as cuckolded by his wife. This prompts Ted Arden to utter a denunciation of the times that reveals, if not a Shakespearean grace of expression, a Shakespearean reverence for stability and a typically Elizabethan sense of the sanctity of marriage: "There's too much of that going on in these parts. Swopping wives. Swopping husbands. It's not right whatever way you look at it" (*RA,* 28). On a later, more tragic occasion, even his language will reveal Shakespearean aspects.

When Denham visits his sister Beryl, he is afforded glimpses of a suburban life that is more stable, although considerably less interesting, than what he sees at the Black Swan. Beryl is the sort of woman for whom a great many television commercials for detergents have been designed: her "unimpaired high-school humour" is revealed in a paradigm framed on her wall: "Je me larf, tu te grin, il se giggle; nous nous crackons, vous vous splittez, ils se bustent" (*RA,* 37). Through Beryl and her equally dreary husband, Denham meets a poetaster named Everett whose harmless versifying habits are of the sort acceptable to the philistine community. Denham's initial impression of Everett seems to reinforce in a curious fashion the connection between Ezra Pound and Selwyn. Everett quotes Pound and, as he does so, a flash of light through his glasses reminds Denham of the Black Swan's eyeless seer (*RA,* 38). Everett has a daughter named Imogen, an attractive but foul-mouthed girl with whom Denham becomes involved as a result of her affair with the cuckolded Winterbottom.

The sad plight of Winterbottom and these brief glimpses of sordid or dreary suburban life are but a prelude to the entrance of a character who provides yet another view of England from the vantage point of Far Eastern experience. This is Mr. Raj, a very handsome Ceylonese gentleman whom Burgess first introduced in *Time for a Tiger.* In that novel, he is presented as "a man of rich culture of which he would give anybody the benefit in long, slow, rolling, monotonous monologues." He is also, like Selwyn, gifted as a prophet. His prophecy that Victor Crabbe will be both "ruined" and "absorbed" by Malaya is fairly close to the mark. Mr. Raj attaches himself to Denham in Colombo in the hope that such a "man of the world" will prove useful in the research he intends to carry out in England. He intends to write a thesis on "Popular Conceptions of Racial Differentiation." Denham is much less than elated to have him for company all the way back to England, but there is no escape. He is given the full "benefit" of Mr. Raj's "rich culture," his knowledge of everything from prescribed techniques of love making to Roman history. Mr. Raj is as extravagantly polite, appreciative, and considerate as he is knowledgeable, and Denham's reasons for wishing to shake him off are not entirely clear. It is more than a matter of being bored with Mr. Raj's worldly erudition or fatigued by his constant show of energy and enthusiasm. Why Denham, for all his experience in the Far East, is quite uncomfortable with Mr. Raj becomes more apparent as their acquaintanceship develops.

That Mr. Raj's research into racial attitudes is going to be not without hazard is shown in the course of his first evening visit to the Black Swan or Mucky Duck. Alice Winter (or Winterbottom), whose husband has run off to London with Imogen Everett, is there with her electrician paramour and his wife, and Mr. Raj decides to bridge some gaps between East and West by getting to know her, if not in a Biblical, at least in a Platonic sense. She happens to be very upset because her husband and Imogen have "broken the rules of the game" and committed themselves wholly to an adulterous love. As in parts of American suburbia, the "rules" will not permit adultery to be anything more than a "game"—blindfolded wives reaching for ignition keys on the coffee table, and so forth. Mr. Raj, sensing an opportunity, thrusts himself upon her with all the confidence to which cultivation, wit, good looks, and radiating virility entitle him. An obstacle immediately looms in the form of the electrician paramour, a rather low type of Englishman generically equivalent to America's "white trash." Similarly, he tends to maintain some rather old-fashioned notions about race relations. Much more to his disadvantage, however, are his old-fashioned notions regarding the most effective means of unarmed assault. As a former boxer and a white native of the Cradle of Boxing, he attempts to chastise an upstart "Wog" with his fists, but Mr. Raj, whose awesome background apparently includes either karate or aikido, if not both, manages to fell him with a very neat front kick to "the goolies." The scene is actually rather symbolic—white Anglo-Saxon manhood endeavoring to vindicate itself against Asia, against that which is Eastern, brown, and therefore effete and degenerate; white Anglo-Saxon manhood with its groin open and therefore vulnerable. (The symbolism should not be lost on American readers.)[2] More violence follows later when Mr. Raj attempts to return to his hotel. He is assaulted by teddy boys and emerges once again victorious. This latter bit of *kumite* is witnessed and recounted by eyeless Selwyn in a kind of sibylline trance even while it is occurring.

As Denham recounts his own experiences and the adventures of Mr. Raj, questions and problems related to the question of stability emerge again and again, chiefly the question of love and the problems of "responsibility." Denham considers them from different angles in the light of some rather strange experiences. When it is time for him to return to Tokyo, he entrusts Mr. Raj with the responsibility for looking after his father in return for lodgings. The old man, who had initially been very much opposed to this plan, is won over by Mr. Raj's masterful cooking. The curries this dark gentleman manages to concoct are orgiastic indulgences that leave the partaker stunned and fearful of great art. Unfortunately, they are also the eventual undoing of the senior Denham, a steady diet of them being too much for his aging viscera to stand. Rightly or wrongly, Denham feels considerable responsibility for this, blaming himself for placing such trust in a man of a dark, alien culture for whom words such as "love," "equality," and "brotherhood" do not mean what they mean in the West. In fact, Mr. Raj has a very clear understanding of what these words should mean in the concrete realm of human affairs, Eastern and Western, as well as in the abstract realm of Eastern or Western idealism, and this is one of the things that constantly gets him into trouble in England. His gastronimic destruction of the elder Denham is actually an act of love, which he tries, too late, to undo with the help of some Indian medical students. Perhaps the most plausible evidence of his love is the fact that he overcomes a strong desire to strangle or poison the old man for being a representative of a generation that had oppressed his people "by their ignorance or tyranny." In thus dissipating his hatred for what Mr. Denham represented, he would have expressed his love for all mankind, including the "good old man" himself. Fortunately, he stifles this somewhat metaphysical impulse, and the death of the "good old man" is, ironically, an accident caused by his devotion.

The question of responsibility is also raised in Denham's mind by the affair of Winterbottom and Imogen. Denham's well-heeled, worldly wise appearance causes the young lovers to turn to him for assistance, mainly financial. Very reluctantly and quite against his principles and all his feelings about stability, he gives them enough money for Winterbottom to acquire a used press and set himself up in his old trade as a printer. His heart is softened to some extent by the romance of the affair, its "attempt at large-scale Arthurian myth," as opposed to cheap little suburban games, but more perhaps by something that the clever, worldly wise Denham does not even recognize—a genuine feeling for Imogen Everett. While he is thus being propelled toward something like a Kantian awareness that truly moral decisions are possible only outside the realm of concrete experience, Denham encounters a clergyman from whom he hopes to learn something about "morality in the world today." When the clergyman finally deigns to take up the question, his battery of references includes an intimidating array of church fathers and scholastic philosophers but nothing to "help put Winterbottom and Imogen more firmly in the moral picture." Denham cannot really be certain that the lovers have sinned against anything but "stability."

Equally unhelpful but, in their way, just as well informed are the discourses Denham hears from a dope-smuggling racketeer named Len whom he encounters in Columbo and Singapore. Len is a "fiercely moral" individual who believes in doing his duty "for the good of humanity." He is opposed to violence in principle, but his sense of "justice" and concern for "humanity" impel him on occasion to administer a "good sharp punishment." This attitude, as Denham reminds him, would be appropriate if he were God. Actually, his moral activism has a kind of Faustian flavor in that he believes it is far better to do wrong than it is to do nothing so long as one is striving to serve humanity in some way. Essentially, the harmless existences of most people involve doing nothing:

> That doesn't lead you anywhere near to what really matters—you know, sin and punishment and ultimate reality and all that caper. That leads you to all your life in a semi-detached and pottering about the garden on Saturdays and cold meat for supper after the boozer on Sunday night. That takes you away from anything that's worth having. (*RA*, 147)

But it is Graham Greene, not Goethe, who has molded his outlook. Greene is his favorite writer, and although he does not refer to specific novels, one gathers that he must have been most profoundly influenced by *Brighton Rock, The Power and the Glory,* and *The Heart of the Matter:* ". . . it seemed to me he was saying that you could only get close to God if you really got down to the real dirt, so to speak" (*RA*, 147). For this reason, he has given up a respectable but meaningless career in insurance and taken up dope smuggling. Denham is quite interested in all this, but when he learns how Len's moral activism has touched Imogen Everett, his interest gives way to revulsion.

Revulsion, anger, remorse—Denham feels all these emotions, but only as a sympathetic, if vaguely sanctimonious and cynical, observer of affairs, never a direct participant. The other characters seek to draw him into direct involvement, but except for dispensing a bit of cash and some not-very-helpful advice, he will not be drawn in. Mr. Raj especially sets great store by his opinions and asks his guidance in forming a relationship with Alice Winterbottom. Urgent inquiries from Mr. Raj, together with reassurances concerning his father's health, meet Denham at nearly every stop on his way back to Japan. But Denham is too involved with hedonistic pastimes aboard his tour ship—eating, drinking, adultery—to reply with anything more than a drunkenly conceived cryptogram advising "COPULATION NOW" (*RA*, 143). Mr. Raj had been willing to settle for a Platonic/Courtly tie not involving the action of the flesh, but fun-loving Denham's drunken injunction is well received. Although Denham may not be directly to blame for the violent expression of Mr. Raj's frustration that follows, he has certainly not helped matters as much as he might have.

The news that his father is dying draws him back again to England, and there he witnesses Mr. Raj's suicide. Since we are never quite sure what's in Mr. Raj's head, we cannot be certain why he puts a bullet through it, but there is obviously more to it than remorse over Winterbottom, whom he has slain, or frustration over his inability to unite East and West by "COPULATION" with Alice. While squeezing the trigger, he winks at Denham, "as though the whole thing were a joke, really; which, for a Hindu, perhaps it was." In a sense, this is all that his research into racial attitudes has yielded—an awareness of the bitter comedy of human afairs. The baffling incongruity of it all he presents in an introductory fragment of the thesis he had planned to write:

> *The capacity of people for hatred can never cease to astonish. This is especially so as it would seem that man is by nature gregarious and that he has created a world which is, in effect, founded on love under various other names. Trust is love, credit is a form of love, reliance on the police force or army of a state is also a form of love. It is easily understandable, of course, that love within and for one group must, of biological necessity, imply quite contrary emotions to those elements outside the group which seem likely to threaten (even when this appearance has no basis in fact) the well-being and security, nay the very existence, of the group. We see this clearly when kittens in baskets hiss and spit, though they are blind and have not been taught the nature of fear or of hate, at a quite friendly dog which sniffs near the basket. All this is understandable and biologically necessary. But what cannot be understood is why man, in being forced by economic necessity, as well as being gently persuaded by the increasing shrinking of the globe through aeronautical advances, to think in terms of larger and larger groups to which he must give allegiance or, in a word, love, is increasing his capacity for hate.*
>
> *Here one is tempted to lay down one's pen and smile pityingly and in lack of comprehension. A spring English day compels the heart to greater love of nature and of one's fellow-beings. The heart in particular expands to the presence of the loved female, and wonders why she too will not love. Love seems inevitable, necessary, as normal and as easy a process as respiration, but unfortunately (RA, 217–18)*

With this fragment, Burgess concludes the novel. Denham realizes it is appropriate for Mr. Raj, not himself, to have the last word. His own lofty, cynical detachment from the sordid affairs of suburban England begins to wear on him, especially after he returns to Japan. He looks in a mirror and finds only the lack of warmth caused by maintaining a safe, sneering distance from his fellows. The events he has seen he tries to dismiss as "just silly vulgar people uncovering the high explosive that lies hidden underneath stability" (RA, 200), but he realizes that the observation of life from such a loveless, safe distance is not the experience of living, and he resolves to do something about it if Imogen Everett is willing to overcome the aversion she has previously shown toward him.

When Denham has completed his account of himself and Mr. Raj, there still remains the Shakespearean presence to be accounted for. By introducing Ted Arden and focusing our attention from time to time on his Shakespearean qualities, Burgess maintains a very real Shakespearean presence throughout the book. Some of the effects of this are fairly obvious. We are reminded of differences between present-day English life and the life Shakespeare knew. The more perilous yet gratifying and, from the standpoint of values, more stable life of the Elizabethan illuminates by contrast the insipid, philistine quality of life in the present age. Ted's attitude toward the life around him is not unlike Shakespeare's in some respects. Although he has a sense of values and deplores things such as mate switching, he views other things, such as ephemeral political causes and ideologies, that other men take seriously, as unimportant. One might also remark on the connection between his Shakespearean presence and Mr. Raj. In many ways the story of Mr. Raj resembles the story of Othello, just as the story of Vythilingam in *Beds in the East* resembles that of Hamlet. Like Othello, Mr. Raj is fond of self-dramatization, although he seems to understand himself better than Othello does. He has, however, the same tendency to idealize in a very unrealistic fashion a golden-haired woman he does not understand, and this makes him prone to fits of insane jealousy that have fatal effects. Again, like Othello, he is under the illusion that he is accepted fully by the fair-skinned society around him only to find, during moments of stress, that those who seem to accept him are, like Brabantio, secretly repelled by his blackness. Although Mr. Raj is not created by Ted Arden, as Othello is by Shakespeare, the drama of his attempt to achieve "contact" with the West is presented largely in the theatre of Ted's establishment, and it is quite appropriate that a man who is himself an authentic piece of Shakespeariana should provide much of the setting for an updated comi-tragic version of *Othello*. Ted provides even more in the way of concrete Shakespeariana. A pirated quarto of *Hamlet* dated 1602 just happens to be among his possessions and brings him a tidy sum from the Folger Library. Of even more interest to Denham, however, and to Burgess's readers as well, is the memory of Shakespeare passed down to Ted through generations of Ardens. The story of Shakespeare and the Dark Lady who leaves him syphilitic and disillusioned, that is, the story of Shakespeare in *Nothing Like the Sun,* has been preserved with shame by his mother's family. It would appear that *Nothing Like the Sun* was twitching itself to life well before the year of the Shakespeare quadricentennial.

The Right to an Answer is indeed a well-filled package. Burgess can incorporate and develop more of the matter of serious fiction in fifty pages than most writers can in five hundred. *The Right to an Answer* is so loaded with fascinating insights and characterization that one has a sense of reading the distillation, the quintessential best, of a much larger work. This is not because anything seems to be missing but because Burgess has presented so much with such faultless economy and wit. The range of subjects treated—from culture clashes to love and moral responsibility—is considerable; yet the relevance of each subject to the others is clearly evident. Denham himself, whose commentaries serve to clarify the connections, is much more than a mouthpiece. He is a well-developed and delightful character, despite his essential selfishness and a rather stuffy conservatism that conflicts, on occasion, with his hedonistic impulses. It becomes clear that what repells him initially about Mr. Raj is his radiating human warmth, a warmth that, by the end of the novel, he longs to acquire himself. But what impresses us the most about Denham, even more than his progress in humanity, is his wit.

In addition to being Burgess's meatiest treatment of love and decay in the West, *The Right to an Answer* is also his funniest. Some of Denham's descriptions of what he sees make one ache with laughter. Even a dreary event such as a Sunday dinner at the house of his sister becomes thoroughly hilarious, and his description of a voyage back to the Orient aboard a Dutch liner is a marvelous piece of comedy worthy of any anthology. We may not share Denham's feelings about what he sees, but we cannot resist being entertained by his descriptions and commentaries. His detached outsider's testimony is a tempting invitation to view England through the eyes of other Burgess protagonists, protagonists who are less witty but more involved with life, love, and decay in the West.

The Doctor Is Sick

For Mr. Tomlin, the long-suffering United Nations adviser in *Devil of a State,* the problems of gaining or maintaining a grasp on "reality" weigh heavily. Faced with impossible tasks, frustrated by irrational human obstacles, looking forward to a retirement even more dismal and meaningless than his last term, he wonders whether he or anyone around him is genuinely aware of what is or is not real. His doubts can be related largely to his "fantasticated" tropical surroundings and the various strange or hostile human types with whom he must associate. However, as another Burgess novel, *The Doctor Is Sick,* suggests, such doubts are by no means peculiar to Englishmen in the tropics. The protagonist of *The Doctor Is Sick,* Dr. Edwin Spindrift, has been in the tropics, in Burma, but when he, like Burgess, collapses on a lecture-room floor, he is flown immediately to England and hospitalized. The action begins in the depressing atmosphere of his hospital ward, a place where all that has previously sustained and protected him in the great world suddenly becomes quite irrelevant and meaningless.

Spindrift is a philologist, holder of a doctorate in linguistics awarded by the University of Pasadena (Cal Tech perhaps?) for a thesis "on the semantic implications of the consonant-group 'shm' in colloquial American speech." A tendency to be inordinately aware of honorifics is quite common among those who have recently gone through the nightmare of gaining a doctorate, but for those who have some other source of inner security and personal dignity, it usually wears off after awhile. For Edwin Spindrift, such a wearing off will be a long process. If anyone is reluctant to honor his request that he be addressed as "Doctor Spindrift," he is prepared to present the ocular proof of a diploma he carries inside his coat pocket, along with all sorts of audible pedantic proof of the knowledge for which the degree was granted. At thirty-eight, he is blessed with the sort of innocence and smug pedantry that can survive only in an hermetically sealed academic atmosphere. For him the only important reality, perhaps the only reality, is within a purely verbal realm. His view of words corresponds, in a sense, to Plato's view of ideas. Just as Plato saw the realm of intelligible concepts as more real and therefore more important than the imperfect tangible phenomena reflecting them, so Edwin Spindrift tends to elevate words above the mere phenomena denoted by them. His resultant inability to cope effectively with the world of tangible percepts is the basic source of most of the troubles he is destined to experience in the course of some informal, although rigorous, postdoctoral studies in the seamier sections of London.

His troubles had begun long before his hasty departure from the Far East. The tangible and intangible realities of his own mind and body had asserted their real presence by failing him even before his collapse. Among other things, he had discovered in himself a total failure of the libido. The only reason this failure becomes a source of distress is his attractive wife, Sheila. Far from frigid, she had looked elsewhere for love, and, although Spindrift is willing to accept sexual infidelity as a reasonable concept, there had been trouble "when promiscuity changed from a concept to a percept." (*DTS*, 15).[3] He had encountered the percept in a hotel in Burma and had had good reason to suspect that the incident was not the first, and that it would not be the last.

Spindrift is also apprehensive about Sheila because of the visitors to the hospital that she either brings with her or sends from a shady little club nearby. Most of them do not appear to be potential rivals, but they are capable of distressing Spindrift simply by being representatives of a world in which comprehension of terms such as *phoneme* and *apocope* is not very important. Indeed, neither the visitors nor Spindrift's healers do much to cheer him up. Among the latter are various crisply permed, white-coated technicians who treat him like a thing, nurses who treat him like a child, and a doctor named Railton who is contemptuously amused at his insistence on his honorific. Before his medical career, Dr. Railton had achieved fame playing the trumpet, but once he had established himself as an M.D., the trumpet had become for him merely a pleasurable avocation, "possibly like," he tells Spindrift, "the study of words to you" (*DIS*, 187).

Most depressing to Spindrift is the news that he must undergo brain surgery. His wife cheerfully consents to the operation in the hope that something will revive his libido, and Spindrift accepts it as something unavoidable. Like a thoroughly demoralized inmate of a concentration camp, he accepts without protest having his head shaved for the operation. After the indignities of excruciating tests and forced regressions to childhood and thinghood, this final indignity is relatively minor. But then, on the very eve of his surgery, he awakens with a determination "that nobody should cut his head open, that there should be no excision of any tumour, that he should live—however briefly—and die—however soon—as he was, whether sick or well" (*DIS,* 61). His determination would mean little if he remained in the power of his healers in the hospital, so it is absolutely essential that he escape, which he does easily.

Spindrift's troubles begin when he is beyond the "safe" confines of the hospital. First he goes in search of his wife, for she has left him nearly penniless and one of her male companions has thoughtfully removed most of his clothing for washing. Consequently, he has been forced to make his escape into the night eccentrically clad like a camp inmate in striped pyjamas, jacket, trousers, and shoes without socks. A woolly cap covers his shaved head. Thus attired, he appears at the London office of his employer, the International Council for University Development, and seeks, without success, to draw a few quid to keep him going. After this, he would certainly not be able to survive long on his own, but he is fortunate enough to fall in with some people who are knowledgeable in the ways of the world, even though they know little or nothing about philology.

One person he meets is a powerfully built mover of opera backdrops and properties named Les, a kindly man who takes an interest in Spindrift. When he is not engaged in projects such as moving Valhalla at Covent Garden, he relaxes at the same shady club where Sheila had become acquainted. Under the big man's tutelage, Spindrift learns the fine art of shove-ha'penny and even manages to win some drinking money. He also meets two characters who are even more knowledgeable than Les in the art of money making: the proprietors of the club, twin Semites named Leo and Harry Stone. The sight of Spindrift's gleaming scalp stimulates their cupidity as they dream of entering him in a forthcoming bald-head competition. But Spindrift, fearful of any more reversions to the thinghood he had known in the hospital, is unwilling to cooperate. He does, however, stay with them and even vindicates his profession by demonstrating its usefulness. When two police investigators enter the club in response to reports of various types of illegal traffic, Spindrift confuses them by giving an impromptu lecture on linguistics. This brief ascent, as it were, to the real world of "forms" leaves Spindrift reluctant to return to the shadowy cave, and he is most distressed when his so-called class returns to furtive drinking without being dismissed by him. A little later, when the officers return, he has another chance to return to his real world via the chalk board, but this ascent, a discourse on folk etymology, ends even more distressingly when he repeats his performance of collapsing in midlecture. Although he revives in time to escape before the policemen can get him into their car, his freedom is brief.

A mad-eyed mobster named Bob, attracted by his apparent "kinkiness" on the assumption it betokens some basic perversion, captures him in a phone booth. Spindrift escapes again briefly but soon is recaptured by Bob and incarcerated in the mobster's apartment. Although Spindrift is innocent, he is not stupid, and he soon realizes he is in the custody of a pervert. He also readily divines the real nature of Bob's "kinkiness"—a masochistic passion for flagellation. Thus freed of any need to explain, the mobster gleefully displays a broad back disfigured by fifty stitches and forces Spindrift to lash him with one of the whips from his large and varied collection. To his utter disgust, Spindrift feels "the joy of the sadist arising in his loins" (*DIS,* 115), and he gives Bob a flogging that gratifies him thoroughly. After this feast, the masochist is quite unwilling to release Spindrift, but Spindrift is saved the chore of a repeat performance that evening by the arrival of another mobster, one of Bob's colleagues in the business of selling smuggled watches ("kettles"). This man, a much disfigured thug, reveals an unexpected interest in Spindrift's precious degree. When the philologist confirms he is indeed a "duckterer fellosserfee," the thug begins an amazing catalogue that, to Spindrift's credit, does not greatly amaze him:

> "Deevid Hüme," said the Gorbals man. "Berrrrkeley. Immanuel Kunt." It was not really surprising to hear such a parade of names from such a person. French criminals would, Edwin knew, quote Racine or Baudelaire in the act of throat-cutting; and Italian mobsters would at least know of Benedetto Croce. It was only the English who failed to see human experience as a totality. "Metterfezzecks," said the Gorbals man, and would have said more had not Bob returned knotting his tie. (*DIS,* 117)

Burgess never seems to tire of ridiculing the smug notion that culture is a province of the formally learned, genteel, and law-abiding. There is a remarkable scene in *A Clockwork Orange* in which the young hero rapes two ten-year-old girls to the accompaniment of Beethoven's Ninth Symphony, and, as we have seen in *The Right to an Answer,* even dope-smuggling racketeers are likely to be fairly well read and interested in things such as theology, ethics, and ultimate reality.

When Bob and his associate go out on business, Spindrift is left confined in the flat, which he proceeds to ravage as throughly as he can, kicking in the TV screen, defacing furniture, and so forth. In this process of aimless destruction, he discovers a hiding place crammed full of £5 notes and helps himself. He also throws Bob's precious collection of whips out the window, except for one that he intends to use on Bob in a totally ungratifying way. Then suddenly he is shocked to think how rapidly he has degenerated. It all occurred so easily and naturally, and he realizes his purely verbal grasp of reality has had something to do with it: "Words . . . words, words, words. He had lived too much with words and not with what the words stood for." His love of words for their own sake had even led him to tell Bob he had served time in prison, even though he had never been near a prison. But his philologists's ear had been gratified by the sound of "tray on the moor," and it had not really mattered because words were "only a game" for him (*IDS,* 119). This disturbing train of thought leads him to conclude that philology has not been for him even an avenue to a greater understanding of words. Quite the reverse, in fact. Since words have their full meaning only with reference to the things they denote in the world, separating words from the world is bound to limit understanding of them, and, as his own case reveals, the moral consequences can be serious: "Let him loose in the real world, where words are glued to things, and see what he did: stole, swore, lied, committed acts of violence on things and people. He had never been sufficiently interested in words, that was the trouble" (*DIS*, 120). Just as he had been treated as a thing in the hospital, so he had "treated words as things, things to be analyzed and classified, and not as part of the warm current of life" (*DIS*, 120).

With the savaging of Bob's flat, escape becomes for Spindrift a matter of life and death. Again, left strictly to his own devices, he would be helpless, but he manages to get word to the Stone twins who, still thinking about the bald-head competition, pick the lock and free him. They then attempt to keep him safely confined with the amiable giant Les and his girl friend until the night of the contest. But Spindrift has a strong desire to see his wife again. He has been, whenever he was not being detained or diverted, in search of her since his escape, mainly because she has all their money. Now, thanks to Bob, he no longer needs her financial assistance, but still he wants to find her. When he hears she has been sighted in one of the innumerable clubs in Soho, he resumes his search immediately.

Spindrift's pursuit of Sheila becomes, among other things, a search for love, or more precisely the meaning of love, and this is one of the many respects in which it parallels the quest of Leopold Bloom through Dublin. It is useful to consider some of the other ways in which *The Doctor Is Sick* can be seen as Burgess's own treatment of the major themes in *Ulysses,* for example, the extent to which Spindrift's descent from disembodied philology into the world of tangible reality is like the progress of Stephen Dedalus from a world of words, in which he is an acknowledged master, to the world of Leopold Bloom. In the third part of the *Telemachia* section of *Ulysses,* Stephen is walking along the seashore pondering the nature of reality and attempting to encompass the shifting, treacherous Protean world of material phenomena in language. To an extent, he succeeds, and through philology, he manages to achieve a partial victory over Proteus. But, as Burgess tells us, it is only

"a sort of victory over Proteus." This is no mere fancy. The chaos of primal matter, of the phenomenal world, is figured in the chaos of language, everchanging, hard to pin down. But language, despite the chaos, has, in a manner, pinned down the world outside. It remains for the poet to impose order on language and, by using the to-and-fro rhythms of the tide, to create an image of organic order, achieve the ultimate pinning-down. Already, at the end of the *Telemechia,* Stephen has come some way towards regaining his inheritance: he rules through words, and even Mulligan fears the lancet of his art, while the sea's ruler, Haines, has a mind to make a book of wisdom out of Stephen's

sayings. But Stephen, though a prince of words, is not yet big enough to write
Ulysses. He needs Leopold Bloom.[4]

Bloom represents the world of the flesh, a world Stephen has not mastered, although he has mastered words and ideas. His fleshly function is
enforced by his association with various bodily organs, especially the kidneys
and genitals. Symbolically viewed, the transition from Stephen's world to
Bloom's is from the spirit to the flesh and also from the more spiritual, in the
sense of disembodied, science of philology to the more fleshly, useful science
of economics. As we are introduced to Bloom, he is shown to be capable of
dealing with problems of household management, although the main problem in this area, his wife, Molly, is beyond his control until their reunion at
the end of the novel. To an extent, Burgess's protagonist parallels this
transition by passing from his world of disembodied words, in which he is an
acknowledged "doctor," to the world of organic and economic reality in
which only the knowledge of medical doctors or technicians or worldly wise
illiterates such as Les and the Stone twins really matters. Correspondences
are by no means exact. For example, Bloom is intellectually gifted and fairly
literate, and Stephen Dedalus actually does succeed in gaining some grasp of
material reality through philology. Such contrasts revealed by attempting to
establish parallels between the two books are in themselves illuminating,
especially the contrasts revealed by comparing Spindrift's quest through
London in search of his wife with Bloom's odyssey through Dublin.

In terms of experiences, Spindrift and Bloom have much in common. Both
have adventures and encounter obstacles that parallel, or rather parody,
those of Odysseus. Spindrift's visit to the office of the International Council
for University Development, for instance, like Bloom's visit to the newspaper office, seems to correspond to the sojourn of Odysseus in the cave of the
wind god Aeolus. Spindrift, like Odysseus, is given a gift of "wind," although
he, unlike Odysseus, actually needs another gift. Both men, like Odysseus,
are detained by monsters and nymphs. The masochistic monster who detains
Spindrift shares with the Cyclops and the Laestrygonians an insatiable perverted appetite and his business of "kettle" flogging may also have analogues
in the *Odyssey.* The Calypso in Spindrift's odyssey is a hardworking London
prostitute who picks him up but finds him a totally unrewarding customer,
except in a financial way. She empties his pockets and leaves him a farewell
note reading "TWISTER" as a token of her fury and frustration, but Spindrift
is cheered by something only he had been able to detect, "an establishment of
definite proof that rehabilitation was possible: a speck of gold in the river"
(*DIS,* 146).

This speck will not be enough to save Spindrift's marriage. Like Bloom, he
is questing toward a reunion with a Penelope who has been unfaithful to him,
but unlike Bloom, he will not be able to revive her love. The reasons become
clear when we compare the two Odyssean wanderers. Like Spindrift, and of

course Odysseus, Bloom is an outsider, but mainly because of his sensitivity, his remarkable although unpretentious personality, and his Jewish heritage, not because he is deliberately detached from the warm current of life. Bloom is in love with Molly and longs to be reunited with her despite her infidelity with Blazes Boylan. In contrast, Spindrift is simply not sure that love has any meaning for him. He tries to focus on its meaning but all that really seems to interest him is "that collocation of sounds: the clear allophone of the voiced divided phoneme gliding to that newest of all English vowels which Shakespeare, for instance, did not know, ending with the soft bite of the voiced labiodental." His next thought is of its origins, "back to Anglo-Saxon and beyond." But this is the extent of his interest in "love." For him there is no real fascination in things such as "its real significance when used in such locutions as 'Edwin loves Sheila' " (*DIS,* 120).

Nevertheless, he wants to be reunited with his wife. He is fairly sure that this desire in itself betokens love, and by the end of the novel, he is willing at least to attempt some sort of basic humanizing change in himself that will cause him to be something more loveable than a sexless, pedantic "machine." But the marriage is beyond salvaging, even if such a metamorphosis were possible. Like a limb without warm circulating blood, it has become gangrenous and dead, and Sheila has chosen to let the warmth in her own blood answer that of her lover back in Burma. She even discourages Spindrift from attempting to replace what had been gangrenous in himself with something artificial: "I don't think it would be right for you to change. You're a kind of machine, and the world needs machines. You're like an X-ray machine, or one of those electrocephalo gadgets you were moaning about. You have a use. But I don't need a machine. Not to live with and go to bed with, anyway" (*DIS,* 198).

In spite of this disappointment awaiting him, Spindrift profits by the quest. He becomes aware of much more than his own inadequacies as a man. For one thing, like characters in *The Right to an Answer, One Hand Clapping,* and *The Worm and the Ring,* he is led by his experiences to an awareness of cultural decline in midtwentieth-century England. His experiences among members of the underworld do not in themselves reveal any sort of decadence, but when the conniving Stone twins finally manage to enter him in the bald-head competition, he does encounter evidence of cultural decay. The contest is held in a cinema, the entrance of which is graced by a huge portrait of "a bald actor with sensual lips and the sardonic eyes of a Mongol, presumably the prototype of all the vying hairless of this evening" (*DIS,* 162). The actual identity of this hairless sex symbol is obvious, and it is significant that he is an American, for, as Burgess reveals in various novels, it is from America that the British have chosen to import much that is cheap, vulgar, silly, brutish, and nasty. Burgess does not blame America for this. It is not America's fault that the British chose to corrupt themselves, nor is it the bald actor's fault that he inspires the utterly ridiculous and somewhat sadistic contest in which

Spindrift participates. It is merely symptomatic of the times that he should be an inspiration and an excuse for Londoners to abandon themselves to cruel and worthless forms of entertainment.

The bald-head competition is the evening's pièce de résistance. Before this event, there is appetizing entertainment provided by various amateur performers, including Leo Stone as a comedian and some teenage pop singers. The latter "artists" anticipate Burgess's devastating satirical portraits of the pop-singing "Crewsy Fixers" in *Enderby Outside.* One of them leaves the girls in the audience in "mid-orgasm" when he virtually rapes the microphone; the other sends them into "fresh screams of abandonment" with a song entitled "A Teenager's Heart." This particular type of corruption has of course flowed both ways across the Atlantic. What seems to depress Burgess is that for over a decade it has been one of the strongest cultural bonds uniting England with America. Throughout this dreary series of spectacles, Spindrift has been barely able to contain his disgust. When he is chosen to be "Mr. Bald Adonis of Greater London," he has an opportunity to express his feelings to the entire telly-viewing public. A rather silly beauty rewards him with a kiss on his baldness and conjectures that this "must be a very big moment" for him, to which Spindrift replies,

> "Not really . . . I've known bigger moments, much bigger. As a matter of fact, I feel somewhat ashamed at having been a party to all this. So typical, isn't it, of what passes for entertainment nowadays? Vulgarity with a streak of cruelty and perhaps a faint tinge of the perversely erotic. Shop girls blown up to be Helen of Troy. Silly little men trying to be funny. Stupid screaming kids. Adults who ought to know better. Here's my message to the great viewing public." He leaned forward and spat full into the microphone a vulgar cruel, erotic word. There was a sensation. History was made. (*DIS,* 168–69)

For all of us who have longed to say essentially the same thing on such an occasion, it is a most gratifying outburst, and it is perhaps Spindrift's finest moment in the novel. It reminds us that, for all his shortcomings as a human being, he is in some ways more in touch with reality than much of the society around him. At least he has been in touch with words and through his experiences with things and people has been growing toward an understanding of himself. The ability to make such progress in this Age of the Telly is by no means common. So many people seem to be like the vacuous creatures that J.W. Denham thinks about, with whom "contact" is impossible because they are fundamentally uninterested in life and tend to greet any talk of it with yawns of boredom "and aimless eyes round the room, looking, in vain, for the real thing, the telly" (*RA,* 193).

Spindrift follows his contribution to history with a mad dash for freedom, made especially desperate by the presence of Dr. Railton, who has been playing his trumpet in the orchestra. Dr. Railton is assisted in his attempt to stop Spindrift by some white-coated institutional toughs, and he seeks additional help from the audience by yelling out a warning that Spindrift's tumor has made him a public menace. Before the evening's events, Spindrift had learned this was a fear shared by his wife to the extent that she was seeking police protection. Thus it becomes clear that all the "agencies of the world" are against him. Outside the cinema, he is reminded that this includes the agencies of the underworld as well: he is recaptured by the flagellate kettle mobster. He soon escapes again but suddenly becomes extremely weary of the whole chase and is ready to surrender. With a farewell double whisky under his belt, he becomes "finally passive, an ultimate thing," to be disposed of as the agencies of the world see fit (*DIS*, 177). Thus resigned, he wanders into a hotel lavatory where he encounters a familiar yet mysterious figure, a former schoolfellow named Aristotle Thanatos from whom he receives a great deal of sympathy and promises of assistance.

With the entrance of this "agency of the world," as he describes him, Burgess begins to introduce a new level of interpretation that may confuse a reader if he overlooks significant details and hints. Perhaps the most important hints are conveyed by the name "Aristotle Thanatos." "Thanatos" means death, and this strengthens the suggestion that Spindrift's three days in the "underworld" have been just that. But Aristotle Thanatos clearly represents more than death itself; he is both literally and symbolically a Dionysian figure. Since his last meeting with Spindrift, he has become a prosperous vintner, and he is in the hotel attending a convention designed to promote Greek wines in England. To grace the occasion, he wears a coronal of vine leaves. Although subsequent events emphasize his association with death, he is also Dionysian in the way in which he seems to hold forth a hope of regeneration. Having assessed Spindrift's wretched condition for himself, he offers not only sympathy but the hope of a public-relations position in his firm. Spindrift, having assessed his own former condition as essentially sterile and dead, is quite receptive to the idea and works to ingratiate himself. Unfortunately, the revulsion and self-contempt he feels concerning his former existence seems to operate in him on a subconscious level to such an extent that he is almost miraculously capable of disregarding even the most basic rules of grammar. When he tries to assure Aristotle Thanatos that he is more at home with "the best people" than his costume would indicate, he horrifies the man by blurting out, "You should see me when I'm got up proper."

Their interview takes place amid a scene of uninhibited Bacchanalian revelry. While another Dionysian figure (fully costumed as Bacchus) staggers about the room with a lifted cup, girls with lifted kirtles crush grapes with their feet. All around them are drinkers draining goblets of golden wine that has been poured from Hellenic jars. Thus it appears that Aristotle Thanatos has, like the Egyptian counterpart of Dionysus, led Spindrift from the underworld into a kind of heavenly realm where he is judged and permitted to make a "Negative Confession" to the effect that he is not as wretched as he appears to be.

Associating Mr. Thanatos with Osiris is not as fanciful as it may sound. If one is familiar with *The Book of the Dead,* one can see Spindrift's progress is parallel to a large extent with the progress of a soul through the underworld with all its perils and monsters into the presence of Osiris himself, the Judge of the Dead, and his sovereign princes and eventually into a state of oneness with the universal being. According to *The Book of the Dead,* the soul, having achieved this last state, is permitted to range the universe at will, even to return to the earth.[5] Spindrift is not actually shown in this transcendent state, but he appears, with the aid of Mr. Thanatos, on his way to achieving it. First, however, he must descend again into the underworld and undergo one more terrible trial. Pitying his homeless, penniless condition, Mr. Thanatos offers him a bed in his own hotel room and Spindrift goes to it willingly with a farewell death wish, "Apothanein thelo." What awaits him is another wretched descent from the realm of concepts to percepts much like the one that had jolted him in Burma. The shock causes him to pass out and plunge into a world of dreams based on his experiences of the preceding three days.

Within his dreams, Spindrift has a sense of confinement, of being "fastened to a bed, absolutely immobile like Odysseus and other Greeks, wine-dark, lashed to the mast to hear unharmable compulsive music of the Sirens." When he awakens, it appears that his entire odyssey, complete with its journey to the underworld, its "Book of the Dead," has taken place while he has been confined to his hospital bed and the operating table. It is not long before Dr. Railton is at his bedside, checking to see how he is recovering from the brain surgery. The physician is still contemptuously amused at the idea of Spindrift's use of an honorific appropriate to one who has grasped the mysteries of a serious field such as medicine but utterly inappropriate to one who devotes most of his energies to a mere hobby "like the study of words." But if Spindrift's claim to the title *doctor* is questionable, what can one say about the role Dr. Railton seems to arrogate to himself? When Spindrift expresses shame and remorse generated by his "dreamt" experiences, Dr. Railton orders him to cast off guilt because it "is a big retarder of recovery." When Spindrift replies by asking for a moral rather than a clinical judgment of himself, Railton answers, significantly: "That doesn't come into the covenant between us" (*DIS,* 187). The word *covenant* suggests that Railton sees himself in a Godlike role with quasi-religious prerogatives and functions as a dispenser of undeserved regenerating grace. In a sense, if we consider what has happened to Spindrift in his "dream," this is justified. We can perceive still another regeneration motif that appears to follow Pauline/Augustinian lines. Spindrift, who has led a sterile life according to the "letter" of his role as a philologist, has been regenerated into the spirit of life itself. If this rebirth has indeed occurred while he has been under Dr. Railton's care, while he was strapped "immobile like Odysseus" on bed and operating table, the doctor may indeed be entitled to view himself as a dispenser or mechanism of "grace."

But what if this is not the case? What if Spindrift has indeed been physically as well as spiritually away from the hospital on a three-day journey through the underworld? What if there has been a kind of conspiracy involving not only Dr. Railton but his wife. Spindrift cannot really be sure what has happened to him. When Sheila visits him, bearing the cheerless news that both she and his employer are through with him, he tries to interrogate her and succeeds in checking a few points, enough to raise doubts in both his mind and the reader's.

The doubts raised by Sheila's visit are not diminished by Sheila's last words to him—a message from Aristotle Thanatos: a request that Spindrift meet with him again as soon as possible. Spindrift appears to be asleep when he hears this, but he soon awakens "with no hint of a margin between sleeping and waking," dresses himself as smartly as he can in clothes belonging to fellow patients, and escapes again into the night: "The city and the land and all the world were there waiting, full of ripe fruit for the picking" (*DIS*, 201). He will, so far as he is able, enjoy it all, and then he will meet again with Aristotle Thanatos wherever he happens to be.

In reintroducing this mysterious figure, Burgess again evokes mythic treatments of death and rebirth, and connected with these regeneration motifs is an "Aristotelian" one we should not overlook. Spindrift, in descending from disembodied philology to a world where words are attached to things, has had to make a plunge analogous to that of Plato's true philosopher returning from the sunlit world of concepts, or "forms," to the cave of percepts. The difference is that Plato's philosopher will supposedly have been granted an infallible grasp of how the world of perceptible things ought to be ordered. Spindrift's career in the immaterial world of verbal forms, on the other hand, had made him simply unable to cope with the world of matter. If he is to get anything at all out of the waiting world, he must completely cast off his old "Platonic" self and assume a new "Aristotelian" one. He must be ready to come to terms with the changing matter in which "forms" are dynamic principles. This "Aristotelian" motif is related to the Joycean parallels mentioned earlier. Stephen Dedalus, too, looks to Aristotle, the great classifier, for assistance in taming the world of matter. It is also related to the *Book of the Dead* analogue in that Spindrift's new "Aristotelian" grasp of reality will draw him toward a state of oneness with the ever-changing universal being, the world of things "ripe for the picking."

In addition, this philosophical motif may help to account for the periodic entrances of a character named Hippo, or rather "Ippo," an illiterate who earns his living by walking about sandwiched between signboards. His name is quite suggestive. One thinks of Hippon, the eclectic philosopher who denied all existence save that of things known through the five senses, a man Aristotle considered too mean intellectually to deserve the name philosopher. One may also, following a hint from Spindrift, think of St. Augustine of Hippo, the great neo-Platonist who came down to earth in his theological writings with consistently profound insights into human psychology. The fact that Hippo steals Spindrift's watch near the beginning of the novel and it is returned by Sheila after the three-day "journey" may be a subtle reference to Book XI of the Confessions in which Augustine considers the nature of time. Spindrift, like Augustine, is greatly exercised over the mystery of so-called past, present, and future. An "Augustinian" presence might also be intended to complement the Platonic/Aristotelian motif by showing how a descent such as Spindrift's, from concepts to percepts, is likely to lead one to a fuller, "Augustinian" awareness of human depravity.

This analysis of interacting theological, mythological, artistic, and philosophical motifs in *The Doctor Is Sick* should not suggest that a reader must bring to the novel a bookish, Spindriftian sensibility in order to enjoy it. If one *wants* to play the professional game of critical exegesis, to hunt for symbols, motifs, and so forth, there is plenty to keep one occupied just digging into aspects of the novel not even touched here. But the book is very nearly as funny as *The Right to an Answer,* and anyone with a feeling for life and language will find it hard to lay aside. Anyone, even a semiliterate, half-lobotomized television addict must be able to appreciate the uproarious, although bitter, comedy in scenes such as the bald-head competition or the episodes in the hospital before Spindrift's escape. The way in which Burgess effortlessly wrings the full comic possibilities out of thoroughly dreary material is continually amazing. What, for instance, could be more dreary than the routine details of daily life in a hospital ward? Yet listen to this:

Just before luncheon another of the legion of the cool, the neat-haired, in a white smock with bare pink arms, came to conduct a sort of pummeling therapy on the Punch-chinned, Punch-humped young man in the winter sports cap. She punched him vigorously, and he responded by coughing profoundly and spitting into a sputum-cup. A brisk trade was done in bedpans. Bottles were called for; sly micturation was achieved under the bedclothes. And then Edwin's afternoon treat was announced.

"A lumbar puncture," said the sister. She was a pinch-nosed Scot who trilled the r's with relish. "They're going to take some of the fluid from your spinal cord. Then they'll take it to the laboratory. Then they'll see what's wrong with it."

"I've had that done already," said Edwin, "twice."

"And," said the sister, "ye'll have it done again." Mistress of repartee, she returned to her office.

Some humorist in the catering department had decided on stewed brains for luncheon. Softer hearted, some other cook had provided potatoes cooked in four different ways, a tiny potato anthology. The black man came with the ice-cream gleaming sardonically at Edwin. Edwin read his philological magazine—a humourless American word-count of *The Owl and the Nightingale.* Stewed brains indeed (*DIS,* 32–33)

The lumbar punctures and other excruciating tests that Spindrift under-goes are in themselves anything but funny, but Burgess's descriptions are irresistibly comic. So it is throughout Spindrift's odyssey. As he has done in so many of his novels, Burgess has exhibited an incomparable wit and verbal wizardry in creating a fictional experience that is at times quite disturbing and provocative but always marvelously entertaining.

Honey for the Bears

Like *The Doctor Is Sick, Honey for the Bears* chronicles a Ulyssean quest for understanding and self-awareness. Set in Leningrad during the Khrushchev regime, it is based in part on Burgess's own experiences there in 1961. Before visiting Russia, Burgess had, like most Westerners, been subtly filled with official and unofficial propaganda depicting Russia as an intolerable, incom-prehensible police state filled with fearful, robotlike workers; diabolical, reptilian secret police; and a general atmosphere of extreme hostility toward anything or anyone from the West. Having arrived, however, he soon be-came aware that the essential humanity of the Russians had in no way been diminished by their ruthlessly enforced march toward a socialist utopia. Even the secret police turned out to be quite human, and Burgess's experiences with them and other Russians filled him with a new sense of humanity's oneness.

To an extent, what Paul Hussey, the protagonist of *Honey for the Bears,* learns about Russia is what Burgess himself learned, and many of his more improbable adventures are based on experiences that Burgess himself had. But this is the fullest extent to which *Honey for the Bears* could be termed autobiographical. Between Hussey and Burgess, there is no appreciable resemblance. Hussey is a rather colorless, apparently asexual antique dealer who goes to Leningrad solely for the purpose of smuggling in twenty-dozen drilon dresses to be sold on the black market at a substantial profit. His motives for engaging in this risky trade are far more complex than simple greed. Mainly it is a matter of doing a favor for a deceased friend named Robert who had planned before his sudden death to sell the dresses himself. Robert's widow, Sandra, needs the money and Paul feels bound to help her. Along with her need, however, is a stronger, related motive. Robert's mem-ory is a constant fond presence and carrying out the venture is a ritual of devotion to it. The real nature of the relationship he had had with Robert is suggested subtly early in the novel but not fully revealed either to Paul himself or the reader until later, when he is about to lose his voluptuous American wife, Belinda, to Russia.

Like her husband, Belinda is concerned about Robert's widow with whom she has had a very warm friendship. Indeed, before Robert's death, the two couples had made a very cozy foursome, enjoying "*such* good fun, harmless Saturday-night larks in one car or the other, country-pub bitter (even gin occasionally, if one or other had had a good week) and kisses and cuddles with swapped partners, the sort of thing considered only decent among people of their class, educated shopkeepers" (*HFB*, 19).[6] This "decent" little relationship has in fact been essential to the preservation of the Husseys's marriage, since it provides them with much of what they cannot give each other, but this is something neither realizes until their encounter with Russia forces awareness upon them.

The opening scene is set on the Husseys's ship the day before it docks in Leningrad. The ship is Russian and its warm-hearted crew and staff give the Husseys a foretaste of what they will encounter in Russia. As in Russia itself, the orthodox Soviet "official dream" of social progress affects the Russian outlook on practically everything, but there is nothing sinister or Orwellian about this. It does not in any way inhibit the kindness and feeling for life that emanate from the Russian soul. Since the Husseys are inhibited by their own official dream of what Russians are like, it takes them awhile to appreciate this. Belinda is filled with terror when Paul reveals to the ship's doctor that she is an American, and Paul, although he responds more readily to the Russian warmth, is apt to let nearly any little suggestion generate visions of "the hammering on the door in the winter night, the brutal boots, the cropped heads, the fists" (*HFB*, 14).

As it turns out, he is more threatened by some of his own countrymen aboard the ship than he is by any of the Russians. A group of leftist British students under the care of a scrawny female lecturer "in very late youth" is outraged by his championing of a persecuted composer named Opiskin whom he knows nothing about beyond what Robert had told him (*HFB*, 25). Robert's fondness for Opiskin's work has been enough to enshrine the composer in a very special place in Paul's heart, a fact that becomes important later in the novel. With the students, however, it nearly costs him a beating, especially when he compounds the offense by crashing their extravagantly blasphemous last-night-of-the-voyage costume party, an affair designed to express, among other things, their contempt for establishment-preserving opiates. Although the costumes of some are titteringly mock clerical, others are frankly sacrilegious.

The idea for this obscene entertainment has come from another Westerner, one who seems to be more sympathetic to Paul's point of view, a mysterious ancient creature in a wheelchair who deliberately baits the students. The most puzzling aspect of this creature is "its" sex, a riddle in no way illuminated by the fact that "it" is never addressed or referred to by any name or title other than the asexual honorific "Doctor." In Paul's mind and the reader's, "it" becomes "Dr. Tiresias." Although "it" isn't actually blind, "its" "oyster-coloured eyes" suggest Tiresian blindness, and "its" role as a seer is suggested early in the novel by "its" recollections of Russia's glorious Tsarist past, which cause "it" to jeer at what it considers the all-pervasive barbarity of life under Soviet rule. Paul's initial impression of "it" is that "it" is something "that philosophy had unsexed, some final Shavian achievement" (*HFB,* 14). As subsequent events prove, however, "it" is driven less by a Shavian involvement with ideas than with a desire to gratify appetites that know no ideology.

Dr. Tiresias does not reappear until near the end of the novel, but "its" sexually ambiguous presence in the novel's opening scenes serves to introduce the inevitably fascinating question of sexual identity. It is a question that has never exercised Paul greatly, but in the course of his adventures through Leningrad it takes on a new and vexing importance. Just as he is never able to guess precisely the sex of Dr. Tiresias, so the mystery of his own sexuality—as well as Belinda's—becomes progressively more insoluble. Initially, although he is willing to admit he is not "a very highly sexed man," he seems to be fairly sure of his masculinity. But when a sudden rare randiness on shipboard prompts him to attempt intercourse with Belinda, he is rendered fearful and impotent by her introduction of a technique not described in "the available literature." Most significant is the fact that an image of Robert is part of the "ugliness" he finds in this erotic novelty (*HFB,* 20). Robert's association with his impotence is something Paul tries to exclude from his consciousness, and he goes on to try, with little apparent success, to redeem himself using "the roast beef of Old England" in a conventional way with this "effete Yankee bastard."

The fact that he is not greatly distressed by these failures is evidence of his lack of self-awareness and understanding. Paradoxically, to safeguard the masculinity of his self-image, he has persuaded himself he is asexual. He has also persuaded himself this does not make him significantly inadequate as a marriage partner. Perhaps if the Husseys had never gone to Russia, if they had remained in England enjoying a cozy suburban existence, Paul would have been able to preserve these fantasies. But cold, humiliating reality is introduced as a result of a skin rash, which afflicts Belinda so severely that she must be hospitalized. Dr. Sonya Lazurkina, a very discerning physician, takes over the case and her diagnosis goes well beyond what might normally be considered strictly relevant to a skin ailment.

Before this, there is an interlude of Leningrad night life. With the doctor's permission, although against her wishes, Belinda is released from the hospital to enjoy what proves to be a very brief euphoria. Paul takes her to a restraurant where they become acquainted with Russian modes of drinking and with some young Leningraders, including a Brooklyn-born would-be hipster named Alexei Prutkov, with whom Paul is destined to become well acquainted. A few hours of friendly drinking generates in Belinda a vindictive impulse to let the whole restaurant see what her sexless husband ignores, and only the more vengeful return of the rash saves Paul from a flesh-flashing, table-top exhibition.

What happens before Belinda's attempted striptease is largely fiction.

What happens immediately after that is essentially what happened to Burgess and his wife one night as they attempted to leave a Leningrad restaurant. There is a terrifying pounding on the front door, and Paul suddenly remembers some scripture: "Bring us the strangers, that we may know them" (*HFB*, 79). Still under the influence of Western propaganda, Paul assumes he and Belinda are being sought by drunken Russians "after foreign blood." As it turns out, however, the hammerers are like nothing one would encounter in a typical Western spy thriller. They are young hoodlums called "stilyagi" who bear a striking resemblance to the "teddy boys" who were then haunting the streets of London. More astonishing the stilyagi and the commissionaires who are straining to keep them out of the restaurant courteously step aside to let the Husseys pass. Then, "to his greater surprise, the *stilyagi* took no advantage. Young toughs in shirt-sleeves (this being no season for *style*), armed with coshes and bottles, they politely made way for the leaving party, waited for the doors to be bolted again, then resumed their batterings and yells. Something to do with the chess-mind" (*HFB*, 81). Witnessing this same ritualized violence gave Burgess the idea for *A Clockwork Orange*.

Once outside, the Husseys are in a very bad way indeed, for there are no taxis and Belinda is in no condition for a long hike back to their hotel. Then, by what would appear to be an incredible piece of conjuring, one of their young friends manages to bring them some transportation in the form of a tiny ambulance. By dazzling coincidence, or so it seems, the little vehicle carries Dr. Lazurkina and two attendants. In fact, there has been nothing thaumaturgical or coincidental about this rescue, and it is strictly for Belinda's benefit. There is no room for Paul in the ambulance, and, although he has no way of knowing, it is the beginning of the end for his marriage.

In addition to Belinda, Paul has two suitcases full of drilon dresses to worry about—his duty to "poor dead Robert." They become especially worrisome when he accidentally leaves them in the "INTOURIST" office in the shipping terminal. This, however, turns out to be one of his happiest accidents since the police have uncovered poor Robert's whole plan and are waiting for him to attempt to contact his Russian middleman, whom they have in custody. When Paul falls into the trap, he is interrogated by two police inspectors, an amiable one named Zverkov and a much less agreeable one named Karamzin. As Paul reflects gratefully upon the "divinity that shapes our whatsits," the inspectors search his innocent baggage. They find nothing, but, like so many of the characters Paul encounters in Russia, they assist him unwittingly in his unwilling search for his sexual identity. They inform Paul that the middleman, under questioning, had revealed that Robert was "gomosexual." Characteristically, Paul refuses to believe that "omnifutuant" (gorgeous Latinism that) Robert had unleashed this side of his "large sexuality" in Russia. Again, we may perceive a resistance to certain truths about his own sexuality. For one thing, his resistance seems to proceed less from indignation at a slur on a friend's name than from a bit of "gomosexual" jealousy and outrage at the thought of infidelity. But Paul is not yet ready to admit consciously that this is the case. Instead, he simply dismisses Robert's alleged deviation as "a lie, of course, an item in the standard litany of vilification" (*HFB,* 81).

He cannot dismiss it for long, however, for when he goes to visit Belinda in the hospital, Dr. Lazurkina is prepared to do some probing that is far more extensive and distressing than the police interrogation. Under "a little dose of pentathol," Belinda has revealed to Dr. Lazurkina that she loathes all men. Paul has a ready explanation for this, one that enables him to preserve the masculinity, such as it is, of his self-image. Belinda's college-professor father, a very unstable man, had attempted incest with her. This and Paul's admission that he is not "what you'd call a very highly sexed man" should satisfy Dr. Lazurkina's curiosity about their sex life (or rather, the lack of it). It should even explain why Belinda has had lesbian relationships with various women, including Robert's widow. This latter jolting revelation, too, has been dredged up while Belinda was under pentathol, although one gathers that Belinda's lesbian tendencies were apparent earlier to Dr. Lazurkina. Paul is actually less astonished by this than he pretends:

> "I had no. . . ." But of course he'd had an idea, he realized. Lugging it up to the light brought shock, but the shock was, for some reason, not all that unpleasant. He tried to feel humiliation but couldn't. Still, he gazed aghast at everything leaping in order to its station. (*HFB,* 93)

The real jolt comes when Dr. Lazurkina presents her own summary of the case:

> "So I explain what your wife has been doing by saying that it is all because you are homosexual and are not honest enough to admit it." Paul gaped to the limit, but still noticed that she did not pervert the h of that bomb of a word to a g. "You have made yourself unaware of it," she smiled in cold scientific triumph. (*HFB,* 94)

Paul tries to deny this, but he cannot be very emphatic. He cannot say he has "never" been homosexual because he had had relations with Robert during the war. The fact that there had been more to their relationship than sexual gratification has enabled him consciously to discount the importance of its sexuality, although the actual importance of this has been repeatedly manifest in his failures with Belinda. He tries to argue, however, that his homosexuality is a thing of the past, nothing more than an ephemeral, almost accidental experience brought about wholly by extraordinary wartime circumstances. Pointing out to Dr. Lazurkina that "It happened a lot during the war," he seeks to take refuge among the considerable numbers of womenless men in various circumstances for whom homosexuality is nothing beyond an experience or two. But Dr. Lazurkina forces Paul to think about his own homosexuality, and she will not let him dismiss it as nothing more than a brief wartime contact; as she perceives it, it is for him an abiding condition. Whether or not he chooses to admit it, he is and always will be a man for whom Eros exists in only one of his many divine forms.

Paul's response to this indicates he is repelled primarily by the idea of being a homosexual. In his efforts to rise above his working-class origins, he has assumed the accent and manners of the upper classes, and, as is frequently the case with those who long for social acceptance, he is much confined in his thinking by conventions. The idea of being a homosexual cannot exist in his mind without a whole accompanying complex of guilt associations, fears of ostracism, and so on. Desperately, he insists that his wartime liaison with Robert had been completely transformed into a legitimate, close friendship that permitted them both to render to their wives their "sexual duties." Dr. Lazurkina pounces on this phrase which, with its connotations of the dreary, the obligatory, the antiseptic, and the unspontaneous, seems to reveal Paul's typical Englishness: "Yes," said Dr. Lazurkina, with an exactly English sarcastic intonation. "Sexual duties. You English are very different from us Russians" (*HFB*, 95). Then, with a few more distressingly accurate observations on what the relationship with Robert had meant to Paul, Dr. Lazurkina goes on to make some generalizations about the Western consciousness:

> "But all this is very interesting. It is most interesting to be in contact again with the Western mind. Incest," she said without irony. "Men with men and women with women. Of course, you all really wish to die. We are quite different here." (*HFB*, 95)

In other words, Dr. Lazurkina sees in the Hussey relationship and Belinda's childhood brush with incest no accidental association. Both aberrations reflect typical Western patterns of thinking. It is in the nature of the Western consciousness to turn incestuously in upon itself, to preserve jealously both the least and the most admirable aspects of its beliefs and culture against intrusion from without, especially from the East. As Burgess reveals in the *Malayan Trilogy*, this incestuous pattern can be seen even when the West moves into the East. Victor Crabbe is shown to be a rare colonial. We can also see some anticipations here of *MF*, Burgess's most thoroughly devastating treatment of the incestuous tendency of the Western consciousness as it is mirrored in art.

Having thus threatened Paul's self-image with total emasculation, Dr. Lazurkina dismisses him. The best way he can find of "cushioning his shocks" is with alcohol and he crawls his way from shop to shop, all the time testing his reactions to attractive young men and women and trying to assure himself he really feels "more for the female than the male." Later, back in his hotel room, he awakens from his bender to the news that his bags full of drilon, poor Robert's wares, have found their way to his hotel from the Intourist office.

With the middleman in custody, Paul must either find another agent or flog the dresses himself. Alexei Prutkov, the would-be hipster, had revealed an interest in saleable Western goods and Paul goes to seek him out. When he finds the young man, he insists on moving in with him, and his reasons for doing so seem perfectly sensible. It will be less expensive than the hotel and the dresses will be safe from Zverkov and Karamzin. He does not consciously admit any other motive. But the fact that he finds Alexei's appearance "very wholesome, very delectable" indicates that his libido is sending him warnings about the dismal epiphany toward which he is being propelled.

While Paul is settling in with Alexei and peddling the dresses, Belinda is recovering nicely in a Soviet hospital. From the beginning, Dr. Lazurkina has sensed the existence in her of "something deeper" in the way of an ailment than the rash and the consequent need of a "very very deep probing" diagnosis. Her conclusions regarding the treatment Belinda needs are determined as much by her own needs as by Belinda's. Like Belinda, she is a lesbian and the cure she prescribes is a long vacation for the two of them together. Although Paul does not anticipate their departure, he is made vaguely apprehensive by his visits with Belinda in the hospital. When he is with her, the insensitivity and selfishness he exhibits tend to deprive him of any sympathy he might otherwise receive from the reader in the course of his subsequent humiliations. Two worries are uppermost in his mind—getting back to the antique shop he had acquired with Belinda's inheritance and doing his duty "in memory of poor dead Robert" by profitably disposing of the dresses. Understandably, Belinda, who is developing a warm, meaningful relationship with Dr. Lazurkina, is not greatly agitated by either concern.

The name "Lazurkina" is very suggestive in terms of what Dr. Lazurkina provides Belinda in addition to lesbian love. The name is cognate with and indeed very close to the meaning of the term *azure* in English. "Azure" is a bright blue shade, the color of lapis lazuli. It also suggests a sky that is cloudless and serene. The name can thus be seen to be quite appropriate in several ways. For Belinda, life with Paul has been, like Paul himself, quite colorless. It has been a life of affected gentility, jolly mate-swapping, and dishonesty about sex. Its sterility, or perhaps neutrality, becomes apparent only when it is placed against the vivid contrast of the Russian feeling for life that she comes to know through Dr. Lazurkina. Neither the "official dream" nor the lack of consumer goods has quenched this feeling, and Belinda longs to share it. Her lesbian lover provides another vivid contrast with Paul simply by her honesty about sex. Her views about deviations from Western sexual mores are utterly unclouded by guilt, and she chides Paul for being, like a typical Westener, full of "guilt about the wrong thing" (*HFB*, 95).

Bearing in mind what Dr. Lazurkina represents helps to account for the name "Belinda" as well. Belinda's incestuous father, a specialist in eighteenth-century poetry, had given her the name because she happened to be born on the same day that his school edition of *The Rape of the Lock* was ready for the press. It is understandable that such a man would be drawn to the poetry of Pope and his age, an age in which the supremacy of reason was never questioned by the most influential writers, although despised emotion had a tendency to assert itself here and there in tasteless, extravagant, or sentimental works of minor writers. It is, however, painfully ironic that the professor's own suppressed emotions should assert themselves at the expense of a daughter named to commemorate his affection for the Age of Reason. Clearly, like the eighteenth-century itself, Belinda's father had been unable to achieve a harmonious balance between reason and emotion. In this same regard, but in a somewhat different way, Paul has been equally disappointing. To suppress his homosexual tendencies, he has suppressed all sexual passion and has persuaded himself it doesn't matter since they have, he fancies, an intellectual rapport: "Companionship, intellectual intercourse— these are the important things in a marriage" (*HFB,* 93). But like the professor, he is destined to be overcome by his suppressed passions, helpless in the face of temptation that appeals directly to his own deviant sexuality. Belinda's revulsion toward men thus becomes readily understandable, as does the attractiveness of Dr. Lazurkina. Lesbian or not, the doctor has a comparatively wholesome, rational attitude toward sex and life in general that makes Belinda quite willing to be spirited away. The appropriateness of Belinda's name can of course be seen again in the fact that her "rape" by Dr. Lazurkina is the climactic event in Paul's mock-epic quest toward self-knowledge.

The doctor's analysis of his case is merely the beginning of Paul's sexual humiliation in Leningrad. When he goes from the hospital to a little dive where he has been trying, with minimal success, to flog the dresses, he encounters a man named Madox, who serves as a companion to the mysterious Dr. Tiresias. Paul, who has taken on the disguise of an extremely seedy appearance, finds he can conceal nothing from this fellow Englishman. To him it is obvious that Paul is up to something "not quite above board," and Madox has been able to recognize him instantly by his walk. Having become hypersensitive about his image as a result of Dr. Lazurkina's assessment, Paul is convinced that he is being picked again as a homosexual. It is actually Paul's own fault that the conversation takes an uncomfortable "sexual turn" because he has been trying to pry out of Madox the sexual identity of his employer. Although Madox distresses him by echoing some of Dr. Lazurkina's injunctions to face life as it is, he is much kinder than most of the people who sense Paul's problem. Like his epicene employer, Madox seems to have a very large understanding of human weakness. He even buys one of Paul's dresses, paying twice as much as he really has to, and gives him a formal invitation to a dinner given by an organization innocuously called "ANGLERUSS." Paul has no way of knowing that ANGLERUSS and its organizer, Dr. Tiresias, will eventually cause him to carry out an exploit that, in its punishable criminality, utterly dwarfs smuggling drilon.

The most painful sexual humiliations await Paul in Alexei Prutkov's flat.

Alexei's girl friend lives with him and bitterly resents Paul, perhaps because she senses a potential rival. When she expresses her contempt by baring her well-endowed torso for a shampoo, Paul takes advantage of Alexei's absence and attempts a vengeful rape. After a brief, spirited resistance, the girl, who seems to be neglected in bed by Alex, settles down to receive him. But then suddenly there is a "power-cut." Desperately he tries to recharge himself with instant compositions of erotica "lashed out" by his imagination, but this is hopeless, for such a process inevitably leads him back to Robert. Hearing Opiskin and smelling the wartime smell of RAF ground capes, he knows he must give up this attempt to know Russia in the flesh.

Humiliating impotence is but a prelude to the emasculating revelations in store during what proves to be his last night in Alexei Prutkov's flat. When the young man returns, Paul's libido again sends him warnings, but there is no real danger of discovery as long as he remains inhibited by his fear of being proven homosexual. Alexei has been given an LP anthology of American jazz by a tourist and he has invited all of his jazz-hungry young friends in to share these officially condemned sounds of Western decadence over cognac and vodka purchased with Paul's money. Unfortunately, thanks to Paul, they are all destined to be treated to a taste of something genuinely decadent from the West. Ironically, it is in the process of establishing his virility, by surpassing the window-sill drinking feat in *War and Peace,* that Paul causes his own undoing. Suspended from a window by one foot, he consumes enough vodka to drown all inhibition. Then, rejoining the jazz symposium, he attempts to arouse the spirit of Plato, or rather Alcibiades, in all the young men present. Alexei's girl friend, the only woman present, is the only one safe.

After this, Paul is allowed to remain in the flat only long enough to sleep off the vodka that has caused him to reveal all. With disgust but also with what appears to be the sympathy of one whose own sexuality is in doubt, Alexei Prutkov drives him out with all his drilon dresses. The young hipster does keep his promise to arrange disposal of the dresses, but this arrangement turns out to be a betrayal to the police. Alex just barely manages to thwart the plan of Zverkov and Karamzin to catch him red-handed in the act of selling the dresses on the street, and the two investigators have the frustrating experience of seeing all the incriminating evidence given away free to passersby on the street. So much for Paul's duty to poor dead Robert.

Although the police have nothing to charge him with, the affair is by no means over. The long-feared interrogation finally takes place, complete with fists. Like any spy-thriller hero from the West, Paul bears up well, but unlike the cropped-headed villains of the same thrillers, Zverkov and Karamzin become very repentant, regretting that Paul's beating is somewhat excessive. Then, having decided to patch him up and send him back to England, Zverkov, the ranking investigator, converses with him pleasantly about the English character that, in his view, has degenerated severely during the last four centuries. Echoing characters in several of Burgess's novels, he observes that "The English are not like the Russians—not any more. They were like the Russians at the time of their Queen Elizabeth I, when they produced their Shakespeare. But not now" (*HFB*, 153). Part of this assessment, the idea that twentieth-century England appears hopelessly effete when compared with Elizabethan England, is something we hear frequently in Burgess's fiction. However, the idea that today's Russians are more like the Elizabethans than present-day Englishmen is something new. Whether or not we are supposed to take it very seriously, there would seem to be some grains of truth in it if we are to accept as accurate the view of Russia that Paul and Belinda gain. The unquenchable feeling for life that shows itself in everything from hearty drinking to the excitement generated by space exploration, a feeling for life that seems to be heightened rather than inhibited by a danger-fraught atmosphere of official dreams and censorship, chauvinistic patriotism, and the sense of being surrounded by enemies is rather like what one finds reflected in the literature of Elizabethan England.

The feeling that he is indeed an effete representative of an effete culture is only one of the many things that depress Paul as he listens to his interrogator. He is penniless, without prospects of getting any money, partly toothless from his interrogation, more than ever aware of his impotence, and generally wretched. Sympathetic, his interrogators arrange for him to have the hospitality of a jail cell for the night, and he is lodged with three friendly prisoners who become even friendlier when they discover he is English. When it is time to turn in for the night, Paul is persuaded to relate a bedtime "English story" in spite of his weariness and his feeble command of Russian. What comes out as he is drowsing off reveals still more of the demoralizing effects of his Russian experiences. It is a simple little allegory involving characters representative of England, Russia, and the United States, but it ends rather oddly with the wife of the character representing England abandoning him for one of the great rival "tsardoms" that are in fact identical with each other. Suddenly all drowsiness is gone, for he realizes he has been vouchsafed a kind of dream view of his own situation. He realizes that he is threatened and must reach Belinda at once, but his "hotel" delays his departure and by the time he reaches the hospital, it is too late.

All that awaits him at the hospital is an incredibly demoralizing farewell note from Belinda. She has departed with her new lesbian lover, but she wants to make the reasons for her "defection" perfectly clear to Paul. In the process of explaining, she savagely indicts not only Paul but the whole "bloodless" culture he represents, ". . . the silly fat ex-wing-commanders running pubs with tankards on the ceiling and going What What and Old Boy. And the people who sneered about me being a Yank. What right did they have to sneer at anybody or anything, little people with light little voices and absolutely bloodless? . . . Yap yap yapping about Deadly Transatlantic Influence and hardly able to lap lap lap it up fast enough. Oh you do so much want to be Absorbed" (*HFB*, 163). For her, England itself has been, like Paul, a colossal disappointment. She predicts it will eventually become nothing more than a "Big American Museum" in which "the men won't have to trouble to breed any more and can just go off with their boy-friends, their dear dead Roberts without feeling guilty or worrying about Duty any more. And what will the women do then, poor things?"

This savage indictment of her adopted culture has been provoked mainly by Paul's failure to provide her with love, security, or warmth. It is made all the more savage by her realization that such things do exist: she has found them in Russia, not merely in the warmth and security of her new lesbian relationship, but in the love that "lies behind" it:

> No, what I mean when I say what lies behind Sonya is something as simple as Love, because Love is about the only thing these people have had to keep them going through all their terrible historical changes, famines and sieges and purges and scorched earth and terrible poverty. And I suppose Love has nearly disappeared in England and the United States of America because there are so many easier substitutes for it. (*HFB*, 164)

By the time Paul reads this she is well beyond reach and he, more wretched than ever, seeks out his fellow countryman Madox. What he wants is a bit of a loan, but Madox begins to think in terms of more substantial assistance, especially when he learns that Paul has a double passport and two return tickets to England. He acquaints Dr. Tiresias with Paul's situation and also with what would seem to be an utterly irrelevant piece of information about Paul—his reverence for the works of Opiskin.

Considering the nature of Paul's progress toward self-knowledge, it is appropriate that the novel's conclusion, like its beginning, should be presided over by this sexually ambiguous figure. On this occasion, the doctor chooses to reveal a great deal about "itself," although little about the mystery of "its" sex. "It" is in fact a kind of genteel racketeer on a fairly large scale. Like Paul, although far more successfully, "it" smuggles consumer goods into Russia, everything from "Mr. Priestley's novels" to cocaine and "questionable post-cards." The appetites "it" gratifies with these items include those of some of the most powerful officials in Leningrad. Smuggling goods in from the West is by no means "its" only source of income. As Paul learns shortly, there are things to be smuggled out profitably as well. The doctor expresses a great deal of sympathy over Paul's misfortunes and it would appear that "its" oyster-colored eyes miss very little. Sensing the strength of Paul's reverence for the memory of Opiskin, "it" plays shrewdly upon it. "It" explains that Paul's double passport and the absence of Belinda offer Paul an opportunity to do something that would thoroughly gratify the ghost of Opiskin. Opiskin is dead, but his son lives, although in perpetual danger of the state's vengeance for the sins of his father. Paul has the opportunity to save the young man by smuggling him out of Russia and Dr. Tiresias will pay him handsomely for the risk involved. Initially Paul resists the plan, but there is really nothing else for him to do if he wants to bring any money at all back to England. As the doctor persuades him, "it" becomes more and more Tiresian. "It" longs for a genuinely Tiresian vision that will close "its" oyster-colored eyes to the broken forms of the light world of the pairs of opposites:

> I am tired of categories, of divisions, of opposites. Good, evil; male, female; positive, negative. That they interpenetrate is no real palliative, no ointment for the cut. What I seek is the *continuum,* the merging. (*HFB,* 176)

A very similar figure, a crippled, smuggling "doctor" of dubious academic qualifications, appears in *MF,* and, although he is not explicitly associated with Tiresias, he has the Tiresian role of revealing the dark secret of incest to a riddling Oedipus figure. The use of a Tiresias in *Honey for the Bears* is similar to the extent "it" assists the hero Paul in his quest for identity. There is another similarity in that the doctor in *MF,* like Dr. Tiresias, assists the hero in discovering the need for a grand "merging."

The escape arrangement Dr. Tiresias has in mind is one whereby Opiskin *fils* will be smuggled out of Russia disguised as Paul's wife. Paul's initial resistance to the idea is partly due to the extreme risk involved but also, perhaps, because he has a dim awareness of how ironically appropriate it will be to have Belinda replaced by a man for the return trip.

Paul is soon won over and the risky, hilarious return voyage begins. Opiskin *fils* turns out to be a very unattractive young brute, "strangely uncultivated for a great musician's son." Paul is led to believe that "perhaps Opiskin *père* had been, like so many great musicians (from Henry VIII to Adrian Leverkühn), syphilitic and had begotten a son whose brain was deeply mined with spirochaetes" (*HFB,* 195). Amazingly, the young Opiskin manages to pass for Paul's wife until the ship is well on its way toward Helsinki. They are, however, betrayed by a steward and young Opiskin appears to be heading into the arms of Russian police who are being flown to Helsinki to meet him. In this predicament, Paul is helped by his memories of melodramatic thrillers dealing with escape from behind the Iron Curtain. There is aboard ship a group of fellow Englishmen returning from a football match in Leningrad, and Paul manages to show them a message through the window of his locked cabin, a message filled with thriller clichés. The football fans, having read or seen the same thrillers, are won over instantly and plot a rescue that they manage to carry out successfully as Paul, young Opiskin, and their guards are disembarking in Helsinki. The Free World has triumphed again, and, although Paul may not be entirely recovered from being cuckolded by a lesbian, he is partially contented by the knowledge that he has done something heroic for his beloved Robert's favorite composer.

But not for long! Among the police who have come to Helsinki to meet Opiskin *fils* are Zverkov and Karamzin. Meeting Paul in a tavern, they reveal that Paul has been duped by Dr. Tiresias and Madox into aiding not the son of a great composer but a thoroughly vicious criminal. Again Paul refuses to believe what he hears, but Burgess gives the reader no reason to doubt that it is the truth. Zverkov asserts that very few truly innocent persons wish to leave the Soviet Union, for what, after all, could they be seeking that was not available within it? When Paul, still influenced by his own orthodox dream, answers "freedom," Karamzin sneers. Zverkov does not sneer. He turns the conversation to the weather, but talk of the coming winter soon turns political, and Zverkov echoes Belinda's prophecy that England will be absorbed either by Russia or by the United States. For all the "little countries," the long winter night will come soon:

> Dark dark dark. You will have to seek the sun and you will find only with us or with the other people across the Atlantic the heat and light you need to go on living. The big countries, the modern states. Soon it will be just one state. (*HFB*, 205)

Paul, suddenly filled with drunken confidence by Finnish ale and moved by the music of Sibelius in the background, answers defiantly that he remains unshaken by what he has suffered in Russia—deprivation of teeth and wife and complete disorientation with regard to his sexual makeup. He will return to his antique shop "to conserve the good of the past, before your Americanism and America's Russianism make plastic of the world." Thinking of his antiques and hearing Sibelius, he is confident that the little countries can still teach those who would absorb them a great deal about "freedom." Not surprisingly, Karamzin sneers at this. More gently, Zverkov muses, "whatever it is," and Paul is suddenly moved to agree, "whatever it is."

Thus ends yet another Burgess treatment of love and decay in the West, as illuminated by contact with the East. There is much in the book that echoes earlier novels, and there are other elements that look forward to later novels such as *MF* and *Tremor of Intent*. But a reading of these novels will not give one any sense of stale rehashing. As Burgess himself says, in reply to the character in Waugh's *The Loved One* who says that one need not read more than one Henry James novel since they are all about the same, "surely a profound theme needs tackling again and again." The same themes do recur again and again in Burgess's fiction, but they are related to complex subjects that cannot be treated exhaustively in even a score of novels.

With regard to the Burgess novels that concentrate on particular subjects, one is tempted to equate some of the views of the West expressed by Burgess's characters with Burgess's own views, especially with regard to England and America. But this could be misleading, for Burgess seems to be mainly concerned with showing how different characters—Russian, American, Ceylonese, and English—are likely to view the West, especially England and America. There is, however, a core of agreement among these widely differing characters on a few aspects of English and American life, and here perhaps we are fairly close to what Burgess feels. There is, for instance, the recurrent idea that the West, especially England and America, is lacking in love and that it, like mad Lear, desperately needs love to be regenerated and saved. Neither the technology of the future (leading to such things as supremacy in space) nor a senseless clinging to the past (to memories of conquered frontiers or colonies or Nazi air power, a past when a stiff upper lip or a ready Colt .45 could win all) will save England or America from decay and the loss of what is most valuable in their cultures.

Paradoxically, the countries such as Russia and England's former colonies that have the most reason to hate the West seem to be the most willing and able to teach it about love. What characters say on this point in *Honey for the Bears* may be very close to the truth. In 1971, at the Western premier showing of the Russian *King Lear,* many delegates to the first World Shakespeare Congress were moved to feel they were seeing the play for the first time. Every aspect of the production—Grigori Kozintsev's direction, the acting interpretations, the background music by Shostakovich—exhibited a feeling for Shakespeare's supreme tragic affirmation of the regenerative power of love that must be without Western parallel. We are probably going to become less and less astonished at the Russian reverence for Shakespeare and the Russian ability to interpret him more movingly than dramatic groups in the West. There may indeed be something in what Inspector Zverkov says about the resemblance of the English "at the time of their Queen Elizabeth I, when they produced their Shakespeare" to the Russians of this age.

There are other recurrent themes related to the progress of decay and the loss of love in the West, themes such as the West's need to overcome its incestuous tendencies by recognizing the oneness of humanity, the very real need to define what it means by "freedom," and the need for England to recognize the real nature of its attitude toward the "Deadly Transatlantic Influence." Burgess had treated them in earlier novels and would treat them again, but not in quite the same ways as in *Honey for the Bears.* Like all his novels, this one is an irresistibly entertaining experience throughout, and one is apt to enjoy it more than, say, *MF* or *One Hand Clapping* because even its satire and criticism are informed by an obvious faith in the regenerative power of love. This is probably due largely to Burgess's feelings for Russia, as opposed to his feelings for the settings of these other novels. It would appear that Russia gave him some hope for the West, while Malta ("Castita" in *MF*) and the America that could breed Miles Faber and export so much of the vulgarity and cheapness that gratify Janet Shirley in *One Hand Clapping* made him wonder whether the West could be saved from the various forms of "incest" mirrored in its racial attitudes and cultural values. Burgess's faith in the regenerative power of love appears again strongly reaffirmed in *The Eve of St. Venus,* but it may be significant that love's triumph in a decadent Western setting requires the miraculous intervention of the goddess herself.

One Hand Clapping

One Hand Clapping first appeared in England in 1960 under the pseudonym Joseph Kell and, largely because of this, failed to attract the attention it deserved. Although it is not one of Burgess's best novels—it is not on the same level with the *Enderby* books and *The Right to an Answer*—it is nonetheless a very competently written, provocative, and entertaining work. Like *The Right to an Answer,* it is a first-person commentary on life in present-day England. What makes it less dazzling and witty than that commentary is not careless craftsmanship but simply the narrator/protagonist Burgess has chosen to use. Instead of someone like the urbane, worldly wise Denham, a highly literate, clever man capable of articulating brilliant insights, we have a very limited narrator/protagonist—an ill-educated young Englishwoman named Janet Shirley who possesses no more than an average share of native cleverness. Burgess thus limits himself from the start both in the ideas he can express and the language he can use to express them. But what he gains is an authentic testimony from a contented product of a decaying philistine culture. Although someone like Denham might win us over by his wit, we are aware of his detachment from the society he is observing and consequently discount some of his feelings about it. Life in suburban England may indeed be dreary and uninteresting, but what does Denham really know about it? He is, as he himself constantly reminds us, an outsider. Janet Shirley, on the other hand, is very much a part of English life today, and her generally uncritical observations on it must be taken seriously. She is, in other words, like Gulliver, a naïve narrator who levels damning criticism without even realizing it. But Burgess is more consistent than Swift. He never drops the mask of his persona and Janet remains herself throughout the novel.

Like Shirley the dramatist, Janet Shirley is living in an age of decaying traditional values and dying art. Her England is more affluent than James Shirley's was, however, and this is part of the trouble. With the coming of televison, the supermarket, and various forms of "Coca-Colization" from across the Atlantic, some things have been lost. Although not exceptionally bright, Janet is bright enough to sense this and to feel a bit cheated by the effects of this loss on her own education. The school she attended appears to have achieved what Dr. Gardner in *The Worm and the Ring* called "the realization of a genuinely democratic education." She has been required to take courses in deportment and dress sense, ballroom dancing, "and what was called Homecraft." Her exposure to the humanities had been very slight:

> None of the teachers knew very much about what they taught and it was pathetic, sometimes, the way they tried to make our schooldays happy. There was young Mr. Slessor with the beard who said he was a beatnik and called us cats and chicks. He was supposed to teach English but said like he didn't dig the

king's jive. Crazy, man, real cool. It was pathetic. Mr. Thornton, who taught
history, said he knew we wouldn't be interested in all those old kings and queens
so he just played his guitar and sang very dull songs, so we weren't allowed to
have any history and I was good at that at the primary. (*OHC,* 8)[7]

Janet is happily married to a good-looking, upright young man named
Howard, who happens to possess an uncommon gift: a photographic brain
that can assimilate an incredible amount of factual material. Not only can
Howard assimilate and regurgitate facts under questioning, he can also
formulate probabilities on the basis of accumulated data. He is, like a
coin-operated computer, capable of dispensing answers without really knowing anything at all about what he is answering. Such a brain can be very useful
in a number of situations. If Howard were a student doing postgraduate work
in English, it might see him through an ineptly administered M.A. com-
prehensive. If he were a secret agent sniffing about among classified documents, he wouldn't need a camera. But Howard is a used-car salesman and has
no need for a photographic brain—until he manages to have himself invited
to be a guest on a TV quiz show called *Over and Over.*

The category Howard chooses is "Books," an area that, for the purposes of
the quiz show, is confined to English literature. Not surprisingly, the questions do not require any real understanding of literature. They are the sort of
factual queries—matching pseudonyms with real names, titles with authors,
occasions with occasional pieces, identifying literary hoaxes—that might
embarrass even a fairly good student but would be answered in any one-
volume survey of English literature on the student's shelf. The only questions
that seem to require actual reading of works—identifications of famous lines
of verse—are answered in most handbooks of famous quotations for the
ornamentation of after-dinner speeches. Howard's brain, well stocked with
handbook data, automatically dispenses perfectly correct answers as the
quizmaster feeds in questions like coins. Successful contestants with a bit of
daring carry on week after week until they reach a limit of £1,000. Howard
arrives at this summit with ease, and his computer brain has not even had a
good workout.

Having gained £1,000 by merely dispensing information, Howard's brain
is put to work multiplying that amount over and over again in the potentially
ruinous game of horse racing. First it is fed a vast quantity of racing data from
a racegoer's encyclopedia and then it is programmed to visualize probable
entries in the next year's edition of the same encyclopedia. His amazing
mental machine triumphs again and he continues to multiply his winnings
until he has gained the sum of £79,000. Suddenly the Shirleys are affluent
and able to enjoy all those things—travel abroad, expensive restaurants,
extravagant clothing—that bear a prohibitive pricetag for the nonaffluent.
Unburdened by any real ties or responsibilities, they are in a position to find
out exactly what money can buy.

The truism that there are some things money cannot buy somehow never quite rings true until one has had the opportunity to test it, and the Shirleys, having the opportunity, soon find that the freer-spending pursuit of pleasure can be as wearisome and ungratifying as any other form of aimless human existence. Howard is less amazed by this than his wife. Indeed, he sets out deliberately to prove to her that money doesn't "make for happiness, really." Their first few weeks of affluency are spent in various types of conspicuous consumption—savoring fine wines, buying luxury items—and giving money away. Howard is actually rather guilt ridden about the way he acquired the money. He sees the bitter irony of the fact that he has been able to capitalize on the works of great writers, to earn more than the writers themselves ever earned, without really understanding them. In a sense, his achievement epitomizes the age in which he lives. Great books are valued because they give quizmasters something to ask questions about, keep consumers glued to the telly, and enable ordinary people, like the consumers themselves, to win big money. Howard is troubled by an awareness that English attitudes and values were not always this way. In the process of boning up for the show, he comes in contact with the literature of the Elizabethan age, and through it he acquires a sense of the age itself, against which his own age makes a rather poor showing:

> He said, "Aaaah, it must have been a damned sight better to live in those days than in these. I mean, they were all red-blooded men and women in those days, drinking down their ale by the gallon—and it was strong ale then, I can tell you—and jogging along on horseback instead of smoking a fag at the wheel of a car, and not reading a lot of lies and tripe put out by the *Daily Window* and gawping at the telly every evening. And no Polaris missiles and all that. Just clean honest healthy living with barrels of sack and canary, and kids looking up to their parents and not treating them like dirt and calling them squares from Cubeville. And when there was a war everybody was in it fighting properly with swords and drawing blood and chopping off heads in a decent clean sort of way, not smashing people who've done no harm to anyone with hydrogen bombs and the like. And when they sang songs they were decent good songs with sensible words, not the bloody tripe you get now with a million records sold to the teenagers. All right," he said, though I hadn't said a word, "you can say it was unhygienic and they were deprived of the bloody blessings of wrapped bread and slices of bacon you can see through all done up in polythene, and they had no washing machines and central heating, but it was still a better life than this one we're living now." (*OHC*, 44)

In fact, Howard's overpowering disgust with his own age will lead him to some very strange decisions concerning what he and Janet ought to do with their lives. But in the meantime, he salves his conscience by giving £1,000 to a reporter on a paper called the *Daily Window* that, like another paper with a similar name, virtually "sums up" the decadence of present-day England

(*OHC,* 180). The reporter is instructed to pass the sum on to starving poets and other transmitters of the great literary tradition that Howard has exploited. This in turn leads to the arrival of one Redvers Glass, a young poet who happens to be writing his autobiography in verse. He is grateful for the £900 he receives, although he shows it in a rather curious fashion, by cuckolding Howard. Unaware of this, Howard leaves him as caretaker of his house while he and Janet go on holiday to America. He also commissions Glass to write a long poem expressing disgust with the times and commemorating the dramatic protest that Howard plans to make with Janet upon their return.

The Shirleys's tour includes a number of major United States cities and the Carribean. The decision to make this pilgrimage to the New World is one they both make, but, in view of subsequent events, one senses their different reasons for making it. Janet is a product of her times, a girl for whom events on television are more real than life itself, a girl who feels cozy in a supermarket and who accepts the word of a woman's magazine that the most characteristic aspects of Elizabethan life had been "smells and disease." Naturally, what one of Burgess's Americans in another novel, *The Worm and the Ring,* calls the "aseptic" land of "chlorophyll and wrapped food and under-arm depilatories" has a strong appeal for her. Indeed, much of what she finds attractive about life in her native land is imported from America. Howard, on the other hand, seems primarily interested in proving that English people are turning themselves "into second-hand Americans." He also wants to prepare Janet for their joint protest against "the cheapness and the vulgarity and silliness and brutishness and nastiness of everything and everybody" that has been bundled for Britain partly in America (*OHC,* 180).

It's not hard to guess, fairly early in the novel, that Howard has suicide on his mind. Janet, being a bit slow, is not aware of it until he informs her that their last day has arrived. It is her birthday and he is going to give her "the finest present anyone could have," death itself. She is not ready for this gift, and when Howard persists in trying to carry out his plan, she is forced in self-defense to kill him with a coal hammer. The whole thing is really quite regrettable because they had in fact loved each other, and Janet had even wanted a baby by Howard.

Janet's slip with Redvers Glass had been just that, a brief transport of concupiscence that she had not intended to repeat. But now Glass, having celebrated in verse Howard's planned end (there are Forsterian themes in the novel), and having tried to warn Janet about it, is very much back in her picture. She really isn't very intelligent, but she's brighter than the poet and cunning enough to be able to convince him that he is hopelessly framed for murder. To avoid taking any chances with the law, they run off to the continent (accompanied by Howard's body in a pigskin trunk), well heeled with the remainder of his fortune. After they are settled in a Paris hotel, they transfer Howard to a camphorwood chest to await further disposal. The two of them seem happy enough, free of guilt and regrets, but one gathers that Redvers Glass had better watch his step. Even if Howard had not been able to make Janet see how life in England has deteriorated, he had still been able to make her see how one Englishman's mind may deteriorate if he thinks much upon the quality of life in the present age. When Redvers Glass begins to indulge in such morbid musing, Janet begins to think about the coal hammer she still keeps, which had saved her from "poor silly Howard."

The limitations of *One Hand Clapping* are not due to any artistic deficiency. To give us an authentic picture of England through a young Englishwoman's mind, Burgess has deliberately handicapped himself considerably, but what he has produced in the process is no mean achievement. There are few male writers in any age who can draw women convincingly. One thinks of Shakespeare, Webster, and Middleton during the Elizabethan Age, and, later on, writers such as Richardson, Thackeray, Henry James, Joyce, and Faulkner. In general, male writers seem to be like Hemingway in this regard—capable perhaps of doing many things well but severely limited in their ability to depict women. Although Janet Shirley is by no means the most interesting female in Burgess's fiction—she is less interesting than the women in *Nothing Like the Sun* and *Enderby*—she is a very convincing portrait of a type of woman that American as well as British readers should recognize readily. Her ways of reasoning, her values, her fears, and her reactions ring true and are not contrived to fit in with themes, as so often happens when a male writer seeks to present a female character as a commentary on a society. A reader may be a bit startled by the callousness and ruthlessness she exhibits near the end of the novel, but this seems to be one of Burgess's purposes. As a product of her society, Janet is so lacking in stable, meaningful values that the transition from loving wife to calculating murderess is quite easy.

The Eve of St. Venus

The most useful critical introduction one can find to *The Eve of St. Venus* is Burgess's own foreword to the American edition that appeared in 1971. Although this book is by no means his most profound treatment of love and decay in the West, it it certainly his most joyful and affirmative. His belief in the power of love to overcome or at least counterbalance the loveless and perverted is happily affirmed in what can be viewed as either an allegory or a straightforward tale of miraculous intervention or both.

The main plot is taken, Burgess tells us, from "an ancient story recounted by Burton in *The Anatomy of Melancholy* (that of the young man who, on the eve of his wedding, places the ring on the finger of a statue of Venus and finds the goddess herself pre-empting the marriage bed)."[8] The title is Burgess's translation of *Pervigilium Veneris,* the joyous and lovely anonymous hymn to Venus that was once thought to be the work of Catullus. By adding the

Christian honorific, he recalls for us as well Keats's poem *The Eve of St. Agnes,* that marvelous lyrical account of how young Porphyro manages to spirit away his fair Madelaine under the very noses of dwarfish Hildebrand, old Lord Maurice, and the others. Indeed, what Burgess does in *The Eve of St. Venus* is similar to what Keats did in this and other poems. He is celebrating love in "pagan" terms within a "Christian" context.

Burgess's tale is set in the country, and this is appropriate, for, as Alan Tate renders the nineteenth stanza of the *Pervigilium:*

> Venus knows country matters: country knows Venus:
> For Love, Dione's boy, was born on the farm.
> From the rich furrow she snatched him to her breast,
> With tender flowers taught him peculiar charm.
>   Tomorrow may loveless, may lover tomorrow make love.[9]

The specific location within the country is the atrociously designed mansion of a Falstaffian baronet named Sir Benjamin Drayton, an edifice that, embraced like an ugly child by "the motherly English countryside," seems to be hideous proof that "England could assimilate anything" (*ESV,* 3).

As the novel opens, Sir Benjamin and Lady Drayton are preparing for the wedding of their daughter Diana, who on the following day is to marry a decent young structural engineer named Ambrose Rutterkin whom she has known since childhood. There appears to be nothing out of the ordinary in the event, but then suddenly things begin to go wrong. For one thing, Ambrose and his best man, a politician named Crowther-Mason, are forced to relinquish the wedding ring to a statue of Venus, which has recently been given to Sir Benjamin. Like the young man in Burton's *Anatomy,* Ambrose has no serious intentions when he places the ring on Venus's finger, but the stone finger slowly curls back in a kind of "obscene invitation" and will not release the ring. There seems to be no remedy, for Sir Benjamin will not permit the statue's finger to be broken.

Then a still more serious threat appears when Diana's best friend and chief bridesmaid, a journalist named Julia Webb, manages to talk her out of the marriage. Ostensibly, Miss Webb is motivated by a desire to see Diana realize her full potential as an artist, but her real motives are apparent to everyone but Diana. She is a notorious lesbian whose hunger for Diana will not be denied. She plans to spirit Diana away to the continent for a tour that will include initiation and entrapment. Miss Webb's will, in every sense of the word, is very strong, and there would seem to be no hope of saving Diana from her spidery grasp. Ambrose is decent enough, but in Diana's eyes his potential offerings make a poor showing aginst the exciting, ego-gratifying charms of her friend.

Nothing less than divine intervention is needed—and divine intervention there is. When Julia Webb imperiously announces the wedding is cancelled, her decent but colorless rival, Ambrose, accepts defeat and retreats to a local pub. After a couple of double whiskies, he is ready to go to his hotel room for a nap, and it is while he is stretched out and still awake that the goddess comes to claim him for her own. She speaks Greek ("but not the sort of Greek people learn at school. It sounded as thought she meant it."). When poor, dull Ambrose fails to respond, she switches to English and tells him he cannot marry Diana, for England "is a mongamous country" and he is already married. Unable to grasp what is happening and presumably hoping to locate a slide rule that will help him, Ambrose switches on the light, which drives the goddess away. He then goes to the Drayton mansion to tell of these strange events to Sir Benjamin, Crowther-Mason, and the Reverend N.A. Chauncell, an Anglican vicar who had been asked to officiate at the wedding.

The responses of the politician and the clergymen to Ambrose's tale are by no means skeptical. Both are greatly excited and their excitement grows as the smell of ozone, the scent of "Foam-born Aphrodite," begins to fill the room. The vicar is especially thrilled, since it appears he will be able to employ professional skills for which he has never had any use. His past study of the origin of devils convinces him that Ambrose must be possessed and in need of exorcism. The pagan gods, he informs his companions, had never died: "They joined the opposition when the new administration took over. Devils were once gods. Devil—the very term means 'little god' " (*ESV*, 63). Like some other present-day clergymen, he has come to believe that sin has virtually disappeared from the modern world. It hasn't been replaced, however, by goodness. Indeed, people are as weak and vicious as ever, but all the "zest" that is so essential to real sinning has gone out of wrongdoing. Crowther-Mason, who has been mildly astonished that an Anglican clergyman would be interested in the subject of sin, agrees:

> It's true enough. . . . The concept of sin seems to be dead. It's been expelled from the Garden. Freud and Marx hold up their flaming swords. (*ESV*, 51)

Although he reveals a conservative, Augustinian bias in his reverence for order, Crowther-Mason believes the explusion of the concept is "a good thing." The vicar disagrees:

> It's an atrocious thing, . . . It's killed both kinds of good living. It's removed a dimension from our lives. We've all lost that incense-laden thrill we used to get from the exciting knowledge that, if you pulled up the floor-boards, you would find a deliciously bottomless pit. What have we instead? Right and wrong, with their interchangeable wardrobes, and the police-courts, temples of a yawning, neutral god with a relish for disinfectants. (*ESV*, 51)

This rather Kierkegaardian meditation is interrupted by the entrance of the trembling Ambrose with his tale of the miraculous. That Crowther-

Mason believes the bed visitor was indeed Venus simply convinces the rather unimaginative engineer that it had all been a cruel, ill-timed practical joke accomplished with the aid of some local whore. It takes a reappearance of the goddess herself outside Sir Benjamin's mansion to convince Ambrose that the "joke," if that is what it is, is "a cosmic joke." His first reaction is one of terror, and he is apprehensive when he is left alone by the vicar and Crowther-Mason, who go to the vicarage for exorcism tools. But he manages to bolster his spirits with brandy and Cointreau, and although the aroma of the sea tells him the goddess is still near, the light in the drawing room makes him feel secure. Then, whether by chance or the machinations of a goddess well skilled in moving men's minds, he takes a volume of Shakespeare's poems and begins reading *Venus and Adonis*. Ambrose is neither terribly bright nor very literate, but the parallel aspects of his case to that of the young boar hunter are not lost on him. Anyone who would flee the goddess of love and beauty in this way must be a "bit of a bore himself, or a boor."

As he sprawls upon the couch, musing upon this and letting the brandy and Cointreau warm his blood, a much less exciting female presence than Venus, the would-be chaste Diana, enters to give him a final pitying farewell before her departure with the all-devouring Julia. The name "Julia," incidentally, like the name "Webb," is suggestive of her role within the fable. The abundance of Latin references in the novel is liable to make one think especially of the profligate granddaughter of Augustus who may have caused the banishment from Rome of Venus's great singer Ovid. Ambrose happens to be in no mood to be pitied by this creature's intended victim, and whatever moral or immoral support he needs to reject it is suddenly provided by Venus, who needs only the darkness of his shut eyes to cover her approach. During a brief interlude of feigned sleep before Diana speaks, he seems to feel "a kind of total embrace of his entire body." Against this sensation, Diana in the glare of the drawing-room lights makes a rather poor showing. To her great dismay, Ambrose is in a mood to laugh about, rather than mourn, his loss of her.

The idea that love can be an avenue to wisdom and knowledge as well as to folly and mad destruction has been articulated by many of love's lovers but usually by those such as Plato and Dante who have little regard for *eros* or the flesh generally. The case of Ambrose Rutterkin suggests that pure *eros* as well as forms of love closer to *agapé* can lead one to a clearer vision of reality. Ambrose suddenly becomes aware of his own stupidity in helping build Diana's image of herself as an unrecognized artistic genius. He is moved to express his resentment at what he has been through with her—his having had to tolerate not only her own pretensions but those of her supposedly artistic friends with their "spurious art-talk and coffee and cooing over canvases" and an even more repulsive new set "reeking of self and halitosis, brown-fingered dyspeptic Fleet Street touts with typewriters in place of the higher cerebral centers. And, of course, Julia" (*ESV*, 72). When she scoffs at him in return, he reveals that he is being pursued by a goddess who haunts his bed. Moreover, he does not wish to have his memory defiled by a "horrible sap" of pity from one who is "a perfectly wholesome but rather insipid creature." The embrace of Venus has given him not only a clearer vision of reality but an eloquence in expressing his disgust and his relief that Diana is leaving him:

> "An undressed salad, that's what you are. A good plain English dinner. You're neither ugly nor beautiful, you're wholesomely neutral. You're two-dimensioned and monochrome. You bore me rather. I'm well rid. Now I'm taking to solid food. The illness is over." (*ESV*, 76)

Putting Diana in her place is for Ambrose an easy and gratifying chore. The sound of his triumphant laughter follows her out of the room as she runs to the arms of Julia. But there remains his new bride—"the laughing-eyed delight of gods and men." As the recent production of *Astarte* by the Joffrey Ballet suggests, she is a bit too much for most mortal men, and when she manages to douse all the inhibiting light in the Drayton mansion, Ambrose is treated to delights that terrify him. By the time Crowther-Mason and the vicar arrive, he is nearly finished, and during the attempted exorcism that follows, he dozes peacefully.

The vicar and Crowther-Mason find the goddess is busy outside of the mansion as well as within. Their car is attacked and driven off the road by pigeons. A short time later, she is also responsible for an attack on Julia Webb's car. Her most delightful prank, however, is mainly at the expense of the vicar. Assuming "the devil's conservative" and attached to "the old faith," he attempts to drive Venus out of Ambrose by reciting the words of exorcism in the original Latin. Instead of being driven out, she proves her total mastery by causing him to recite instead the prayer to Venus with which Lucretius opens *De Rerum Nature*. The vicar's defeat plunges him into despair and, over the strenuous objections of Crowther-Mason and Sir Benjamin, he tears off his clerical collar as a token of surrender and recognition that a "glorious [Anglican] tradition of compromise" has made him wholly unfit to engage in a struggle with the enemies of God. But then suddenly all of his faith in himself is restored by a bolt from Heaven. Lightning strikes an elm, and the falling tree destroys most of Sir Benjamin's pantheon, including Venus. Both the ecstatic vicar and the dismayed Sir Benjamin are certain that it has been an act of God brought on by the vicar's blasphemous utterances of despair when his exorcism fails. Crowther-Mason is not so sure, and the reader is liable to share his doubts in the light of subsequent events. All that is certain is that Ambrose is suddenly freed of his divine love. He is free, but his freedom gives him little joy. With Venus out of his life, there remains only the flat, dull "monochrome" existence he had known before. He shambles off to bed, resigned and depressed.

Moments later, his first bride, the would-be praised as well as chaste Diana, wanders in, having fled the clutches of Julia. Although she does not realize it, she, too, has felt the touch of the goddess of love. One of the tires on Julia's car had been punctured by "a sort of dart" or "arrow," and with the tire, her whole image of more-than-masculine self-sufficiency has been deflated. Against Diana's image of Ambrose as a strong, competent male, Julia's ineffectual struggling with the tire made a poor show. Having decided that "if you want a masculine principle you should seek it in a masculine body," she is ready to patch things up with Ambrose. She assumes it will be a simple enough matter to get him back merely by granting him the privilege of approaching her on his knees for an appropriate rebuke. She has no way of knowing that Ambrose, having slept with Venus, is much less than ready to crawl to any woman. He asks Crowther-Mason to inform Diana that she must crawl to him, although only his "pity" and "magnanimity" will make him accept her.

The stormy reconciliation of Diana and Ambrose is left to the reader's imagination. They are only two of many characters who feel the goddess's touch in the course of this same evening. Venus, it seems, by means of her destruction on Sir Benjamin's lawn, has performed a kind of Dionysian regenerative rite. Crowther-Mason notices a strange green-blue light in the sky that appears to be an earth satellite, one of the many sent up by "the Russians and the Americans vying with each other as young boys vie with each other, arching higher and higher, in school urinals" (*ESV,* 125). But soon he realizes the truth: it is the planet Venus, appearing miraculously some sixty years ahead of its next scheduled transit, and he interprets it to mean that "Venus was obviously, after her stone death and the dissolution of her earthly marriage, intent on rising to heaven, showering warmth, odor and light on the world as a witness of the power of love" (*ESV,* 126). He notices as well the effects within himself, the sensation that his whole body is "turning into some Oriental or Silver Latin book on amation" and his sudden inclination to embrace the leader of the opposition. Suddenly the vicar appears, "dancing across the garden, his arms held out as for an embrace." Rather like St. Paul, heaven-struck by the truth after assisting at the martyrdom of Stephen, he is filled with a yearning to glorify Venus, to preach sermons in praise of nothing but love: "Love. *Sanctificatur nomen tuum, Venus Caelestis, per omnia saecula saeculorum,*" he sang. "And if that's blasphemy, I'm past caring, but I somehow don't think it *is* blasphemy" (*ESV,* 128). His past life, in which he has fulfilled his role as Christian teacher by meeting the modern world on its own loveless terms, discoursing on love as he had discoursed on sin, with intellectual detachment—this has been "the real blasphemy." No sermon could express what he feels:

> I could sing, but none of the hymns I know—a wilder music than the four-square dirges of Ancient and Modern, a faun-like music, full of flutes and unsubmissive to text-book harmony, full of the dreadful primal innocence. (*ESV,* 128)

Crowther-Mason, fully sensitized and aware of how rare and sacred such moments are, urges the vicar to join with him in surrendering completely. The remarkable fact that their speech has been "verging on verse" throughout the evening suggests that they were being prepared to utter fitting song, and indeed from both of them, song comes forth—*Pervigilium Veneris* itself, sung in the original by Crowther-Mason and translated by the vicar. When they have completed a dozen verses drawn from various parts of the hymn along with a verse or two from Lucretius, Lady Drayton suddenly appears and, prompted obviously by the goddess, continues the translation with some additional interpolation:

> Tomorrow shall be love for the loveless,
> and for the lover love
> The scrubbing and dusting,
> the worry about what to eat,
> The stretched elastic of wages
> and housekeeping money
> Ready to snap, the vertigo vista of debt
> Shall no longer seem important;
> the housewife's fingers
> Shall lose their creases of grime;
> the husband's hair,
> Receding, will give him a look
> of Shakespeare

The translation becomes even freer with the entrance of Sir Benjamin:

> Tomorrow shall be luck for the luckless,
> and for the lucky luck
> The luckless punter will have
> unbelievable luck
> And the bookmaker doubt his vocation.
> Houses will echo
> With a fabulous smell of frying onions, steaks
> Will be featherbeds of salivating thickness.
> Beer will bite like a lover and prolong its caress
> Like cool arms in a hot bed. And clocks
> Shall, in the headlong minute before
> closing-time,
> Not swoop to the kill, but hover indefinitely,
> Like beneficient hawks. (*ESV*, 129–32)

It would be strange if Ambrose and Diana did not make their own contributions to the hymn and indeed they soon join the others to sing in anticipation of Venus's greatest joys. One could imagine the hymn welling out of these inspired singers until the dawn of the wedding day. But the songs of lovers will always be interrupted by the loveless for whom no tomorrow brings love, and this hymn is brought to a frigid conclusion by the reentrance of Julia Webb. As gracefully as the situation permits, she accepts defeat and seeks to be reconciled with Diana. Although she is no longer a serious threat to the lovers, her very presence causes Venus to retreat. A warm light that has transfigured everyone quickly fades out. The smell of ozone disappears. There is simply no room for the goddess in the same house with Julia Webb, and although the group would vastly prefer the goddess to Miss Webb, they are much too civilized to throw her out.

Although the triumph of love has been a trifle diminished by Miss Webb's return, overall the situation has been decidedly improved. All that is needed is the return of the ring that had been grasped by the hand of Venus. No sooner do they think of this than the ring is brought in by a servant girl. It had arrived by pigeon, a carrier that is a kind of emblem of the pentecostal descent of the goddess upon this English country mansion.

There is nothing new in the way of a "message" in *The Eve of St. Venus,* no themes that Burgess has not developed in other novels, and it does not probe very deeply into the complexities of life. By Burgess's own criteria, *The Eve* is more "entertainment" than "serious literature."[10] It is, however, splendid entertainment, and an examination of its thematic relationship to his other, more serious novels is illuminating. In nearly all of them, Burgess manages to express his abiding belief in the regenerative power of love, especially sexual love. In *Tremor of Intent,* for instance, the protagonist (Hillier) reflects in Augustinian pessimistic fashion upon the atrocities of Nazi Germany as an expression of humanity's general will and concludes that "a decent bout of sex in the chapel" might be a healthy way of sweating out the perverse attractions of such horrors. In other words, given the Augustinian view that unregenerate man is enslaved to self-serving, self-devouring, destructive appetite, which he expresses in every conceivable ghastly fashion that circumstances permit, the only hope for him, other than miraculous infusions of divine grace, would seem to be love that expresses, or at least dissipates, this appetite benignly. The importance Burgess attaches to physical love can also be seen as one of the sources of his intense dislike of the various forms of "incest," that he finds reflected in Western culture. As he suggests in *MF,* the Western tendency to cling to racial identities is an obstacle to what could be Venus's greatest triumph—a grand miscegenation that might save not only Western culture but mankind itself. Indeed, to heed the injunction of *MF* to "start thinking in terms of the human totality" and avoid incest would mean, among other things, placing service to Venus well above allegiance to race, state, or ideology.

The same message is presented in different ways in *The Right to an Answer,* *The Doctor Is Sick,* and *Honey for the Bears.* Mr. Raj is an emissary of Venus, and his suicide is ultimately the result of his being unable to convey her message to the English suburbs in any way other than by means of the fragment of writing that Denham finds. Like Hippolytus, the protagonists of the other two novels suffer the wrath of Venus in various ways, including the infidelity of their wives, because they ignore her. By failing to render her the worship she deserves, they fail not only as husbands but in other human relationships as well. In Spindrift's case, even his competence as a philologist is severely limited by his inability to love. Paul Hussey's unrelieved series of humiliations in Russia are all either directly or indirectly results of his inability really to love anything but the delicious memory of his friend Robert.

The treatment of love in *The Eve of St. Venus* differs only in that it is a positive celebration rather than a bleak revelation of the frustrations and emptiness of life without love. In a sense, it might be likened to the "Venus" movement within Gustav Holst's *The Planets*. In that great suite, immediately after the long, brutal "Mars" movement that conveys so effectively the composer's vision of war's horror and stupidity, we have the irresistibly lovely tribute to the goddess as Bringer of Peace. In the same way, Burgess's joyous little novel provides a laughing-eyed alternative to the various forms of loveless stupidity that he illuminates so unsparingly in the other novels.

5

PELAGIUS AND AUGUSTINE

A desire to ascertain the "liberalism" or "conservatism" of writers who have provided us with significant commentaries on human experience is frequently an efficient cause of much of the critical exegesis of their works. In the case of many of the most significant commentators—Shakespeare and Conrad, for example—the issue can never be resolved. They transcend any possibility of categorization in these terms, no matter how the terms are limited or applied. Shakespeare and Conrad have both been termed "aristocratic" and "politically conservative" in their attitudes, but the adherence of these labels, or their opposites, must depend upon a selective reading of their works. Although none of Shakespeare's works could reasonably be termed *antiaristocratic,* it is nonetheless clear that he has illuminated fallacies underlying aristocratic attitudes and values. Coriolanus's personal magnificence and his apt comments on "the mutable rank-scented many" must be balanced against his willful blindness and the folly bred into him as an aristocrat. Similarly, Conrad's observations on the futility of revolution in his preface to *Under Western Eyes* must be balanced against more "liberal" observations in his essay "Autocracy and War."

So it is with Burgess. The temptation to label him in these terms is especially strong because so many of the conflicts in his novels are between *Pelagian liberals* and *Augustinian conservatives.* By his use of these *terms,* Burgess intends to remind us of the ultimate origins of much of the so-called liberalism and conservatism in Western thinking. In Burgess's view, the liberal's optimism, his belief in the fundamental goodness and perfectability of man, derives from an ancient heresy—the Pelagian denial of original sin. Not surprisingly, he believes the doctrinal bases of much of the pessimism pervading Western conservative thinking can be traced to Augustine's well-known refutations of Pelagian doctrine. In view of the frequency of clashes between Pelagians and Augustinians in Burgess's fiction, it is worthwhile to review their principal differences.

The Seminal Debate

Pelagius, a British monk who resided in Rome, Africa, and Palestine during the early decades of the fourth century, set forth doctrines concerning human potentiality that virtually denied the necessity of Divine Grace and made the redemption a superfluous gesture.[1] Such an assault on basic Christian doctrine does not, however, seem to have been part of his original design. What he sought to promote initially was an awakening of Christians from the sinful indolence into which they had fallen, largely, he thought, as a result of underestimating their spiritual potentialities as human beings. He believed that just as the Roman ideal of preeminent heroic virtue, embodied in the term *virtus,* was attainable by any Roman who applied himself, so the Christian ideal was attainable by any Christian through his own efforts, using his own natural gifts.[2] If this were not the case, how could we account for the virtuous, self-denying lives of the pagan philosophers? What about the Patriarchs? What about Job? The fact that they were able to please God without the explicit guidance of the Torah is indisputable evidence of the natural goodness of humanity. It cannot be denied of course that the evidence of man's innate goodness became less plentiful after the time of the Patriarchs, but this, in Pelagius's view, would explain the necessity of the explicit revelation of God's law. The law, hitherto unnecessary, was revealed to guide men back to the path of righteousness that their forefathers had followed by natural inclination.

It is not surprising that Grace, in its most widely accepted orthodox sense, as an infusion of the Holy Spirit, did not occupy a very prominent place in the Pelagian scheme of salvation. Pelagius likened it to a sail attached to a rowboat in which the oars, the only essential means of locomotion, might be likened to the human will. The sail makes rowing easier, but the boat could reach its destination without it: *"Velo facilius, remo difficilius: tamen et remo itur."*[3] In short, as W.J. Sparrow-Simpson observes, "Grace in the sense of supernatural strength imparted is obviously superfluous in the Pelagian view."[4] Man rows the boat, and by his own unaided exertion on the oars, he merits God's approval.

Pelagius's cavalier treatment of Divine Grace was a concomitant of his total rejection of orthodox doctrines concerning original sin: "Everything good and everything evil, in respect of which we are either worthy of praise or of blame, is *done by us,* not *born with us.*"[5] He and his less discreet disciple Coelestius were also condemned for teaching that Adam's sin injured no one but himself and that he would have been mortal whether he had sinned or not. His sin has no effect on new-born infants, who are in the same spiritual condition that Adam was in before the Fall. Since they are in a state of prelapsarian innocence, they may attain eternal life even without baptism. Moreover, just as it was not through Adam's sin that men became mortal, so it is not through Christ's resurrection that they may have life beyond the grave. The fact that men such as Job and the Patriarchs had led sinless lives before Christ's coming indicated that the law, as well as the gospel, could lead men to God's kingdom.

Augustine was horrified by these teachings. Recognizing them as essentially an abandonment of Christianity itself, he devoted fully as much energy to discrediting them as he had previously given to refuting the Manichees. In mounting his attack, he relied heavily upon scripture, especially the Epistles of St. Paul, but his fervor and the intensity of his insistence on the helplessness and fundamental wickedness of man without Divine Grace cannot be accounted for simply in terms of his objective appreciation of the soundness of Pauline doctrine. Clearly, he was also moved by the memory of his own early slavery to sin, which he describes so vividly in the *Confessions.* In these spiritual memoirs, he looked back with bitter revulsion at his wanton, aimless youth when he was motivated only by vanity and appetite and, contrary to all fashionable moral theory, capable of delighting in evil for its own sake: "Foul soul, falling from Thy firmament to utter destruction; not seeking aught through the shame, but the shame itself!"[6] Without the Grace of Baptism and the assurance of Christ the Mediator's intercession, his damnation would have been assured. At one point, filled with a sense of his helplessness without Grace, he uttered a prayer that outraged Pelagius: "I have no hope at all but in thy great mercy. Grant what thou commandest and command what thou wilt."[7]

In Augustine's view, it is impossible for any man to choose the path of righteousness without divine assistance. He has been created with freedom of choice and God's law has been revealed to him, but these gifts cannot save him unless he also receives the free gift of the Holy Spirit, the Grace "whereby there arises in his soul the delight in and the love of God, the supreme and changeless Good." Without this divine infusion and the accompanying delight in pleasing God, an awareness of the law serves only to accelerate one's progress toward damnation, for it merely increases one's desire for whatever it has prohibited and fills him with the guilt of transgression when he yields to the desire. Moreover, if a man obeys the law out of fear or any motive other than the love of God, he has done nothing meritorious.[8] Augustine found the whole question of the relationship of the law to Divine Grace summarized in St. Paul's text, "the letter killeth, but the Spirit giveth life." This dictum might be taken to mean that literal interpretations should not be enforced upon the figurative sayings of scripture. But it must also be taken to mean "that the letter of the law, admonishing us to avoid sin, kills, if the life-giving Spirit be not present. . . . The apostle's aim is to commend the grace which came through Jesus Christ to all peoples, lest the Jews exalt themselves above the rest on account of their possession of the law." Had there been no redemption, there could be no justification. If, as the Pelagians say, men can achieve salvation simply by exerting their natural gifts in conformity with the law, then as St. Paul says, "Christ has died for nought."[9]

Man's feeble condition, in Augustine's opinion, was not any basis for complaint about the justice of the Creator. The origin of evil itself, he argued, could be located in the free will of rational creatures, and man's total culpability for sin could be explained in terms of original sin. God, it is true, created man's nature, but we must realize that as a result of the Fall, there are essentially two types of human condition that may be designated by the expression *human nature*. There is (or rather was) the condition of prelapsarian innocence in which man, as created, had complete freedom and ability to pursue the path of righteousness. As a result of Adam's sin, however, human nature has been vitiated and corrupted. This latter condition, a "penal" state in which man is impeded from pursuing righteousness by ignorance and an inability to overcome the urgings of his flesh, is also termed "human nature." Actually, we should restrict the expression to that state of innocence and freedom man enjoyed before the Fall. Man freely abandoned that condition, and, as he is now, lacks both freedom and goodness: "Because he is what he now is, he is not good, nor is it in his power to become good, either because he does not see what he ought to be, or, seeing it, has not the power to be what he sees he ought to be."[10]

So much for the seminal debate. If we are willing to share Burgess's vision and set aside, or at least look beyond, the narrowly theological aspects of it and view "Augustinianism" and "Pelagianism" in terms of their broad philosophical implications, we can see that the council of Carthage in A.D. 418, which condemned Pelagianism, was by no means the end of it. The debate has in fact continued in the West with periodically varying degrees of intensity down to our own time. Its more vigorous sessions include the fourteenth-century clash between Bradwardine and Ockham and the conflict three centuries later between the Jansenists and the Jesuits. Outstanding Augustinian spokesmen include Luther, Calvin, Jansen, Pascal, Racine, Hobbes, Swift, and Edmund Burke. Some of the more notable Pelagians are Shaftesbury, Corneille, Hume, Rousseau, Jefferson, Thomas Paine, Marx, Hegel, John Stuart Mill, Edward Bellamy, and most of the major English and German romantic poets. The validity of these classifications depends of course upon a willingness to view the debate in terms of its social and political as well as its religious implications.[11]

When the debate is viewed in broader terms, the nature of man emerges as the pivotal issue, and one can see that the diametrically opposed assumptions of Augustine and Pelagius could be taken as premises of diametrically opposed political philosophies as well as attitudes toward social progress as far removed as hope and despair. The Pelagian view of humanity justifies optimism and a Rousseauvian trust in *la volonté générale* (the general will). Indeed if one could accept Pelagius's sanguine estimates of human potentiality, one might hope to see Heaven on earth. For surely, if men can achieve spiritual perfection and merit eternal salvation solely through the use of their natural gifts, the solutions to all problems of relations within earthly society must be well within their grasp. They need only to be enlightened properly, and their fundamental goodness will inevitably incline them toward morally desirable social goals. The realization of a universally acceptable utopia would not depend upon the imposition of any particular social structure. Rather, humanity, if properly enlightened, could be trusted to impose upon itself a utopian social scheme.

To say the least, there is a good deal less hope implied in Augustine's doctrines than in Pelagius's. One can readily see that Augustine's fundamentally pessimistic view of human potentiality, his basic distrust of human nature, could be taken as the basis of policies of rigorous enforcement in human affairs. A utopia organized upon Augustinian premises must necessarily be a police state and in this connection, it is certainly no accident that the human community most closely approximating such a utopia was Geneva in the time of Calvin. Calvin, like Luther, relied very heavily upon Augustine in the formulation and support of his doctrines, and it would appear that the enormous importance he attached to the enforcement of discipline within the Christian community derived largely from his fundamental agreement with the Augustinian view of human nature.[12]

Burgess's view of the debate encompasses its broadest implications, and some awareness of these implications, especially within social and political spheres of Western thinking, is essential to an appreciation of his social satire. In *The Wanting Seed,* for instance, we are shown a fascist police state of the future emerging from the ruins of a future socialist democracy, and emerging with it are eager entrepreneurs, "rats of the Pelphase but Augustine's lions." The full irony of this metaphor cannot be grasped simply with reference to Augustinian doctrine in its pre-Calvinist, pre-Gilded Age purity. Burgess intends to remind us of the ways in which Augustinian/Calvinist doctrines on grace, election, and unregenerate human nature have molded the socioeconomic ethics of Calvin's intellectual and spiritual heirs both in the Old World and the New.[13] In this same novel and in his other proleptic nightmare, *A Clockwork Orange,* he also reveals some likely doctrinal developments of the future. The forces that contend for governmental mastery are labelled "Pelagian" and "Augustinian," but they are more obviously Rousseauvian and Hobbesian. It is natural that their conflicting philosophies should seem to echo *Leviathan, De Cive (The Citizen), Du Contrat Social (The Social Contract),* and the *Discours sur l'inégalité (Discourse on the Origin of Inequality),* rather than the treatises of Pelagius and Augustine, since both novels are set in a future in which the issue of Divine Grace and indeed theology have been virtually forgotten. Augustinianism without theology becomes Hobbism, and Pelagianism even in its original form was not far removed from romantic primitivism. In short, Burgess's satiric vision encompasses the entire debate—past, present, and future—and one may find, especially in his dystopian books, echoes of the writings of all the participants I mentioned here and a good many more.

The Wanting Seed

The Wanting Seed is Burgess's fullest and most explicit treatment of the

Augustinian/Pelagian conflict. In this Orwellian/Malthusian proleptic night-mare, he presents a cyclical theory of history—as essentially a perpetual oscillation or "waltz" between two philosophical "phases"—a Pelagian phase and an Augustinian. As the novel opens, we behold a world in which our undernourished descendants have little more than standing room. England, as suffocatingly crowded as the rest of the world, is under the benevolent guidance of a "Pelagian" government. Official attitudes and policies are, however, more distinctively Rousseauvian than Pelagian. Indeed, the shock-ing vision of the Malthusian nightmare itself may remind one of Jean-Jacques's pronouncement that "the government under which, without exter-nal aids, without naturalization of colonies, the citizens increase and multiply most is beyond question the best."[14] Just as the folly of this assumption is revealed, the incredible naïveté of the Pelagian government's Rousseauvian political philosophy is also revealed. According to Rousseau, "The general will [*La volonté générale*] is always in the right, but the judgment that guides it is not always informed";[15] hence it follows that laws must be provided, not as restrictions, but as signposts pointing men toward the greatest common good, the object of their natural inclinations. Burgess's sardine-can civiliza-tion comes into being largely because the government has been unshakable in its trust in *la volonté générale*. Despite massive proof to the contrary, it maintains an optimistic belief that "the great liberal dream seems capable of fulfillment." Coercion is officially eschewed. Laws exist merely as guidelines to lead the cramped citizenry to "precise knowledge of the total needs of the community." Since the official faith dictates that a desire to act for the common good is a basic component of human nature, "it is assumed that the laws will be obeyed" and that an elaborate punitive system is unnecessary.

The fact that the economy is totally controlled by the state does not indicate any official lack of trust in the people. On the contrary, it is believed that without capitalism, the state is more securely subject to the general will. Tristram Foxe, the history teacher/protagonist, informs his pupils that as civilization approaches the liberal millenium, these tokens are thought to be manifest:

> The sinful acquisitive urge is lacking, brute desires are kept under rational control. The private capitalist, for instance, a figure of top-hatted greed, has no place in Pelagian society. Hence the State controls the means of production, the State is the only boss. But the will of the State is the will of the citizen, hence the citizen is working for himself. (*TWS*, 18)[16]

This is of course another feature of the society that would please Rousseau and some of the other "Pelagians" mentioned above.

Pelagian faith is not, however, in itself the principal reason the world has become so cramped. Rather, this is a major factor in man's failure to deal realistically or responsibly with the main problem, which is his own procre-ative instinct. Because of man's failure to control his sperm, the world has become overpopulated beyond Malthus's most fearsome imaginings. All of

Malthus's positive and preventive "checks"—through "misery," "vice," and "moral restraint"—are destined to be brought into play, and it is clearly demonstrated that even in England circumstances could make them much less distinguishable from each other than the good Anglican demographer had assumed.

During its Pelagian phase, England relies heavily upon what Malthus would call checks through "vice" and "improper arts." Homosexuality, castration, abortion, and infanticide are all encouraged by a desperate government. The Pelagian leaders share Malthus's belief that the educated classes can be persuaded by reason to act for the common good while the proletariat cannot. Hence, although the state makes little attempt to sway the "proles," it seeks to influence the more "responsible" classes by education, propaganda, and social pressure. Everywhere posters blare *"It's Sapiens to be Homo."* A "Homosex Institute" offers both day and evening classes. People are able to improve their social and economic positions only if they can maintain a reputation either of "blameless sexlessness" or nonfertile sexuality. The protagonist misses a deserved promotion because, as a superior tells him, "A kind of aura of fertility surrounds you, Brother Foxe." Among other things, Tristram has fathered a child, and, although each family is legally allowed one birth, "the best people just don't. Just don't" (*TWS*, 31). Necessity has thus completely inverted sexual mores, and whereas Malthus would have termed these measures checks through "vice" and "improper arts," this cramped society sees them as checks through "moral restraint."

Overpopulation is the main cause of this inversion, but clearly another important causative factor is the present-day liberal trend toward sympathy for the homosexual. Burgess has remarked that "the homosexual is on the rise in the west."[17] If Western popular entertainment is a valid indicator, the point is hard to dispute. Movies such as *That Certain Summer, The Staircase,* and *A Taste of Honey* and television plays such as *Who's Art Morrison?* emphasize the warm humanity of homosexuals and the injustice of their being rejected by society. Popular singers, such as the Rolling Stones and Alice Cooper, whatever their personal sexual inclinations in fact, present images of sexual ambiguity, and their appeal may be accounted for partly in terms of it. The rigid, mutually exclusive classification of humanity into raw masculinity and ultrafemininity has been seen as a source of psychic disorder. Less popular entertainment, that is, serious literature, has of course always included some sympathetic presentations of homosexuality, but the sympathy, not to mention the example, of serious writers could never offer homosexuals generally the hope for acceptance that they may now enjoy. It takes no great imaginative exertion to see that if the homosexual's sexual bias could be found to be socially useful, something more than acceptance might follow. Indeed, his or her bias might well become a desired norm. If this seems far-fetched, it might be well to recall that the ancient Greeks were not faced with a comparable population explosion. Man's sexual mores, like his economic ethics, are extremely flexible and in a state of constant metamorphosis. The attitudes of medieval moralists toward concupiscence appear as quaint and rationally indefensible to us as their attitudes toward usury.

In spite of steadily diminishing rations and standing room, the Pelagian government remains committed to an official faith of optimism and progress that assumes citizens will be reasonable enough to modify their sexuality for the common good, and that they will do so more or less voluntarily. There is a large, well-trained, mostly epicene force of population police (the "Poppol") that discreetly encourages people to conform to official moral standards, but its role is more persuasive than coercive, at least until the advent of the great "DISAPPOINTMENT." Pelagian liberalism, as Tristram Foxe tells his pupils, inevitably breeds "DISAPPOINTMENT," and the government itself becomes vulnerable as soon as there is compelling evidence that people are more selfish than the official credo dictates they should be. The evidence becomes significant when basic appetitive needs are denied. Although the "best people" may be willing to unsex themselves or to rechannel their sexuality, not even the most public-spirited can transcend the need for food. The food shortage caused by irresponsible procreation is made even more severe by a worldwide scourge of blights and animal diseases.

The Pelagian government's official faith in man has necessitated an official denial of the existence of God, but this scourge has the all-encompassing character of an expression of divine wrath, and eventually even the Pelagian leaders are driven to prayer. In addition to praying, the government hastily organizes a rather brutish police auxiliary, the "greyboys" (who strongly resemble the *Gris* force employed by the Spanish civil government under Franco)[18] to assist the Poppol in maintaining order. However, neither prayer nor a beefed-up police force can prevent the most gruesome consequences of overpopulation. Without domestic animals, seafood, or edible crops, people turn to each other, and widespread cannibalism is the most ghastly aspect of the chaotic "Interphase" that follows the complete breakdown of Pelagian methods of civil control. People are murdered and devoured by anthropophagic "dining clubs." Frequently these cannibal feasts are followed by heterosexual orgies "in the ruddy light of the fat-spitting fires." Tristram, wandering about the countryside in search of his wife, occasionally takes part in both feasts and orgies. He also witnesses a fertility ritual strongly reminiscent of ancient Dionysian festivals and, not surprisingly, a rebirth of drama. Indeed, in some respects the Interphase brings refreshing improvements—freedom of religion (including some rather grisly bits of breadless "transubstantiation"), open heterosexual love, and a revival of folk culture.

But chaos, "indiscriminate cannibalism and the drains out of order" (TWS, 171) cannot long be borne by a whole society of once-civilized people. The time is ripe for a coup, and the "Augustinians" do not hesitate. Seizing the reins of government, they quickly create an army and restore order. They then deal with social problems in the light of what they consider to be a more

realistic assessment of human nature. Unlike the Pelagians, they acknowl-
edge the reality of sin and, like Augustine himself, they recognize it as an
"abiding condition" in which a sizable percentage of their fellow men are
hopelessly fixed by their very nature.[19] Burgess labels these pessimistic
reformers "Augustinians," but their cynicism and bottomless contempt for
humanity are more Hobbesian (or perhaps Swiftian) than Augustinian. Certainly their impaired moral vision, resulting from their total preoccupation
with social stability, reminds us more of Hobbes than of Augustine.

It soon appears that the experience of cannibalism has suggested to the
Augustinian leaders new methods of achieving social stability. Essential to
their scheme is a re-creation of war as it had been fought long before, during
the twentieth century. As they see it, war can be both a social "drainage
system" and a partial solution to the problem of hunger in an overpopulated
world. Social misfits of one kind or another, male and female, are drafted into
the army, trained in complete isolation from the rest of the population, and
then shipped for extermination to carefully contrived "battlefields." The
actual slaughtering method used is simply a contrived World War I-type
battle in which ignorant armies go over the top and clash by night. In the
typical "extermination session" witnessed by Tristram Foxe, male and female
armies destroy each other completely. The remains are then gathered up to
be processed in tins for human consumption. There is a widely held assumption that canning makes cannibalism a relatively civilized affair. "It makes all
the difference," as one soldier tells Tristram, "if you get it out of a tin" (*TWS,*
172).

Only the government and civilian contractors know that the heroes are
bound for this dismal Valhalla. The rest of the population, not unlike some of
their ancestors, simply cheers them on, content to be totally ignorant of the
objectives of the war, the character of the enemy, and the nature of the
warfare devouring its soldiers. Understandably, the ruling class exhibits a
Hobbesian annoyance at any attempt on the part of soldiers or citizens to
become informed or involved. Tristram receives a nearly fatal military assignment because he holds discussions with his men concerning the issues of
the war in which they are involved and the nature of the enemy. The officer
who makes the assignment obviously subscribes to the military ethic summarized in Stephen Decatur's famous toast to his country, but he also
represents the Hobbesian attitude of the ruling class. In his *De Cive (The
Citizen),* Hobbes specifically excludes moral assessments of governmental
policy from the duties of citizenship, and in *Leviathan,* he draws wistful
distinctions between well-ordered societies of insects and human societies in
which there is always a troublesome tendency of citizens to seek involvement
in their own government.[20]

The "drainage system" and the rest of the governmental functions must of
course be in the hands of responsible individuals, and in a latter-day "Augustinian," that is, neo-Calvinist or Hobbist, state, the most responsible
individuals are directors of corporations. "Private enterprise," we are told, is

the "beginning of Gusphase," and "election," that is, economic significance, is proven by efficient, functionally significant involvement in the military/ industrial complex. In fact, the "War Department" itself is a corporation with a renewable charter. Its indisputable success in remedying previously insoluble problems makes its employees confident that the charter will be renewed perpetually. They believe that so long as there is an army to absorb "the morons and the enthusiasts," "the ruffians, the perverts, the death-wishers," and the "cretinous [female] over-producers," it is possible to maintain "a safe and spacious community. A clean house full of happy people." There is a suggestion that the protagonist, like the man whose surname he shares, may chronicle the fate of exterminated martyrs to social stability, but one gathers that such a chronicle would accomplish little toward accelerating the advent of a new Pelagian phase. As the example of Nazi Germany suggests, in a well-fed, martially involved "clean house full of happy people" citizens *are* apt to look the other way and close their nostrils to the smell of burning flesh.

Parenthetically, in connection with this last point, we can perhaps see another reason why Burgess relegates capitalism to Gusphase. The militaristic Augustinian society with its acceptance of (if not indifference to) mass murder for the sake of social stability obviously resembles Nazi Germany, and it is generally agreed that Hitler's rise would have been much less meteoric without the help of Bolshevik-fearing industrialists. It may also be remembered that some imaginative German entrepreneurs fattened their purses designing and building camps, and even during the last years of the Third Reich profits were still being made by those who could design the special pitch forks, ovens, and other appliances needed to facilitate a stepped-up extermination process. This seems to be the sort of "civilian contractor" Burgess has in mind.

The Wanting Seed concludes on a note that may or may not be optimistic. We see the Pelagian prime minister, surrounded by his catamites, enjoying a pleasant exile in a seaside villa, calculating the moment of his return to power. But even more significant than his personal optimism is the optimism of scientists who are forging ahead in their efforts to locate nonanthropophagic sources of food. They are preparing to ferret them out in the abysmal depths of the sea: "Untouched life lurked, miles down, leagues down" (*TWS*, 270). Successful conquests of natural elements encourage a belief in man's ability to control nature completely and a concomitant belief that man can control himself by an exercise of reason. The advent of another Pelagian phase may be delayed, but it will come. The "waltz" never ceases.

The great drama of the "waltz" itself is the main focus of the novel, but we are also shown some of its effects on particular individuals, especially the history-teacher protagonist. His given name emphasizes with heavy irony the nonheroic quality of this future age. Like Tristram of old, he embarks on a quest that carries him throughout much of England, but there the resemblance ends. Instead of cuckolding his uncle, he is himself cuckolded by his brother. Instead of hacking and thrusting his way to immortal martial glory, he has the distinction of being the only soldier to escape an "extermination session" and entombment as canned meat. There is irony, too, in that he is a historian whose understanding of the "waltz" is more complete than that of any other character in the novel. For all his understanding of historic process, he is tossed about helplessly, unable to control his own destiny in any way until he flees the battlefield. In one sense, he does illustrate the idea of Marx and Hegel that man's freedom depends upon, indeed consists in, his awareness of some inevitable historic process. In another, he contradicts these great Pelagians who saw in "man's" growing awareness cause for optimism. Tristram's awareness, which is large to begin with and increases considerably, gives neither him nor us much cause for optimism since it leads him only to foresee endless repetitions of the cycle and no static millenium.

History teachers are not the only ones who understand the cycle. Consummate Machiavellian bureaucrats, such as Tristram's treacherous brother Derek, adapt chameleonlike to the moral standards officially promoted during each phase and thrive. During Pelphase, Derek—his name suggests cold-blooded support—is impeccably epicene. No one except a not-too-bright, would-be rival even suspects he is cuckolding his brother. Tristram's wife, Beatrice-Joanna, also has a suggestive name, and in a novel as full of comic/ironic literary allusions as this one, we have much to gain by following hints. Beatrice-Joanna is the name of the passionate heroine in Thomas Middleton's best-known play *The Changeling*. The term *changeling* can refer to a child or thing substituted by stealth, especially an elf child left by fairies. Derek, the Machiavellian pseudofairy, unintentionally impregnates his sister-in-law and thereby substitutes his own offspring for Tristram's child, whom she has recently lost. This piece of Pelagian bad luck is very much to his advantage later on during the "Gusphase" when it is important for rising bureaucrats to prove their heterosexuality and potency. He rises quite as rapidly in the Augustinian Ministry of Fertility as he had previously risen in the Pelagian Ministry of Infertility.

Although these characters are certainly far from being Burgess's subtlest psychological studies, they serve admirably to convey his ideas in a novel that is a major contribution to the subgenre known as the dystopian "novel of ideas." Surprisingly, the novel's initial critical reception was not terribly enthusiastic. That is, although some reviewers were and are enthusiastic, the book seems to have antagonized the more influential critics. Brigid Brophy, for one, termed it "half-baked." Another critic, assessing it more favorably, considered it "heavy-handed" as a piece of satire. In fact, a careful reading of *The Wanting Seed* fails to support either of these hyphenated strictures, and one is tempted to wonder about the extent to which this novel's unfavorable reception was caused by an awareness that it had been produced in some haste along with several others. The novel's only significant weakness proceeds from Burgess's tendency to be too entertaining and too witty. (Although he didn't wish to apply it, W. H. Pritchard's phrase "debilitating cleverness" is well chosen.)[21] The novel is full of playful references to

Burgess's fellow novelists and other literary figures. There is, for example, the description of the bearded giant atop the Government Building, which is identified from time to time with various figures of cultural and political importance, including "Eliot (a long dead singer of sterility)" (*TWS*, 20). The reports of cannibalism include the account of how "a man called Amis suffered savage amputation of an arm off Kingsway," and how "S. R. Coke, journalist, was boiled in an old copper near Shepherd's Bush; Miss Joan Waine, a teacher, was fried in segments" (*TWS*, 160). In themselves, these allusions and fantasies are delightful, but they combine with occasional flippancies of tone to deprive the book of some of its potential impact. As with the black-comic film classic *Dr. Strangelove,* the hilarity of presentation occasionally tends to make it difficult to bear in mind the seriousness of the themes.

Excessive hilarity is not, however, a ruinous weakness, either in *Strangelove* or *The Wanting Seed.* Ours is an age in which gallows humor is invaluable as a safeguard of our sanity, and as one reads the dark comedies of Burgess, Evelyn Waugh, Nabokov, and more recent "black-comic" effusions, such as Romain Gary's *The Dance of Genghis Cohn,* Kurt Vonnegut's *Cat's Cradle,* or even Gore Vidal's scabrous *Myra Breckinridge,* one must be impressed by the soundness of Thomas Mann's observations on modern tragedy and comedy in the preface to his translation of Conrad's *The Secret Agent.* Mann felt that "broadly and essentially, the striking feature of modern art is that it has ceased to recognize the categories of tragic and comic, or the dramatic classifications, tragedy and comedy, with the result that the grotesque is its most genuine style—to the extent, indeed, that today that is the only guise in which the sublime may appear."

The Wanting Seed is, in Mann's sense, a "grotesque" drama, and, like Shakespeare's sonnets, it is a relatively late but fresh and enduring contribution to a subgenre that seemed to have been worked to death. It antagonized some influential critics but is greatly admired by more youthful intellectuals, especially in America, who see in it a book that passes the test of "relevance," not merely because it depicts some possible consequences of the population explosion we all fear, but also because it gives a horribly convincing picture of the alternatives modern man may face at some time in the near future in his endless quest for social stability: If he isn't, in one sense or another, "eaten" by a military/industrial complex, he will be persuaded to castrate himself, in one way or another, for the sake of social stability.

A Clockwork Orange

Even before Stanley Kubrick's brilliant and faithful rendering of *A Clockwork Orange* in film, this was probably Burgess's most widely read novel. This does not greatly please Burgess, who values some of his other novels much more. Like *The Wanting Seed,* it is a proleptic nightmare with dystopian implications. Although it can be read as an answer to and a rejection of the main ideas of B. F. Skinner, the author of such works as *Walden Two* and *Beyond Freedom and Dignity,* Burgess seems to have been directly influenced less by Skinner's ideas in particular than by accounts he had read of behaviorist methods of reforming criminals that were being tried in American prisons with the avowed purpose of limiting the subjects' freedom of choice to what society called "goodness." This struck Burgess as "most sinful," and his novel is, among other things, an attempt to clarify the issues involved in the use of such methods.

The setting of *A Clockwork Orange* is a city somewhere in either western Europe or North America where a civilization has evolved out of a fusion of the dominant cultures east and west of the Iron Curtain. This cultural merger seems to be partly the result of successful cooperative efforts in the conquest of space, efforts that have promoted a preoccupation with outer space and a concomitant indifference to exclusively terrestrial affairs such as the maintenance of law and order in the cities. As it does in *The Wanting Seed,* Pelagian faith in *A Clockwork Orange* also accompanies Promethean fire. Appropriately, there is shop looting on Gagarin Street, an avenue of this Western metropolis, and a victim of teenaged hoodlums is moved to ask, "What sort of a world is it at all? Men on the moon and men spinning around the earth like it might be midges round a lamp, and there's not no attention paid to earthly law nor order no more" (*A CO,* 20).[22]

In light of recent events, a reader is apt to assume Burgess was thinking of the United States when he envisioned this situation of the future. In fact, he was more directly influenced by what he had seen during his visit to Leningrad in 1961. At that time, Russia was leading in the space race, and the gangs of young thugs called "stilyagi" were becoming a serious nuisance in Russian cities. At the same time, London police were having their troubles with the young toughs known as the "teddy boys." Having seen both the stilyagi and the teddy boys in action, Burgess was moved by a renewed sense of the oneness of humanity, and the murderous teenaged hooligans who are the main characters in *A Clockwork Orange* are composite creations. Alex, the fifteen-year-old narrator/protagonist, could be either an Alexander or an Alexei. The names of his three comrades in mischief, Dim, Pete, and Georgie, are similarly ambiguous, suggesting both Russian and English given names.

A reader may miss these and other hints completely but what he cannot overlook is the effect of culture fusion on the teenage underworld patois in which the story is narrated. The language itself, Burgess's invention, is called *nadsat,* which is simply a transliteration of a Russian suffix equivalent to the English suffix *teen,* as in "fifteen." Most, although by no means all, the words comprising nadsat are Russian, and Burgess has altered some of them in ways that one might reasonably expect them to be altered in the mouths of English-speaking teenagers. There is, for instance, the word *horrorshow,* a favorite adjective of nadsat speakers meaning everything from "good" to "splendid." The word sounds like a clever invention by an observer of teenagers who is aware of their fondness for films such as *I Was a Teenage Werewolf* and *Frankenstein Meets the Wolfman*. Actually it is an imagined development from *kharashó,* a Russian adjective meaning "good" or "well." The initial consonant, an unvoiced velar fricative (IPA/x/), is nonexistent in English, and the supposition that it would become a voiceless glottal fricative in the mouths of British or American teenagers is quite in accord with phonetic probability, since the aspirate is already contained in the Russian phoneme. This is not to say that *horrorshow* is purely the result of phonemic or phonetic change. Juvenile fondness for cinematic shockers has obviously had something to do with it and has indeed modified the Russian word further by adding new associations. Something that is "good" in the view of these young savages is something that thrills or shocks, like a film about Dracula. Well-delivered blows ("tolchocks") to the head or groin, fast cars, and ample female bosoms are more than "good"; they're "horrorshow."

A similar "loanshift" can be seen in the nadsat word *rabbit,* a verb meaning "to work." Alex and his *droogs* (transliteration of the Russian word for friend or comrade) are contemptuous of any gainful employment other than burglary or "shop-crasting," and the word itself obviously suggests that one who "rabbits" must be something of a rabbit, habitually meek and scared. Rabbit is a modified form of the Russian verb *rabotat,* which means the same thing without the pejorative connotation, but we may reasonably conjecture that one of the reasons for its adoption into nadsat is its relation to the word *rab,* meaning "slave," as well as the English/Czech word *robot,* meaning "mechanical slave." The law compels all able-bodied adults, male and female, to work, but Alex and his friends consider one who does so to be as spiritless as a robot.

Implements of street warfare, such as bicycle chains, knives, and straight razors, bear their unaltered Russian names, which seem much more suggestive of the objects themselves than their English equivalent. A bicycle chain, for instance, its shiny coils shaken out along a sidewalk or whizzing through the night air, is so much more like an "oozy" than a "chain." There is something much more murderous about a "cutthroat britva" than a "cutthroat razor." This increased suggestiveness can also be seen in the loan names for parts of the human body. The primary social function of the tongue is strongly implied in the word *yahzick,* although not in the English equivalent. An orifice full of decaying "zoobies" is indeed more like a "rot" than a "mouth." The term *glazzies* is so much more suggestive than "eyes." A reader with a modicum of sensitivity can see that Burgess has not merely transliterated at random a lot of Russian words. He has carefully chosen words that are immensely more evocative to an English or American ear than their English equivalents, and he has, as I have said, modified some of them very plausibly. The word *grood,* for instance, might reasonably be expected to become "groody," even as one of its mildly vulgar English equivalents becomes "titty."

A good many of the non-Russian words in nadsat are derived from British slang. For example, a member of the city's finest, the ineffectual safeguard of law and order, is referred to as a "rozz." Although the word may be related to *rozha*, a colloquial expression roughly equivalent to "ugly mug," its direct ancestor is the English slang term *rozzer*, meaning "policeman." Tracing the origins of the nadsat vocabulary is an absorbing exercise for anyone with a feeling for language.[23] The American edition of the novel has a glossary, prepared without any consultation with Burgess, which is not entirely accurate either in its translation of nadsat words or in the information it gives concerning their origins. The word *yarbles*, for instance, is glossed as a non-Russian word meaning "testicles." Indeed, it is used by Alex and his friends to designate the street fighter's favorite target of opportunity, but it is derived from the Russian word for apples (sing. *yabloko*). The Russian word itself occurs virtually unchanged in Alex's irreverent greeting to a high-ranking government official: " 'Yarbles,' I said, like snarling like a doggie, 'Bolshy great yarblockos to thee and thine' " (*ACO*, 175). Actually, after a few pages of the novel, a reader of even moderate sensitivity should not need a glossary, and he will do well to refrain from consulting this one, whose translations, even when they are accurate, may anchor him to terms that lack the rich onomatopoeic suggestiveness of Burgess's language. The following passage, for instance, in which Alex describes the orgiastic pleasure he derives from a violin concerto, would lose everything in translation:

> As I slooshied, my glazzies tight shut to shut in the bliss that was better than any synthemesc Bog or God, I knew such lovely pictures. There were vecks and ptitsas, both young and starry, lying on the ground screaming for mercy, and I was smecking all over my rot and grinding my boot in their litsos. And there were devotchkas ripped and creeching against walls and I plunging like a shlaga into them, and indeed when the music, which was one movement only, rose to the top of its big highest tower, then, lying there on my bed with glazzies tight shut and rookers behind my gulliver, I broke and spattered and cried aaaaaaah with the bliss of it. And so the lovely music glided to its glowing close. (*ACO*, 38)

The novel is much more than a linguistic tour de force. It is also one of the most devastating pieces of multipronged social satire in recent fiction, and, like *The Wanting Seed*, it passes the test of "relevance." Although most people have been made aware of the assumptions of behavioral psychology through the recent uproar caused by Skinner's polemical restatement of his ideas in *Beyond Freedom and Dignity*, it is perhaps less generally realized that Skinner's schemes for imposing goodness on the human "mechanism" are among the less radical of those being proposed by behavioral technologists. As of this writing, a sociologist, Professor Gerald Smith of the University of Utah, is engaged in promoting the development of a device that can be implanted within the person of a paroled convict. The device, which measures adrenalin, is designed to send signals to a receiver in the home or office of his parole officer if the convict becomes excited by committing a crime. How this gadget would separate criminal stimuli from activities such as love making that might signal "false positives" has not been revealed. What is certain, at least in the mind of the sociologist, is that the beneficial effects of such devices would completely justify their use. A convict would lose nothing, since, as a prisoner, he is already without freedom, and the benefits to society would be incalculable.

It is this line of thinking that Burgess challenges in *A Clockwork Orange.* He had been reading accounts of conditioning in American prisons, and it happened that as the teddy boys were being replaced on the streets by the mods and rockers, and youth was continuing to express its disdain for the modern state, a British politician put forward very seriously a proposal that obstreporous British youth should be conditioned to be good. At this point, Burgess says, "I began to see red and felt that I had to write the book." His protagonist Alex is one of the most appallingly vicious creations in recent fiction. Although his name was chosen because it suggested his composite Russian/English identity, it is ambiguous in other ways as well. The fusion of the negative prefix *a* with the word *lex* suggests simultaneously an absence of law and a lack of words. The idea of lawlessness is readily apparent in what we see of Alex's behavior, but the idea of wordlessness is subtler and harder to grasp, for Alex seems to have a great many words at his command, whether he happens to be snarling at his droogs in nadsat or respectfully addressing his elders in Russianless English. He is articulate but "wordless" in that he apprehends life directly, without the mediation of words. Unlike the characters who seek to control him and the rest of the society, he makes no attempt to explain or justify his actions in terms of abstract ideals or goals such as "liberty" or "stability." Nor does he attempt to define any sort of role for himself within a large social process. Instead, he simply experiences life directly, sensuously, and, while he is free, joyously. Indeed, his guiltless joy in violence of every kind, from the simple destruction or theft of objects to practically every form of sexual and nonsexual assault, is such that the incongruous term *innocent* is liable to come to a reader's mind.

Alex also has a fine ear for European classical music, especially Beethoven and Mozart, and although such widely differing tastes within one savage youngster might seem incongruous, they are in fact complementary. Knowing his own passions, Alex is highly amused by the idea that great music is any sort of "civilizing" influence:

> I had to have a smeck, though, thinking of what I'd viddied once in one of these like articles on Modern Youth, about how Modern Youth would be better off if A Lively Appreciation Of The Arts could be like encouraged. Great Music, it said, and Great Poetry would like quieten Modern Youth down and make Modern Youth more Civilized. Civilized my syphilised yarbles. Music always sort of sharpened me up, O my brothers, and made me feel like old Bog himself, ready to make with the old donner and blitzen and have vecks and ptitsas creeching away in my ha ha power. (*ACO,* 45–46)

The first third of the novel is taken up with Alex's joyful satiation of all his appetites, and as rape and murder follow assault, robbery, and vandalism, we are overwhelmed by the spectacle of pleasure in violence. Although it might be argued that such psychopathic delight could not be experienced by a sane person, there is no implication in the novel that Alex is anything but sane—sane and free to choose what delights him. Since his choices are invariably destructive or harmful, it appears that society's right to deprive him of his freedom, if not his life, could hardly be disputed. What the novel does dispute is society's right to make Alex something less than a human being by depriving him of the very ability to choose a harmful course of action.

Partly as a result of his own vicious activities and partly as a result of struggles between Pelagian and Augustinian factions in government, Alex is destined to experience life as a well-conditioned "good citizen." The labels "Pelagian" and "Augustinian" are not used, but it is not very difficult to recognize these factions by their policies. The Pelagian-controlled government that is in power as the novel opens is responsible by its very laxness for the enormous amount of crime that occurs. When Alex is finally caught (while attempting to escape from a burglary involving a fatal assault on an old woman) it is mainly because his gang has betrayed him and facilitated the capture. He is sentenced to fourteen years in prison, and it is here that he will feel the effects of a major change in government policy.

The failure of liberal methods of government generates the usual DISAP-POINTMENT and the concomitant yearning for "Augustinian" alternatives. Realizing that the terrorized electorate cares little about "the tradition of liberty" and is in fact quite willing to "sell liberty for a quieter life," the government seeks to impose order by the most efficient means available. Unlike the Augustinian-controlled government in *The Wanting Seed,* this body does not resort to mass murder. Instead, it relies upon the genius of modern behavioral technology, specifically the branch of it that aims at the total control of human will. Alex, who brings attention to himself by murdering a fellow inmate, is selected as a "trail-blazer" to be "transformed out of all recognition."

The purpose of Alex's transformation is to eliminate his capacity to choose socially deleterious courses of action. Psychological engineers force upon him what Professor Skinner might call "the inclination to behave." Strapped in a chair, he is forced to watch films of incredible brutality, some of them contrived and others actual documentaries of Japanese and Nazi atrocities during World War II. In the past violence has given him only the most pleasurable sensations; now he is suddenly overcome by the most unbearable nausea and headaches. After suffering a number of these agonizing sessions, he finds that the nausea has been induced not by the films but by injections given beforehand. Thus his body is being taught to associate the sight or even the thought of violence with unpleasant sensations. His responses and, as it were, his moral progress are measured by electronic devices wired to his body. Quite by accident, it happens that his body is conditioned to associate not only violence but his beloved classical music with nausea. The last movement of Beethoven's Fifth Symphony accompanies a documentary on the Nazis and the connection of the two with bodily misery is thus firmly fixed.

Finally, when his rehabilitation is complete, he is exhibited in all his "goodness" before an audience of government and prison officials. What is demonstrated on this occasion beyond all argument is that his body will not permit his mind to entertain even the thought of violence. When a hired actor insults and beats him, Alex must force himself to respond in a truly "Christian" manner, not only doing but willing good for evil. In a desperate effort to ease his misery, he literally licks the man's boots. This ultimate expression of submission will become, incidentally, one of the most memorable scenes in the Kubrick film. If one were seeking an illustration to place above a Skinnerian caption, such as "The Inclination to Behave" or "Operant Conditioning" or "Beyond Freedom and Dignity," one could hardly find one more vivid and arresting than the picture of Malcolm McDowell in the role of Alex licking the sole of the actor/antagonist's shoe.

A further demonstration proves that Alex is above sexual violence as well. When a ravishing, thinly clad young morsel approaches him on the stage, he is filled momentarily with an old yearning "to have her right down there on the floor with the old in-out real savage," but again his visceral "conscience" prevents him and he is able to stop the nausea only by assuming an almost Dantesque attitude of noncarnal adoration. Having thus gratified his rehabilitation engineers with proof that he is a "true Christian," Alex is free to enter society again—if not as a useful citizen, at least as a harmless one, and as living proof that the government is doing something to remedy social ills and thus merits reelection.

Alex is not only harmless but helpless as well, and shortly after his release he is the victim of a ludicrous, vengeful beating by one of his most helpless former victims, an old man assisted by some of his ancient cronies. Unable to endure even the violent feeling needed to fight his way clear, he is rescued by three policemen. The fact that one of his rescuers is a former member of his own gang and another a former leader of a rival gang suggests that the society is experiencing a transitional "Interphase" as it progresses into its Augustinian phase. These young thugs, like the "greyboys" in *The Wanting Seed,* have been recruited into the police force apparently on the theory that their criminal desires can be expressed usefully in the maintenance of order on the streets.

Again, we are tempted to suppose that Burgess was influenced by conditions in some American cities where, as he has remarked, the police seem to represent little more than "a kind of *alternative* criminal body." To some extent, he may have been influenced by such conditions, but the political phenomena of which these hoodlum police are a symptom could be observed in practically any society passing into a phase of Augustinian reaction. The government accepts as axiomatic that order must be *imposed* and that its imposition will probably require some form of violent force. It is actually far less interested in suppressing crime than in simply maintaining stability and the appearance of order. Few citizens will question the use of a hoodlum police force unless they happen to be its victims, and those few include citizens whose opinions count for less than nothing with an Augustinian government, since they are, for the most part, advocates of Pelagian alternatives. One of the marks of Augustinian government is its total intolerance of political opposition. In this connection, we hear a very significant remark by the minister of the interior at the time Alex is selected for conditioning: "Soon we may be needing all our prison space for political offenders" (*A CO,* 92). Again, as in *The Wanting Seed,* here, too, we are reminded how Augustinianism may become fascism. We are reminded of Nazi Germany where most of the imprisoned were political offenders, and where common criminals in SS uniforms were the guardians of order.

Not surprisingly, Alex's former associates find his new situation ideal for settling some old scores. They drive him down a lonely country road and administer more than "a malenky bit of summary" with their fists. Then, in a battered and even more helpless condition, he is left to drag himself through pouring rain toward a little isolated cottage with the name HOME on its gate. This little cottage happens to have been the scene of one of the most savage atrocities he and his droogs had carried out before his imprisonment, and one of the victims, a writer named F. Alexander, is still living in it. F. Alexander had been beaten up by Alex and his gang and forced to watch the four of them rape his wife, who had died as a result. The writer has remained in the cottage devoting all his energies to combatting the evils of "the modern age." Rightfully blaming government failure as much as teenage savagery for his wife's death, he seeks to discredit the government sufficiently to have it turned out of office in the next election.

F. Alexander's political and philosophical ideals incline toward Pelagian liberalism and he has remained, in spite of his experience as a victim of human depravity, committed to the belief that man is "a creature of growth and capable of sweetness." Because of this, he remains unalterably opposed to the use of "debilitating and will-sapping techniques of conditioning" in criminal reform. To some extent, he is an autobiographical creation. Like Burgess, he has written a book entitled *A Clockwork Orange* with the purpose of illuminating the dangers of allowing such methods. The fact that he has had the sincerity of his beliefs about criminal reform tested by the personal experience of senseless criminal brutality is something else he shares with Burgess. We recall that during the war, while Burgess was stationed in Gibraltar, his pregnant wife was assaulted on a London street by American deserters and suffered a miscarriage as a result. But here the resemblance ends. Although Burgess believes man is capable of sweetness and should not be turned into a piece of clockwork, he is no Pelagian and his book, unlike F. Alexander's, is no lyrical effusion of revolutionary idealism ("written in a very bezoomy like style, full of Ah and Oh and that cal" [*ACO*, 157]). Most important, Burgess, unlike F. Alexander, is not blinded to concrete human realities by his political and philosophical ideals.

Since Alex and his droogs had been masked during their assault on HOME, F. Alexander does not recognize him. Filled with indignation against the state, he sees only another "victim of the modern age" who is in need of compassion. It soon occurs to him, however, that Alex can be used effectively as a propaganda device to embarrass the government—an example of the dehumanizing effects of its crime-control methods. He calls in three associates who share his beliefs and his enthusiasm for this idea. Although F. Alexander and his friends seem motivated by the loftiest of liberal ideas, it soon becomes apparent that they are incapable of seeing Alex as anything but a propaganda device. Like Swift's "projectors," they are so full of the abstract and the visionary that they have little concern for the suffering or welfare of individual human beings. To them Alex is not an unfortunate human being to be assisted but "A martyr to the cause of Liberty" who can serve "the Future and our Cause." When Alex asks F. Alexander to explain how he, as a will-sapped victim of the government, will benefit by being used as a propaganda device, the man is confused and unable to answer:

> He looked at me, brothers, as if he hadn't thought of that before and, anyway, it didn't matter compared with Liberty and all that cal, and he had a look of surprise at me saying what I said, as though I was being like selfish in wanting something for myself. Then he said: "Oh, as I say, you're a living witness, poor boy. Eat up all your breakfast and then come and see what I've written, for it's going into *The Weekly Trumpet* under your name, you unfortunate victim." (*ACO*, 160)

Although he is in no position to object, Alex realizes he is being treated "like a thing that's like got to be just used" (*ACO*, 163) and is bitterly resentful.

In his anger, Alex lapses from polite, respectful English into snarling nadsat, a slip that, along with a few others, causes F. Alexander to remember the night his home was invaded. Although he cannot be certain that Alex was one of the attackers, his suspicions begin to grow, and it is apparently because of this that a change is made in the plan for using Alex. The revolutionaries had originally planned to exhibit Alex at public meetings to inflame the people, but now they decide to make him a real martyr to their cause. Lest the people not be sufficiently shocked by the destruction of Alex's moral nature, they decide to have him destroyed completely by the government. As a dead "witness," he will be even more damning than a "living" one. They lock him in a flat and fill it with sounds of a loud and violent symphony in the hope he will be driven to suicide. Since he had already been considering suicide, the plan is immediately successful and he dives out a window, severely although not fatally injuring himself.

Among other things, this episode effectively underlines what Pelagian idealism shares with Augustinian cynicism. The Pelagian preoccupation with the tradition of liberty and the dignity of man, like the Augustinian preoccupation with stability, will make any sacrifice for the good of man worthwhile, including the destruction of man himself. But of course the revolutionaries do not view Alex as "man"; he is merely a human being who counts, as he himself perceives, for nothing more than a means to implement in a small way the great Pelagian scheme for the future. This ill-defined yet glorious dream, which causes these revolutionaries to use in such a fiendish and cynical manner the responses implanted in Alex by the Augustinian psychologists, might be equated in some respects with "The Idea" inspiring the revolutionaries in Dostoevsky's *The Possessed.* Dostoevsky's revolutionaries are of course nihilists, not Pelagians, but Burgess's implication seems to be that Pelagian revolutionary fervor is not far removed from nihilism. There is underlying both forms of enthusiasm a shared assumption that once the government is overthrown and corrupt institutions are destroyed, "man" will be saved. If individual men are obstacles to the salvation of man on earth, so much the worse for them. If they can be used as means to achieve the end, so much the better for the cause.

The Pelagian scheme very nearly succeeds, and while Alex is recovering in a hospital from his death dive, a power struggle rages. The government receives ample amounts of embarrassing publicity concerning the attempted suicide, but somehow survives. One day Alex awakens to find himself fully as vicious as before his treatment. More psychological engineers, using "deep hypnopaedia or some such slovo," have restored his moral nature, his "self," and his concomitant appetites for Beethoven and throat cutting. As he listens to the "glorious Ninth of Ludwig van," he exults,

> Oh, it was gorgeosity and yumyumyum. When it came to the Scherzo I could viddy myself very clear running and running on like very mysterious nogas, carving the whole litso of the creeching world with my cut-throat britva. And there was the slow and the lovely last singing movement still to come. I was cured all right. (*A CO,* 177)

The Augustinians are delighted. In this "depraved" condition, he cannot embarrass them further.

At this point, the American edition of *A Clockwork Orange* ends, and Stanley Kubrick, following the American edition very closely, ends his film. In its earlier British editions, however, the novel has one additional chapter that makes a considerable difference in how one may interpret the book. This chapter, like the chapters that begin the novel's three main parts, opens with the question, "What's it going to be then, eh?" Indeed, this is the question the reader has been left to ponder. We have seen Alex's depraved "self" replaced by a well-behaved "not-self," which is then replaced by the old "self" when he is "cured." We are led to believe that, aside from imprisonment or hanging, these two conditions are the only possible alternatives for Alex. The omitted chapter, however, reveals yet another alternative. Alex and a new squad of droogs are sitting in his old hangout, the Korova Milkbar, drinking hallucinogenic "milk-plus mesto" and getting ready for the evening. This is exactly the way the novel began, but whereas the opening chapter is a prelude to violence, this one reveals Alex becoming weary of violence. He leaves his gang and wanders alone through the streets reflecting on the changes in his outlook. Although the behavioral engineers have managed to restore his old vicious self, he is becoming sentimental and starting to yearn for something besides the pleasure of indulging himself in classical music and the "old ultra-violence." What it is, he does not know, but when he encounters a member of his old gang who has married and settled down to a completely harmless, law-abiding existence, he realizes that this is what he wants for himself. He wants to marry and have a son. He will try to teach his son what he knows of the world, but he doubts that his son will be able to profit from his mistakes:

> And nor would he be able to stop his own son, brothers. And so it would itty on to like the end of the world, round and round and round, like some bolshy gigantic like cheeloveck, like old Bog Himself (by courtesy of Korova Milkbar) turning and turning and turning a vonny grahzny orange in his gigantic rookers. (*A CO*, 188)

Burgess's explanation for the omission of this chapter in the American version is as follows:

> He [Kubrick] followed the American edition which, in a kind of reverse version of Gresham's Law, will drive out the British version. The American edition has 20 chapters while the British edition has 21, and in the 21st chapter we have a scene enacted two years later than the final scene of the film. Alex is getting tired of violence and he meets one of his old friends who appears in the film, and sees him with a young girl going off to a wine and cheese party to play word games. So Alex thinks it's about time he got a girl and thought of getting married and having a son of his own, and he envisages the circle going around, the Orange turning in the paws of God, the Orange of the world turning. My American publisher in 1962 said, "I recognize that you are British and hence tend to a more pragmatic or milk-and-water tradition than we Americans know. We are tougher than you and prepared to end on a tough and violent note." And I said: "Well, if this is one of the conditions for publishing the book, get on with it."[24]

This explanation, from an interview published in *Penthouse* magazine, suggests that Burgess tends to agree with his publisher, at least with regard to the superiority of the truncated American version. Certainly the omission of that twenty-first chapter causes the book to end on a very "tough and violent note."

The recurrent question, "What's it going to be then, eh?" becomes more difficult to answer because the dilemma posed by the book is a true one, *tertium non datur*. Assuming that Alex remains as he is when he awakens "cured," the society has the choice of either permitting him to exist as he is until, presumably, he kills someone else and is again confined, or imposing "goodness" and thereby being guilty of a moral evil more enormous than any of Alex's crimes. For political (not moral) reasons, of course, the government in the novel first impales the society on one horn and then on the other. Yet, even from a strictly moral standpoint, the choice can be very difficult. Although the Judaeo/Christian ethic clearly dictates that society should be governed on the assumption that man is and should remain an autonomous, responsible moral agent, this is by no means the last word on the subject for a great many individuals who, rightfully, consider themselves ethically sensitive. If one tries to persuade, say, a utilitarian that diminishing a criminal's ability to choose by conditioning or implanting gadgets is invariably evil and never justifiable from a moral standpoint, one is likely to become involved in lengthy and ultimately inconclusive debate. Utilitarian arguments in favor of achieving the greatest happiness for the greatest number by conditioning and, if you will, dehumanizing a few, can only be refuted if the Kantian principle that a person must be treated according to "the concept of a human being" and an end in himself, never a means, is accepted. Alex is no rule deontologist, but he objects to being used "like a thing that's like got to be just used." His outburst effectively illuminates the real question underlying the whole debate over conditioning: can it *ever* be right to use any human being as a nonhuman means to achieve an end, however noble or beneficient that end may be?

If the answer is "yes," we had better listen to Professor Skinner, for he and his behaviorist colleagues are seeking to provide the most effective and humane methods of using "man the mechanism" as a means of achieving the end of a stable culture. Although Skinner insists the culture he would design would be for "man," he also admits that man must be redesigned to fit this culture. He states explicitly in *Beyond Freedom and Dignity* that the culture he would design is "not for man as he is now" but for man as he may become under the benevolent shaping hand of science.[25] If we are a bit chilled by this and change our answer to "ideally no but perhaps yes under extreme circumstances"—for example, a state of lawless chaos on the streets—we had still better listen to Professor Skinner, for once a society knowingly permits the dehumanizing use of one human being to achieve an end, it has effectively set in motion a process that must eventually involve all of its members. This is the warning Burgess gives us in *A Clockwork Orange,* and he gives it again in his essay *Clockwork Marmalade,* written shortly after he viewed the Kubrick film:

Hitler was, unfortunately, a human being, and if we could have countenanced the conditioning of one human being we would have to accept it for all. Hitler was a great nuisance, but history has known others disruptive enough to make the state's fingers itch—Christ, Luther, Bruno, even D. H. Lawrence. One has to be genuinely philosophical about this, however much one has suffered. I don't know how much free will man really possesses (Wagner's Hans Sachs said: *Wir sind ein wenig frei*—"we are a little free") but I do know that what little he seems to have is too precious to encroach on, however good the intentions of the encroacher may be.[26]

This essay contains some very revealing explanations that should help a great deal to clarify the meaning of Burgess's book and Kubrick's film for those who misunderstood their parable as little more than a glorification of violence. Burgess explains the novel's arresting title as follows:

In 1945, back from the army, I heard an 80-year-old Cockney in a London pub say that somebody was "as queer as a clockwork orange." The "queer" did not mean homosexual: it meant mad. The phrase intrigued me with its unlikely fusion of demotic and surrealistic. For nearly twenty years I wanted to use it as the title of something. During those twenty years I heard it several times more—in Underground stations, in pubs, in television plays—but always from aged Cockneys, never from the young. It was a traditional trope, and it asked to entitle a work which combined a concern with tradition and a bizarre technique. The opportunity to use it came when I conceived the notion of writing a novel about brainwashing. Joyce's Stephen Dedalus [in *Ulysses*] refers to the world as an "oblate orange"; man is a microcosm or little world; he is a growth as organic as a fruit, capable of colour, fragrance and sweetness; to meddle with him, condition him, is to turn him into a mechanical creation.[27]

I quote this passage in full because it explains a good deal more than the title. It also explains the inclusion of that rather optimistic last chapter in the original British version. Again, Burgess is no Pelagian. Like most of his more perceptive characters, he "accept[s] the myth of the Garden of Eden and the Fall of Man."[28] But if he has an Augustinian view of man as a fallen creature, he also has a great deal of non-Augustinian hope for him as a creature of growth and potential goodness. The message of the chapter that was omitted is that, if there is hope, it is in the capacity of individuals to grow and learn by suffering and error. Suffering, fallen human beings, not behavioral technology or the revolutionary schemes of idealists, bring "goodness" into the world. Awaiting this development is of course far less efficient or satisfying to some than imposing a design that ensures "goodness," but there is reason to hope that the wait will be worthwhile. Burgess is far more optimistic than Skinner, who has obviously lost all faith in man as he is and as he may become without the imposition of goodness.

In this same connection, Burgess continues his essay:

Viewers of the film have been disturbed by the fact that Alex, despite his viciousness, is quite likeable. It has required a deliberate self-administered act of aversion therapy on the part of some to dislike him, and to let righteous indignation get in the way of human charity. The point is that, if we are going to love mankind, we will have to love Alex as a not unrepresentative member of it. The place where Alex and his mirror-image F. Alexander are most guilty of hate and violence is called HOME, and it is here, we are told, that charity ought to begin. But towards that mechanism, the state, which, first, is concerned with self-perpetuation and, second, is happiest when human beings are predictable and controllable, we have no duty at all, certainly no duty of charity.[29]

He concludes with a note on the language, which, he says

. . . is no mere decoration, nor is it a sinister indication of the subliminal power that a Communist super-state may already be exerting on the young. It was meant to turn *A Clockwork Orange* into, among other things, a brainwashing primer. You read the book or see the film, and at the end you should find yourself in possession of a minimal Russian vocabulary—without effort, with surprise. This is the way brainwashing works. I chose Russian words because they blend better into English than those of French or even German (which is already a kind of English, not exotic enough). But the lesson of the *Orange* has nothing to do with the ideology or repressive techniques of Soviet Russia: it is wholly concerned with what can happen to any of us in the West, if we do not keep on our guard. If *Orange*, like *1984*, takes its place as one of those salutary literary warnings—or cinematic warnings—against flabbiness, sloppy thinking, and overmuch trust in the state, then I will have done something of value.[30]

That he has given us something of value cannot be disputed. Whether or not we choose to agree with the book as "a sermon on the power of choice," we have been forced to view clearly the implications of limiting that power. It is providential that the Kubrick film should come out in the same year as the publication of *Beyond Freedom and Dignity*. For those who were disturbed by Skinner's book but unable to articulate a refutation, Burgess and Kubrick have provided an eloquent answer.

Burgess's Position

Pelagius and Augustine appear in several of Burgess's other novels, and his treatment of their endless debate is consistent. Clearly, he views philosophical extremes—Pelagian, Augustinian, or whatever—as avenues to moral blindness and collective insanity, but any tendency to promote a generalized view of human nature is also liable to be a butt of his merciless satire. His satiric implication seems to be that both Pelagius and Augustine, as well as many of their philosophical heirs, have been hopelessly myopic in their analyses of the human condition. Their views of man have been determined and severely limited by preconceived notions about "man" that leave little room for the uniqueness of individual men. True, many of Burgess's most sympathetically drawn protagonists, such as Victor Crabbe in the *Malayan Trilogy,* Richard Ennis in *A Vision of Battlements,* and Mr. Woolton in *The Worm and the Ring,* are liberals, but they are totally ineffectual human beings. They are believers in social progress through the liberation of beneficent human energies, but they themselves can accomplish nothing, largely because they fail to understand the human beings around them. In fact, Burgess's most appealing characterizations, Hillier in *Tremor of Intent* and the Shakespeare/Burgess composite hero in *Nothing Like the Sun,* actually lean toward Hobbist/Augustinian pessimism. The latter's pessimism may be due in part to the syphilis he catches from the Dark Lady, although he would not, in any case, accept the naïve Pelagianism of Southampton and the other supporters of Essex who seek to accelerate social progress through revolution. Most of his Hobbist/Augustinians, though, such as Dr. Gardner in *The Worm and the Ring* and Theodorescu in *Tremor of Intent,* are thoroughly repellant. They have a Hobbesian contempt for humanity and cynically assume that all power may and indeed should be gained by the manipulator who fully understands human weakness and malleability.

Pelagianism and detheologized Augustinianism actually share a great deal, as Burgess suggests in his first novel, *A Vision of Battlements.* We hear an American army officer describing how the Pelagian denial of original sin had spawned "the two big modern heresies—material progress as a sacred goal; the State as God Almighty." The former has produced "Americanism" and the latter, "the Socialist process." The officer points out that not only do the two heresies derive from the same ultimate source, they have also had essentially the same long-range consequences: "supra-regional goods—the icebox and the Chevrolet or the worker, standardized into an overalled abstraction at a standardized production belt" (*AVOB,* 122–23). In other words, by exalting human potentiality and discarding Divine Grace, Pelagius and his heirs have actually reduced individual human significances immeasurably. For when Divine Grace has no place, when sin in the Augustinian sense doesn't exist, when man is in need of nothing but a greater exertion of his will to improve his moral and spiritual condition, the only significant distributors of "grace" in any sense are the managers of the earthly communities wherein the effort must be made. It is these managers—corporation heads, "projecting" social scientists, commissars, bureaucrats, and others—who are most desirous of standardizing humanity, of bringing its affairs within the compass of their finite wisdoms. When Pelagianism really gains the upper hand, dominating the self-images of whole societies, civilization itself is threatened. This is what Mr. Enderby tries to convey in his long allegorical poem about the Minotaur, and in *The Worm and the Ring,* we hear Christopher Howarth suggesting the same thing in a drunken conversation with an American. For Howarth, America is a kind of clean-limbed, odorless, football-playing

Theseus, and the Minotaur is original sin. The labyrinth is civilization itself (*WR*, 173–76). That this line of thinking is close to Burgess's own can be seen from his reflections on the Mei-lai massacre and the resultant national remorse. In his view, America had at last "discovered sin." It was, he seemed to feel, a not unhealthy discovery, for it is his belief that "a society that loses its sense of guilt is doomed."[31]

Burgess's own leaning appears to be toward Augustinianism; yet he has clearly shown that the Augustinian tradition is just as inimical to the dignity of man, although it at least acknowledges a distinction between regenerate and unregenerate human nature. Since present-day Augustinian thinkers, like the Pelagians, have largely abandoned traditional orthodox Christian concepts of grace, the categories "regenerate" and "unregenerate" have meaning only with reference to social stability. One must subordinate one's "self" to the social machinery, become functionally or economically significant as a part of it, to be of the elect. The individual "self," asserting its existence by purely self-determined actions, is sand in the machinery of Augustinian society. In the detheologized Augustinian view, which is still very "Christian" in some respects, moral evil and self-assertion are so inextricably bound up with each other that they tend to be identified. As the murderous young hero of *A Clockwork Orange* tells us:

> More, badness is of the self, the one, the you or me on our oddy knockies, and that self is made by old Bog or God and is his great pride and radosity. But the not-self cannot have the bad, meaning they of the government and the judges and the schools cannot allow the bad because they cannot allow the self. And is not our modern history, my brothers, the story of brave malenky selves fighting these big machines? I am serious with you, brothers, over this. But what I do I do because I like to do. (*ACO*, 44)

"These big machines" are both Pelagian and Augustinian, and the contest between them, which manifests itself in the debates of intellectuals, and the actual "waltzing" of governments from blind conservatism to blind liberalism and back are symptomatic of Western man's acceptance of a faulty dilemma. Presumably, sanity and vision could lead men to a rejection of both "Pelagian" and detheologized "Augustinian" extremism and a recreation of society based upon realistic assessments of individual human potentiality. Without an increase of sanity and vision, Western man will become progressively dehumanized by Pelagian and Augustinian machines that seek to destroy the "self" to save "man." Eventually, he may be forced into the dilemmas Burgess has presented in these dystopian books. Once he, "man," is thus confined, it will not be up to the "malenky selves" to choose between the dehumanizing alternatives available.

6

BETWEEN GOD AND NOTGOD

Tremor of Intent

In 1966 Burgess, having already experimented successfully with a wide variety of subgenres of the novel—mock epic, historical romance, picaresque, proleptic satire—turned his hand to a type that seems to be, by its very nature and purpose, fatally constricting to a writer with Burgess's philosophical and artistic concerns. *Tremor of Intent* is a spy thriller. If one reckons literary success purely in terms of sales, unquestionably Ian Fleming has been the most successful creator of spy thrillers. (By the same criterion, of course, Elvis Presley was the greatest musical success of the last two decades.) But one wonders about just how many generations of readers will be thrilled by the exploits of James Bond. The tag "sensation novelist" is so much more appropriate to Fleming and his imitators than to the Victorians—Collins, Dickens, Charles Reade—who first wore it. For there is virtually nothing but sensation in the James Bond thrillers. Fleming seems to have defined the limits to the type of novel he was writing in *Casino Royale* and then to have stayed within those limits throughout the rest of his canon.

The Bond formula is potent in terms of its sensation-stirring impact. The hero, a supervirile specimen, is epic to the extent that the fate of his nation or race rests on his broad shoulders. He is also of epic stature in that he embodies most of the virtues idealized by his race. Bond is as characteristically Anglo-Saxon as Beowulf—courageous, cool-headed, prudent, possessing a sportsman's sense of fair play, utterly uninhibited by intellectual subtlety, a man of "action" not words. He also has characteristically Anglo-Saxon vices that further endear him to his audience—a fondness for eating, drinking, and wenching and the ferocious pleasure of destroying an enemy with his own capable hands. Invariably, the Bond formula calls for trials by pleasure and trials by torture, usually contrived by the brilliant but overly subtle and warped intellect of a supervillain. The hero, unlike Spenser's Guyon, does not immediately destroy the bowers of bliss he encounters. On the contrary, he enters them wholeheartedly with every hormone of his being, thus transporting readers with vicarious concupiscence. Other trials by pleasure include gastronomic interludes designed to leave readers helplessly salivating. However, before the readers' appetitive responses have been utterly used up, the "thrilling" usually begins. The hero, despite his cool wits, his mastery of karate and other martial arts, and the elaborate gadgetry that Western technology has placed at his disposal, is trapped by the supervillain and rendered helpless in his grasp. The villain, too vain intellectually to take simple measures, must then make the blunder of devising an overly involved means of disposing of the hero. This permits the hero to devise a counterplan that is invariably successful. So it happens that Goldfinger's man Oddjob is sucked out of an airplane and Bond winds up in bed reviving the heterosexuality of Pussy Galore. The Free World has been saved again.

Burgess is by no means the only novelist to perceive that Fleming and his imitators had not exhausted the possibilities of the spy thriller. John le Carré, among others, has written spy novels (*The Spy Who Came in From the Cold; The Looking-Glass War*) containing serious moral and psychological investigations. There has been, however, nothing to compare with Burgess's *Tremor of Intent*. Upon the well-worn framework of the Bond formula, he has fleshed out and molded a tale of intrigue that must fire the senses of even the most Bond-weary aficionado of the spy thriller. The typical Bond feats of appetite are duplicated and surpassed, sometimes to a ridiculous extent. The protagonist, Denis Hillier, has bedroom adventures that make Bond's conquests seem as crude and unfulfilling as an acneed adolescent's evening affair with an issue of *Playboy*. His gastronomic awareness is such that Bond is by comparison an epicurean tyro. In addition, Hillier possesses a mind that is good for something besides devising booby traps and playing games with supervillains. Unlike Bond, he has a moral awareness that extends beyond ideology. In his view, the specter of nuclear holocaust that causes East and West to tremble before each other, ponder genocide, and play their murderous little pranks is illusory:

> It's all been a bloody big game—the genocidal formulae, the rocketry, the foolproof early warning devices mere counters in it. But nobody, sir, is going to kill anybody. This concept of a megadeath is as remotely unreal as specular stone or any other mediaeval nonsense. Some day anthropologists will comment in gently concealed wonder on the ludic element in our serious flirting with collective suicide. (*TI,* 3)[1]

His growing awareness that the whole accompanying business of international intrigue is not only extremely nasty and degrading but childish and pointless as well causes him to announce his retirement.

However, before he abandons his long, generally successful career as "a void, a dark sack crammed with skills" (*TI,* 4), he must carry out one more mission. He must play the game of make-believe again—he must carefully disguise himself as a typewriter salesman vacationing on a luxury cruise, sneak behind the Iron Curtain at a Black Sea port, and kidnap a British scientist who has defected to Russia. The scientist, Dr. Edwin Roper, happens to be an old friend whom Hillier has known since their school days at a Catholic college in Bradcaster. In a kind of unwritten epistle to his superiors, Hillier recounts the history of their friendship. Roper's brilliance in the physical sciences had manifested itself early and was one of the things that had made it impossible for the good fathers to keep him within the fold of the church. Hillier, too, had left the church at an early age, although his own intellectual bent was humanistic, his principal gift being languages. For Hillier perhaps the most repulsive aspect of the church was its attitude toward the flesh, the belief of some of its teachers that "all the evil of our modern times springs from unholy lust . . . the fount of all other of the deadly sins" (*TI,* 6). Hillier believes that much of the youthful moral confusion he and Roper experienced might have been avoided had they simply "sweat it all out in a decent bout of sex in the chapel" (*TI,* 13).

Antipathy toward the Holy Mother Church is, however, the only attitude Hillier and Roper share. At an early age, their beliefs concerning the human condition had begun to diverge toward the poles that Burgess has elsewhere labelled Pelagian optimism and Augustinian pessimism. Hillier tells his superiors, "if he's a heretic at all it's your heresy he subscribes to—the belief that life can be better and man nobler. It's not up to me, of course, to say what a load of bloody nonsense that is" (*TI,* 2–3). Roper, having acquired the Promethean fire of a trilogy of sciences, came to see good and evil only in terms of knowledge and ignorance. The diabolical actions of the Nazis were for him merely the result of their being "politically ignorant." Actually, as Hillier perceives, Roper's scientific education had propelled him toward moral idiocy: "He was becoming both full and empty at the same time. He was turning into a *thing,* growing out of boyhood into thinghood, not manhood—a highly efficient artefact crammed with non-human knowledge" (*TI,* 13). In contrast, Hillier retains a strong Augustinian belief in original sin and the existence of evil and a strong Augustinian sense of "what a bloody Manichean mess life is" (*TI,* 22).

In some of his earlier novels, as we have seen, notably in *The Wanting Seed* and *A Clockwork Orange,* Burgess had already shown that a Pelagian/Promethean outlook can be conducive to moral idiocy, but in *Tremor of Intent,* there is an immediacy and a shock of recognition more powerful than the shock generated by proleptic visions. For Roper is, as Lear says of Edgar, "the thing itself," man at his most brilliant and simultaneously most idiotic. He is Mary Shelley's Dr. Frankenstein, J. Robert Openheimer, and the many scientifically great minds who served *der Führer* and, after him, his conquerors on both sides of the Iron Curtain. He is, whenever Hillier sees or hears from him, full of moral outrage but always remarkably lacking in moral sense. He has the unforgettably ghastly experience of cleaning up Nazi death camps, of seeing concrete, palpable evil beyond the power of his scientific rationalism to explain. Yet shortly thereafter, he is easily persuaded, with the aid of some toothsome Teutonic flesh, that fascism was fundamentally right for western Europe, that Russia, not Germany, was the real enemy of Western civilization. It is not long after this that he veers sharply to the left, becomes a pamphleteering Socialist, and, a short time later, is persuaded to defect to Russia.

Part of Roper's motivation for this last ideological shift is a curious desire to have some vengeance on Capitalist/Protestant England for martyring one of his Catholic ancestors in 1558. Like the man whose surname he shares, he preserves the memory of a martyr to the old faith, but while he was under the influence of his busty ex-Nazi wife, his ancestor was "a fool" who should have "shut up about" his faith. When he defects to Russia, he is easily persuaded that his ancestor was a heroic victim of Western capitalism, which is inextricably bound up with Protestantism. The Russians have reason to be confident that he will never seek to check out all the relevant historical data. Roper is appropriately thorough in his scientific research but, like so many Pelagians, is willing and eager to place his faith in a hazy, simplified scheme of history. The startling information that his ancestor was actually a Protestant martyr simply causes him to view the Reformation in a new, more favorable light, as an important step toward the growth of a classless society.

Roper is, however, much less interesting intellectually than Hillier, and this would seem to be the case with Pelagian and Augustinian minds generally. The Pelagian view of human nature, economics, history, or whatever requires a certain amount of willed naïveté, a willingness to overlook contradictory experience. The resultant state of optimism cannot really be termed simplemindedness, for it may involve an elaborate, subtle compartmentalization of awareness, but it is usually conducive to simplistic interpretations of events, such as Roper's explanation of the Nazi atrocities in terms of political ignorance. Augustinians, such as Hillier, are more complex and more capable of intellectual growth because they are not inhibited by simplistic formulae that Pelagians find convenient for explaining away subtle human problems. They also have, unlike the Pelagians, a sense of the great cosmic forces beyond human control:

> "Beyond God," said Hillier, "lies the concept of God. In the concept of God lies the concept of anti-God. Ultimate reality is a dualism or a game for two players. We—people like me and my counterparts on the other side—we reflect that game. It's a pale reflection. There used to be a much brighter one, in the days when the two sides represented what are known as good and evil. That was a tougher and more interesting game, because one's opponent wasn't on the other side of a conventional net or line. He wasn't marked off by a special jersey or colour or race or language or allegiance to a particular historico-geographical abstraction. But we don't believe in good and evil any more. That's why we play this silly and hopeless little game. . . . We're too insignificant to be attacked by either the forces of light or the forces of darkness. And yet, playing this game,

we occasionally let evil in. Evil tumbles in, unaware. But there's no good to fight evil with. That's when one grows sick of the game and wants to resign from it."
(*IT*, 119–20)

As he plays the game for the last time, Hillier learns still more about evil. He finds it is not merely in the degradation and nastiness, having to destroy foreign agents one respects to protect pop singers and other Free-World citizens one loathes and despises. The real wellspring of evil uncapped by this miserable children's game is neutrality, a state of self-serving noncommitment in which an especially contemptible group of human beings exist and thrive as parasites on the bodies of their committed fellows. In the course of his last mission, Hillier becomes aware, as never before, of the "neutrals" and what they represent. Theodorescu, the pederastic supervillain who becomes his major opponent, is not, technically, one of the enemy. He serves neither East nor West, neither the MGB nor Her Majesty's Secret Service. Instead, he merely buys and sells information to both about each other. The consequences of these transactions concern him not a whit, so long as he receives payment from the highest bidder. His physical presence is an accurate index of his character. Strikingly reminiscent of Sidney Greenstreet in a film version of *The Maltese Falcon*, he

> . . . was of a noble fatness; the fat of his face was part of its essential structure, not a mean gross accretion, and the vast shapely nose needed those cheek-pads and firm jowls for proper balance. The chin was very firm. The eyes were not currants in dough but huge and lustrous lamps whose whites seemed to have been polished. He was totally bald, but the smooth scalp—from which a discreet odour of violets breathed—seemed less an affliction than an achievement, as though hair were a mere callow down to be shed in maturity. . . . His body was so huge that the white dinner-jacket was like a moulded expanse of royal sailcloth. He was drinking what Hillier took to be neat vodka, a whole gill of it. (*TI*, 65)

He is insatiable appetite personified, a tick waxed to bursting with the blood of agents and other counters in the game of espionage. As Hillier finds out, in games of appetite, he is unbeatable. In the first of these, Burgess replaces the typical Bond interval of gastronomic indulgence with an eating contest. Both Theodorescu and Hillier exhibit menu mastery and wine connoisseurship that Bond would envy, but Hillier never really has a chance. While Theodorescu relaxes in victory as if "he'd merely dined on a couple of poached eggs," Hillier reels toward "that traditional vomitorium," the sea. Shortly after this, Theodorescu scores another victory with the aid of his assistant, a Tamil love goddess in the flesh named Miss Devi. In addition to a fondness for good food and drink, Hillier's fleshly weaknesses include satyriasis, and he finds Miss Devi an avenue of erotic delights beyond the imaginative powers of the authors of the *Kama Sutra*. But Miss Devi is merely an appendage of the lord of appetite, Theodorescu, and while Hillier is borne aloft in orgasmatic transport, she gives him an injection of truth serum that enables Theodorescu to pump out vital information for his next secret "auction." Hillier is utterly unable to resist effectively, and when the great tick has siphoned enough to satisfy his thirst of the moment, Hillier is left in a state of impotent shame.

But Hillier's education has just begun. He has yet to perceive just how extensively the ring of evil-spawning neutrality actually surrounds the children's game of which he is a part. He would in fact be utterly destroyed by it without the aid of two persons who are quite literally children. One is Clara Walters, a beautiful sixteen-year-old girl who seems to represent for him a kind of opposite pole to Miss Devi. Hillier falls in love with her but is loathe to remove her innocence, partly because she is so extremely innocent and partly because he sees in her a potential avenue to respiritualization. Indeed, she becomes for him a sort of Beatrice image, a "clear bright one" toward which he ascends in a Dantesque journey from the "hell," both figurative and, in an Elizabethan sense, literal, of Miss Devi. The other child is her thirteen-year-old brother, Alan, an appallingly precocious youngster who is able to see beneath all the disguises and pretensions of the so-called adult world. More than anyone else, he is able to share Hillier's loathing for the "neutrals" and his awareness of how fundamentally "unreal" the whole game of espionage actually is.

With the assistance of Clara, Hillier is able to sneak into Russia as planned and contact Roper, but at that point, he finds that all his planning has been wasted effort. His real purpose in being sent on this mission has been nothing he would ever have contemplated. His superiors, "gentlemen, who, when they're not on the golf-course, worry about security," have decided to make his retirement a perfectly safe one. Their instrument is another of the ubiquitous neutrals, an employee of a neutral agency known as Panleth that specializes in political assassination. This same creature is also being paid by a British cabinet minister to eliminate Roper, who could be a source of embarrassment if he were brought back to trial and it was revealed that the cabinet minister's appetite for Teutonic flesh, that is, Roper's wife, had been instrumental in causing the scientist's defection. Thus through an assassin's revelation and, later, the autobiography of Roper, Hillier is vouchsafed a dismal epiphany. When one is no longer a functional piece of equipment, one's own government may choose to dispose of one like so much obsolete, potentially lethal material. But far from being an incorruptible body whose overall rectitude might palliate the liquidation of corruptible, therefore potentially lethal, sensualists, the government itself is partly run by "bloody neutrals," such as the cabinet minister, who will serve their own appetites before they serve their country.

These revelations would be even more staggering to Hillier if his whole mental outlook and spiritual condition, like James Bond's, were bound up with his function as an instrument of espionage, but he has already, in the words of the Panleth assassin, begun "to opt out of the modern world." As a devout sensualist, he has partially blotted out the "Manichean mess" of the world by immersion in the flesh. There may be some truth in the assassin's suggestion that his sensuality has been "a kind of substitute for faith." But his idealized image of Clara has stimulated a respiritualizing process that will eventually lead him back to his first faith, Roman Catholicism, an influence on his life that, according to the assassin, has been another factor causing his superiors to doubt the wholeheartedness of his patriotism.

Before his encounter with the assassin, Hillier had begun to think about his immortal soul, but it was Clara, not the church, who kindled a longing to save it. To be worthy of her, he "needed, in a single muscular gesture to throw that luggage of his past self (blood-and-beer-stained cheap suitcases full of name-less filth wrapped in old *Daily Mirrors*) on to the refuse cart which, after a single telephone-call, would readily come to his gate, driven by a man with brown eyes and a beard who would smile away a gratuity (This is my job, sir). He was creaking towards a regeneration" (*TI*, 142). He does in fact make the gesture and the phone call under the very muzzle of the assassin's gun. While the Pelagian Roper swears lustily, disdaining any communication with the world beyond science that may be awaiting him, Hillier makes an act of contrition. The two men are not, however, destined to be "vouchsafed the final answer" at this time. A miraculous rescue puts off the reckoning for both, and Hillier is able to return to the cruise ship and the girl who has been in his thoughts throughout the whole ordeal. Naturally he abandons his plans to kidnap Roper, who is now indeed more fortunate than he, in that the country that Roper has chosen to serve has not yet chosen to discard him.

Having undergone a purgatory of terror, disillusionment, and repentance, Hillier feels that he is more worthy of approaching Clara, but he has a Dantesque fear of shattering his idealized image by knowing her too fully in the flesh. He finds, however, that the flesh cannot be avoided. She is only a woman, as fleshfast and ready as the scores of women he has known before. He initiates her into a world of experience that he himself is about to abandon, but neither his own growing spiritual vitality nor her well-being can be served by any further knowledge, and he drives her away in a fit of shame and revulsion.

Another ex-secret agent in Hillier's position, with his knowledge of be-trayal by his government, might choose to retaliate by joining Roper and the enemies of that government. But Hillier is finished with the meaningless games. The real sources of the evil that has very nearly devoured him cannot be touched by a player merely switching sides. If he would strike a blow that is worthy of any moral qualification such as good or evil, he must strike that blow at the self-serving neutrality that gluts itself on the game itself. Theodorescu, literally the grossest embodiment of neutrality he has encoun-tered, has made himself available for further transactions in Istanbul, and before Hillier opts out of the modern world completely, he wants to cleanse it a bit. He contacts Theodorescu in Istanbul and, as before, that worthy lord of appetite has Miss Devi waiting to prepare Hillier for their encounter by draining all of the potency out of him. But the brief regenerating glimpse of paradise Hillier has had with Clara, although disappointing and illusory, has removed any desire to plunge again through "the heat of a beneficient hell" to her "earth's centre" (*TI,* 89). He wants only "a simple tune, not a full orchestra," and Miss Devi, stung by a humiliating awareness that her well-schooled charms have been eclipsed by those of an inexperienced rival, coldly rejects him. He is now more ready for Theodorescu than he had been on the cruise ship, even without the truth serum.

Hillier's plan for flushing this gross piece of neutral sewage out of the world is simple. He will let the great tick fill himself to bursting with all the choicest bits of information at his command, and then he will use his pistol, already stained with the blood of another neutral, to ventilate and drain the great putrescent carcass. But Theodorescu is no tyro at this game. Although his appendage, Miss Devi, has failed to weaken Hillier with her charms, she has made sure he has no harmful weapon at his command. Hillier finds himself as impotent as before, capable only of fulfilling the first part of his scheme, much to the gratification of Theodorescu. A rather ludicrous combat sequence follows in which Hillier finally prevails, but his victory emphasizes again the fundamentally childish character of the game of international intrigue. The wizardry of Western chemistry enables him to make Theodorescu regress to his boyhood in an English public school. Then Hillier, masquerading as a jeering school chum, manages to destroy him by nimbly accomplishing a boyish stunt that is impossible for the great-bodied neutral. Theodorescu, his boyish vanity scourged by Hillier's juvenile taunts, leaps into a watery grave, and Hillier's last mission is accomplished. There is, however, no suggestion that "the Free World has been saved again." Theodorescu carries with him evidence that would incriminate another neutral, the cabinet minister, and as Hillier lights a victory cigar, he imagines that worthy dancing in, "thumbing his nose, going Yah like a schoolboy" (*TI,* 228).

Recognizing that the physical destruction of a few "bloody neutrals" is nearly as fruitless a children's game as espionage is, Hillier refrains from any further stunts. Nothing will satisfy him now save meaningful action against neutrality itself—a meaningful commitment to one of the great nameless opposed cosmic forces. Although government agencies and most other human organizations are unable to provide satisfactory avenues of commitment, there is a body in whom some clear recognition of the conflict exists—the church of Rome. Within this body, one can develop an understanding of the opposed forces without being hindered by "historico-geographical abstractions." Such ideological impedimenta and indeed the actions of some self-serving neutrals have occasionally corrupted and hindered the church, but their corrosive effects have not been fatal. Nothing has ever prevented the church from remaining committed to seeking an understanding of the great conflict and participation in it. For some of its members the whole thing can be summed up in the traditional concept of the struggle between the forces of good and the forces of the Devil, but there are others who recognize the possible inadequacy of this explanation.

Hillier, for one, thinks new terms are needed: "God and Notgod. Salvation and damnation of equal dignity, the two sides of the coin of ultimate reality" (*TI*, 237). He still believes "the evil" must "be liquidated," but experience has taught him it will not be found among those who serve either God or His opposite. Instead, it will be found among those who serve only themselves and deliberately maintain a cynical indifference toward the outcome of either the great conflict itself or any of the "temporal wars" that figure it. Damnation without dignity awaits these neutrals, and when Alan Walters objects that Hillier is veering perilously close to Manichaeism, Hillier replies:

> "If we're going to save the world . . . we shall have to use unorthodox doctrines as well as unorthodox methods. Don't you think we'd all rather see devil-worship than bland neutrality?" (*TI*, 238)

The only truly unorthodox implication of Hillier's teaching is that God's opposite is coeternal with and independent of God. This notion is, as Alan observes, part of the Manichean heresy that was so attractive to the youthful Augustine until the stupidity of Faustus discredited it for him.[2] It is a rather handy way of explaining Christianity's perennial embarrassment, the problem of evil, but it does not fit very neatly with traditional Christian concepts of the nature of God. In other respects, Hillier is quite orthodox in his thinking. Certainly Jesus Christ had little use for neutrals. The intolerable lukewarm stuff He would spit out of His mouth is "bland neutrality." The suggestion that devil worship is preferable to bland neutrality is almost in keeping with a Pauline emphasis on the primacy of conscience. The Pauline dictum "whatever is not of faith is sin" enjoins commitment towards the good as apprehended. One's conscience may or may not be well informed; the important thing is to heed whatever it dictates. Neutrals like Theodorescu have a moral sense, are even aware of their own rottenness, but they simply don't care. Appetite, not conscience, determines their actions.

Burgess has accomplished something rather amazing in *Tremor of Intent.* He presents violence and a variety of sensual experience with an evocative linguistic verve that must dazzle even the most jaded sensibility. At the same time, he makes some very provocative eschatological statements and conjectures. This in itself is amazing because the spy thriller by its very nature tends to avoid eschatology. If a reader is compelled to think about what may occur long after the Pentagon and the Kremlin are reduced to rock dust, he may find it difficult to worry about whether James Bond or Matt Helm can win another round for the Free World. Indeed, in the hands of a less competent novelist, any involved religious or philosophical questions would be a fatally distracting burden, but *Tremor of Intent* is such a brilliantly integrated package that somehow we pass quite easily from an irresistible, corrupting vicarious involvement in gastronomy, fornication, and bloodshed to involved questions of ethics and eschatology and back again.

The entire novel is integrated around the character of Hillier and again, in this characterization, we can see that Burgess has brilliantly succeeded in doing something that few writers of thrillers would even attempt. Hillier undergoes a radical spiritual transformation, a total relinquishment of a self that has been subordinate for a very long time to the exigencies of espionage. In less competent hands, such a rapid spiritual progress might not be convincing, but Burgess enables us to accept it without difficulty. Types of experience that make up nothing more than an involved obstacle course for a Bond or a Helm become for Hillier stages in a Dantesque/Augustinian spiritual progress. (I have already mentioned some of the Dantesque motifs.) Hillier's progress can also be seen as roughly analogous to that of the young Augustine. At the beginning of the book, in his epistle to his superiors, he says, "Look in my glands and not in the psychologist's report. I am mentally and morally sound. I tut-tut at St. Augustine, with his 'O God make me pure but not yet.' Irresponsible, no appointment duly noted in the diary, the abrogation of free will" (*TI,* 4). But Hillier is destined to receive the regenerating grace (or call it what you will) to rise miraculously like Augustine above aimless satyromania and slavery to appetite. Like Augustine, he becomes more and more preoccupied with the problem of evil, and he agrees with Augustine that its origin lies within the free will of self-serving rational creatures.[3] The major difference in their thinking concerns Manichean dualism. Hillier, like Augustine, is drawn to it, but, unlike Augustine, he seems to visualize ways in which either Manichaeism can be made compatible with orthodox Roman Catholic doctrine or vice versa.

In any case, whether or not Hillier's theology is sound, there can be little doubt that his story will be read and relished long after most of the contemporary spy thrillers have become literary curiosities of interest only to historians and idea-hungry dissertation writers. A critic in the *Saturday Review* aptly described it as "a feast for the senses, a banquet for the mind." It is certainly that, a total reading experience inviting complete sensual and intellectual involvement. It is in fact very nearly as gratifying a feast as *Nothing Like the Sun* and, like that masterpiece, must be ranked among the very best novels in the Burgess canon.

7

INCEST AND THE
ARTIST

MF

In a number of his novels, notably *The Wanting Seed, The Eve of St. Venus, The Worm and the Ring,* and *Enderby,* Burgess builds deliberately upon mythic frames and, like his master Joyce, even reveals some mythopoeic tendencies. Many of Burgess's characters are ironically modified archetypes who undergo archetypal experiences or ironic parodies of such experience. In addition, we find literal goddesses as well as goddess figures intervening in human affairs in order to revive and regenerate. However, none of these novels fits wholly within a mythic frame, presumably because Burgess found such archetypes too confining for his purposes. In *MF* he seems to have found a framework large enough to accommodate his total artistic design. He has fused incest myths—Algonquin Indian and Greek—and given them new meaning as a devastating satiric indictment of contemporary Western cultural values that goes well beyond the criticisms levelled in the *Enderby* novels.

The novel's title, *MF,* derives in part from the initials of the narrator/protagonist, Miles Faber. It also stands for "male/female," a valid human classification that the book implicitly contrasts with various false taxonomies, and it has another, related significance with reference to the all-encompassing theme of incest, especially when certain racial factors, bases of false taxonomies, are revealed in the conclusion. As everyone knows, the term *motherfucker* has a wide range of usages in the North American black idiom, and Burgess reveals that the range can be widened further to encompass totally the maladies currently afflicting Western culture.

As the novel opens, Faber is recalling a scene in a room of the Algonquin Hotel in New York City. He had been young then, an affluent orphan not yet twenty-one, and a student at an American Ivy League university. Like many of his fellow students, he had been perpetually filled with moral outrage by various more or less vaguely defined social and political injustices— "tyrannical democracies, wars in the name of peace, students forced to study

. . . skeletal Indian children eating dog's excrement" (*MF*, 4)[1]—and on one occasion he had sought to express his outrage in an unoriginal, ineffectual, yet satisfying manner—by public copulation in front of the university library. Like the creator of a recent play featuring copulation on the American flag, he and his cheering student supporters had apparently hoped to make the American establishment see that this form of "obscenity" was much less obscene than its own obscenities of social and political injustice. His social conscience was not, however, his only or even his strongest motivation. To be able to protest one type of naked obscenity by means of another, using one's social conscience as an excuse, is an exhibitionist's dream, and Faber, as he readily admits, is a sexual exhibitionist. The exotic flesh of his partner in protest, Miss Ang, was another major stimulus to his social conscience.

As Faber casually defends his actions to the lawyer in charge of doling out his inheritance, we find he has been gifted with an Oedipean skill as a riddler. This talent in itself emphasizes his role as an archetypal MF, and it becomes more and more important as the mythic design of the novel is revealed. Like "that poor Greek kid" who had been crippled and left to die, he is propelled unwittingly but inexorably toward a solution to the riddle of his own origins and destiny. The gods have managed to place him under the influence of a professor who introduces him to the works of one Sib Legeru, a poet and painter who had lived, created, and died in almost total obscurity on the Carribean island of "Castita." The samples he has seen of Leguru's work lead Faber to hope that the main corpus will reveal the "freedom" he passionately yearns to see expressed in art—"beyond structure and cohesion . . . words and colors totally free because totally meaningless" (*MF*, 11). To be vouch-safed this vision, he must make a pilgrimage to the island and seek out a kind of museum where Legeru's works have been decently interred.

The process of reaching this shrine is long and arduous. Initially, Faber is delayed by the efforts of the lawyer, who, it turns out, is seeking to prevent fulfillment of a curse of incest that hangs over the house of Faber. The young man is told that he is the offspring of an incestuous union of brother and sister, and that this same union has produced a sister he has never been allowed to meet. One of the chores laid upon the executors of his will by the remorseful incestuous father has been to maintain a safe distance between young Faber and his sister. By what would seem to be an incredible coinci-dence, her hiding place happens to be the island home of the late Sib Legeru. Actually, as Faber is destined to discover, there is much more than coinci-dence involved.

Prodded on by the insatiable curiosity of a riddler, he will not be persuaded to delay his pilgrimage until the occasion of sin can be removed. His haste is stimulated to some degree by a desire to see the sister who has been so deceitfully hidden away from him, but this does not overshadow his main goal, that of visiting the Sib Legeru shrine, there to imbibe true artistic "freedom." This experience will, he hopes, enable him to liberate his artistic energies, which will in turn enable him to cram together all the masses of inconsequential, unrelated data whirling about within the "junkshops" of his young brain so "inconsequentiality" will be forced to "yield significance." His choice of a medium to express his vision is dictated by his exhibitionism. He will write a play, the like of which, he fancies, has never been written. It will contain such memorable glimpses of the inconsequential as this scene:

> GEORGE: Half-regained Cimon the spider-crab.
> MABEL: A pelican fish of herculean proportions. The three Eusebii in baskets, I mean Basque berets.
> GEORGE: Yes yes. The thundering legions.
> These words to be spoken on a bed, with copulation proceeding. The significance, of course, would lie in the inconsequentiality. (*MF,* 57)

As he looks back on this youthful dream, Faber realizes that such scenes, charged with this sort of "significance," would hardly have made him one of the avant-garde among twentieth-century dramatists. But he had been young then, filled with blinding, formless "vision" and, like so many of his form-despising peers, utterly unable to grow in wisdom. Only after he has completed his pilgrimage and unravelled the great Sib Legeru riddle will he be able to see things clearly and divine the real "significance" of "inconsequentiality."

On the last leg of his journey to Castita, Faber sails as a galley hand on a yacht with two homosexuals who have little to do besides cruising about the Carribean in "desperate sexual bondage to each other" (*MF,* 55). One of them, the skipper, is a woman-hating ex-fashion designer. His faithless, helpless mate is a would-be poet. *MF* is not really a "contrived" book, but this voyage, like everything else in it, fits within the archetypal framework. Its archetypal function is emphasized during a storm, which very nearly finishes all three voyagers and which Burgess manages to draw with Conradian vividness and authenticity:

> God, like a dog, hearing his name, leapt in a great slavering joy upon us. The sea cracked and ground at the bones of the bows in a superb accession of appetite. We rode rockinghorse the quaking roof of the waves. Aspinwall cried:
> —God Jesus Christ Almighty.
> There was an apocolyptical rending above us and then the thudding of wings of a tight and berserk archangel. Aspinwall bounded for the deck, sandwich in hand, and I lurchfollowed. Brine spray spume jumped on us ecstatically. He threw his sandwich savagely into the rash smart slogger, which threw it promptly back, as he gaped appalled at the fluttering flagrags of old laundry on the bolt ropes, stormjib eaten alive, trysail sheetblocks hammering. He had time to look at me with hate before yapping orders that the wind swallowed untasted. A war, a war, or something. No, a warp. But what the hell was a warp? He tottered to the forecastle himself, cursing, while I clung to a rail. Then I saw what a warp was: a sort of towline. He and I, he still going through a silent-

movie sequence of heavy cursing, chiefly at me, got the trysail down and then
furled it with this warp to the main boom. There was no sail up at all now. The
yacht just lolloped moronically in the troughs. It was a complicated torture of an
idiot child tossed by one lot of yobs in a cloth, another gang of tearways singing
different songs loudly and pounding him, her, it with ice-lumps that turned at
once to warm water. Night, as they say, fell. At the helm I left Aspinwall,
whipped by warm water that broke in heads of frantic snowblooms, and went
below, being scared of being washed overboard. (*MF*, 62–63)

Shortly after he goes below, Faber is knocked unconscious by a piece of loose
furniture, but just before he goes under, he senses the significance of what is
happening to him. The would-be poet is cringing below, not actually praying
but wearing a sports shirt patterned with the utterances of mystical writers
that seems to pray for him. One saying that catches Faber's eye expresses
resignation and hope in the Resurrection: *"If He is found now, He is found then.
If not, we do but go to dwell in the City of Death"* (*MF*, 63). Immediately after
Faber notices this, the "oyster-ballocked poetaster" expresses both his terror
and his sense of the archetypal in one brief exclamation: "Jonah." At first
Faber seems to reject the notion of himself as a "Jonah," but a few moments
later, as he is plunging into insensibility, he accepts the role: "that inner pilot
was doused as I went down into slosh and debris, the belly of Jonadge, black
damp whaleboned gamp" (*MF*, 64). Faber is, in fact, going through an
essential stage in his progress toward knowledge. According to Joseph
Campbell, who has managed to discern a single archetype behind Jonah,
Oedipus, Hiawatha, Finn MacCool, and a thousand other faces in world
mythology, such plunges into darkness signify a hero's arrival at a "threshold"
of awareness:

> The idea that the passage of the magical threshold is a transit into a sphere of
> rebirth is symbolized in the worldwide womb image of the belly of the whale.
> The hero, instead of conquering or conciliating the power of the threshold, is
> swallowed into the unknown, and would appear to have died.[2]

Faber emerges from the dark womb of unconsciousness to clear daylight
and the landfall that means Castita. As he gropes about below deck, an
utterance that seems to be from the poetaster's shirt impinges itself upon his
brain: *"The fear of solitude is at bottom the fear of the double, the figure which
appears one day and always heralds death"* (*MF*, 66). Significantly, he can't find
this text anywhere on the shirt itself. It is in fact a message from the unknown
revealed to him while he was on the threshold of awareness awaiting a rebirth
of consciousness. It will have no meaning for him until he has solved the
riddles of Castita.

It is useful to review briefly the myths that Burgess has fused in construct-
ing his archetypal framework. His fusion of Algonquin Indian and Greek
incest myths has been noted. The Greek myth, the story of Oedipus, is quite

well known. Depending upon one's own assumptions, one can say it has
thrown both light and darkness over the fields of psychoanalysis and literary
criticism. There is something irresistibly fascinating about the story of the
brilliant riddler doomed by the gods, his own weaknesses, and his own
cleverness to parricide and an incestuous marriage. Everyone, including
Oedipus himself, is determined to prevent fulfillment of the curse, but
everyone plays completely into the hands of the gods. As many commentators have pointed out, it is not merely Oedipus's skill as a riddler or the
various coincidental happenings that lead to his entrapment. He is trapped
from the moment of his birth by the very blood in his veins. The son of a king
can hardly be expected to exhibit meekness when he is rudely ordered off a
road by a surly charioteer, and later, when he is offered a crown, the regal
blood in his veins will not let him refuse. All that is needed in addition is his
instinctive skill as a riddler, which enables him to destroy the Sphinx, but
which also accelerates the process of his own destruction by driving him on to
solve the riddle of Laius's murder and the plague afflicting Thebes.

The inevitability of the whole process and the inescapableness of the act of
incest are perhaps the most stimulating aspects of the myth. Joseph Campbell
views this and other incestuous unions in mythology as indicative of the
hero's arrival at a summit of awareness beyond the "threshold" previously
described:

> The mystical marriage with the queen goddess of the world represents the
> hero's total mastery of life; for the woman is life, the hero its knower and
> master. And the testings of the hero, which were preliminary to his ultimate
> experience and deed, were symbolical of those crises of realization by means of
> which his consciousness came to be amplified and made capable of enduring the
> full possession of the mother-destroyer, his inevitable bride. With that he
> knows that he and the father are one: he is in the father's place.[3]

However, neither Campbell nor Lord Raglan nor Sir James Frazer nor even
Emile Durkheim has satisfactorily accounted for all aspects of the Oedipus
myth.[4] They have not, for instance, suggested any logical connection between the hero's gift of riddling and his incestuous entrapment. Establishing
this connection was a task that remained for Claude Lévi-Strauss. In developing his theory, Lévi-Strauss was proceeding from his own doctrine that
archetypal myths are shared by cultures so widely separated that there could
be no direct exchange of ideas between them—as widely separated as, say,
aboriginal New England and Greece. His conclusions with regard to this
particular myth are most convincing, and one of the people he has convinced
is Anthony Burgess.

Burgess seems to have first encountered Lévi-Strauss's theory in the
latter's inaugural lecture as a newly appointed professor of the Collège de
France. In that lecture, subsequently translated into English as *The Scope of
Anthropology,* Lévi-Strauss recounted the following piece of Algonquin Indian folklore:

The Iroquois and Algonquin Indians tell the story of a young girl subjected to the amorous leanings of a nocturnal visitor whom she believes to be her brother. Everything seems to point to the guilty one: physical appearance, clothing, and the scratched cheek which bears witness to the heroine's virtue. Formally accused by her, the brother reveals that he has a counterpart or, more exactly, a double, for the tie between them is so strong that any accident befalling the one is automatically transmitted to the other. To convince his incredulous sister, the young man kills his double before her, but at the same time he condemns himself, since their destinies are linked.

Of course, the mother of the victim will want to avenge her son. As it happens she is a powerful sorceress, the mistress of the owls. There is only one way of misleading her: that the sister marry her brother, the latter passing for the double he has killed. Incest is so inconceivable that the old woman never suspects the hoax. The owls are not fooled and denounce the guilty ones, but they succeed in escaping.[5]

As Lévi-Strauss observes, the thematic parallels between this myth and the story of Oedipus are startling. For one thing, "the very precautions taken to avoid incest actually make it inevitable." Moreover, in both myths, much depends on the fact that two characters, supposedly distinct, become identified with each other. In the Indian myth, the hero is not technically related to his double; yet he and the double are one to the extent that the murder is a kind of suicide. Similarly, Oedipus has two distinct personalities—a condemned child long thought to be dead and a triumphant hero. Lévi-Strauss views the incest between brother and sister of the Iroquois myth as "a permutation of the Oedipal incest between mother and son." These parallels might of course be purely coincidental. More proof that we are dealing with the same archetype is needed, and Lévi-Strauss provides it by establishing that the owls in the Indian myth are a transformation of the riddling Sphinx destroyed by Oedipus. He notes that puzzles, proverbs, and riddles are rare among North American Indians. There is, however, in the Southwest a Pueblo ceremony in which clowns set riddles to the spectators. According to Pueblo myths, these clowns were born of an incestuous union. More significant perhaps is the fact that among the Algonquins themselves are "myths in which owls, or sometimes the ancestor of owls, set riddles to the hero which he must answer under pain of death." The fact that the sorceress in the myth is a mistress of owls, rational creatures capable of solving the riddle of her son's murder, strongly suggests a correlation between riddling and incest.

The nature of the correlation can be seen if one considers what a riddle is. It may, according to Lévi-Strauss, be defined simply as "a question to which one postulates that there is no answer." To make the definition more all-embracing, one may consider all the possible transformations of it. One may even invert its terms to mean "an answer for which there is no question." He points out that there are a number of myths that derive their dramatic power from this "symmetrical" inversion. The death of the Buddha follows inevitably upon the failure of a disciple to ask an expected question, and in some of the Grail myths, much depends upon the timorous reluctance of heroes in the presence of the vessel to ask, "What is it good for?"

Riddling and incest have become associated in myth because they are both frustrations of natural expectation. Just as the answer to a riddle succeeds against all expectation in getting back to the question, so the parties in an incestuous union—mother and son, brother and sister, or whatever—are brought together despite any design that would keep them apart. One can see the relation as well in that the hero himself is a living riddle whose solution is simultaneously a discovery of incest. Frequently, as in the case of Oedipus, discovery is hastened by the reaction of an outraged Nature: "The audacious union of masked words or of consanguines unknown to themselves engenders decay and fermentation, the unchaining of natural forces—one thinks of the Theban plague—just as impotence in sexual matters (and in the ability to initiate a proposed dialogue) dries up animal and vegetable fertility."[6]

Burgess was greatly stimulated as well as convinced by Lévi-Strauss's argument. In an essay entitled *If Oedipus Had Read His Lévi-Strauss,* he observes that a theme common to both the Algonquin myth and the story of Oedipus—that one may avoid incest by avoiding riddles—is also developed in Joyce's *Finnegans Wake.* Guilt-ridden Earwicker, whose name during his waking hours is Porter, transmits his obsessive passion for his daughter to his two sons, Shem and Shaun. Shem, who is to be identified with Joyce himself, is saved from incest with his sister by his inability to solve a riddle put to him by a chorus of angelic, "not quite human" girls. His failure is a humiliation, but it removes him from temptation. If Oedipus had not humiliated the Sphinx, he would have been devoured, but he would have been saved from incest. Burgess found additional evidence that the "riddle-incest nexus" is deep in human consciousness in his own writing. In his eschatological spy thriller *Tremor of Intent,* the hero is saved from a kind of incest by his refusal to listen to the decoding of a message.[7]

The riddle/incest bond was not one of Burgess's major concerns in *Tremor of Intent.* As with some of the most interesting themes in Shakespearean drama, it seems to have emerged on its own while the author was consciously preoccupied with something else. In *MF,* however, the theme of incestuous entrapment through riddling is everything. The adventures of Faber parallel both the story of Oedipus and the Algonquin myth. One may even discern figures of the Algonquin owls and the Theban sphinx. Professor Keteki (Sanskrit for "riddle"), who introduces Faber to the works of Sib Legeru, is remembered by him in very feathery terms, "cranelike in body, owl-headed, ululating a mostly unintelligible lecture, with the smell of Scotch as a kind of gloss" (*MF,* 6). The fact that he is engaged in a study of "Volitional Solecisms in Melville" seems to tie up with the novel's Jonah theme. Like one of the Algonquin owls, Keteki puts a riddle to his class that Faber manages to solve by an incredible suprarational process of association. Later, when Faber finds himself answering riddles to stave off starvation on Castita, he faces Dr. Gonzi, a riddling creature whose appearance is more lionlike than human. It is the misery of looking less than human, rather than the humiliation of being outwitted by Faber, that causes this creature to follow the example of the Theban sphinx in self-destruction.

Having overcome this latter riddling peril, Faber is led inexorably on toward a meeting with his double, a repulsive, foul-mouthed creature named Llew, whose taste in art runs to pop songs and pornography. What Llew represents is suggested by his mispronunciation of the name of the street where Faber is looking for the Sib Legeru museum. Llew encounters and attempts to rape Faber's sister in a house on the same street. Its name, "Indovinella," is Italian for "riddle," but Llew gets it out as "indiarubber," suggesting that he himself is a plastic creation, erasable, and dedicated to infertility, rather than a man. Llew's death at the hands of the girl's protector causes Faber little grief initially, but it is destined to force him into abandoning his identity and being trapped in incest.

As in the Algonquin myth, Faber is tested by a mistress of birds and is threatened by the birds themselves. Eventually, the curse of incest is exorcised. When this is accomplished, the real "meaning" of *MF,* the connection between incest and the maladies currently afflicting Western culture, especially art, is made clear. Although an awareness of the mythic framework and the influence of Lévi-Strauss is useful, such information is not essential to an appreciation of *MF,* any more than, say, a knowledge of Vico's theories of history is essential to an appreciation of *Finnegans Wake.* No writer of lasting quality is dependent to any degree on the exegesis of academic critics.

One way or another, Burgess reaches those who are capable of responding to serious literature with or without glosses. The most useful service an academic critic can perform for readers of a novel such as *MF* is to provide them with hints to aid them in increasing the sensual and intellectual enrichment they may find in any event. Such a truism may be a kind of reassuring answer to one of Faber's asides to the reader near the end of the novel:

> Don't try distilling a message from it, not even an expresso cupful of meaningful epitome or a sambuca glass of abridgement, *con la mosca.* Communication has been the whatness of the communication. For separable meanings go to the professors, whose job it is to make a meaning out of anything. Professor Keteki, for instance, with his *Volitional Solecisms in Melville.* (MF, 240–41)

As a member of the scribbling, riddling crew "whose job it is," I want to declare the purity of my intentions in presuming to discuss and evaluate *MF.* I would not attempt to extract any "separable meaning from it, any more than I would try to distill one from *The Wanting Seed.*

Like *The Wanting Seed, MF* is an invitation, an exhortation perhaps, to view

Western culture within an illuminating framework. Just as it is easier to comprehend two radically different, yet similar, philosophical and political avenues to insanity within the framework of an archetypal theological debate, so it is easier to see much of what ails Western culture within the framework of archetypal myth. If the academic exegete has any useful function at all, it is merely to encourage the reader to accept the invitation and test the adequacy of the framework even as he experiences the vision.

Burgess's mythic framework encompasses much of Western culture and especially those branches that seem to be flowering currently in North America. It is clear that Burgess's American experiences, perhaps as much as his reading of Lévi-Srauss, have had a great deal to do with generating his vision of incest. According to Miles Faber's grandfather, who may or may not be expressing Burgess's point of view, incest "in its widest sense" signifies "the breakdown of order, the collapse of communication, the irresponsible cultivation of chaos" (*MF*, 235). This same character, who has a Tiresian vision of the world's corruption as a result of a long lifetime's immersion in it, observes that the totally free (because totally meaningless) "works of Sib Legeru exhibit the nastiest aspects of incest. . . . In them are combined an absence of meaning and a sniggering boyscout codishness. It is man's job to impose order on the universe, not to yearn for Chapter Zero of the Book of Genesis. . . . Art takes the raw material of the world about us and attempts to shape it into signification. Antiart takes that same material and seeks insignification" (*MF*, 235).

For a number of reasons, one is liable to suspect these are Burgess's own sentiments. For one thing, they echo sentiments expressed by the autobiographical Shakespeare (WS) in *Nothing Like the Sun*. In refusing to support Essex's revolt, WS explains that "the only self-evident duty is to that image of order we all carry in our brains," and this duty has a special meaning for the artist: "To emboss a stamp of order on time's flux is an impossibility I must try to make possible through my art, such as it is" (*NLS*, 199). We might also recall the opposition between the honest, technically competent poetry of Mr. Enderby and the utterly chaotic, meaningless drivel of the chaos and acid-inspired makers who scorn him. But one need not go beyond *MF* itself to find Burgess's sympathies with the view that art demands discipline, not an incestuous abandonment to an illusion of freedom. One need only look at young Faber himself, a pedantic, thoroughly obnoxious, confused product of a culture that exhibits a curious fondness for chaos, which it tends to equate with freedom. In the realms of art especially, there is a reluctance to label the chaotic and undisciplined according to data gathered by sense and intellect. Take, for instance, the case of the linguistic team who gave their computer a free hand in turning out a volume of "poetry" and then sent the volume around to some *soi-disant* literati. One set of readers offered the "poet" a full university scholarship. Others expressed concern for his mental and emotional well-being. Happily, a few *poets* were able to tell that the verse had not been written by a human being. Or take the case of the painter who spreads his oils with the rear wheel of his motorcycle. Or the respected composer who offered an audience a symphony of total silence. As *MF* suggests, this chaos obsession and reluctance to call *merde* by its proper name shows itself most insidiously on the campus, frequently in the attitudes of people such as Professor Keteki who should know better because they have the cultural yardsticks of the past at their command. All too frequently, the students are seriously taken in by works such as those of Sib Legeru, but occasionally they are not. Recently, I was delighted to overhear two undergraduates extemporizing between fits of laughter a scene from an imagined play by a respected Legerulike writer. It sounded quite a bit like the scene Faber imagines in his projected play. Their healthy laughter was one of the most reassuring sounds I have heard in months.

The focus of *MF* is broader than art—much broader. The whole pattern of Western culture, as Burgess sees it, is incestuous. Race consciousness in particular, which has in no way diminished in recent years, is symptomatic of an incestuous pull. In Burgess's view, "the time has come for the big miscegnation."[8] All of the races must overcome their morbid preoccupation with color identity and face the merger that is inevitable in any event. As *The Wanting Seed* suggests, population pressures will make any notion of racial compartmentalization utterly absurd in the not-too-distant future. But aside from this, Burgess sees race consciousness itself as fundamentally absurd, and he has illuminated the absurdity in a number of books. In *A Vision of Battlements,* for one, he has Richard Ennis imagining how life in postwar England would be for him and the beautiful Spanish girl he loves:

> . . . Concepción in the fish queue, the "bloody foreigner" in the English village, the "touch of the tar brush" from the tweeded gentry. He foresaw the ex-prisoner-of-war Luftwaffe pilot, flaxen, thick-spoken, absorbed into the farming community playing darts with the boys ("That were a bloody good one, Wilhelm"), Concepción and himself in the cold smoke-room ("That foreigner that there Mr. Ennis did marry"). (*AVOB,* 71)

Throughout the *Malayan Trilogy* race consciousness is shown to be the major factor that will inhibit cultural progress in the new Malaysia. In *MF* Burgess focuses on what he regards as the absurd and incestuous black preoccupation with race. Some months before he began writing *MF,* he observed "that it's about time the blacks got over this business of incest, of saying they're beautiful and they're black, they're going to conquer, they're going to prevail."[9] In *MF* itself, he attempts to jolt his readers out of their race consciousness by allowing them to finish the entire novel before he reveals a racial factor that most writers would feel compelled to clarify on their first page.[10] One of the "alembicated morals" he mockingly offers the reader is "that my race, or your race must start thinking in terms of the human totality and cease weaving its own fancied achievements or miseries into a banner. Black is beauty, yes, BUT ONLY WITH ANNA SEWELL PRODUCTS" (*MF*, 241).

Burgess has invited us to recognize, if we can, the incestuous pattern on the racial plane as it mirrors the incestuous yearning in art or, rather, antiart. The two are directly related in that they both reveal a colossal willed ignorance and laziness on the part of Western man. Just as it's a good deal easier to shirk the burdens of true art in the name of "freedom," so it is easier to allow oneself to be defined and confined by a racial identity so the search for truths that concern "the human totality," truly a "man's job," can be put off. Both the "freedom" of the artist who incestuously allows his own masturbatory "codishness" to create for him and the "identity" of the black or white racial chauvinist are pernicious illusions that the artist, perhaps more than anyone else, is bound to expose.

To the extent that it deals with the role of the artist, *MF* can be seen as a continuation of the explorations in *Enderby*. The works of Sib Legeru, like the insipid wailing of Yod Crewsy or the supposedly "relevant" babbling of the acid heads, are pseudoart or antiart. Their acceptance as real art has been encouraged by such revered "prophets" as Marshall McLuhan, but, as an *Enderby* persona suggests, we need not fear that posterity will be fooled. *MF* reassures us of the same thing by affirming a faith in basic sense experience. All the spurious creation of Sib Legeru "stinks" in a metaphorical sense, and some of it stinks quite literally, and only a pseudointellectual little wretch like Faber, or one of his professors like Keteki, could be taken in indefinitely.

MF can also, as suggested, be seen as a continuation of those novels in which Burgess focuses on Western man's myopic view of his own nature. In his dystopian books *A Clockwork Orange* and *The Wanting Seed* especially, he focuses on Western man's insane compulsion to generalize about the nature of "man" at the expense of any true understanding of human problems. As social order is sought on the basis of preconceived "Pelagian" or "Augustinian" notions about the nature of man, society is propelled toward moral chaos. Similarly, in *MF* we see that the yearning for freedom through chaos is actually a yearning for slavery. Another "alembicated moral" Faber offers his readers is that "a mania for total liberty is really a mania for prison, and you'll get there by way of incest" (*MF*, 241). Taking the application of this at its broadest, one realizes that Western man's failure to understand himself causes him to develop a spurious concept of freedom and to seek ruinous avenues to that freedom. Narrowing the focus to America (and *MF* invites this focus), one can see a strong tendency to preserve "freedom" through incestuous avenues. The "yellow horde" must be kept back in Asia and controlled in Latin America. Non-American cultures must either be resisted or Americanized. World federalism, the concept of world government, is viewed as un-American and dangerously subversive. This incestuous tendency of America, this feeling that it can be saved only if it turns in upon itself and either excludes or converts the corrupting influences from the great world outside, is not an avenue to freedom. It imprisons America. Many supporters of the recent "crusade" in Indo-China, who considered it essential to the preservation of American liberty, would like to see Washington politicians replaced with generals. Only in this way, they feel, can America be "free."

Some readers may think: "You're reading all of this into Faber's 'alembicated moral?' He was only talking about the 'mania for liberty' and the incestuous impulse in art, and, to some extent, race consciousness." However, as Burgess says, we may take what we please from his story, "any damned nonsense" we "happen to fancy." He has defined incest for us and invited us to find it where we will. Some readers will find it elsewhere in the American or Western consciousness. The only thing a reader will not be able to do is deny that "incest" is practiced.

Most readers will probably enjoy *MF* less than some of Burgess's other books, not because it is inferior artistically, but simply because it is a devastating satire with so much of Western culture as its object. Satire that cuts in so savage and sweeping a fashion and at the same time demands too much in the way of intellectual involvement will almost always be less "enjoyable" than gentler entertainments. But just as a strong-stomached and agile-witted playgoer can find *Troilus and Cressida* or *Measure for Measure* more rewarding than Shakespeare's early romances, so a reader can find *MF* more rewarding, as well as challenging, than Burgess's lighter entertainments. (If one is repelled by *MF,* one had better avoid Petronius and Ben Jonson and Swift and Nabokov.) Like nearly all of Burgess's novels, it is a piece of linguistic wizardry that delights and never wearies. If one objects that Faber does not sound like a typical twenty-year-old university student, one is overlooking the clearly indicated fact that Faber is *not* a twenty-year-old student but a highly literate middle-aged man looking back upon his youth and remembering imperfectly the ways in which he spoke.

When Burgess wants to give us the sounds of youth, he is quite capable of doing so, as he did in *A Clockwork Orange.* If one happens to be an American and finds the directions of the satire unsettling, one may take some comfort in the fact that the objects of attack are much broader than America. One can see much of Western culture in general being satirized. One may even discern the outlines of Burgess's former residence, Malta, in the island of "Castita." Look in a gazetteer and you will not find Castita, but if you try an Italian/English dictionary, you will find "chastity." There is plenty of irony in the name, and the picture of the island and its government is not flattering. The abundant references to things Maltese and bits of "Castitan" history point strongly to that island. One might mention in particular the name "Gonzi," which the archbishop of Malta shares with the riddling, lionlike creature who attempts to trap and kill Faber.

For all its bitterness, however, *MF* does contain the seeds of Burgess's great affirmation of the power of the creative will in his next novel, *Napoleon Symphony.* Like Ben Jonson's *Poetaster,* it spares no spleen in attacking the enemies of art, but, like that comedy, it affirms the power of art itself to triumph. Faber does, after all, grow in wisdom to an understanding of the difference between art and antiart, even as the court of Augustus is enlightened by Jonson's autobiographical Horace. Jonson, however, never went very far beyond this limited affirmation to depict the divine power of a truly great artist "to impose order on the universe." It remained for his greatest contemporary to dramatize (in *The Tempest*) the power of art informed by love. Burgess's faith in the power of art, as we see in *Napoleon Symphony,* is much stronger than Jonson's, more like Shakespeare's. Even when he produces yet another *Poetaster*-like satire against the enemies of art, in his *Clockwork Testament,* the same affirmation is implicit.

8

THE ARTIST AS CONQUEROR: *NAPOLEON SYMPHONY*

One of Beethoven's biographers, John N. Burk, remarks that "those who have listened to the 'Eroica' Symphony have been reminded, perhaps too often, that the composer once destroyed in anger a dedication to Napoleon Bonaparte."[1] In Burk's view, the Symphony No. 3 in E Flat, Opus 55 "is entirely incongruous as applied to the vain and preening Corsican and his bloody exploits."[2] Indeed, as one listens to the symphony, described by Paul Henry Lang as "the greatest single step made by an individual composer in the history of the symphony and the history of music in general,"[3] and tries to hear its heroic movements as a celebration of the little tyrant's career, one readily perceives the incongruity, and musicologists now seem to agree that the music looks well beyond Napoleon. Although it may have been conceived as a portrait of Bonaparte, it became a portrait of Beethoven himself, a defiantly heroic assertion of his willpower and freedom as an artist when first confronted with the threat of total deafness.[4]

Like Beethoven, Burgess has defiantly asserted his own willpower as an artist more than once: answering the threat of imminent death by an unprecedented outpouring of novels; satirizing, in *Enderby* and *MF,* the enemies of art and purveyors of pseudoart; and asserting, in *A Clockwork Orange* and *The Wanting Seed,* his own sense of freedom in an age that would generalize "man" into mechanical thinghood. It is no coincidence that Alex, the demonic protagonist of *A Clockwork Orange,* should have a special fondness for Beethoven. When he recovers both his freedom to choose and his passion for classical music, he calls for "the glorious Ninth of Ludwig van," and the novel, a celebration of the capacity of "brave malenky selves" to overcome the will-sapping tyranny of modern society's "big machines," concludes appropriately with the imagined sound of the *Ode to Joy.*[5]

Burgess's *Napoleon Symphony* is an assertion of his willpower as both musical and literary artist. He has sought to impose the form of the *Eroica* upon the whole course of Napoleon's life from the marriage with Josephine until his death. Although there have been many attempts in the past to musicalize literature—Eliot's *Four Quartets* and Aldous Huxley's *Point Coun-*

terpoint, for instance—Burgess's imposition of musical form seems to go well beyond most of these. *Napoleon Symphony* is, as he explains, in the "shape" of the *Eroica:*

> On the most general level this means that the book is in four movements, just as a symphony is in four movements. But it means a little more than that. It means that the proportions of each movement are exactly matched in the novel itself. What I did was to play the symphony over on the phonograph and time each movement, and I worked out a kind of proportion of pages to each second or five seconds of playing time. So there is a correspondence between the number of pages and the actual time taken for the thing to be performed. But more than that, I've worked with the score of the *Eroica* in front of me, the orchestral score, and I've made each section within a given literary movement correspond to a section within the *Eroica,* so that a passage of eight bars would correspond to so many pages in the novel. And not only the length, the number of pages, but the actual dynamics, the mood and tempo.[6]

As with Burgess's translation of Wagner in *The Worm and the Ring,* the discrepancy here between subject matter and heroic musical form suggests that the book is to be viewed as burlesque.[7] Indeed, the *Eroica* is even more "incongruous" as applied to Burgess's characterization of Napoleon (N) than it is to the Napoleon preserved by historians and biographers. But the label "burlesque" is unsatisfactory for a number of reasons. For one thing, Burgess's portrait of N is no caricature but a plausible and, at times, sympathetic presentation of the man. Burgess has maintained throughout his novel the heroic tone and dimensions of the symphony. He has not, as it were, reduced Beethoven to a lower, Napoleonic level. Rather, he has exalted the little tyrant to a truly heroic plane by fusing him with the Promethean, perhaps autobiographical, hero of the symphony. Comparison of *Napoleon Sympathy* with *The Worm and the Ring* may be fruitful in this regard. In *The Worm and the Ring,* one of his bitterest works, Burgess translates *Der Ring des Nibelungen* into a power struggle for the control of a grammar school in a little English borough. The mean, unheroic or antiheroic, petty nature of the strife is effectively emphasized by the Wagnerian heroic framework, even though the novel does conclude with something like a Wagnerian affirmation of hope in the redemptive power of love. *Napoleon Symphony,* too, is not without its share of bitter irony, but the ironic perspectives are conveyed in ways other than the mock heroic, and indeed the essentially heroic quality of the protagonist's aspirations and struggles is not questioned.

In the verse epistle to the reader that concludes the novel, Burgess says flatly:

> This is a comic novel and it must
> Be read as such, as such deemed good or bad—

He explains why he did not entitle it "The Napoleon Comic Symphony":

A name that reason forced me to reject,
Since *comic* leads the reader to expect
Contrivances of laughter: comic taste,
Like the term *comedy,* has been debased.
Arousing mirth—this is not what I'm at:
What's comedy? Not tragedy. That's that. (*NS,* 362)[8]

Viewing the novel as a whole suggests that Burgess's sense of "comedy" is vaguely Dantesque. It begins in the "hell," in an Elizabethan sense, of his passion for Josephine, moves on through purgatorial campaigns in Italy, Egypt, and Russia, and finally concludes, not with his death on St. Helena, but with a resurgence of an earlier triumphant mood as his partial fulfillment of the dream of a united Europe is prophesied, with even the British, "those bastards incorporated into the Great European Family. . ." (*NS,* 359). Within comedy of this kind, there is room for a great deal more than there is in the types of comedy recognized by modern taste and evaluated in terms of hilarity achieved. There is certainly room for hilarity and the farcical, the arousal of mirth and contrivances of laughter, but there is also room for representing a wide variety of human experiences, some arousing pity or sadness or even horror rather than mirth. This is the comedy of the Elizabethans, as well as Dante, the comedy of Marlowe, simultaneously exalting and mocking Promethean aspiration in *Tamburlaine* and *Faustus,* or Shakespeare in *Troilus and Cressida.* It is the comedy of Burgess in *Nothing Like the Sun, A Clockwork Orange,* and the *Malayan Trilogy.*

Napoleon Symphony is introduced by an overture in which we hear the reflections of three wedding guests awaiting, in company with the bride and a dozing registrar with a wooden leg, the arrival of the bridegroom. It is the evening of 9 March 1796. The tardy bridegroom is Napoleon. The bride-to-be is Josephine, and the three guests who will be witnesses are gentlemen who have shown themselves to be her good friends. By deft allusion, Burgess indicates the ways in which these men have proven their friendship, but a reader unfamiliar with Josephine's history might easily overlook some of these allusions and the concomitant playful ironies of the overture.[9] To one of these men, Jean Lambert Tallien, Josephine owes her life. Tallien was the man who courageously attacked Robespierre on the floor of the Convention and precipitated his downfall, thus serving France as well as rescuing Thérésia, the woman he loved and later married, from the guillotine. He also rescued his friend Josephine, then awaiting execution with other aristocrats in the Carmelite prison. Another guest/witness is Josephine's former lover Paul Barras, who has promised Napoleon command of the Army of the Alps as a wedding present if he marries Josephine. Barras hopes to solidify his own position as one of the five directors through the marriage:

And did not the way to the Alps lie (this was coarse, he admitted) between her legs? Take it another way and be calm: they were all three of them aristocrats, though those two from disregardable island colonies, speaking very provincial French, language with no kiss in the vowels. They all three had, in a sense, to cling together in a world ruled by the middle-class. A cast-off mistress settled in a reasonable marriage, a friendly man who took deep breaths and had a brain clever with cannonballs. The two were, so to speak, engines of his own survival. (*NS,* v)

Also present is Jérôme Calmelet, Josephine's lawyer, who has given her marriage encouraging approval after her notary, Raguideau, had tried strenuously to dissuade her and had deeply offended Napoleon. Thus within the brief space of the overture, we are reminded of much that has gone before, how Josephine has been led to this marriage and how France itself has been prepared for the same messianic "bridegroom." (One of Calmelet's irreverent little jokes likens N to the heavenly bridegroom for whom the virgins have been waiting.) When he finally strides in with a fourth witness, his aide-de-camp Lemarois, and commands the registrar to "Begin!" we are ready for the *Allegro con brio.*

Burgess's allegro opens with N in Italy, "midway between the navel of Nice and the genitals of Genoa" (*NS,* 7). Italy is a woman to be enjoyed, ripe to be ravished, and the passions that fill the young Napoleon are very much those of the ravisher. His honeymoon with Josephine has been all too brief, leaving him in a state of frustration and longing so manifestly obvious that his generals have secretly dubbed him "Wet Dream." The entire campaign, from his first victory at Montenotte to the fall of Mantua and the defeat of the last great Austrian offensive, is largely an expression of his passion for Josephine. Whether he happens to be immersed in complicated strategic planning or actually conducting a battle, she is never out of his thoughts. Indeed, he views the engaging of armies at Montenotte as emblematic of his love for her:

I take out your image and rain weeps on the crystal. I kiss the rain away and look down to see the interlocking of the blue and white ants. Three blue to two white, hand to hand, mostly bayonet-fighting, we have no problem. Your slim white back, I must imagine, is turned against the musket-puffs and the thin noises that rise from below. I lock you again in the warmth of my breast, out of the rain and slaughter. (*NS,* 9)

In presenting Josephine as the source of Napoleon's energy in this campaign, Burgess is not inventing. Vincent Cronin, a recent biographer of Napoleon, asserts that "Josephine, by inspiring Napoleon, was in one sense the heart of the Italian campaign."[10] His conclusion is based on the published *Lettres de Napoléon à Joséphine.*[11] Burgess goes well beyond the letters in revealing N's passion, for his primary concern is to capture not merely N's passions but those conveyed by Beethoven in the allegro of the symphony.

Richard Wagner's description of the passionate development of the allegro in the *Eroica* is to some extent an accurate summation of the emotional interplay in the "first movement" of Burgess's novel:

> The *First Movement* embraces, as in a glowing furnace, all the emotions of a richly-gifted nature in the heyday of unresting youth. Weal and woe, lief and lack, sweetness and sadness, living and longing, riot and revel, daring, defiance, and an ungovernable sense of Self, make place for one another so directly, and interlace so closely that, however much we mate each feeling with our own, we can single none of them from out the rest, but our whole interest is given merely to this one, this human being who shows himself brimful of every feeling. Yet all these feelings spring from one main faculty—and that is *Force*. This Force, immeasurably enhanced by each emotional impression and driven to vent its overfill, is the mainspring of the tone-piece: it clinches—toward the middle of the Movement—to the violence of the destroyer, and in its braggart strength we think we see a Wrecker of the World before us, a Titan wrestling with the Gods.[12]

Through Burgess's swift-paced narrative, we experience the "daring, defiance, and an ungovernable sense of Self" in victory after victory. N's tremendous exhiliration is infectious, especially in the description of the daring gamble at the Lodi bridge. As Cronin observes, this victory was achieved largely as a result of Napoleon's success in nettling and goading his soldiers, playing upon their "horror of opprobrium" until he had them worked up to a reckless pitch of courage and they were ready for the suicidal storming of the bridge.[13] Burgess relates this episode from the points of view of N himself and the giant Savoyard Dupas who actually led the charge. Again, he goes well beyond where any biographer or historian could tread to describe how N *must* have felt:

> God almighty it was a near thing, Bonaparte was thinking, God almighty it wasn't planning this time, it was taking a chance, it was impossible gambling that came off, and it tastes like brandy, it feels like that delirious flying moment when you spend into her thighs, now that I know I am a living spirit and a very special one as well as a military library and a craftsman and a machine as modern as a semaphore telegraph or a hydrogen balloon. And suppose the cavalry had not been able to ford that river? They almost did not, almost, *almost*. It is in the region of Almost that the blood sings. We won, my love. Sixteen guns and nearly two thousand prisoners. Prisoners, my love, are such a nuisance. War feeds on war; what do prisoners feed on? (*NS,* 12–13)

Interlaced with these moments of supreme exhiliration are the woeful moments when Napoleon is filled with doubts and worries about Josephine. Even the delirious orgasmic joy of victory at the Lodi bridge is mixed with anguish as he takes out his miniature of her to kiss and discovers the crystal has been broken. Being superstitious, he assumes she is either "very sick or very unfaithful." This incident actually occurred and was related by Napoleon's aide-de-camp Marmont, but it did not occur until long after the victory at Lodi, on the date Joachim Murat arrived in Paris to escort Josephine to join Napoleon in Italy. Burgess, to achieve the close interlacing effect remarked by Wagner in the first movement, places it immediately after the battle.

The "force" that Wagner considers the mainspring of the first movement is conveyed by Burgess in various ways. The rapid tempo of events contributes to the effect, as does the juxtaposition of action scenes in Italy and Egypt with scenes in Paris involving little action. In some of the latter, we hear Barras, Talleyrand, and other politicians debating Revolutionary policy, philosophizing about history and entertaining the illusion that they can control N. In others we hear Josephine enjoying her lover Lieutenant Charles, and trying to cope with her husband's frightening, "not civilized" passion for her.

Josephine, certainly the most attractive and sympathetically drawn character in the novel, is simply unable to understand N's dynamism and her own role as inspiration. Her affair with Charles is well documented, and Burgess's invented conversations in her bed and elsewhere are probably close to what was actually said. Much of the lieutenant's success seems to have been due to his ability to make Josephine laugh, something Bonaparte could seldom do. She especially enjoyed his puns, as for example: *"Buonaparte est sur le pô, ce qui est bien sans Gênes* (Buonoparte is coolly performing on the Po [chamberpot])."[14] Burgess alters and improves this one considerably when we hear it amidst the swish of silk and the clink of medals at a ball celebrating one of N's victories: *"General Bonaparte has got off the Po and is now busily wiping up"* (*NS*, 14). Burgess's portrait of Josephine is somewhat reminiscent of Molly Bloom in *Ulysses,* and, like Joyce, he lavishes his most beautiful verbal music upon his heroine and her thoughts. In the overture, we do not hear her but only the appreciative reflections of Barras and the others. Later we hear her thoughts and are compelled to sympathize with her in her infidelity. N, for all his passion and sexuality, is a poor lover. He translates his lightning tactics of the battlefield to the bedroom, hardly bothering even to remove his sword in the transition:

> He floods in me like a river, she thought. Like urine.
> "Oh my God oh my. Angel oh my heart's. Blood. How I've been able to. Sustain this. Long time of waiting only God. And the angels know. And even now, my celestial vision, it is. As it was at the beginning. A snatch of heaven in your arms and then. Back to it."
> "To what?"
> "The war, Würmser, the Austrians. . . ."
> "We must have children of our own. *We will.*"
> And, straight to the target again, as ever, pushing the snarling bundle away, the reserves pouring in fast and joyful, he was back on to his angel and heart's blood. She tried to think of Charles, but it was difficult. The one did not fit easily into the other's body, not even in the dark. (*NS*, 17–18).

Like N, Josephine becomes both a historic and a mythic character. Noting Beethoven's fondness for Plutarch's *Lives* and the apparent influence of the parallel *Lives* upon the design of the *Eroica,* Burgess makes her assume the identities of both Cleopatra and Aphrodite. The two are brought together in the *Marcia Funebre* within the lyrical dream section that immediately precedes N's announcement that he is divorcing her. The two are already brought together by Plutarch in the famous description of Cleopatra on her barge that Shakespeare follows so closely in *Antony and Celopatra:*

> She was laid under a pavilion of cloth-of-gold of tissue, appareled and attired like the goddess Venus commonly drawn in picture; and hard by her, on either hand of her, pretty fair boys, appareled as painters do set forth god Cupid, with little fans in their hands with the which they fanned wind upon her. Her ladies and gentlewomen also, the fairest of them, were appareled like the nymphs Nereides (which are the mermaids of the waters) and like the Graces, some steering the helm, others tending the tackle and ropes of the barge, out of the which there came a wonderful passing sweet savor of perfumes that perfumed the wharf's side, pestered with innumerable multitudes of people. Some of them followed the barge all along the river's side, others also ran out of the city to see her coming in, so that in the end there ran such multitudes of people one after another to see her that Antonius was left post-alone in the market place in his imperial seat to give audience. And there went a rumor in the people's mouths that the goddess Venus was come to play with the god Bacchus for the general good of all Asia.[15]

Josephine's dream is a kind of surrealistic parody of this description ("NON-SENSE, NATURALLY, BUT RATHER CHARMING PLAYED ON flutes and oboes" [*NS,* 142]) in which she sees herself floating on a barge and wondering "whether she was being worshipped as a queen or as a goddess." Instead of floating toward a Bacchus, she is annoyed by a hirsute Silenus with the face of Tallien, "gibbering and really obscenely parodying the sacred act of love" (*NS,* 143). This appearance of Tallien in her dream is not really as "strange" as it appears to her, for the dream itself reveals what his preservation of her has enabled her to become—a comic Venus wedded to a comic Mars. Significantly, she becomes virtually identified in the dream with water, the life-giving element that Napoleon fears and that will contribute so much to his downfall. Like N in his own "water" section, Josephine hears, anachronistically, the sinister rhyme from Orwell's *1984*—"Here come a candle to light you to bed," and so on—in French translation. It may also be significant that the description of her riding foam-borne like Aphrodite with "a really beautiful shell-like pavilion" at her back echoes the description of the barge carrying Leicester and Elizabeth in *The Wasteland* (III, lines 280–85). This section of "The Fire Sermon" in Eliot's poem, it will be recalled, almost immediately precedes "Death by Water."

Upon waking, Josephine thinks with longing of the islands she had known as a girl, and again Burgess enforces her identification with both water and Venus:

> To get to Paris meant that horrid jolting over land, somehow very *male* in its roughness. The sea, the warm spicy sea, she never feared the sea, the sea was her element, the sea was a woman, *la mère la mer,* and lapped round a man and enclosed him and made him yield, yes, yield all. And now the sea had failed her. (*NS,* 146–47)

Josephine's trusting attitude toward the sea recalls the natural faith of another Burgess heroine, Beatrice/Joanna, whose prayer to the sea concludes *The Wanting Seed.* Like Beatrice/Joanna, Josephine symbolizes the unreasoning instinctual forces that will not be controlled by the imposition of abstract ideas such as "stability" or the "general good." For Josephine, facing the catastrophe of divorce, the only thing to be considered is the *fact* that Napoleon still loves her, and she is utterly unresponsive to the torrent of abstractions that he uses to console and justify himself:

> "The stupidity lies in in, where does the stupidity lie? Fate? Destiny? The force of history?" Those big words which were *abstract* were making him tremble less. . . . The national interest . . . National welfare . . . considerations of state. . . . (*NS,* 148–49)

Her union with Napoleon is actually a grotesque parody of the mythic union of Mars with Venus and what it symbolizes, the union in elemental strife of the forces that move the universe—creation and destruction—and the interplay between desire and conflict. She can subdue N, as Venus could subdue Mars, but, unlike Mars, N is capable of escaping from her.

The capacity to escape from distressing concrete reality into an agreeable metaphysical haze of abstraction is one of the key traits of Burgess's Napoleon. When, for instance, he is caught in a potentially humiliating situation in Egypt, surprised in bed with a young officer's wife by the officer himself, he treats the young man to a lecture on metaphysics in which he asserts his own ability to control history by choosing whether or not to allow events to remain upon the "terrain" of time. Later, addressing his weary officers during the retreat from Moscow, he quickly glosses over the appalling facts of their situation and moves on to justify the mad expedition in heady terms: "the principles of the Revolution," "the Eternal Spirit of Reason," the "Empire of Man," "Fraternity," "Equality . . . and . . . the other thing," as well as "our simple pure and, yes, *Christian* doctrine" (*NS,* 201). Then, with a final warning against an unidentified "Antichrist," he embraces them all and leaves them to extricate the Grand Army without him.

That abstract ideals are potential avenues to moral idiocy is one of the most recurrent themes in Burgess's fiction. It is most fully developed in *The Wanting Seed* and *A Clockwork Orange,* in which he satirizes both "Pelagian" revolutionary idealism and "Augustinian" reactionary cynicism, opposing philosophical stances that share an inability to come to terms with the realities of human experience on any plane but the abstract.[16] "Liberty" and the other abstract ideals of the Pelagians based upon an optimistic view of "man" and his potential are naturally a good deal more attractive than those of Augustinians, who tend to be preoccupied mainly with achieving an ideal of "stability." They are also more conducive to hazy thinking and indifference to concrete perceptual reality. Napoleon, an intellectual heir of the Age of Reason and the Rousseauvian tradition, is very much a Pelagian and in some ways, as one character tells him, "nihiliscient." The unwillingness of so many of his fellow Europeans to accept his design for a united Europe utterly baffles him.

Pelagianism, as Tristram Foxe, the history-teacher protagonist in *The Wanting Seed,* tells his class, breeds "DISAPPOINTMENT," and the second movement, the Marcia Funebre, in *Napoleon Symphony* is integrated about the theme of disappointment. The coda in the allegro is brought to a triumphant conclusion with N crowning himself emperor and Josephine empress. The second movement opens with a passage in verse:

> There he lies
> Ensanguinated tyrant
> O bloody bloody tyrant
> See
> How the sin within
> Doth incarnadine
> His skin
> From the shin to the chin (*NS*, 125)

In attempting to capture the mood and tempo of the *Eroica,* Burgess uses a great deal of verse, and it is possible frequently to discern the particular passage he is following in the orchestral score. This passage, for instance, is clearly the statement of theme that opens the second movement and recurs, either whole or in part, throughout it:[17]

Marcia funebre Adagio assai ♪= 80
sotto voce
Oboe
Violin I
Violin II
Viola
Cello
Bass
pp
Ob.
Vl. I
Vl. II
Vla.
Vc.
Cb.
p
sf

The same theme is stated by the slightly varying verse passages presenting Josephine as Cleopatra and/or Aphrodite:

> See the re-
> Incarnate Cleopatra
> Barge burning on the water.
>   Bare
> Rowers row in rows.
>   Posied rose. (*NS,* 156)

This particular passage is printed parallel to the "Ensanguinated tyrant" passage at the end of the section in which N announces the divorce. He and Josephine are lying in bed together after passionate love making generated by the awful word *divorce.* The two passages also lie side by side making very different verse statements but stating musically the same theme of death and disappointment. The same theme is stated also in verse passages woven through the flashbacks dealing with the Russian campaign:

> See a fif
> ty mile long column shuffle
> through
> Borovsk and Vereya (*NS,*172)

Comparison with the corresponding passages in the orchestral score reveals that Burgess has made each syllable of his verse passages correspond to a note in Beethoven's theme statement. The passages of orchestral score must, however, be copied to leave some space for the words. Burgess's own notation reveals the necessary spacing:[18]

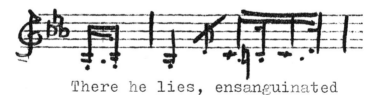

Maintaining his spacing throughout the theme statement enables us to perceive the total correspondence of Burgess's verse passages:[19]

There is a significant addition in Burgess's verse rendering—the bitter, indeed "sneering," tone that mocks rather than mourns its subject. This and the incarnadining "sin" are not to be found in Beethoven's statement expressing sorrowful acceptance of a great man's death.

To conclude our brief examination of correspondences, we may observe that the second subject of the Marcia Funebre is in the major and has words to it like this:[20]

O Deutschland arise.   Light is rising in the

When Beethoven recapitulates the theme, he adds a note. Adhering to every note, Burgess produces the following: "Light is rising in the *echt* Deutschlander skies" (*NS,* 211).

By these recurrent theme statements Burgess maintains, musically as it were, the sombre mood of the Marcia Funebre while his N reviews, chiefly by means of flashbacks within dreams, the disastrous retreat from Moscow and a series of lesser disappointments. The Russian invasion was a humiliating failure for Napoleon, but he emerged from it unscathed to raise still another huge army to fight the Prusso-Russians. But what of the Great Army that followed him into Russia? What of the thousands he left behind, killed in battle or left to face castrating Cossacks and freezing temperatures? Burgess presents all the horrors of the retreat from their points of view. An especially memorable horror, as it is narrated by participants of various ranks, is the celebrated crossing of the Berezina, a feat described by Cronin as "one of the most remarkable . . . in the history of warfare."[21] Cronin is one of the few historians to turn his attention away from the cool brilliance of Napoleon

long enough to mention that most of the four hundred pontoneers who made
this remarkable feat possible "were to die as the result of the icy twenty-four
hours they spent bridging the river."[22] Burgess interweaves the imagined
recollections of one of the few surviving pontoneers with what appears to be
either a historian's account or an official report based upon more detached
observation, set forth perhaps in the snugness of a study or a staff officer's
quarters:

> General Eblé spent a great deal of the night attempting to clarify the situation to
> the apathetic and ragged companies, who did not appear to understand either
> plain language or gesture, namely that orders from Imperial Headquarters had
> been received for the firing of the bridges immediately after the transit to the
> western shore of the rearguard of the Ninth Corps. Arguing all fucking night
> with them and himself near dropping with the fatigue while the rest of us
> bivouacked down after we'd melted ice and made stews of the frozen horseflesh
> that we'd hacked hacked away at. It was hard for some of us to get any sleep at
> first because we'd had the figures about the Engineers, we were down from four
> hundred to about forty, no wonder the work had seemed to get tougher all the
> time. Forty of us, Jesus Christ. (*NS*, 187)

Musically, "the crossing of the Berezina is an exact double fugue, corresponding to the one in the Marcia Funebre."[23]

This nightmare is followed by the descriptions of some typical heroic
deaths during the remainder of the retreat. One man represents the confusion of many as he spends his final thoughts upon a supposed purpose of the
invasion, to strike a blow at England and coerce Russia into supporting the
Continental System:

> Sergeant Huppe knew at odd intervals that they were evacuating Russia and had
> crossed a big river to do it and as soon as they saw the Niemen again they would
> be really on their way home, but he knew that the main enemy was England and
> why in God's name had they had to march into Russia in order to fight England?
> Because Russia was not supporting the Continental System. And what was the
> Continental System? It was everybody all being forced to band together to stop
> England exporting the things she manufactured into Europe, that was to say the
> French Empire. So you marched over half a million men into Russia to make the
> Czar or Tsar start supporting the Continental System again. But if supporting
> the Continental System was the most important thing in the world, then why
> was the Great Army not supporting it? Sergeant Huppe had had undeniable
> proof until very recently that army boots were coming from England—a tag in
> the inside of the boot said NOTTINGHAM, now disintegrated along with the
> boot, N and TT and NGH and M lowing like ghost-cows through the steppe
> winds. Sergeant Huppe composed himself for death inside the frozen shell of a
> horse. I am your little shuddering foal, give birth to me, huppe huppe, gee up,
> whoa, Continental System. (*NS*, 188.)

Although N survives the Russian campaign, he is forced throughout the
novel's second movement to come to terms with his own mortality, to face

the concrete fact of death against which no *"abstract* nonsense," as Josephine terms it, will protect him. Before the Russian invasion, at the Battle of Regensburg in 1809, he had been wounded in the foot by a musket ball, and shortly afterwards, at Schönbrunn during a review of the troops after the Wagram victory, a Saxon student, Frederick Stapps, had tried to kill him. Questioned, Stapps admitted he would have tried to kill Francis of Austria too, "but Francis had sons to succeed him."[24] More than ever, Bonaparte became desperate to produce an heir, hence the divorce with Josephine and the search for a new empress who could bear children as well as strengthen alliances. Burgess imagines a conversation between Stapps and Bonaparte, which the latter recalls while he is drowzing in the Kremlin bedchamber. The attempted assassination itself is a reminder of his own personal mortality, but the dialogue with Stapps that follows is even more disturbing as N is forced to view the possibility that everything he has sought to achieve, everything he represents, is equally mortal. Stapps tells Bonaparte that he is living in the eighteenth century, blind to the "change and science" that will transform Europe in the nineteenth. Stapps's conception of "change and science," however, is completely bound up with his German nationalism, his sense of the *Volk* and its destiny. (Stapps refers to the Germans as *Der Volk,* not *Das Volk,* and thus provides an important musical hint. The *DER* is meant to jolt the alert reader into seeing that S, which is German for E flat and used as such in Schumann's "sphinxes," is not there. We are not, in other words, in the minor mode just now, but in the major—with the E natural [dEr] sticking out.)[25] His vision helps Napoleon believe what he wants to believe, that his would-be assassin is mad, blinded by an illuministic vision that could not be reached by an exercise of reason, "the true French commodity." He proceeds to lecture Stapps on "what our modern history is all about," excluding nationalism as a factor and asserting confidentially that a "glorious piece of modern history is still proceeding" as Europe continues to free itself of the "dirty past." To counter this optimistic discourse, Stapps need only remind N of the reluctance of some countries, notably Spain and England, to free themselves of the "dirty past" and accept a Napoleonic liberation.

There are many such dialogues about history in Burgess's fiction. Typically, as in *A Vision of Battlements* or *The Wanting Seed,* it is less of a dialogue than a lecture to listeners who contribute little in reply. What makes Napoleon's exchange with Stapps so memorable is the irony arising from the fact that both men are simultaneously right and wrong. N has indeed failed to reckon with nationalism as a significant obstacle to the achievement of his great designs. He does, however, have the uneasy feeling "that what he was doing for Europe was teaching it the most efficient techniques for rising against him" (*NS,* 135). Having swept away or reformed so many venerable institutions and social structures in the name of freedom, he has shown to revolutionary forces (including nationalism) the vulnerability of all institutions and structures, including his own creations. For his part, Stapps is so full of ideology and the dream of Aryan supremacy that he cannot appreciate Napoleon's vision. Ironic, too, is the fact that both tyrant and would-be assassin represent in their thinking many of the same hideous dehumanizing forces of the future. Burgess strengthens this suggestion by having Stapps anachronistically quote from Hans Sachs's monologue at the end of *Meistersinger,* which is not to be written (by Wagner) for another sixty years. Under the illusion that they stand merely for opposed ideals, they actually represent complementary modes of "modern" thinking that will make possible the great genocidal horrors of the twentieth century.

Stapps sounds like a Nazi as he discourses on the necessity of keeping Aryan blood free of Jewish and other admixtures from "lower races." Failure to maintain this purity will cause Jesus Christ to turn His back on the German race. He argues against the imposition of a *Pax Gallica* as "inimical to the evolution of the German, that is to say human, race." His authority for the latter argument is Napoleon's great enemy, Baron von Stein.[26] He simply rejects N's suggestion that either Christ or Stein could have any blood in their veins other than "the *echt* blood of the Aryans." Thus he represents, in addition to the types of idealism that will cause future Germans to become Nazis, a kind of typically modern willed ignorance made possible by either a compartmentalization of awareness or what Orwell labelled "doublethink." Anything that conflicts with the ideology or self-image a people wants to maintain can simply be shut away in a sealed compartment of the mind, as the concentration camps were shut out of the consciousness of wartime Germany. Or as in the case of America in Vietnam, a people can entertain simultaneously contradictory ideas regarding its national purpose and resist all attempts to illuminate the contradiction.

Napoleon, too, represents the doublethinking idealism of the future, but this is shown more clearly earlier in the novel, when he orders the slaughter of four thousand Turkish prisoners at Jaffa. This particular atrocity was necessitated by the French army's insufficient food supply and the inability of the Turks to grasp the idea of parole in war. In fact, Napoleon did not give the orders for the slaughter until after he had consulted with his senior officers for two days and the majority of them had decided there was nothing else to do. Burgess does not leave out this council of war, but the reader is not left with the impression that Bonaparte is yielding to the majority's will. A fleeting image of the Marquis de Sade, whose name he cannot remember, crosses his mind as he addresses his staff at the conclusion of the two-day discussion:

> "We have to decide now how to execute a regrettable duty, putting out of our minds the humane philosophies on which our Revolution is based, thinking only, as soldiers should, of the technic or method." A man full of dreams of slaughter and earthquakes, frotting his yard with glee as he dreamed. (*NS,* 47)

The affair gives N a vision of a near future in which efficiency is the only god and morality based on other considerations is a mere sentimental hangover from bygone ages:

> "Think about it, gentlemen." He took on a visionary look that the fires made devilish, angelic. "Conceivably a thesis might be written, a considered conspectus drawn up. The army's functions expand, we have our *Institut,* we need theory, thought, speculation, philosophy, all within the army. Consider, for instance, the efficient annihilation of a whole disaffected city. The unventilated room crammed with subjects—we must not think of victims, prisoners, the terms being emotive—and the introduction, by a simple pumping device, of some venomous inhalant. Our army chemists may work on such things. New methods, gentlemen, for new wars. We are done with dancing minuets." (*NS,* 48)

Significant in this regard is Napoleon's almost inhuman freedom from guilt. Like Hitler, he is human enough in his relationships with women, but, like Hitler, he is capable of abandoning every human feeling that might restrain implementation of a policy, and the suffering he causes comes not near his conscience. On the eve of his coronation as emperor, when he and Josephine are about to be remarried within the church, he encourages her to go to confession but dismisses her suggestion that he too confess: "My conscience is clear, I think. I think my conscience is clear. Venial sins, perhaps. No more" (*NS,* 118). In a recent interview, Burgess remarked that "the sense of guilt is essentially human, and any society which doesn't know guilt is probably a doomed society." He observed that America had only recently "learned to be guilty," had only recently experienced a sense of sin, as a result of the Mei-Lai massacre.[27] But there is a tendency, remarked by one of Burgess's characters in *The Eve of St. Venus,* for any people living in the twentieth century to lose its sense of sin: "The concept of sin seems to be dead. It's been expelled from the Garden. Freud and Marx hold up their flaming swords" (*ESV,* 51). There are other sword holders—high priests of the god Efficiency, social engineers, and other diminishers of the individual, responsible self—and these, too, Burgess has represented, or introduced, in his bloody but guiltless little tyrant, ensanguinated herald of the modern age.

N's sense of disappointment and the mortality of his dreams are in no way diminished when he returns to Paris from Russia. To find out what the citizens really think of their emperor and his policies, he goes out in disguise into the streets and cafés. There he finds little sense of national purpose, small regard for the continental system, and neither gratitude toward nor admiration for himself. He and his new empress, Marie Louise, are the subjects of a businessman's bawdy joke. A satirical "history" by the frustrated Madame de Staël revealing his sodomitic perversions is being relished by some nesh intellectuals. Then he is subjected to another lecture on history and the future by a cousin of the late Frederick Stapps. Burgess's apparent purpose in inventing this cousin and his conversation with Napoleon is to provide some answers to questions raised in the earlier dialogue with Stapps. Stapps's cousin, like Stapps, believes it is "the time of the Germanic peoples now," but his sense of the future is not limited by German nationalism. For him the future lies in synthesis, *"Synthetisch zuzammenfassen."* What Stapps means is something completely different from the unified Europe that N envisions under his own control. Stapps believes in a Goethean Europe in which the glories of all the European peoples are manifest. In some ways, this lecture echoes the recollections of Miles Faber near the conclusion of *MF,* specifically his explanation of how the incestuous pattern in racial conscious- ness mirrors incestuous yearnings in art or antiart. The artist, perhaps more than anyone else, is bound to think and compel thinking in terms of the human totality and to resist the kinds of racial consciousness that lead to chaos. Both Napoleon and Frederick Stapps lack the vision of the artist, the vision of a Goethe that goes beyond pernicious, chaos-producing trivia such as the dream of Aryan supremacy or the tyrant's dream of total lock-step control. The conversation with Stapps's cousin effectively illuminates what is missing from the first conversation, an alternative vision of a united Europe, one that is neither Teutonically dominated nor subject to the tyranny of one man's ego.

The superiority of the artistic vision is indeed a major theme of the novel as a whole, and Burgess underlines it in his concluding verse epistle. Having told the reader how to regard Napoleon, he calls attention to another presence:

> *Standing behind him, though, or to one side,*
> *Another, bigger, hero is implied,*
> *Not comic and not tragic but divine,*
> *Tugging Napoleon's strings, and also mine,*
> *Controlling form, the story's ebb and flow—*
> *Beethoven, yes: this you already know. (NS, 362)*

This theme is related to, indeed part of, the theme of the creative will. N manifests a Promethean creative will, but his achievement is so very paltry compared to the achievement of Beethoven in commemorating it.

Just as the musical statement of Burgess's verse passages differs from Beethoven's theme statement by expressing mockery rather than sorrow, so the conclusion of his second movement differs from Beethoven's. Al- though the pianissimo concluding the Marcia Funebre: Adagio assai seems to suggest that peace may be found in the resigned acceptance of sorrow,[28] the conclusion of *Napoleon Symphony's* second movement ends with N in bed with his estranged Josephine dreaming of his funeral, which turns out to be "quite an amusing affair, really." The last word in the movement is provided by Josephine's parrot: "Bonaparte. Ahahahaha, Bonaparte. Booonapaaaaaaaahahah!" (*NS,* 246).

In the *Eroica,* both the scherzo and the finale seem to deal with Prometheus. While he was writing the novel, Burgess remarked that "the sound of the *Scherzo* is very much the sound of fire. And then you get the hunting horns as though the gods are chasing Prometheus, and in the last movement, Beethoven puts all his cards on the table because it is a series of variations on a theme taken from his own ballet about Prometheus and his creatures."[29] His own scherzo in *Napoleon Symphony* deals with Napoleon in his Promethean aspect in a more or less surrealistic manner with a number of historic events merged into a parachronic pattern. It opens with festivities commemorating his crowning as emperor. The festivities include a masque depicting the crucifixion of Prometheus by Jupiter and the Olympians. The allegory is clear enough to Napoleon as he drowses in the audience, but it gives him little pleasure. The Olympians represent "a doomed and discredited régime," apparently anti-Napoleonic Europe still adhering to ancient principles opposed to those of the revolution. N guesses that Prometheus represents himself, but he is distressed to learn from Duroc, grand marshal of the palace, that the myth is being followed to its ancient conclusion with Hercules rescuing Prometheus and the two announcing the end of the reign of the old gods. Duroc does not reassure him by tactfully suggesting that Prometheus is actually the spirit of man and Hercules is Napoleon. N insists upon his identity as a Titan and also upon an alteration of the myth to include a victory of his Titanic strength over the Olympians. He must snap his own chains. This willful rewriting of the script reveals a great deal about N, about the limitations of his vision. By rejecting a Herculean identification he rejects not only apotheosis but the idea of reconciliation with the Olympians and the forces they represent. He does not realize that reason and Titanic force alone cannot prevail against the tyranny of the Olympians, even though they are decrepit and discredited. Something else is needed, perhaps the love that, as Shelley says in *Prometheus Unbound,* "makes the reptile equal to the God" or some Herculean redemptive agent, as Aeschylus suggests, in *Prometheus Bound.* But N cannot understand or imagine any revolutionary force other than force itself directed by reason. He demands that the actors in the masque improvise a new concluding act in which Prometheus manages to incinerate all of the Olympians with stolen fire. To one who has "improvised a whole civilization," this appears to be asking little.

N's confidence that he can remake the myth he is playing out must be grouped with his earlier boast that he can control time and history as an expression of an attitude somewhat beyond hybris, but in a sense his confidence is justified. The modern age he heralds will be one in which Promethean fire will achieve many victories over outmoded institutions without the aid of love or the intervention of any redemptive agents. The second section of the scherzo is played out with "Promethapoleon" chained to the crags of Elba while his victorious foes attempt to restore Europe to its pre-Napoleonic condition. Interwoven flashbacks in verse summarize the little titan's career up to this point; then the section concludes with his triumphant return and the Battle of Waterloo. Like Thackeray handling the same battle in *Vanity Fair,* Burgess conveys a great deal with a few deft strokes, mainly from the point of view of N as he directs the battle. With the battle lost, attention shifts to the victorious allies entering Paris. A weary Wellington hears his own report played back to him in the drumming of his mount's hoofbeats: "Most desperate business I ever was in ever was in. . ." (*NS,* 279). Marching feet and clattering hoofbeats mingle with other sounds: "Horns and trumpets in hollow hunting harmonies, drums drums drums. All over" (*NS,* 279). Again, we can see that Burgess is adhering to the score of the *Eroica,* following the epilogue of the scherzo in which, as Donald Ferguson remarks, Beethoven's "keen sense of the meaning that may reside in the sound of the drums is likewise made clear."[30] Whatever "meaning" Beethoven intended to convey—and there is some disagreement among commentators—Burgess's meaning is clear enough. The pounding of hooves and boots anticipates the pounding of the hammers that will rechain Prometheus to another rock.

The finale is filled with pastiches of Sir Walter Scott, Wordsworth, Tennyson, Henry James, Dickens, and G. M. Hopkins, among others. The reason for this is that "Beethoven's last movement is a set of variations—viz, different ways of looking at a couple of themes. In the Henry James section, we have to remember that James believed he was N when he was dying, and here N returns the compliment. The reason why you have Hopkins and Henry James jostled together in the Finale is again to suggest counterpoint."[31] Largely by way of flashbacks, the finale brings together the themes related to Napoleon's Promethean aspect as it builds toward a climactic resurgence of the old triumphant mood. One of them is the theme of the cross, which Burgess finds in the last movement of the *Eroica,* a rising and falling statement "that sounds a bit like a cross."[32]

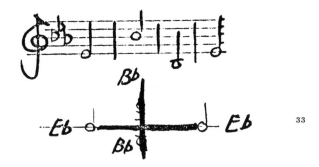

This suggests INRI, which appears as an acrostic in every piece of rhymed verse in this section of the novel. We should also recall that St. Helena is named after the woman who discovered the purported "true cross" of Christ. Napoleon has been nailed to this rocky cross by the four major powers, who might be viewed as representing the points of the cross. All of this enables us to view N as a comic Christ.

There is also the theme of "gardening" expressed in the helpless Titan's yearning to create a garden on the barren island and to impose order on its growth. In handling these themes, Burgess is able to adhere fairly closely to history. Aside from dictating his memoirs, Napoleon's main projects to while away his time on St. Helena were the cultivation of his garden at Longwood and his "last battle," as Cronin describes it, with Sir Hudson Lowe.[34] Burgess presents Napoleon's conflict with Lowe as a mock epic struggle during which the two adversaries converse like combatants in a medieval romance. Napoleon becomes "Lion of the Valley" (this is what his name actually means) confronting the "Knight of the Doubtful Countenance," Sir Hud, and their parlance is that of knights in the novels of Sir Walter Scott and Tennyson's *Idylls of the King.* Burgess may have been prompted to handle the struggle in this way by something in the score of the finale. More likely, he is emphasizing the pathetic irony in that Napoleon's will to conquer remained with him and drove him on to wage a relentless war of nerves with Lowe, who, in spite of his power over Napoleon as governor of the island, was hardly a worthy antagonist. In fact, both prisoner and jailer seem to have viewed their petty strife with each other in terms of all-out war, losing all sense of perspective as the contest wore on.[35]

Within the Promethean thematic framework, Sir Hud is the eagle pecking at N's liver, and again it is interesting to see how much Burgess is able to draw from historical fact in presenting his theme. When Lowe would not allow him to go horseback riding without being followed by a British officer, Napoleon simply gave up riding, and the lack of exercise, combined with a clammy climate, caused him to become liverish.[36] In a very real sense, then, Sir Hud was a kind of eagle pecking at Napoleon's liver, and Burgess has the identification made explicit in the remarks of a sympathetic redcoat sergeant:

> If ever I see the Hand of Death in a man's face, in his I see it. Liver, I'd say it is, that being first to crumble when it's starvation. You see the yellow in him as it might be a Eathen Chinee. Liver, that is. Peck peck peck at it, goes Sir Haitch Hell, like any pecking bird that I see. (*NS,* 314)

But again, as in the preceding three movements, Burgess's main guide is the *Eroica,* the creative will of Beethoven manifesting itself. Burgess includes three long scenes with women in his fourth movement, suggesting that his own impressions of Beethoven's themes in his fourth movement, as in the first, are not unlike those of Richard Wagner. Discussing the fourth movement, Wagner remarks how about a theme of "firm-set Manly individuality, there wind and cling all tenderer and softer feelings, from the very onset of the movement, evolving to a proclamation of the purely Womanly element; and to the manlike principal theme—striding sturdily through all the tone-piece—this Womanly at last reveals itself in ever more intense, more many-sided sympathy, as the overwhelming power of *Love*."³⁷ The "womanly element" is ubiquitous in Burgess's fourth movement, and there is a confrontation of male and female.

Near the onset, N is in the garden of Mr. Bascombe awaiting transfer to Longwood. Actually, the "Bascombe" family should really be the Balcombe family. Burgess changed the name for musical reasons: "There the S (E flat) sticks out to remind us what key we're in."³⁸ Bascombe's young daughter Betsy brings out a tender side of him that appears only in the company of women. He tells her of the garden he had cultivated and defended fiercely while he was a young cadet at Brienne. It is one of the many scenes in the novel in which we experience the personal charm of Napoleon, a factor that must be reckoned with to explain his almost inexplicable success in having his way long after a less persuasive tyrant would have been tried and shot as a war criminal by his own people. There is also, even in this charming scene with Betsy Bascombe, an element of mockery as N, expecting a lock of her hair, receives instead a carven caricature of himself as a monkey ascending a pole. Later, in his dreams (the only escape from Sir Hud's vengeful pecking), he relives one of his most joyous affairs with the loving, sympathetic womanly element. If Marie Walewska was not Napoleon's greatest love, she was his loyalest mistress. It is likely that Napoleon, abandoned by his empress, Marie Louise, did indeed dream fondly of the passionate girl who had followed him to Elba and again after Waterloo had wished to follow him into exile. Again there is the note of mockery as delicious scenes of love making in the Polish snows and the heat of Elba give way to a dream of love making with Betsy Bascombe, who becomes in turn Marie Louise. The dream ends appropriately with a near escape from drowning in another ever-threatening womanly element, the British-dominated sea.

As he did in the scherzo, Burgess again merges events in a parachronic pattern. While Napoleon's doctors quarrel over whether he will be given milk, a potentially lethal gift from Sir Hud, the dying tyrant relives in a dream his bloody triumph at Austerlitz. There follows a storm in which his carefully tended garden is utterly destroyed and then yet another entrance of the womanly element. Again, he is in a garden and a girl approaches him bearing a basket of flowers. Clearly, she is an allegorical figure, but what precisely she represents is difficult to say. She may be a combination of all the women with whom he has failed. The fact that she asks N for a summary of his achievement for posterity suggests that she may, like the school mistress in *Enderby*, be the voice of posterity. But there are suggestions that imply her identification with something else as well. Like posterity in *Enderby*, she judges, and like the mysterious muse figure who appears near the end of the same novel, she seems as well to be a representative of artistic inspiration who is capable, like posterity, of putting would-be artists in their place. Perhaps she is to be identified with Clio, the Muse of history. The description of her entrance is laced lightly with allusion to Gerard Manley Hopkins's sonnet "The Wind-hover," and she greets Napoleon with "O my chevalier."

The significance of these allusions is not readily apparent. Certainly, to some extent, they are ironic. Hopkins's soaring falcon is both Jesus Christ and himself the poet, as well as a literal embodiment of "brute beauty." Initially, its archetype or "inscape" radiates itself to the poet. But then the greatness, "the achieve of, the mastery of the thing," is suddenly, as it were, dethroned: "Brute beauty and valour and act, oh, air, pride plume, here/ Buckle!" As Romano Guardini remarks, "However the word 'buckle' may be explicated, it includes the meaning that what was before free in the heights, surrounded by light, unlimited . . . must now yield to or become a thing that dwells in the lower darkness, constricted, care-worn, yet in truth, greater."[39] Burgess's crucified Napoleon realizes that he, too, must "buckle" with his own mortality, "with joints that . . . were now unmeet for straddling the charger or striding the conference room" (*NS*, 339). He realizes this without regret, for he has a sense of fulfillment: "The nature of the hero has to be made manifest"(*NS*, 342).

Anticipating Raskolnikov's Napoleon theory, he feels justified as a "being of exceptional qualities, the man above men in the intensity and scope of thought and ability" (*NS*, 342). When the mysterious lady replies with a simple, disconcerting "Why?" he adds without hesitation a teleological jus-tification: "To the end of disseminating the word of republican enlighten-ment" (*NS*, 343). When the lady dismisses this "decidedly jejune and at the same time positively elephantine, certainly demagogic summation of the whole, so to put it, *tissage*," he points with pride to the actual achievement, the replacement of outmoded social and governmental structures with "an aristocracy of sheer merit." Unwittingly, he describes how far his ideal actually deviated from any truly "republican" ideal: "The state much like the army, with merit rewarded, medals, pensions, duchies and principalities. Indeed, the state hardly to be distinguished from the army" (*NS*, 344). Like the general in Norman Mailer's *The Naked and the Dead,* he is ostensibly a defender of democracy but is in fact a champion of fascist dictatorship.[40]

The lady does not bother to illuminate the contradiction for him, but she tries to bring him to the devastating realization that "the whole, so to put it, *tissage*," was really unnecessary. Although it may be granted that heroic images are necessary to nourish the imagination, it may not be necessary for the heroic image to manifest itself in action, which may be, indeed usually is, needlessly wasteful and destructive. The heroic image may itself be created by an heroic imagination. Again, as in every other part of the novel, the presence of "another, bigger, hero is implied." Beethoven, a greater hero and a truer republican, could have created his heroic symphony without Napo-leon. He could "have made" Napoleon himself or at least that part of his "Promethean" achievement that was worthy of celebration. As it was, Napo-leon's achievement in his "own Promethean manner" was, like that of Marlowe's Tamburlaine, another frustrated Promethean, far more destructive than creative. Napoleon lost his chance to become a part of a truly heroic achievement when "he [Beethoven] tore up the dedication" (*NS,* 347).

The ironic significance of the "Windhover" allusions seems to be that N is under the illusion that in fulfilling himself, he has fulfilled a heroic archetype. In fact, the archetype or "inscape" of the heroic has been truly fulfilled only by Beethoven. The "sheer plod" of Napoleon's conquering creative will could, in a sense, have been sanctified by the dedication, even as, for Hopkins, the incarnation has sanctified all material things, however common or mean.[41] The imagination of Beethoven manifested in the *Eroica* reveals the paltriness, not only of Napoleon's achievement by comparison, but of any achievement in the sphere of human action. One is reminded here of the opening lines of Burgess's poem on the first moon landing:

> Imagination is your true Apollo.
>   In our translunar skulls the moon's small beer.
> Fact's crippled fancy. Acts are slow to follow
>   Words (small cheese, I meant—small green cheese).
>   We're
> Too long beyond the moon. The moon's too near.[42]

This scene effectively emphasizes what has been the thrust of the novel as a whole, a celebration of the creative will and imagination of the artist. The novel concludes with a resurgence of the old triumphant mood as Napoleon is greeted by his cheering troops. His dream of a united Europe has been partly fulfilled in his own lifetime and will be fulfilled much later. But even this, if we bear in mind the Goethean vision referred to earlier, can be seen as part of the celebration of the artistic imagination.

In assessing the novel as a whole, we should heed at least some of the pleas and modest avowals in the concluding verse epistle. Like Ben Jonson, Burgess is concerned and worried, perhaps unduly, that his artistic purposes will not manifest themselves clearly enough to be understood by his audience. He is worried that some critics may compare his portrait of Napoleon with Tolstoy's in *War and Peace.* Such comparisons diminish unfairly Hardy's achievement in *The Dynasts,* and he seems to fear the same fate for *Napoleon Symphony.* Such a comparison would of course be pointless because it would be apple and orange, both in terms of subject and subgenre. Burgess's subject is ostensibly Napoleon, but his real, "implied," subject is Beethoven, the creative will of Beethoven manifesting itself in an achievement that utterly dwarfs that of its ostensible subject. Burgess asks that the novel be judged as a "comic novel," but he does not wish to have it assessed in terms of hilarity generated by contrivances. In short, Burgess is asking his critics to have a *sense de mesure* and a *sense de métier.*

Fair enough. Let us restrict our comparisons to works within his own canon. As a historical romance, or rather, a celebration of artistic genius within the framework of an intimate fictional portrait of a great man, *Napoleon Symphony* is less successful than his *Nothing Like the Sun.* The reasons for this are obvious. In *Nothing Like the Sun,* Burgess is celebrating the genius of Shakespeare, the unparalleled master of language. Burgess's own linguistic genius is necessarily exercised to the full in this celebration, availing itself of all the riches of Elizabethan English. Moreover, in *Nothing Like the Sun* ostensible and real subject matter are one. We become intimately involved with Shakespeare and are made to perceive the connections between his personal life and his art. Whether or not we agree that his great tragedies and bitter comedies were probably the fruits of syphillis, we are made to see the plausibility of the theory by the brilliant interweaving of Burgess's insights and Shakespeare's within the medium of the latter's language. In *Napoleon Symphony,* on the other hand, he is celebrating musical genius by framing musically a comic treatment of a nonmusical subject. For all Burgess's ubiquitous musical reminders that the subject is Beethoven's genius, we are mainly absorbed in Napoleon as a comic character to the extent that we must be reminded explicitly and nonmusically in N's dialogue with the muse/posterity or Clio figure that there is "another, bigger, hero . . . implied." The reader is urged to "hear" Beethoven imaginatively as he reads. Indeed, this is possible, and it is greatly facilitated by the ingenious syllable-to-note correspondences of the verse passages, as well as other devices of correspondence between mediums. But when all is said and done, the reader could derive nearly as much pleasure from the novel without being aware that it attempts to "translate" the *Eroica.* He could also, without hearing Beethoven in it, perceive its main thematic designs.

Thematically, *Napoleon Symphony* does not represent any "new directions" in Burgess's fiction. As in *MF* and *Enderby Outside,* he is mainly preoccupied with summarizing and clarifying his views concerning the role of the artist in the modern world. *Enderby* defines the artist in terms of his concerns and identifies the forces that threaten him. *MF* is a satirical polemic against antiart and pseudoartists that also attempts to define the role of the artist. *Napoleon Symphony* carries the definitions of these novels somewhat further by exalting the true artist's creative will and imagination, which could have created perhaps a better modern world without Napoleon. It is a much subtler handling of the theme than either *MF* or *Enderby,* but in some ways it is more successful than both. Although all three novels emphasize the theme of the artist's role with didactic dialogues near their conclusions, we are perhaps more likely to be convinced by *Napoleon Symphony,* in which the didacticism is not overheavy. We see the actual historical would-be creative exploits of "Promethapoleon" being molded by the artistry of Burgess into comedy richer than mere hilarity. We are then made aware that the artist who has, in a sense, "controlled" this figure is himself controlled by a greater artist, "Tugging Napleon's strings, and also mine." Here Burgess has made his point regarding the awesome powers and concomitant responsibilities of the artist far more effectively than he has in the other two novels by such devices as having a muse figure quote Shelley on the role of the poet as unacknowledged legislator of the world or having a protagonist discourse directly to the reader on the irresponsibility of antiart.

The fact that Burgess is mainly preoccupied with redeveloping themes developed in earlier novels and revealing their relationships to each other should not lead us to think he is anywhere near the end of his revels. As he says in defending Henry James against a sly dig in Waugh's *The Loved One,*

> Read *The Ambassadors,* and you can confidentally say that you have read Henry James. But surely a profound theme needs tackling again and again? A painter may paint nothing except apples, but there are innumerable facets of apples to be treated artistically, even though the apple remains an apple.[43]

It can be argued that Burgess deals with essentially the same themes in nearly all his novels. What *Napoleon Symphony* reveals is that the themes are inexhaustible when subjected to the will and creative genius of a true artist.

Notes

Chapter 1
ENTER POSTERITY

1. Readers of Burgess's novel *Enderby* will recognize the above as a respectful parody of the opening scene in which a strange persona leads a tour of schoolchildren through the poet Enderby's bedroom.

2. From an interview with Thomas Churchill in the *Malahat Review* 17 (January 1971): 117–18.

3. Interview with Geoffrey Aggeler in Stratford, Ontario, July 30, 1969.

4. Ibid.

5. Ibid.

6. Dick Adler, *Sunday Times* (London), Color Supplement, April 2, 1967.

7. Letter to Geoffrey Aggeler, October 10, 1969.

8. Taped lecture at Simon Fraser University, Vancouver, B.C., March 5, 1969.

9. Interview with Geoffrey Aggeler in Stratford, Ontario, July 30, 1969.

10. Letter to Geoffrey Aggeler, May 3, 1976.

11. Letter to Geoffrey Aggeler, April 22, 1977.

12. Interview with Geoffrey Aggeler in New York City, September 16, 1972.

13. Ibid.

14. Letter to Geoffrey Aggeler, April 22, 1977.

15. Interview with Geoffrey Aggeler in New York City, September 16, 1972.

16. Letter to Geoffrey Aggeler, August 9, 1970.

17. Interview with Geoffrey Aggeler, September 16, 1972.

18. Ibid.

19. Letter to Geoffrey Aggeler, April 22, 1977.

20. Ibid.

21. Letter to Geoffrey Aggeler, May 3, 1976.

22. Anthony Burgess, *Beard's Roman Women* (New York: McGraw-Hill, 1976), p. 61.

23. Letter to Geoffrey Aggeler, April 22, 1977.

24. Interview with Geoffrey Aggeler, September 16, 1972.

25. Ibid.

26. Ibid.

27. Interview with Geoffrey Aggeler, Stratford, Ontario, July 30, 1969.

28. Ibid.

29. Ibid.

Chapter 2
IN QUEST OF A DARKER CULTURE

1. Anthony Burgess, *A Vision of Battlements* (New York: Ballantine Books, 1966), intro., p. vii. All quotations are from this edition.

2. In this connection, see Burgess's discussion of *Ulysses* in *Re Joyce* (New York: Ballantine Books, 1966), pp. 105–231.

3. Anthony Burgess, *Time for a Tiger,* in *Malayan Trilogy* (London: Pan Books, 1964), p. 49. All quotations are from this edition, and subsequent references will be given in the text with page numbers and abbreviation.

4. Anthony Burgess, *The Enemy in the Blanket,* in *Malayan Trilogy* (London: Pan Books, 1964), p. 201. All quotations are from this edition, and subsequent references will be given in the text with page numbers and abbreviation.

5. Anthony Burgess, *Beds in the East,* in *Malayan Trilogy* (London: Pan Books, 1964), p. 336. All quotations are from this edition, and subsequent references will be given in the text with page numbers and abbreviation.

6. William H. Pritchard, "The Novels of Anthony Burgess," *The Massachusetts Review* VI (Summer 1966): 527.

7. John Gross, *New Statesman,* November 24, 1961, p. 28.

8. Anthony Burgess, *The Novel Now* (London: Faber & Faber, 1967), p. 212.

9. Anthony Burgess, *Devil of a State* (New York: Ballantine Books, 1968), p. 151. All quotations are from this edition, and subsequent references will be given in the text with page numbers and abbreviation.

10. Letter to Geoffrey Aggeler, November 2, 1971.

11. John Burgess Wilson, *English Literature: A Survey for Students* (London: Longmans, Green & Co., 1965), p. 288.

12. Interview with Geoffrey Aggeler in New York City, September 16, 1972.

13. Anthony Burgess, *The Worm and the Ring* (London: Heinemann, 1970), p. 149. All quotations are from this edition, and subsequent references will be given in the text with page numbers and abbreviation.

14. A.A. De Vitis observes that "the Worm of the title then is the boy Albert Rich—in the opera, Alberich transforms himself into a great snake; and the ring is the confusion forged by the incorrigible boy." *Anthony Burgess* (New York: Twayne, 1972), p. 97. For reasons indicated, I believe Gardner is more clearly identified as the worm.

15. Interview with Thomas Churchill, *Malahat Review* 17 (January 1971): 116.

16. Ibid.

Chapter 3
DESCENT OF THE GODDESS

1. Anthony Burgess, *Nothing Like the Sun* (London: Penguin Books, 1966), p. 19. All quotations are from this edition, and subsequent references will be given in the text with page numbers and abbreviation.

2. Anthony Burgess, *Inside Mr. Enderby* (London: Penguin, 1966), p. 61. All quotations are from this edition, and subsequent references will be given in the text with page numbers and abbreviation.

3. Taped lecture at Simon Fraser University, Vancouver, B.C., March 5, 1969.

4. Interview with Geoffrey Aggeler in Stratford, Ontario, July 30, 1969.

5. Anthony Burgess, *The Novel Now* (London: Faber & Faber, 1967), p. 212.

6. Anthony Burgess, *Enderby Outside* (London: Heinemann, 1968), p. 22. All quotations are from this edition, and subsequent references will be given in the text with page numbers and abbreviation.

7. Letter from Anthony Burgess to Geoffrey Aggeler, July 3, 1969.

8. Robert Graves, *The White Goddess* (London: Faber & Faber, 1967), pp. 388–91.

9. Anthony Burgess, *The Clockwork Testament, or Enderby's End* (New York: Alfred A. Knopf, 1974), p. 15. All quotations are from this edition, and subsequent references will be given in the text with page numbers and abbreviation.

10. Eleanor Ruggles, *Gerard Manley Hopkins: A Life* (Port Washington, N.Y.: Kennikat Press, 1969), p. 129.

11. B.F. Skinner, *Beyond Freedom and Dignity* (New York: Alfred A. Knopf, 1971), p. 165.

12. Cf. Fyodor Dostoevsky, *Notes from Underground,* chapter 7.

13. See especially chapters 6, 7, 8, 9 of *Beyond Freedom and Dignity.*

14. Anthony Burgess, "A Fable for Social Scientists," *Horizon* 15 (Winter 1973): 15.

15. Compare this with the following:

"What is being abolished is autonomous man—the inner man, the homunculus, the possessing demon, the man defended by the literatures of freedom and dignity.

"His abolition has long been overdue. Autonomous man is a device used to explain what we cannot explain in any other way. He has been constructed from our ignorance, and as our understanding increases, the very stuff of which he is composed vanishes. Science does not dehumanize man, it dehomunculizes him, and it must do so if it is to prevent the abolition of the human species. To man *qua* man we readily say good riddance. . . . Krutch has argued that whereas the traditional view supports Hamlet's exclamation, 'How like a god!,' Pavlov, the behavioral scientist, emphasized 'How like a dog!' But that was a step forward. . . . Man is much more than a dog, but like a dog he is within range of a scientific analysis" (*Beyond Freedom and Dignity,* edition cited, pp. 200–201).

16. Burgess, "A Fable for Social Scientists," p. 15.

17. See chapter 7.

18. Interview with Geoffrey Aggeler in New York City, September 16, 1972.

19. Ibid.

20. See chapter 5 and my article "Pelagius and Augustine in the Novels of Anthony Burgess," *English Studies* LV (February 1974): 43–55.

21. Henry Bettenson, ed., *Documents of the Christian Church* (Oxford University Press, 1967), pp. 52–53.

22. Ibid., p. 58.

23. Martin Luther, "The Bondage of the Will," in *Martin Luther,* ed. John Dillenberger (New York: Anchor Books, 1961), p. 187.

24. John Burnaby, trans., *The Spirit and the Letter,* in *Augustine: Later Works,* (London: Library of Christian Classics, 1953), p. 201.

25. Interview with George Malko, *Penthouse Magazine,* June 1972, p. 116.

26. Cf. the "Diapsalmata" section of *Either/Or.*

27. I have discussed Burgess's uses of the Joycean mock epic structure in "The Comic Art of Anthony Burgess," *Arizona Quarterly* 25 (Autumn 1969): 234–51.

28. Interview with Thomas Churchill, *Malahat Review* 17 (January 1971): 125.

29. Ibid., p. 111.

30. Ibid.

31. Interview with Geoffrey Aggeler, New York City, September 16, 1972.

32. In "The Canonization."

33. See note 20, this chapter.

Chapter 4
LOVE AND DECAY IN THE WEST

1. Anthony Burgess, *The Right to an Answer* (New York: Ballantine Books, 1966), pp. 35–36. All quotations are from this edition, and subsequent references will be given in the text with page numbers and abbreviation.

2. Cf. Norman Mailer, *Why We Are in Vietnam* (New York: M. McCosh, 1967).

3. Anthony Burgess, *The Doctor Is Sick* (London: Pan Books, 1963), p. 15. All quotations are from this edition, and subsequent references will be given in the text with page numbers and abbreviation.

4. Anthony Burgess, *Re Joyce* (New York: Ballantine Books, 1966), p. 133.

5. See Joseph Campbell, *The Hero with a Thousand Faces* (New York: Meridian Books, 1949), chapter IV.

6. Anthony Burgess, *Honey for the Bears* (London: Pan Books, 1963), p. 19. All quotations are from this edition, and subsequent references will be given in the text with page numbers and abbreviation.

7. Anthony Burgess, *One Hand Clapping* (London: Peter Davies, 1961), p. 8. All quotations are from this edition, and subsequent references will be given in the text with page numbers and abbreviation.

8. Anthony Burgess, *The Eve of St. Venus* (New York: Ballantine Books, 1971), p. ix. All quotations are from this edition, and subsequent references will be given in the text with page numbers and abbreviation.

9. L. R. Lind, ed., *Latin Poetry* (Boston: Houghton Mifflin, 1957), p. 311.

10. Anthony Burgess, *The Novel Now* (London: Faber & Faber, 1967), pp. 206–7.

Chapter 5
PELAGIUS AND AUGUSTINE

1. Quotations from the writings of Pelagius are taken from Henry Bettenson, ed., *Documents of the Christian Church* (London: Oxford University Press, 1967). In summarizing Pelagian doctrine, I am heavily indebted to the analyses by W.J. Sparrow-Simpson in *The Letters of St. Augustine* (New York: Macmillan, 1919), and John Burnaby, trans., *The Spirit and the Letter*, in *Augustine: Later Works*, vol. 8 (London: Library of Christian Classics, 1955).

2. Burnaby, *The Spirit and the Letter*, p. 183.

3. Quoted by Sparrow-Simpson from a sermon, *Letters of St. Augustine*, p. 131. Literally: "With a sail (it is) easier, with an oar more difficult; nevertheless with an oar it goes."

4. Ibid., p. 130.

5. Bettenson, *Documents*, p. 53.

6. *Confessions*, II, 9, trans. Edward B. Pusey (New York: Modern Library, 1949), p. 29.

7. Ibid., X, 40.

8. Burnaby, *The Spirit and the Letter*, p. 196.

9. Ibid., pp. 199–212.

10. John H.S. Burleigh, trans. *On Free Will*, in *Augustine: Earlier Writings*, vol. 6 (London: Library of Christian Classics, 1953), p. 201.

11. The reader who wishes to follow this debate in detail may find the following

works of interest: Jacques-François Thomas, *Le Pelagianisme de J.-J. Rousseau* (Paris: Librairie Nizet, 1956); Gordon Leff, *Bradwardine and the Pelagians* (Cambridge University Press, 1957); Ray B. Browne, ed. *The Burke-Paine Controversy* (New York: Harcourt Brace & World, 1963); Basil Willey, *The Seventeenth Century Background* (New York: Doubleday Anchor, 1962) and *The Eighteenth Century Background* (Boston: Beacon Press, 1961).

12. As R.H. Tawney observes: "Having overthrown monasticism, its [Calvinism's] aim was to turn the secular world into a gigantic monastery, and at Geneva, for a short time, it almost succeeded. . . . Manners and morals were regulated, because it is through the *minutiae* of conduct that the enemy of mankind finds his way to the soul; the traitors to the Kingdom might be revealed by pointed shoes or golden ear-rings, as in 1793 those guilty of another kind of *incivisme* were betrayed by their knee-breeches. Regulation meant legislation, and still more, administration. The word in which both were summarized was Discipline. Discipline Calvin himself described as the nerves of religion, and the common observation that he assigned to it the same primacy as Luther had given to faith is just" (*Religion and the Rise of Capitalism* [New York: Mentor Books, 1958], pp. 101–2).

13. In this connection, see Gail Kennedy, *Democracy and the Gospel of Wealth* (Boston: D.C. Health, 1949).

14. Jean-Jacques Rousseau, *The Social Contract,* book 2, trans. G.D.H. Cole (New York: Everyman's Library, 1968), chapter 9, p. 69.

15. Ibid., book 2, chapter 6, p. 31.

16. Anthony Burgess, *The Wanting Seed* (New York: W. W. Norton, 1963), p. 18. All quotations are from this edition, and subsequent references will be given in the text with page numbers and abbreviation.

17. Interview with Geoffrey Aggeler, Vancouver, B.C., March 5, 1969.

18. Burgess informed me that their uniforms were also symbolic of the "Inter-phase," the chaotic passage from one philosophical extreme to the other. Interview in Stratford, Ontario, July 30, 1969.

19. Sparrow-Simpson, *Letters of Augustine,* p. 133.

20. *De Cive or The Citizen,* chapter 12; *Leviathan,* part 2, chapter 17.

21. W.H. Pritchard, "The Novels of Anthony Burgess," *Massachusetts Review* 6 (Summer 1966): 529.

22. Anthony Burgess, *A Clockwork Orange* (London: Pan Books, 1962), p. 20. All quotations are from this edition, and subsequent references will be given in the text with page numbers and abbreviation.

23. Robert O. Evans has published a brief analysis of nadsat: "Nadsat: The Argot and Its Implications in Anthony Burgess' *A Clockwork Orange,"* *Journal of Modern Literature* I (1971): 406–10.

24. Interview with George Malko, *Penthouse,* June 1972, p. 115.

25. B.F. Skinner, *Beyond Freedom and Dignity* (New York: Alfred A. Knopf, 1971), p. 223.

26. Anthony Burgess, "Clockwork Marmalade," *The Listener,* December 1971, p. 21.

27. Ibid., p. 22.

28. Interview with Malko, p. 115.

29. Burgess, "Clockwork Marmalade," p. 22.

30. Ibid.

31. Interview with Malko, p. 116.

Chapter 6
BETWEEN GOD AND NOTGOD

1. Anthony Burgess, *Tremor of Intent* (New York: W.W. Norton, 1966), p. 3. All quotations are from this edition, and subsequent references will be given in the text with page numbers and abbreviation.

2. See *Confessions,* books III, IV, V.

3. See Augustine, *On Free Will,* an early treatise against the Manichees.

Chapter 7
INCEST AND THE ARTIST

1. Anthony Burgess, *MF* (New York: Alfred A. Knopf, 1971), p. 4. All quotations are from this edition, and subsequent references will be given in the text with page numbers and abbreviation.

2. Joseph Campbell, *The Hero With a Thousand Faces* (New York: Meridian Books, 1949), p. 90.

3. Campbell, *Hero,* p. 121.

4. Cf. Lord Raglan, *Jocasta's Crime: An Anthropological Study* (London: Methuen, 1933); Emile Durkheim, *Incest: The Nature and Origin of the Taboo,* trans. Edward Sagarin (New York: L. Stuart, 1963); Sir James Frazer, *The Magic Art and the Evolution of Kings,* part I, vol. 2 of *The Golden Bough* (London: Macmillan, 1922), chapter XI.

5. Claude Lévi-Strauss, *The Scope of Anthropology,* trans. Sherry O. Paul and Robert A. Paul (London: Jonathon Cape, 1967), p. 35.

6. Lévi-Strauss, p. 39.

7. Anthony Burgess, "If Oedipus had read his Lévi-Strauss," in *Urgent Copy: Literary Studies by Anthony Burgess* (New York: W. W. Norton, 1968), pp. 260–61.

8. Interview with Geoffrey Aggeler in Stratford, Ontario, July 30, 1969.

9. Ibid.

10. Burgess explained:" In my novel *MF* the hero does not have his race defined at the beginning because I consider the race to be irrelevant. At the very end of the book, he defines himself as black. This is supposed to come as a surprise to the reader and the reader is intended to read the book again and see this chief character as a black man instead of white. There should be no difference. Nothing is changed. Color is an irrelevance, and what we have is a kind of synthetic person who has absorbed all the elements of culture he needs, who is totally unconscious about race and thinks of himself primarily as a human being. In other words, the book is about taxonomies, about ways of classifying things. There are true classifications and false ones. The man-woman or M-F classification is true and valid. The black-white classification is a false one, probably the falsest of all" (Interview with Geoffrey Aggeler in New York City, September 16, 1972).

Chapter 8
THE ARTIST AS CONQUEROR: NAPOLEON SYMPHONY

1. John N. Burk, "Program Notes for Boston Symphony Orchestra," quoted in

The Beethoven Companion, ed. Thomas K. Scherman and Louis Biancolli (New York: Doubleday, 1972), p. 546.

2. Ibid., p. 547. See also his *Life and Works of Beethoven* (New York: Modern Library, 1946), chapter 9.

3. Paul Henry Lang, *Music in Western Civilization* (New York: W.W. Norton, 1963), p. 763.

4. Burk, "Program Notes."

5. In the American edition. The British edition has an additional chapter.

6. Interview with Geoffrey Aggeler in New York City, September 16, 1972.

7. See chapter 2, this book.

8. Anthony Burgess, *Napoleon Symphony* (New York: Alfred A. Knopf, 1974), p. 362. All quotations are from this edition, and subsequent references will be given in the text with page numbers and abbreviation.

9. Useful biographies for a reader's reference are Emil Ludwig's *Napoleon* (New York: Modern Library, 1933), and Vincent Cronin's *Napoleon Bonaparte: An Intimate Biography* (New York: William Morrow, 1972).

10. Cronin, *Napoleon Bonaparte,* p. 129.

11. J. Bourgeat, *Lettres de Napoléon à Joséphine* (1941).

12. Quoted in *Beethoven Companion,* p. 553.

13. Cronin, *Napoleon Bonaparte,* p. 119.

14. Ibid., p. 132.

15. *Plutarch's Lives,* trans. Sir Thomas North (1579); "The Life of Marcus Antonius," in *The Sources of Ten Shakespearean Plays,* ed. Alice Griffin (New York: Crowell, 1966), pp. 268–69.

16. See chapter 5, this book.

17. Based on notation by Mr. John Payne, Department of Music, University of Utah.

18. Based on notation by Anthony Burgess in letter to Geoffrey Aggeler, December 24, 1974.

19. Based on notation by John Payne according to instructions by Anthony Burgess in letter to Geoffrey Aggeler, December 24, 1974.

20. Based on notation by Anthony Burgess in letter to Geoffrey Aggeler, December 24, 1974.

21. Cronin, *Napoleon Bonaparte,* p. 328.

22. Ibid., p. 328.

23. Letter to Geoffrey Aggeler, December 24, 1974.

24. Cronin, *Napoleon Bonaparte,* p. 306.

25. Letter to Geoffrey Aggeler, December 24, 1974.

26. For a description of Stein see Ludwig, *Napoleon,* book 4, chapter 6.

27. Interview with George Malko, *Penthouse Magazine,* June 1972, p. 116.

28. Hermann Scherchen, jacket cover *Symphony No. 3 in E Flat* (Westminster Recording Co.)

29. Interview with Geoffrey Aggeler in New York City, September 16, 1972.

30. Donald N. Ferguson, *Masterworks of the Orchestral Repertoire* (Minneapolis: University of Minnesota Press, 1954), quoted in *Beethoven Companion,* pp. 555–59.

31. Letter to Geoffrey Aggeler, December 24, 1974.

32. Interview with Geoffrey Aggeler in New York City, September 16, 1972.

33. Notation by Anthony Burgess in letter to Geoffrey Aggeler, December 24, 1974.

34. Cronin, *Napoleon Bonaparte,* chapter 26.

35. Ibid.

36. Ibid.

37. *Beethoven Companion,* p. 554.

38. Letter to Geoffrey Aggeler, December 24, 1974.

39. Romano Guardini, "Aesthetic-Theological Thoughts on 'The Windhover,' " in *Hopkins: A Collection of Critical Essays,* ed. Geoffrey H. Hartman (Englewood Cliffs: Prentice-Hall, 1966), p. 78.

40. In this connection, see Burgess's comments on *The Naked and the Dead,* in *The Novel Now* (London: Faber & Faber, 1967), pp. 49–52.

41. See William Y. Tindall, *Forces in Modern British Literature* (New York: Vintage, 1956), pp. 177–78.

42. Anthony Burgess, poem in *New York Times,* July 21, 1969, the day the men walked on the moon.

43. Burgess, *The Novel Now,* p. 205.

Index